MW00816677

Birth of the Geopolitical Age

Birth of the Geopolitical Age

Global Frontiers and the Making of Modern China

Shellen Xiao Wu

STANFORD UNIVERSITY PRESS

Stanford, California

Stanford University Press
Stanford, California

© 2023 by Shellen Xiao Wu. All rights reserved.

No part of this book may be reproduced or transmitted in any form or by any means, electronic or mechanical, including photocopying and recording, or in any information storage or retrieval system, without the prior written permission of Stanford University Press.

Printed in the United States of America on acid-free, archival-quality paper

Library of Congress Cataloging-in-Publication Data
Names: Wu, Shellen Xiao, 1980- author.
Title: Birth of the geopolitical age : global frontiers and the making of
    modern China / Shellen Xiao Wu.
Description: Stanford, California : Stanford University Press, [2023] |
    Includes bibliographical references and index.
Identifiers: LCCN 2022060493 (print) | LCCN 2022060494 (ebook) |
    ISBN 9781503636415 (cloth) | ISBN 9781503636842 (paperback) |
    ISBN 9781503636859 (ebook)
Subjects: LCSH: Borderlands—China—History—19th century. | Borderlands—
    China—History—20th century. | Geopolitics—China—History—19th
    century. | Geopolitics—China—History—20th century. | Colonization—
    History—19th century. | Colonization—History—20th century. |
    Imperialism—History—19th century. | Imperialism—History—20th century.
Classification: LCC DS737 .W79 2023 (print) | LCC DS737 (ebook) |
    DDC 320.1/20951—dc23/eng/20230112
LC record available at https://lccn.loc.gov/2022060493
LC ebook record available at https://lccn.loc.gov/2022060494

Cover design: Martyn Schmoll
Cover image: W. & A.K. Johnston Limited, *Chinese Empire*, Library of Congress Geography and Map Division, G7820 190- .W2.
Typeset by Elliott Beard in Latino URW 9.75/14

CONTENTS

ILLUSTRATIONS

PREFACE

When much of the US shut down during the Covid-19 pandemic in the spring of 2020, like many people, I found myself unexpectedly spending a long uninterrupted stretch of time at home. Conferences and workshops were canceled. The university where I worked shut down the campus. Unable to access my office, I headed down to my basement, in the company of shelves of books and notes I had gathered over many research trips. In the time of stillness that I might otherwise have spent on trains, planes, and in cars, I reminisced about memorable trips I had undertaken in the past. During the time that I had planned for further travel to archives and libraries, I started to write.

As I wrote what became this book, I thought often of a trip I had undertaken years earlier. I had lived in Beijing in 2007–2008 while on a Fulbright scholarship and doing research for my dissertation. In the late spring of 2008, a friend and I traveled west, following the outlines of trade routes that have connected China to the rest of the world for millennia. Lines of camel trains no longer ply the Silk Road, but with the Open Up the West campaign starting in 2000, followed by the Belt and Road Initiative in 2013, China has continued to engage with the outside world through its western frontiers in a series of campaigns and development initiatives. The Chinese government has invested heavily in the building of infrastructure in the region, from railroads to newly paved roads and entire cities of high-rises surrounded by empty sandy stretches. To travel west, I realized as the horizons widened, was to see China and Chinese identity from a wholly different perspective. I was hardly the first person to come to that conclusion. From exiled officials in the imperial era to early twentieth-century academics and writers, travels to the west often induced a sense of dislocation and personal epiphanies. One of the joys of travel is to untether from the routine of daily life, familial and work obligations, and to experience the world from a new vantage point. As the horizons opened it was suddenly possible to imagine a different China from the familiar coastal cities.

From Beijing my friend and I traveled to Gansu province and the city of Dunhuang at the edge of the Gobi Desert. At first glance a dusty outpost, the city is known for the Buddhist caves carved into the cliffs along the Dachuan River, where travelers and merchants along the Silk Road had once prayed for safe passage before heading into the sand dunes to unknown western lands. The caves had been left to quietly fade into the desert when the British explorer Aurel Stein arrived in 1907. In the last years of the Qing dynasty centralized control over the edges of the empire frayed. Stein was able to win over the trust of the caretaker of the caves, who eventually allowed Stein to remove twenty-four cases of manuscripts and 40,000 scrolls, including the world's oldest printed text, the Diamond Sutra, dating to 868 AD. The discovery and removal of the scrolls, notorious even at the time, quickly caused an outcry and spurred growing Chinese nationalism in the early decades of the twentieth century.[1] Although Chinese historians conform to narratives of China's victimization by imperialism in a "century of humiliation," what is remarkable is the extent to which a few early and notorious incidents like Stein's removal of the scrolls from Dunhuang became the catalyst for a strong nationalist response. From the outrage grew support for modern archaeology as one of the first efforts to develop a national science in China.

A century later, in 2008, my friend and I found ourselves the only visitors at the caves of Mogao outside Dunhuang. The voluptuous figures of Bodhisattvas glowed cerulean blue in the cool semi-light of the caves—the rare blue of turquoise imported from Afghanistan, painted in the Indian style, likely by Indian artisans. Their eyes were scratched out, a desecration dating to the period after the Uyghur people of the region converted to Islam and corporeal depictions of Buddhist deities became anathema to their religious beliefs. The quiet retreat of green and shade in an arid landscape had once drawn people and resources from across the region. Their stories are forgotten but their work remains, these blind Buddhas waiting in dimly lit caves for the end of times.

We traveled onward by car to Jiaohe in the Yarnaz Valley. In this long-abandoned city baking in the sun we walked through ancient hearths, courtyards, and marketplaces, which had once thronged with people in the ninth century. In the long centuries since, the city had steadily eroded into the light yellow of the surrounding sands. Through flat, desert landscapes we passed by lonely obelisks in the sand, the remnants of watchtowers from the Han dynasty (202 BCE–220 AD), when these arid regions were the frontiers of the empire.

In Urumqi, the capital of the Xinjiang autonomous region, we went to the Xinjiang Museum, where a plain little exhibition room held one of the famous mummies unearthed from the Tarim Basin. Preserved by the dry climate, the 3,000-year-old mummy resurrected from the desert displays Caucasoid facial features and blond hair. These mummies have become part of a swirling controversy and debate over the racial and ethnic history of the western regions and the origins of Chinese civilization. Historians and archaeologists have long argued for the multicultural and mixed origins of the "Han" race that makes up the largest majority in China, based on findings such as the mummies. These complexities, however, run counter to the dominant narrative of Chinese nationalism. In the months leading up to the Beijing Olympics, the government clamped down hard on any signs of unrest in the country. The first Olympics hosted by China announced the country's arrival as a great power and had to go off without a hitch, much like the tightly choreographed performances of the opening ceremony.

Xinjiang was already getting restive, although nowhere near the level of disturbances and repression that have since enveloped the region. In the spring of 2008 the government cut back on domestic tourism in the region—which explains in part why my friend and I often found ourselves the only people at major sites. In the years since, conditions in Xinjiang have become far more contentious. The Chinese government has turned the entire region into a surveillance state using the latest technologies in facial recognition and the older technology of incarcerating ethnic Uyghurs in reeducation camps, ostensibly to quell domestic terrorism.

The ethnic tensions in Xinjiang and in other borderlands are rooted in China's modern history. The origins of the conflict date back to before the founding of the communist regime. In the 1920s archaeology became one of the top priorities for a newly organized national academy of sciences, Academia Sinica, which was formally founded in 1928, right after the Nationalist Party unified the country and reestablished its capital in Nanjing. Unearthed artifacts provided incontrovertible proof of ancient Chinese civilization, in turn bolstering nationalist claims over the territorial expanse. When scientists discovered the Peking Man fossils at Zhoukoudian, a small town outside of Beijing, in the 1920s, it quickly became a national sensation, although some found it difficult to assimilate an exalted history of ancient China with its distinctively simian features.[2] A few years later, starting in 1928, archaeologists at Academia Sinica oversaw the excavation at Anyang, the site of an ancient Chinese civilization, and hailed it as one of the signal achievements of Chinese science in the Republican period. Science and history became entwined with Chinese nationalism and inscribed across the landscape. The interest of the Han Chinese majority, however, did not necessarily coincide with the interests and demands of minority populations in the borderlands. From the Northeast to the Southwest, violent encounters ensued.

By the time we reached Kashgar, on the border with Pakistan, I had grown comfortable with the lulling rhythm of extended travels: a string of hotel rooms; waking up each day in a new place; the long, quiet stretches of time spent in various modes of transportation. The men driving donkey carts, the densely packed old city of twisting lanes, and perilously stacked houses were the furthest removed I had been from Shanghai and the Jiangnan area I was most familiar with in China. The feeling of vast distances and cultural untethering marked the journey, which remained in my memory long after we returned to Beijing and eventually the US. It is this side effect of journeys to induce personal epiphany and, in a larger context, to change the geographical conception of the nation along with the preservation of empire, or at least the imperial territorial expanse, that is the starting point of this book.

In the years after my return from that trip to Xinjiang, I started a tenure-track job at the University of Tennessee, Knoxville in the foothills of the Smoky Mountains; I received a Luce/ACLS China fellowship that saw me travel to Taiwan and China; and two stints of residential fellowships at the National Humanities Center and the Institute of Advanced Studies. My travels to various archives and libraries continued in spurts until the pandemic suddenly brought life to a standstill. But the journey that began in western China took me to the global frontiers that shaped the emergence of the modern world.

FIGURE 0.1: The long-abandoned city of Jiaohe in Xinjiang. Photo taken by author in 2008.

ACKNOWLEDGMENTS

This book would not have been possible without the considerable help and advice I have gotten over the years from participating in workshops, conference panels, and from many casual conversations with colleagues and friends. Various sources of inspiration include the 2014 AHA panel chaired by Jeremy Adelman and his invitation to take part in the PIIRS conference on empire and the social sciences at Princeton; the AAS panel on borderland agricultural studies chaired by Sigrid Schmalzer, with Peter Lavelle, Yingjia Tan, and Yi Wang; and the 2020 AHA panel chaired by Stefan Tanaka, with David Ambaras, Tze-hi Hon, and Jo Guldi. I have been inspired by other conversations over the years with Fa-ti Fan, Zuoyue Wang, Eugenia Lean, Arunabh Ghosh, Chuck Wooldridge and others at the Columbia Modern China colloquium, Lijing Jiang and the Johns Hopkins History of Science colloquium, Victor Seow, Michael Gordin, and Yulia Frumer and her beloved cat Merlin.

Marta Hanson encouraged me to use Ruth Rogaski's work as a model and to coin a new term—*geo-modernity*. Kate McDonald and David Ambaras's Bodies and Structure project was deeply inspiring. Dagmar Schäfer and the LoGaRT team at the MPIWG, including Shih-Pei Chen, Sean Wang, and Calvin Yeh, provided an amazingly productive environment for the *tu* group of Ken Hammond, Anne Gerritsen, Jiajing Zhang, and myself. I got countless ideas from conversations with Tansen Sen, Shengqing Wu, and Bin Xu at Fudan; Miriam Kingsberg Kadia, April Hughes, Michael Gordin, Noriko Horiguchi, Laura Nenzi, Tom Rawski, Han Qi, Aaron Moore, Jennifer Altenhenger, Margaret Tillman, Denise Y. Ho, Brigid Vance, Maria Repnikova, and Doug Howland. My Princeton mentors Sue Naquin, Ben Elman, and Sheldon Garon continued to provide helpful advice after my graduation. My colleague in geography Shih-Lung Shaw introduced me to human dynamics studies. My initial research was funded by the ACLS Luce China fellowship; a year at the National Humanities Center; and a pandemic year spent writing at the Institute of Advanced Studies, with Zoom colloquiums presided over with aplomb by Nicolas di Cosmo. A virtual manuscript workshop with Nicolas di Cosmo, Myles Jackson, Bin Wong, Charles Maier, and Tore Olsson helped guide me in my revisions. Sidney Lu, Peter Zarrow, and Lynn Sacco were kind enough to read the entire manuscript and offer comments and suggestions.

My editor at Stanford, Dylan White, has been a joy to work with in the past year. Jan Berris and the Public Intellectual Program of the National Committee on US China Relations introduced me to the best Sinologists in the country. My PIP cohort continues to deeply inspire me. I had the great honor of getting to know the late Ezra Vogel through the program. Jon Lowet from the NCUSCR led a study trip to China with a delegation of congressional aides in December 2018. As the academic guide on the trip, I had the opportunity to encounter the landscapes in Guizhou that I had read about in archives. The help provided by the hardworking staff at all the various libraries and archives I visited was essential. My editor Audra Wolfe helped me to wrestle the manuscript into shape. In the end, the only mistakes that remain are wholly my own.

Birth of the Geopolitical Age

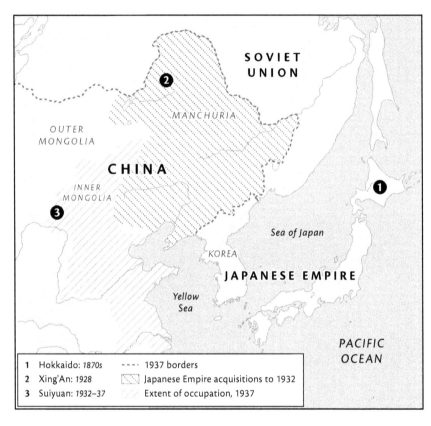

MAP 0.1: Military frontier settlements (*tunken* 屯墾) in Asia in the nineteenth and early twentieth centuries.

INTRODUCTION

Why Empires Matter in the Age of the Nation-State

At first glance the images appear interchangeable. Neatly tended and clearly demarcated fields stretch into the horizon; flat expanses dotted with tractors and bales of hay; contented cows and pigs; and, when they're not mere dots in the distance, hale men and women who exude a healthful glow from laboring outdoors. Only the captions betray the specificity of time and place. These are not images of any one place or time, but rather Xing An, in northeastern China in 1928, Hokkaido in the 1870s, Eastern Europe in the 1930s, and Soviet Central Asia in the 1920s. The visual similarities dissolve upon closer examination of the individual political and historical contexts for these frontier settlements. Like small pieces of a much larger puzzle, together they tell a story of a significant global shift in state power, boundary making, and the way internationalism and nationalism became entwined and mutually rein-forcing by the end of the nineteenth century. The rise of modern science and social sciences served as the connective thread in this global trend. A dense network of social scientists aided the global spread of ideas on the purpose and uses of inner colonization and frontier development. The fields of geography and agricultural science, in particular, evolved and maintained close relationships with state institutions invested in the concept of empire and the planned settlement of borderlands. This geopolitical reordering of the world took place in a global context with China as a central protagonist of the story.

Birth of the Geopolitical Age is the product of many journeys—actual travel to western China, Europe, and throughout the United States—and an intellectual journey that brought me to think deeply about how and why frontiers mattered to the modern state. This book is about how disciplines like geography and agricultural science, which straddle both premodern forms of knowledge and the rise of modern science, played essential roles in changing how states viewed frontiers. The adoption and adaption of these areas of knowledge, along with the need to adjust to an international order based on national sovereignty and fixed borders, ushered China and the rest of the world into *geo-modernity*. From the edges of empires, experimental stations in scientific governance and forced settlement of borderlands formed the modern state. The geopolitical remaking of the world took place from the outside in.

Geo-modernity, I argue, is the foundation for modern geopolitical concerns. Geo-modernity is defined by clearly demarcated borders and the use of the latest science and technology to develop borderlands through agriculture and the intensive exploitation of natural resources. The concept speaks to the central role of science in the reordering of the modern world order. The term is distinct from *geopolitics*, which was coined at the turn of the twentieth century by the Germanophile Swedish political scientist Rudolph Kjellén (1864–1922) and circulated broadly during the interwar period. While geopolitics focuses on the strategic goals of state actors, geo-modernity addresses the wider cultural, social, and scientific context that gave rise to geopolitics. The distinction is important because commentators and even historians often use the term *geopolitics* loosely and without providing the historical context of its emergence. Yet, geopolitics as a mode of analysis would not exist without the rise of modern science and a series of developments in new technologies and scientific disciplines like geology and agricultural science. The last great push to reach the North and South Poles in 1909 relied on dogs, Siberian ponies, and human labor. Since then, polar exploration, as well as frontier development in extreme environments around the world, has relied on new technologies to counter harsh conditions. In that sense, geo-modernity and the extension of the frontier occurred in tandem, with science and technology the essential tools to support human settlement of lands previously inhospitable to development and the intensive exploitation of natural resources.

In China, discussions of scientific settlement and frontier management frequently focused on resource extraction. For Qing officials and writers from the late nineteenth century, coal became an essential fuel of imperialism and the foundation of a new industrial economy.[1] In the twentieth century, some of the same figures repeatedly returned to the question of how to exploit natural resources, secure energy sources for industries, and most effectively redistribute the population. Political leaders and social scientists described in sometimes exuberant detail how the open spaces and rich natural resources on the frontiers could absorb excess populations in the interior and provide the economic basis for the development of the entire country. These debates clearly drew from external influences even while grappling with specifically Chinese historical legacies and geographical conditions.

In 2013–2014, I spent the year in Shanghai and Taiwan, working my way through databases of Chinese journals and archives of government documents in the Republican period in the first half of the twentieth century. I discovered that the contemporary Chinese term for geopolitics, *diyuan zhengzhi xue* 地緣政治學, only began circulating in the 1930s, but the underlying ideas that connect geography, natural resources, and social Darwinian competition had circulated much earlier in late Qing translations from the Japanese.[2] As I continued my research in Chinese archival sources, I realized that the documents revealed a historically and geographically specific story about how modern China came into existence that only made sense in a larger global context about frontiers, state formation, and the deployment of science and technology to those ends. By incorporating Japan and China, as well as Germany and the United States, into the story of how China retained the territorial extent of its last empire while assuming the political form of a nation-state, I illustrate the various ways that, from the nineteenth century, each of these countries engaged with new interpretations of empire to accommodate the rise of the nation-state. I demonstrate how frontier practices shaped the emergence of the modern Chinese state in a global context.[3] China entered geo-modernity with a global cohort of other countries adjusting to the displacements and turmoil created by industrialization and the rise of modern science.

Much of the scholarship on frontiers focuses on the early modern period and the nineteenth century, operating under the assumption that by the end of the nineteenth century most of the open spaces around the world had been enclosed by national boundaries. My readings convinced me that frontier discourse not only continued to play an outsized role in China and in other parts of the world, but also took on new dynamics with changing technologies of communication and transportation. Over the next few years, in archives in Taipei and Nanjing, Berlin and Koblenz in Germany, Washington, DC, Lexington, Kentucky, Baltimore, and New Haven, I steadily read what seemed a vast and endless literature on frontiers around the world. I traced the steps of various figures through their diaries, correspondences, and their often voluminous and dense writings. From these scraps of a jigsaw puzzle, spread out in fifteen libraries and archives across three continents, emerged a larger global story about territory and power and the continued importance of empire in the modern age.

From the 1850s until the mid-twentieth century, a period marked by global conflicts and anxiety about dwindling resources and closing opportunities after decades of expansion, the frontier became a mirror for historically and geographically specific hopes and fears. Around the same time that the American historian Frederick Jackson Turner made the American West the defining feature of a new national history, the Prussian government undertook an inner colonization program in the East from 1886 to 1920. Japan took its first steps towards empire in the northern island of Hokkaido, followed by ventures in Korea, Taiwan, and finally, the Asian mainland. Russia (then the Soviet Union) sponsored efforts aimed to extract natural resources from the Arctic, Siberian, and Central Asian frontiers. The global circulation of concepts about science, race, territory, and modern statehood helped to shape the trajectory of colonial expansion into these borderlands as countries around the world struggled with industrialization and new technologies of transportation and communication. Of these countries, China is the only one to successfully navigate through the twentieth century with its imperial territorial expanse largely intact. How that came about is the subject of this book, which focuses on the global transformation of frontiers into colonial laboratories and the scientists and social scientists who made it possible, including many at great personal cost.

To the Frontiers!

The *frontier* is a loaded and relational term—it assumes the presence of a core area for there to be a periphery. To talk about the frontier is to assume a hierarchy of space. Western China was exotic and strange to me because of my background as an ethnically Han Chinese American born in Shanghai. In the imperial era, crossing into borderlands was the unenviable fate of exiled officials, who often wrote tearful poems to mark the solemn occasion of leaving behind ordered civilization for the wilderness beyond. From the 1930s, however, Han Chinese writers began to describe the frontiers as filled with untapped treasures, in ways that often diverged significantly from the reality on the ground. The American West was only the frontier to the Anglo settlers who relentlessly pushed indigenous peoples from their lands through a series of wars, treaties, and removal efforts. Cherokees, among other tribes, found themselves forcibly marched from hilly, forested homelands in the southern Appalachian Mountains to the flat, arid stretches of Oklahoma. In the Southwest, Comanches adopted horses, an Old World species, to build their own empire based on raids and the exchange of goods with settlements. They had no concept of the "frontier."[4] From the mid-nineteenth century, German writers frequently compared Eastern Europe to the American West and Poles to the "primitive" Indians. The comparison was both intended and understood to be metaphorical. Russians attempted to carve agricultural productive landscapes out of the steppes of Central Asia in environmental conditions with marked similarities to the American Midwest, but also in a region where they encountered the Great Game interests of the British Empire and the Qing Empire in the nineteenth century. In the same period, the Japanese frontier shifted from islands to the south and north to the Americas, and finally, the Asian continent and the conflagration of its continental empire during World War II. The fascination with the frontier transcended geographical and environmental differences. These are not separate stories, but part of a connected global narrative.

The frontier is only the first of multiple terms I will introduce in this work with shifting meanings and significance in the period covered in the book, including a host of other related terms such as *settlement*, *reclamation*, *geopolitics*, and finally *science*. Despite various efforts by intellectuals and political leaders to embed these terms in a cloak of inevitability and immovability, these are shifting concepts created during a period of remarkable global flux. Particularly in Asia, these ideas underwent further transformation through processes of translation and a succession of actions and reactions in response to the arrival of Western imperial powers, the rise of the Japanese Empire from the late nineteenth century, and the political fracturing in China that followed the collapse of the Qing Empire in 1912.

Through translations beginning in the late nineteenth century, China adopted a number of neologisms coined in Japan, including *kexue* 科學, the kanji for "modern science."[5] In the post-Meiji period, Japanese students studied in the US and Europe and brought the latest agronomic theories back with them on their return to colonize the northern island of Hokkaido.[6] The Japanese agronomist Nitobe Inazo (1862–1933) helped to create a new vocabulary of colonization and empire and coined the term *shokumin* 植民, "planting people," for these new efforts to extend the Japanese Empire.[7] The botanical reference drew not only from Nitobe's educational background but also exposed the undercurrents of the global circulation of concepts about race, territory, and modern statehood. *Shokumin* more directly corresponds to the German term *Verpflanzung* than the English word *colonization*.[8] An etymological search for *Verpflanzung* in the Grimm's dictionary shows that the word originated in the fifteenth century, strictly referring to the transplantation of floras.[9] By the early nineteenth century its usage expanded to include the settlement of people. This broadening coincided with the Napoleonic invasions and efforts across the German-speaking lands to promote a sense of nationalism in the detritus of the Holy Roman Empire, including ridding the German language of foreign loan words. The term was also used in the context of inner colonization in East Prussia in the nineteenth century. Through translation and the works of geographers and historians, ideas about inner colonization traveled to imperial Russia.[10] Terminology mattered for German, Japanese, and Chinese writers and political leaders because language was an essential part of becoming a nation.

In China, however, broad resistance against foreign imperialism imprinted an appeal to the country's ancient imperial past with a modern twist. Twentieth-century Chinese writers rarely ever referred to Han settlement efforts using the Japanese neologism for colonialism, *shokumin*, preferring the classical Chinese terms for "frontier military settlements" and "land reclamation," *tuntian* 屯田 and *kaiken* 開墾 respectively, or a newly coined word for "military colonies," *tunken* 屯墾.[11] Related to the terms *tuntian* and *kaiken,* both of which appear frequently in historical records dating from the Han dynasty, *tunken* did not come into vogue until the 1920s.[12] The same writers who used *tunken* in their Chinese language works, employed *inner colonization* in English. The etymology of the term strongly suggests that *tunken* was popularized as a response to China's perceived besiegement from imperialist powers. Translated works of literature aided the circulation of new language. As Japan expanded its presence in Northeast China in the 1930s, both Japanese colonial officials and Chinese writers and journalists began to use the term *virgin lands* (Ch. *chunüdi* 處女地)to refer to frontier territories. In the Chinese case, the use of "virgin lands" dates from the translation of the works of the Russian writer Mikhail Sholokhov (1905–1984).[13] From the 1920s onward, journalists, writers, propagandists, and Nationalist or Guomindang (GMD) party bureaucrats alike crafted claims to the Northwest as the birthplace of Chinese civilization and argued that Han Chinese occupation of the region dated back several thousand years. The circular logic of the era declared the region both as a permanent part of Chinese civilization and an apparently depopulated virgin land awaiting conquest and settlement. The evolution of terminology, including neologisms and foreign loan words, point to the importance of the nation-state and fixed geographical boundaries as the definition of state sovereignty in the language of modernity in the twentieth century.[14]

In the nineteenth and twentieth centuries, global elites often presented one set of ideas to Western audiences in English or European languages and wholly different concepts in their native languages. These disparities make more difficult the global historian's task. What may appear at first glance to be a flattening effect of globalization turns out not to be the case after all. To domestic audiences, these educated elites filtered and altered the ideas that they picked up over the course of their education and travels overseas. The underlying actions—the building of infrastructure and modern transportation, transforming areas previously seen as pasture or wastelands into agriculturally productive zones, and the aggressive exploitation of mineral resources—were the same. These same means underlay the geopolitical remaking of the world in the twentieth century. Carried out with new technologies of development, transportation, and sciences, geo-modernity enabled a global realignment. We're still living in its fallout.

Time, Space, and the Global History Perspective

In addition to the multiple meanings brought about by the process of translation, this work also plays with concepts of space and time. In doing so, I am taking up Stefan Tanaka's call for historians to "embrace the richness and variability of different times that exist throughout our lives," and against what Michel de Certeau enjoined as a conflation of time and chronology, an unthinking surrender to the alibi of time.[15] Most of the comparative literature on frontiers focuses on the early modern period and ends in the nineteenth century because of the perception that the most important settlement policies date to this earlier foundational period. Great frontiers around the world, in North and South America, South Africa, and Australia, had closed by nineteenth century's end.[16] Yet, the disciplines most important to globally circulating ideas about settlement, including geography and agricultural science, did not professionalize until the late nineteenth century, at the tail end of this first frontier rush. What happened in the German East, the American West and South, the Japanese Empire, and the Chinese Northeast and Northwest took place in different historical, environmental, and political contexts. Nevertheless, what happened in these borderlands was connected by people and ideas that crossed both national boundaries and historical eras.

The broad time frame and disparate cultural histories and geographical conditions of these places appear to strain the comparative approach. The historian Marc Bloch argued for revealing the larger patterns of historical change through "a parallel study of societies that are at once neighboring and contemporary, exercising a constant mutual influence, exposed through their development to the action of the same broad causes just because they are close and contemporaneous, and owing their existence in part at least to a common origin."[17] The limitations of this approach are already apparent in his suggestion to examine neighboring societies from the same time period. The rise of global history in recent years offers a methodological alternative to comparative studies. Global history focuses on connections rather than parallels. The rise of science and the social sciences in the nineteenth century created the space for such connections. Instead of using the comparative methodology of quantitative and qualitive study of frontiers, I am taking a global history approach by tracing the network of connections between individuals whose ideas on frontiers and development crossed from academic debates to policy changes.[18] Tracing the lives of individuals, however, means that I do not follow any standard periodization of national histories. As the following pages will show, lives and ideas do not follow neatly bounded geographies and time periods.

The combination of these two perspectives—global history and studies of individuals—places my work in conversation with two seemingly opposing trends in historical scholarship. On the one hand, the school of micro-histories and histories from below has traced the life of individuals and provided a much-needed human face to historical developments and given voice to women, working people, and others who have been left off the pages of history. The rise of global history, on the other hand, incorporated aspects of longue durée histories and expanded the lens to reveal global dynamics and shifts. The broader lens, however, raises other issues. Racism and sexism are inescapable in both the contemporary academic literature and the document trail of frontier settlements. Decisions about the fates of millions of people were made in rooms of men from elite backgrounds. While encouraging the poor and working class to take up the challenge of settling the borderlands, the academic and political elites in countries around the world did not see the need to experience conditions on the frontiers for themselves, other than on short research and fact-finding expeditions. Geopolitics, both in its first stages of development in the early twentieth century and its post–Cold War revival, positioned people like chess pieces across a global stage. Male agronomists, geographers, and bureaucrats often mentioned women in terms of their reproductive capacities and as the means to tie down male settlers in secure familial bonds. Although some bemoaned the gender imbalance on the frontiers, they did not go so far as to admit women to the decision-making process. Geopolitics, along with agronomy and geography, were all disciplines dominated by men who, through the social networks built over the course of their education and careers, promoted those with similar backgrounds. The few exceptions, including the American geographer Ellen Semple, benefited from family wealth and social class, which considerably blunted the constraints of gender.

These disparities cut directly to the heart of fundamental issues with global history. Global history has drawn criticism in recent years for its lack of diversity among its practicing ranks and the flattening effect of its materialist focus. I would like to propose a middle way: a global history that encompasses individual agency; an intellectual history that addresses the racism and misogyny built into much of frontier discourse from the nineteenth and twentieth centuries; a history that acknowledges the exclusions built into archives and written records but also the way that these unpalatable pasts created the modern world in which we live. The use of multiple and intersecting biographies as a global history method breaks down the flattening effect of larger historical narratives into the individual trajectories of lived lives along with all their associated messiness, triumphs, and reversals of fortune. Individual lives give texture to broader concepts of empires, frontiers, and nations and cross the temporal and spatial boundaries we have created in the professionalization of modern history writing.[19]

The focus on specific individual social scientists emphasizes the way that ideas about empire, nation-state, and modern state-making crossed political divides and periodization of national histories. It is also my intentional choice to locate agency for historical change on a global scale with individuals. The concept of "national" history is itself a product of this formative age in the making of the modern state.[20] Moreover, while certain events brought out global echoes—from the revolutions of 1848 to both World War I and II—the events covered in this book did not arise from any specific moment but as both the cause and effects of globalization, including industrialization, the rise of modern science and social science, and new technologies of communication and transportation.

The Resilience of Empire

Empires were the dominant state form for 2,000 years before the rise of the nation-state.[21] In their magisterial overview of empires throughout world history, Burbank and Cooper argued that as a state form empires have been remarkably flexible in setting the political context of their transformation over time, both inspiring and constraining leaders and followers.[22] As such, empires and imperial concerns continued to influence leading political thinkers and bureaucrats in their reimagining of the post-imperial state in the twentieth century. Despite growing popularity of nationalist movements around the world, on the ground the situation in borderlands was often far more complex than central governments would have liked to acknowledge. To assert control over contested territories and to consolidate borders, politicians, military leaders, and social scientists sought to deploy science and technology as the means to overcome adverse environmental conditions on one hand, and at the same time, to control recalcitrant nomadic populations. As the concepts of the nation and nationalism gained purchase in the nineteenth century, advocates for empire recalibrated their rhetoric and, in some instances, disguised imperial methods under a cloak of nationalism or avoided altogether using the term *empire*. Nevertheless, imperial structures conferred certain advantages.

I began this project with curiosity over why twentieth-century Chinese regimes have continued to lay claims over Qing territories while rejecting its flexible frontier policies. What was in the beginning a simple question about the continuity in territory between the last empire and the current Chinese state turned to an examination of the way that the sciences, particularly the fields of geography and agricultural science, as well as the social sciences, shaped this transitional period in the late nineteenth and early twentieth centuries, between the height of imperial reach and the rise of the nation-state. The transition was hardly a clean break—empire continued to influence the formation of the nation-state long after its supposed obsolescence. Geographers, anthropologists, economists, archaeologists, agronomists, and historians worked to craft the ideas that informed political and military leaders to adapt the best features of empire (and unintentionally, some of the worst) to the age of the nation-state. The years around World War I saw swept away not only the Qing, but no less than four other historically land-based empires, including the Ottoman Empire, Austria-Hungary, the German Empire (only formed in 1870), and Imperial Russia. By war's end, the great age of empires appeared to wane. The age-old state form would be replaced by the rise of the nation-state and the principle of self-determination. Empire, however, continued to cast a long shadow after its alleged demise. Not coincidentally, all five empires mentioned above struggled over the course of the nineteenth century with the social and political disruptions of modernization.

In the twentieth century, Germany attempted to reconstitute empire under the National Socialists. The Nazi vision for Eastern Europe borrowed much from precedents in the nineteenth and early twentieth centuries. The Soviet Union adopted a minorities policy that drew from Leninist anti-imperialist rhetoric to establish a multinational federation of nationalities. The rhetoric of equality and a united front against imperialism, however, ran hollow and contrasted against the reality of sponsored efforts aimed to extract natural resources from the Arctic, Siberian, and Central Asian frontiers. The Soviet policy influenced the People's Republic of China's designation in the 1950s of fifty-six ethnic groups and regions like Tibet and Xinjiang as autonomous zones rather than provinces.[23] China also drew from its own imperial tradition, dating to the first unification in 221 BCE.

The United States is usually not mentioned in the same category as the European empires. Nevertheless, a large and growing body of literature on US international relations has pointed to the rise of an American empire from the nineteenth century.[24] The United States took the lead in the opening of Japan in the mid-nineteenth century. Within decades, the acquisition of territories like the Philippines in the 1898 Spanish-American War and the annexation of Hawai'i in the same year brought American expansion across the Pacific. As the American empire expanded through overseas territorial acquisitions, geographers and agricultural scientists played key roles in informing the public and popularizing the newly acquired territories, all the while making a concerted effort to avoid using the word *empire*. In the twentieth century, geographers like Isaiah Bowman, director of the American Association of Geographers and the president of Johns Hopkins University from 1935 to 1948, took the lead in reconceptualizing the notion of empire and steering the US in the post–World War II period of Pax Americana to a deterritorialized empire led by corporate interests.

The complex politics of the era obscured the ways that both China and Japan reacted to global dynamics of power in the golden age of imperialism and the nation-state and structured their response using similar language. From the late nineteenth century, Japanese social scientists and geographers began to construct new disciplines of colonial science and to conduct extensive fieldwork and surveys on the Asian mainland. By the 1930s, the Japanese colonial empire had expanded from Hokkaido to Taiwan, Korea, and Northeast China. Japan's continental ambitions entered a new phase with Manchuria, where the colonial administration established collective farms while the Japanese home government promoted the region as an industrial and modern Eden.[25] Less successful in realizing their plans, the GMD government, as well as certain regional warlords, adopted similar measures to modernize the Chinese border-lands and bolster national defense.

As Japan extended its influence in Manchuria and eventually launched into an invasion of all of China in 1937, a new fervor for fron-tier settlement crossed the Japanese / Chinese divide. Indeed, the image of happy peasants turning apparently unpopulated wasteland into pro-ductive agricultural tracts turned up everywhere from the Nazi push into Eastern Europe, the Japanese controlled puppet state of Manchu-kuo, Soviet Siberia, to the largely unrealized GMD settlement plans for the frontiers.[26] While Japan exercised its interpretation of imperialism on the Asian continent, Chinese intellectuals turned their colonial gaze upon their own frontier regions. As John Fitzgerald puts it, "The nation-alist discovery of China mimicked the explorations of European adven-turers because it was part of the dialogue with the civilizing mission of European imperialism."[27] In this internal imperial project, geography and mapping became an essential part of the ideological formation of the Republic. The territorial imaginary created during this period survived the Chinese civil war and the Communist victory in 1949. Global inspi-rations clearly influenced twentieth-century Chinese territoriality, even as historians and social scientists of the era self-consciously mined the Chinese past for relevant models. Various reformers, military leaders, and social scientists reinterpreted China's own imperial past to accom-modate new ideas about the nation-state to achieve scientific modernity. At the same time, they eagerly took note of parallel developments in other parts of the world. *Geo-modernity* in China emerged from this fun-damental spatial reconceptualization of territoriality.

After the collapse of the Qing Empire in 1912, Han Chinese control over the border regions of Xinjiang, Tibet, Manchuria, and parts of the Southwest grew increasingly tenuous under combined pressures from powerful local warlords and foreign encroachment. Yet, a succession of regimes retained control, at times entirely fictive, over these border-lands. The ubiquity of a finely nuanced frontier discourse in the upper echelons of the GMD bureaucracy and military, in the Chinese Com-munist Party, and among the ranks of cosmopolitan and well-educated scientific circles, strongly indicates that these ideas echoed throughout the twentieth century, gained purchase across political divisions, and underlie China's territorial claims today.

The growing prominence of a New Qing history in the last two decades placed China into a global spectrum of early modern empires while engaging with ways the Manchu-ruled dynasty both expanded and redefined a multiethnic imperial ideology.[28] Qing historians like Peter Perdue and James Millward have examined the importance of the western frontiers for the Qing state.[29] At the same time, mainland Chinese scholars, most prominently the Chinese Academy of Social Sciences in 2015, have attacked New Qing history. The Marxist influence on Chinese historiography in the twentieth century has resulted in the almost complete elision of the influence of China's own imperial past on its twentieth-century process of state-making. In this view, China is the victim of imperialism in the nineteenth and early twentieth centuries but never an active participant in the marginalization of its own minority populations. *Birth of the Geopolitical Age* aims to fill this lacuna and restore a narrative of continuity by examining Chinese history in a global context.

China, of course, was not the only country navigating the transition from empire to nation-state in the twentieth century. In an early work, Prasenjit Duara placed in tandem the impact of Western capitalism's penetration into the Chinese countryside with the extension of state control into rural society as the two key historical processes of the twentieth century.[30] Both processes connected China to global forces but remained tethered to specifically Chinese local dynamics from the late imperial period.[31] The focus of this work on the US, China, Japan, and Germany makes clear that this transition was hardly a clear-cut one of displacement and replacement. Old imperial ideas remained, if only in the minds and memories of those who actively sought new ways to adapt empire to the modern age. After a quick spurt of overseas territorial expansion at the turn of the century, the US seemed to pull back. In the 1930s President Franklin Roosevelt reaffirmed the United States' noninterventionist stance in Latin America with the Good Neighbors Policy, emphasizing economic cooperation and trade. By sending American expertise overseas to aid in mining and resource surveys, however, the United States simply expanded its influence through other means than territorial annexation.[32]

The downfall of the Third Reich brought a quick end to a central European empire dominated by Germany. The dream of a *Mitteleuropa,* and an economic and territorial bloc in the heart of Europe dominated by a German powerhouse, had circulated from the time of Friedrich

List in the nineteenth century. The liberal German politician Friedrich Naumann proposed a *Mitteleuropa* plan in 1915.[33] During World War II, research in the newly coined field of "East Research" or *Ostforschung*, helped the regime articulate a plan for the development of the East based on the promotion of settlement by ethnic Germans.[34] The questionable political loyalty of these social scientists helped them to evade responsibility after the demise of the Third Reich. The long-held dream of a unified European economic bloc came to fruition with the formation of the European Union, still dominated by Germany as an economic anchor. Empire never disappeared; under different guises and in different forms, empire has come roaring back in the twenty-first century. The infrastructure created by empire, particularly the means to control, extract, and transport natural resources, has remained intact.

The rise of nationalism in the nineteenth century was entangled with empires and the pervasive impact of imperialism, distracting from the underlying global and transnational forces that linked the two.[35] The tensions between these two seemingly conflicting trends, nationalism and empire-building, play out most trenchantly on the frontiers. Aided by elite intellectual and military discourse (often articulated by those with extremely cosmopolitan educational backgrounds, learned in the tools of empire and social sciences), policies on frontier settlement often appear deeply embedded in historical and nationally specific contexts and cloaked in ardently nationalistic rhetoric. Yet, the national specificity of these ideas on frontiers and settlements often turns out to be smoke and mirrors. Take away the bombastic nationalism and one is left with a certain framework of development and borders (as accepted under international law), which grew from the global expansion of European maritime empires and in turn informed the world order that took shape by the late nineteenth century and remains in place today. In that sense, the apparent end of free land—the closure of frontiers, including the iconic American West—did not merely signal the end of one era, but also the start of a new age, still hinged upon the frontiers.

Empires of Knowledge

Ideas about territory are deeply entrenched in the history and culture of a country. What made this global trend possible was the rise of science and social sciences and their adoption by a ruling and academic elite around the world. The members of this elite were not, for the most part, well-known nor necessarily politically powerful figures. The people I examine are not unknown—in fact, some figures have received a fair amount of attention from historians in specific fields. These accounts, however, offer only a brief and incomplete snapshot of these figures without a narrative that connects them in the making of new global norms—of agricultural development and frontier settlement, science, education, and boundary-making. This book is about the missionaries of improvement who drove these initiatives. They came not just from Western countries, but also from Japan, to other Asian peoples, and from China, to its own minority populations. In doing so, my approach not only decenters Europe, but also holds the United States, Japan, and China answerable for their roles in colonialism, both formal and informal, external and internal.

Geographers and agronomists were part of a global educated elite and active participants in international networks put in place by the professionalization of their disciplines. The successive collapse of formal empires in the early twentieth century appeared to herald the end of this era of transnational, professionalized experts on empire. Nevertheless, empire remained on the minds of social scientists and played into their reimagining of a post-imperial world. Hitler did not draw up schematics for farm communities in the East. Planning for the occupied East fell to geographers and agronomists. In China, Nationalist party leader Chiang Kai-shek's famed 1943 political tract *China's Destiny*, which laid out his territorial vision for modern China, was ghostwritten by the party historian Tao Xisheng. The details of Chiang's ghostwritten vision were enacted by geographers and agronomists who continued to shape the country's territorial expanse long after Chiang lost the civil war to communist forces and fled to Taiwan in 1949. The American Century, the term coined by *Time* publisher Henry Luce, was set in motion by the global reordering forged by two twentieth century world wars, with geographer Isaiah Bowman as its consigliere. Ideas about frontiers and development shaped the modern state and territoriality. They did not originate with political leaders but did help to mold their ideas about territory, power, and empire. In many instances the intellectuals who formulated these ideas were consumed by the very forces they helped to unleash.

Empires had long provided the infrastructure for the circulation of knowledge. In his work *Green Imperialism,* Richard Grove traces the rise of a global state environmentalism to the early modern period, in particular the rise of climate theories and conservationism from the European encounter with the tropics and the settlement of oceanic islands.[36] As part of European territorial expansion, islands like St. Helena to Mauritius were integrated into global intellectual, economic, and trade networks, through which new scientific ideas and climate theories circulated. In the period between the French Revolution in the late eighteenth century and the Indian Mutiny in the mid-nineteenth century, the state became increasingly interventionist in shaping environmental policy through the institutional diffusion of professional science and the active engagement of the colonial peripheries with the metropoles.[37] Far from marginal, the new species discovered and knowledge gained in the colonies proved essential for the formulation of new scientific theories.

The importance of the frontier was clear to early modern states around the world. John Richards's environmental study of frontiers around the world pointed out broad similarities in the way that early modern states annexed frontier areas and dispossessed indigenous peoples. Lands occupied by nomadic peoples were emptied first on the map, marked as *terra nullius.* Settlers then moved in and, with plans of improvement, staked claims of ownership. In nearly every world region, technologically superior pioneer settlers invaded remote lands sparsely occupied by shifting groups of cultivators, hunter-gatherers, and pastoralists. Encouraged, directed, and subsidized by expansive states, surplus populations moved to new areas promising fertile land and opportunities for enrichment. In turn, expanding early modern states imposed new types of territoriality on frontier regions. Settlers and colonial regimes refused to recognize any existing property rights among indigenous peoples (or if they did so initially, these were soon abrogated). Instead, they viewed these lands as empty, to be claimed by the encroaching state.[38]

Richards demonstrates how various disparate states, including Russia, the New World colonies, Qing China, and Japan settled excess populations on the frontiers, as both part of internal colonization and migration to external territorial acquisitions. He, like Grove, emphasizes the environmental consequences of these frontier settlements. In all these cases, efforts to settle the frontiers involved extending cultivation of the newly settled lands and bringing water control and irrigation to facilitate the process. These efforts to change the ecologies of regions brought about long-term changes in settlement patterns and climate of these areas. The environmental approach notably differs from the way that Alfred Rieber has studied Eurasian borderlands as "shatter zones," contested areas between the Habsburg, Russian, Ottoman, and Qing empires that witnessed significant conflict from their rise to their collapse around the time of World War I. Despite differences in how they approached the concept of empire, these works share a comparative approach and connect frontiers to the expansion of early modern empires. Little attention, however, is paid to the people who crossed empires and assisted in the circulation of knowledge.

By the mid-nineteenth century, European empires and the colonial governments they administered around the world had deployed a series of innovations to confer homogeneity and "improvement" to newly settled territories. These innovations included irrigation projects to bring agriculture to arid regions and survey, registration, and land reallocation policies that provided acreage, tax relief, and other forms of subsidies to these frontier settlements.[39] In the twentieth century, the environmental imprint of empire took on new dynamics with changing technologies of communication and transportation. Global examples of frontier settlements in the twentieth century, from Germany to the Soviet Union and China, illustrate how authoritarian regimes particularly favored these frontier "experiments" as testing grounds for resource extraction and radical development plans. These plans looked good on paper, but in real life conditions exacted huge costs on the environment and the lives of those who took up the challenge of settling the frontiers. The long-term impact of twentieth century global frontier efforts is only now becoming apparent. What happened on the frontiers did not stay in the peripheries. The events covered in this book created the world we live in today, along with all the inequalities and disparities between and within countries and their populations.[40]

The infrastructural knowledge networks of empires were hardly one-way affairs. Empire also created an infrastructural network that served as a conduit for indigenous ideas. The French physiocrat Pierre Poivre was heavily influenced by Chinese works on the relationship between forests and soil erosion. The German counterpart to physiocracy, cameralism, was similarly shaped by the participation of Germans on global expeditions, some sponsored by other European states. In turn, the publications of well-known naturalists like Alexander von Humboldt, Georg Forster, and others guided the rise of a global environmental consciousness that took root in Europe based on knowledge and inspiration from across the world.

The professionalization of the sciences played an integral role in creating global views on the environment and in defining the relationship between scientists and the state. Organizations such as the Royal Society, the British Association for the Advancement of Science, and academies of sciences across the European continent allowed for the circulation of ideas within and between empires. From its founding, the newly independent United States joined these circles. Thomas Jefferson's well-known interest in natural history, for example, connected him to the leading scientific minds of his time, including Comte de Buffon at the Jardin du Roi in Paris, the leading naturalist of his age.[41] By the mid-nineteenth century, the United States was striking out on its own, sending its own expeditions around the world with joint diplomatic, economic, and scientific goals. In the late nineteenth and early twentieth centuries, Asian countries like Japan and China followed suit and established their own academies of sciences as the means to achieve parity with the West.

The disciplines of geography and agronomy bridged the divide between premodern categories of knowledge and modern science. These fields internationalized as they adjusted to fulfill the universalist claims of modern science. The importance of agriculture to premodern states made it an essential area of knowledge. The prominence of agricultural texts among the works the Jesuits brought to China from the sixteenth century onward makes clear the topic's importance in Europe, Asia, and elsewhere.[42] By the nineteenth century, natural scientists on global scientific expeditions regularly collected seeds and potentially economically valuable plants at every stop; in the twentieth century, professional plant hunters and agronomists in government institutions like agriculture departments filled the same role. As a discipline, geography helped to create a hierarchy of space central to the reordering of the world in the nineteenth and twentieth centuries. Concepts such as central place theory provided an explanatory model for how we understand the rise of megacities like New York, Chicago, Tokyo, and Shanghai, as well as the spatial organization of rural hinterlands in an ascending hierarchy. Central place theory originated in Germany in the nineteenth century. In the early twentieth century, German economists and geographers were among its earliest proponents to theorize the spatial organization of industrial development. In time, American historians like William Cronon used central place theory in the analysis of Chicago's development, and Sinologist G. William Skinner employed it to study the rural organization of the Chinese countryside.[43] Among its most important theorists was the German geographer Walter Christaller, who spent World War II as a Nazi researcher in the field of *Ostforschung*, the study of Eastern Europe.[44] At the same time, geographers themselves were embedded in internationalized professional networks during a period when the field began to assume its current boundaries and navigated the tricky boundaries between natural and social science.

These global trends were not solely limited to the European empires. As the effects of capital-intensive globalization spread, so did science and the globalizing influence of educational networks, which brought elites from Asia, the Middle East, Africa, and the Americas to a select number of institutions of higher learning and conversely brought professionalized scientific disciplines and their applications in geography, agriculture, and economic development to various corners of the world. Geography and agriculture are both widely recognized as areas of knowledge foundational to the function of the premodern state and had long been the focus of state support or regulation in different parts of the world.

In China, these global examples of frontier settlements refracted through its unique history to form a new territoriality that informed the process of modern Chinese state formation. A politically charged discussion of the frontier became deeply entangled with the impetus for modernization and development. These ideas about the frontier survived the political transition to the People's Republic of China and are still evident today. I argue that *geo-modernity* emerged from this fundamental spatial reconceptualization of Chinese territoriality and drew from the unique dynamics during a turbulent transitional period from empire to nation-state. The subsequent reshaping of Chinese geopolitical ambitions in the twentieth century continues to reorder the power dynamics in East Asia and the world in the twenty-first century.

The epistemological change and incorporation of traditional areas of knowledge into the categories of modern science are central to this transition to geo-modernity. The imperial Chinese state staffed its bureaucracy based on a vaunted civil examination system, which privileged knowledge of the classics over areas of practical application. Nevertheless, members of the literati class that peopled the civil bureaucracy viewed geography and agriculture as appropriate areas to cultivate learning and knowledge. In the nineteenth century, these interest circles came into contact with global networks. Translations of geography and agricultural works from the West introduced these topics as sciences but would not have elicited much surprise or resistance because of their long-standing acceptance as part of the practical knowledge necessary to the successful administration of empire. There are broad similarities to the transmission of the new science of geology in China. These similarities to existing knowledge opened the way to broad assimilation of modern science.

In my earlier work I have argued that the familiarity with mining of large segments of the Chinese population, from scholar-officials, to merchants, to peasants, helped to usher in acceptance of geology and new conceptions of natural resources foundational to industrialization. China similarly has a long history of innovations in geography and agriculture. For scholar-officials, interests in these areas were not only accepted but encouraged as essential knowledge for the proper administration of the state. This broad acceptance can be seen in the inclusion of these new sciences in local gazetteers, a form of knowledge compilation that had been in place since at least the Tang dynasty in the tenth century, flourished during the Ming and Qing dynasties, and continued throughout the twentieth century. These gazetteers frequently featured administrative maps, lists of local products, schools, and temples. From the late nineteenth century, new features like agricultural experimental zones, new types of schools, including for girls, and new cartographic innovations imported from the West showed up in these local gazetteers across the country and often in places far from the coastal treaty port cities. The inclusion of these changes in a traditional medium illustrates how existing networks of scholars and officials quickly adopted and adapted new knowledge. These changes carried over from the last decades of the Qing dynasty to the Republican period in the early twentieth century and the communist era after 1949.

In the twentieth century, influences from abroad, including the importation of scientific disciplines and ideas about race and nationalism, combined with long-running domestic concerns to form a potent new justification for territorial control over peripheral regions. There is no question that the twentieth century and modern period brought momentous change to China. Classical Chinese gave way to vernacular; the nation replaced empire; science became the savior of a nation in decline. Yet, some of these dynamics of change were also deceptive. The language changed, but the territorial expanse of empire did not. This work draws out some of the underlying continuities between "traditional" Chinese geography and twentieth-century developments, when Chinese geographers attempted to remake geography into a science, to make the argument that geo-modernity emerged from this fundamental spatial reconceptualization of Chinese territoriality.

There were new names given to these new disciplines—agricultural science, agricultural economics, and the study of Earth (*dixue* 地學)— alongside the old designations of geography (*dili* 地理) but with a "new" appended to indicate its newly acquired scientific bona fides. These works on "new" geography employed empirical study and statistical methods versus the kind of historical geography that literati with allegedly stultifying and rigid classical training had engaged in previous eras. Yet, upon closer examination, one couldn't help but notice the superficialities of these designations of newness and some underlying continuities. At the heart of the discussion is the issue of semantics—and the varying gray areas between classical Chinese, neologisms from Japan, and the various translations of ideas from international law to the language of science which so occupied missionaries and Chinese translators alike in the late nineteenth century.

Chinese scientists of the early twentieth century, who proudly viewed themselves as part of a New Culture movement that rejected tradition, often discovered modernity in the close reading of Chinese classics, in medicine, and in the traditional compilations of local information, the gazetteer. They dusted off these findings and, using adopted new methods from the West, repurposed this knowledge to craft the sciences necessary to build a modern nation.[45] Early twentieth-century Chinese scientists and intellectuals used the phrase *kexue jiuguo* 科學救國, "science saves the nation," to appeal to nationalism and promote science.[46] The very success of these efforts laid the foundations for some of the current conflict between the United States and China, each vying for dominance in science and technology and neither acknowledging the more unpalatable history of dispossession and violence on the frontiers. The histories of these two continental powers have been entangled from the nineteenth century, as one rose and the other declined in the international order. In the twenty-first century, they appear headed for collision as each laid claim to great power status. From conflict to collaboration, both the US and China share in the reluctance to discuss the common influences of their respective frontier experiences.

Network Science as Structure

This work operates on several registers: as a history of multiple lives whose arcs crossed and crisscrossed through time, and at the level of discourse about empire and frontiers. We live in a world created from the outside in, where state-making processes took place on the frontiers. The peripheries became the testing places for the expansion of interventionist state policies. Network theories have gained favor in recent years with the rise of social media. What Facebook and Twitter make visible, however, are the connections that were always present, just as global travel existed long before the invention of trains and airplanes and the adoption of fossil fuel–based economies and trade connected far corners of the world well before people came up with the concept of globalization. Around the year 2000, in the first wave of research on the internet, researchers discovered something interesting and unexpected about the World Wide Web and its connections: it was not spread out evenly but rather clustered around a few nodes.[47] The internet apparently worked in the same fashion as the underground connections between trees in the whimsically dubbed "world wood web." The underground fungal connections, a means of communication between trees, are not evenly spread out. Instead, a few old-growth anchor trees function as important hubs for an entire forested area.[48] The mysteries of human history and the circulation of knowledge mimic the ways of subterranean mycelial networks.

I have adapted these insights from network and mushroom science to a historical narrative to break away from a purely chronological narrative of the nineteenth and twentieth centuries. Each chapter is based on the concept of a hub—points in time and space, both physical and conceptual, at which an entangled web of individual lives and events intersected and then diverged. Chapter 1, for example, begins with the year 1852, a date that does not seem to occupy any place of prominence for historians but was a point of intersection for a variety of figures from Commodore Perry and Horace Capron in the United States to Zuo Zongtang in China. By the mid-nineteenth century, the forces of capitalism had penetrated to the far corners of the world and underlay growing global turmoil. Chapter 2 examines the proliferation of agricultural experimental stations across Asia from the late nineteenth century. Chapter 3 moves on to the development of modern geography as a discipline and its contributions to the understanding of the ideal spatial organization of the modern state. Chapter 4 begins at Versailles, France, at the post–World War I peace negotiations and from this physical hub, analyzes the subsequent flourishing of geopolitics in the interwar years through global intellectual networks. Chapter 5 begins with the efforts by the big American philanthropical institutions to promote the global spread of democracy and the scientific modernization of countries like China, Mexico, and India. On the other side of the political spectrum, regional warlords in China also led rural reconstruction efforts. With different goals in mind, both the American NGOs and Chinese warlords sought to deploy science to achieve their ends. Chapter 6 scrutinizes settlement plans during World War II proposed by both the Nazi planning offices for the conquered Eastern Europe and besieged wartime Chinese government for the Northwest and Southwest. Finally, chapter 7 explores geographers' and agronomists' contributions to the making of the Cold War world order.

Dozens of figures appear in these chapters, mostly geographers and agronomists. Many of these people met tragic ends, used by their regimes and those in power and then consumed by the very forces they helped to unleash. What endured were imperial structures and aims repackaged as uniquely national and with their historical and global contexts erased. What follows is a narrative that moves through time and space, the lives of individuals, and empires' rise and downfall and rebirth.

ONE

1852 and the Afterlife of Revolutions

> Each age must be studied in the light of all the past; local history
> must be viewed in the light of world history.
>
> *Frederick Jackson Turner*[1]

In the annals of history, 1852 fades into the background in the roiling agitations of the century. A few years earlier, in the spring of 1848, a wave of revolutions had swept across Europe, built on the disruptions and discontent caused by industrialization. The son of a large textile industrialist in England and his native Prussia, Friedrich Engels, directly observed the conditions of the working class in Manchester in 1842–1844. The resulting account vividly described the crowded slums of the working class, where the unpaved streets were littered with refuse and stagnant wastewater and wracked by waves of disease that sped through these tightly packed and poorly ventilated residential quarters.[2] The fetid conditions of these industrial slums fed into the discontent that rose to a fevered pitch in 1848.

As the calls for revolution spread in 1848, Engels partnered with an admiring German philosopher named Karl Marx to publish a rousing manifesto for workers to overthrow the shackles of their capitalist oppressors.[3] For a brief period in 1848, it appeared as though the long-awaited revolution was finally taking place. In an unusually warm spring, crowds gathered in protest in European capitals across the continent. The coalition of reformers, working class, and the bourgeoisie, however, did not hold, and by 1852, a conservative reaction had set in place. To the great disappointment of observers like Marx and Engels, revolutionary gains were quickly reversed, and the status quo reinforced. The aborted revolution notwithstanding, vast changes were clearly under way that would transform the world in the years to come. We begin, then, with this temporal hub as the starting point for multiple protagonists who raced to deal with the fallout from the widespread social and environmental disruptions around the world created by the twin forces of industrialization and capitalism.

Cultivating the Qing Frontiers

On the other side of the world from the protests in Europe, a different sort of rebellion had begun to gain traction. Starting in the late 1840s, the failed civil examination candidate and Christian convert Hong Xiuquan (1814–1864) had agitated for the overthrow of the Qing dynasty and built up a formidable force of followers.[4] Born in 1814, Hong was the fourth of five children in rural Guangdong province, in a region of the country most affected by the growing encroachment of Western powers, and a member of the Hakka minority, the "guest people" who migrated south from central China centuries earlier. The civil examinations promised entry to the bureaucracy and prestige for the entire lineage. Like many in China who saw the civil examination as the path to social mobility, Hong's extended family had pooled their resources to fund his education and exam preparation. Hong repeatedly disappointed their hopes.

After passing the preliminary exams, in the 1830s Hong failed two attempts to advance to the next level. In 1836, on one of his trips to take the exams in the city of Guangzhou (Canton), Hong encountered a Protestant missionary, Edwin Stevens, who had arrived from the United States. The exams were grueling, multiday ordeals that taxed the limits of physical and mental stamina. Before the examinees entered special examination sites filled with small cubicles, they were searched for crib notes (nevertheless, many tiny handwritten cheat books made their way through, hidden in food, writing brushes, and utensils). Through days and sleepless nights, examinees wrote the responses that would determine their fates. After a third failure in 1837, Hong returned home and fell gravely ill, during which he suffered prolonged bouts of fever and delirium. The death of his lifelong dream nearly brought about his physical collapse.

Six years later, Hong failed the exam for a fourth time. He read the pamphlets he had picked up years earlier from Stevens and had a revelation that his feverish dreams years ago in fact featured God, Jesus Christ, and himself as the younger brother of Christ. A life of failure suddenly found its purpose. With newfound clarity, Hong moved to Thistle Mountain in Guangxi province in southwestern China to preach his revelations to anyone willing to listen and to form the Society of God Worshippers.

It had been over two hundred years since the Manchus, a nomadic tribe from the northeastern region bordering Russia and Korea, had conquered all of China, expanded control over borderlands to the northwest, west, and southwest, and reigned over a multiethnic empire.[5] The Qing experienced a period of unprecedented prosperity and peace in the eighteenth century. A confluence of external and domestic threats, however, ushered in an extraordinarily turbulent nineteenth century. Faced with growing threats from Western empires on the eastern coasts and domestic unquiet in the interior, Hong's millenarian preaching struck a chord. As his base grew exponentially, Hong built an army and marched out of the Guangxi mountains to take aim at all of China.

In January 1851, Hong declared himself the Heavenly King of the Taiping Kingdom. The two characters for Taiping, 太平, denote "great peace"—an ironic moniker for an uprising that would eventually cost 20 to 30 million lives and lay waste to vast stretches of agriculturally fertile lands over the course of roughly a decade and a half. Two years later, in March 1853, the former Ming capital of Nanjing, in the wealthiest middle region of China, fell to the rebels. That same year, when it appeared that the Qing Empire would quickly collapse in the face of escalating military losses, Karl Marx published an article in the *New York Daily Tribune* that argued for external causes, first and foremost imperialism and the predations of the global market, for the great rebellion.[6] His hopes in Europe dashed, Marx looked in vain to Asia. The Qing would eventually suppress the Taiping at great cost in lives and damages and limp on in power for another five decades before its final dissolution in 1912. The great rebellion undoubtedly unleashed forces that ultimately contributed to the demise of the dynasty. In 1852, however, this calamity was still in the making, its outcome too murky to prognosticate. Karl Marx was unfamiliar with the domestic issues, including a fast-growing population and environmental depletion, that had built up pressures on the Qing state.

For a millennium China was connected to the outside world through various trade routes that crossed Central Asia to Persia and beyond. From the sixteenth century these trade networks expanded through the cargoes of ships that plied the ocean routes between Europe, Africa, the New World, and Asia. The Age of Discovery brought silver to Asia from the mines of South America, loaded onto galleon ships that plied the Pacific.[7] The use of silver in the Chinese currency made Asia the most lucrative market for the New World metal. On return trips, these ships carried teas and silks from China to satisfy growing demands in Europe. The merchants who funded these risky journeys, susceptible to the vagaries of weather, rough seas, and pirate attacks, attained great wealth through this trade triage. The Spanish and Portuguese gave way to the Dutch and British. As it harnessed the power of carbon and led the way in the mechanization of manufacturing, the British Empire became the dominant European power in Asia in the nineteenth century.

Environmentally, both Europe and China entered a period of intensifying use of natural resources in the sixteenth century. Deforestation in Europe meant that the large logs used to build ships had to travel longer distances to reach the port cities from forests in remote frontiers.[8] England had already switched to the use of coal in the sixteenth century for heating and metallurgy. Similarly, major centers of the porcelain industry in China, in Jingdezhen in Jiangxi province, for instance, turned to coal to fuel its kilns as the surrounding countryside became denuded of large forests. To satisfy growing population demands, women and children resorted to piecework and home weaving for extra income. Increasing efficiency in human labor nevertheless failed to fully counter ecological constraints: the limited supplies of commodities, such as cotton for homespun, and of energy sources like firewood.[9]

At this critical juncture, the New World and its seemingly limitless frontiers of wilderness and pristine forests opened a fresh resource frontier for Europe.[10] The route to modern capitalism cut through the frontiers. China did not have the good fortune of discovering New World resources to break through its ecological constraints. To feed a rapidly growing population, particularly in the seventeenth and eighteenth centuries, the late imperial Chinese state and bureaucracy saw the intensive exploitation of nature as a solution to the exponentially escalating demand for fertile lands. In the late eighteenth century, the renegade official Hong Liangqi warned of impending crisis from an unchecked rise in population and exhaustion of natural resources. Much like the English author Thomas Malthus, Hong argued that "the amount of [available land and housing] has only doubled, or at the most, increased three to five times, while the population has grown ten to twenty times. . . . the resources with which Heaven-and-earth nourish the people are finite."[11] Chinese officials, however, did not look outwards for solutions to the issue of environmental depletion. Instead, eighteenth- and nineteenth-century officials subscribed to a statecraft school of governance, which emphasized the cultivation of practical knowledge, including ways to improve agriculture and manufacturing, to foster economic growth.[12] The focus on practical knowledge (*shixue* 實學) created the foundations for the adoption of science.[13]

Despite a devoted coterie of provincial officials who sought to provide practical solutions for problems in the areas under their jurisdiction, the rapid growth of the Chinese population created increasing ecological constraints by the late eighteenth century. By examining both Chinese and Jesuit discussion of agricultural practices in the late imperial period, the historian Mark Elvin has argued that, based on contemporary accounts, most of China's areas of intensive cultivation did not practice fallowing, a prevalent agricultural practice in Europe. Population pressures created the need for fields to produce yearly, without off-years for the soil to naturally recover lost nutrients. Restoration of soil fertility relied on intensive application of fertilizers. Given the paucity of large draft animals in most parts of the country, farmers relied on human excrement as the primary fertilizer. Farmers applied fertilizer not just to the most important crops, but every plant, multiple times during the growth cycle. Jesuits traveling in parts of the country outside of the capital in Beijing and major cities noted arid and desolate landscapes, vulnerable to flooding and landslides.[14]

Ecological collapse and rural dispossession in China led to the transpacific coolie trade in the nineteenth century. By the mid-nineteenth century even the intensive application of fertilizer only brought marginal benefits as ecological damage forced farmers off the land. Impoverished Chinese peasants resorted to finding employment in the international coolie trade, joining the global circulation of labor. Chinese workers risked dangerous conditions working with explosives and blasting through mountains building the Transcontinental Railroad across the United States. Conditions in South American plantations that employed coolie labor were brutal and akin to slavery—in fact, Chinese workers replaced some of the labor shortages caused by the demise of the trans-atlantic slave trade. Few of those recruited in the coolie trade returned home alive. Workers endured hellish working conditions on guano farms along the South American coast. The guano served as the raw ma-terials for fertilizers and gunpowder before the invention of chemical alternatives. Countless workers committed suicide by throwing them-selves off cliffs rather than continue to work in inhumane conditions.[15] Sugar plantations in South America and mines in Southeast Asia were hardly better. Mine owners in Southeast Asia offered cheap opium dregs to workers to alleviate their bodily pains, trapping workers in a vicious cycle of addiction and debt until they worked themselves to death.[16]

The overuse of the farmlands compounded the effects of natural di-sasters that struck with frightening frequency. In the third decade of his life in the 1830s, a man named Zuo Zongtang (1812–1885), who would go on to play a leading role in the suppression of the Taiping rebels, already experienced a series of significant floods, crop damage, and droughts in his home county of Xiangyin in Hunan province.[17] Hunan was long con-sidered the agricultural heartland of the country. The repeated natural disasters contributed to Zuo's interest in the study of subjects loosely grouped under "practical learning" (*shixue*), including various ways to improve agriculture. Although not considered part of the classics, the essential works which all young Chinese men who aspired to pass the civil examinations needed to master, agricultural knowledge was a time-honored field of study for the learned elite, the literati, of imperial China.

China had become an empire in the 200s BCE, when the first emperor of the Qin dynasty defeated rival kingdoms and unified the country. For most of its long imperial history, the state recognized the importance of agriculture. Works dating to antiquity attest to an enduring tradi-tion in agricultural knowledge. The earliest extant work, *Qimin Yaoshu* (*Essential Techniques for the Peasantry*), dates to ca. 535 AD, contains over 100,000 characters, quotes from 160 other works, and describes in great detail the practical knowledge necessary to running an agrarian state, including the cultivation of commercial and food crops, sericul-ture, animal husbandry, as well as the various household manufactur-ing which supplement peasant livelihoods.[18] The later classic *Nong Shu* (*Agricultural Treatise*) by Wang Zhen in the early fourteenth century includes detailed illustrations of farming implements and agricultural technologies like the watermill.

The third great agricultural work in the imperial era was written by the official Xu Guangqi (1562–1633) close to the end of the Ming dynasty. Xu had befriended the Jesuit missionaries who arrived in China in the sixteenth century and became one of their most high-profile Chinese converts. (The Vatican announced the beatification of Xu on April 15, 2011.) In the seventeenth and eighteenth centuries, Jesuit priests followed a top-down approach in their proselytizing efforts and used mathematics, astronomy, and other European technical innovations of their time to gain access to the Ming and Qing courts. Jesuit efforts included the translation of European works they saw as of potential interest to the Chinese. Matteo Ricci (1552–1605) with the help of Li Zhizao and Xu Guangqi translated the first six chapters of Euclid's *Elements of Geometry* (*Jihe yuanben*) and the *Complete Map of the Myriad Countries on the Earth* (*Kunyu wanguo quantu*), along with assorted other works.[19] The Ricci map, as it became known as, is today one of the most famous legacies of this earlier period of exchange.

Works on agriculture were an important part of this corpus that resulted from the early modern circulation of knowledge. In his work *Nong Zheng Quan Shu* (*Complete Treatise on Agricultural Administration*), Xu drew upon his considerable experience in agricultural administration and technology, as well as experiments with Western irrigation techniques he learned from the books the Jesuits brought with them. Among the new technologies which Xu tried to promote in his work was the Archimedean screw, which he had learned from the Jesuits, to be used in irrigation works. Over a century later, Xu's work and other classics would have been the starting point for Zuo's education in agriculture. Beyond these well-known works, other writings circulated privately among scholarly circles with shared interests in the practical application of technologies.

By the late 1830s, Zuo had mastered an extensive library of Chinese agricultural knowledge and wrote his own treatise. At this critical stage, his hopes for a career in officialdom stalled. While the population grew threefold from the start of the dynasty in the seventeenth century, the size of the bureaucracy remained stagnant. By the nineteenth century, it had become increasingly difficult to get a foothold in officialdom and nearly impossible for someone like Hong Xiuquan, who lacked the social

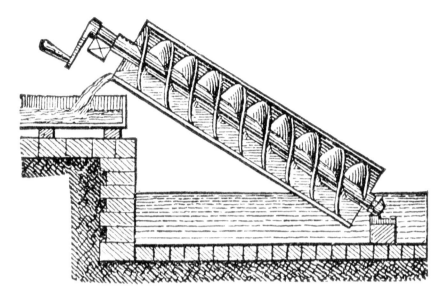

FIGURE 1.1: Illustration of an Archimedean screw, one of the new technologies from the West which the Ming official Xu Guangqi tried to promote in his work. Image from William Dwight Whitney, *The Century Dictionary, an Encyclopedic Lexicon of the English Language* (New York: The Century Co., 1902), I:297.

and scholarly networks for entry. For Hong, that frustration fed his growing rage against the ruling Qing dynasty. Even for talented and well-connected young men like Zuo Zongtang, the path to officialdom became increasingly fraught. These external conditions that led Hong to revolt, in Zuo brought about a quiet resignation. In the 1840s Zuo moved to a property in Liuzhang in Hunan to experiment on cultivation methods and test ways to improve productivity on his land. If he could not become a scholar official, then he would transform into a rural scholar and work on his gardens and fields.

The fates, however, had other plans for Zuo. As the Taiping rebels marched out of the southwestern mountains, they found a disaster-stricken Hunan province ripe grounds for recruitment. In October of 1852, as a member of the learned scholar-elites, Zuo was summoned by the governor to the provincial capital of Changsha to join in the fight against the rebels.[20] For these Confucian scholars, the rebels represented an existential threat—not only did Hong inveigh against the Manchu rulers, which might have garnered him supporters among the majority Han population, he also called for an egalitarian redistribution of land

and equality for women (on paper, at least) that struck some later historians as heralding a proto-communist ideology. The destruction of the main moral principles upholding society was a bridge too far for the Confucian elites to stomach. They now closed ranks with the Manchu court to suppress the rebels. The massive rebellion and an initially botched government response provided Zuo with his first official posting. Zuo Zongtang's life would come to be defined by his role in quelling the great rebellion.

Such was Zuo's effectiveness as a military commander that he was later placed in charge of Gansu province in the West, where a Muslim-led rebellion had festered at the same time as the Taiping. Before he left for his new posting, Zuo helped establish a naval shipyard on the south-eastern coast that aimed to build ironclad ships. A new age was dawning, bringing with it new technologies and sciences that would transform so-

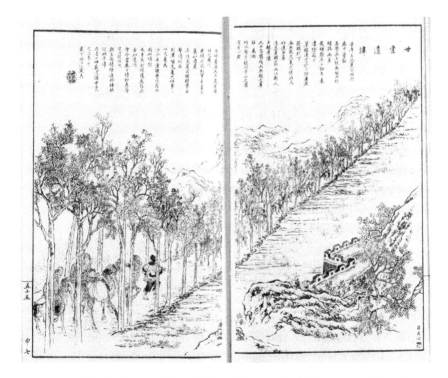

FIGURE 1.2: Illustration and description of trees planted by army of Zuo Zong-tang along roadways in Gansu province. Shanghai: Ji cheng tu shu gong si, Xuantong 2 (1910). From Cornell University Rare Book and Manuscript Collections, open access.

cieties around the world. Zuo and other reformist Qing officials recognized the need to adapt this new knowledge for the empire to survive.

It was a far cry for a scholar who once thought he would live out his life experimenting with farming techniques on his secluded estate. But he didn't entirely leave behind his agricultural interests. Zuo introduced cotton cultivation in the Northwest in his effort to stamp out opium. In the arid Gansu province, he had planted along main avenues neat rows of trees, a reminder perhaps of his verdant Hunan home and the path not taken. Zuo was not the only scholar-official of his generation who recognized the importance of meeting the challenges of the age by adopting new technologies and scientific knowledge from the West, as well as reinforcing the empire's control over its borderlands. These two goals were entwined in efforts to introduce new crops, farming techniques, and manufacturing machinery in the development of borderland regions, including in Western China. Provincial officials were aware of the growing threat posed by the British to Tibet, the French to the Southeast, the Russian Empire in the Northwest and Northeast, and at the end of the century, the Japanese in the Northeast.

One potential solution from the imperial toolbox presented itself as acceptable to both reformers and conservatives—the planned settlement of contested borderland areas by Han Chinese agriculturists. Officials viewed peasants as the stable base of society. Such reclamation plans enjoyed broad support, although many overestimated the willingness of able-bodied settlers to move to harsh new environments and difficult terrains in exchange for slight incentives. To counter these adverse conditions, local officials became particularly interested in importing new agricultural technologies and crops.

The empire was large, with varied geographies and climate zones, and change takes time over such a multitude. As the nineteenth century progressed, time was not on the side of the Qing. In 1852, Marx knew none of the trials of this Qing literatus on the other side of the world, but he picked up on the vague tensions in the air as global forces transformed societies around the world. In these tinderbox conditions, all it took was an unusually warm spring in 1848 and an aggrieved examination candidate to set in motion cataclysmic unrest in Europe and Asia.

To the Texas Borderlands

A disastrous century for the Qing was a period of prosperity and growth for the new nation on the move across the North American continent. The year 1852 saw the start of a journey to the American southwestern borderlands. A few years earlier, in 1846, the United States had gone to war with its southern neighbor Mexico over a territorial dispute in Texas.[21] The land dispute served as a pretext for Americans eager to pursue an expansionist agenda. In the Treaty of Guadalupe Hidalgo, signed on February 2, 1848, Mexico ceded 525,000 square miles of territories to the US, relinquished all claims to Texas, and recognized the Rio Grande River as the boundary between the two countries. The war briefly satisfied the expansionary appetites of its advocates, while papering over the differences, particularly over the issue of slavery, that would lead to another great domestic conflagration of the mid-nineteenth century a decade later. One of the Americans who rushed to volunteer for the Mexican-American War was a man named Horace Capron (1804–1885).

In the Spring of 1852, US President Millard Fillmore appointed Horace Capron as Special Agent for Indian Affairs along the newly negotiated Texas-Mexico border. To reach his destination, Capron traveled by multiple means of transportation, moving across the space and time of an industrializing nation. Leaving Washington, DC, on April 10, 1852, Capron took the train from Washington to Wilmington, North Carolina. At Wilmington, he transferred from railroad to ferry and took to the coastal sea route from Wilmington to Charleston. At Charleston, he again transferred modes of transport and turned inland, first by rail then stagecoach down the Alabama River to Mobile. From Mobile he took a steamboat to New Orleans, across the Gulf of Mexico to Galveston, and finished the final leg of his journey, the last 160-mile stretch to San Antonio, Texas, by stagecoach. It was a long journey, but one that was already made significantly shorter from just a few decades earlier by sections of railroad and steamship, the two coal-fueled transportation technologies ushering the world into the modern global age.

Capron had started his journey across a still frozen Potomac River. In South Carolina he delighted in the perfume of magnolia and roses in the early southern spring. He sweltered in heat and dust on the stagecoach journey across Texas.[22] At the end of his cross-country trek Capron arrived at San Antonio, "more Mexican than American," a frontier town of desperadoes, whose "cheerfulness was often broken in upon by assassinations, street fights, and other interesting pastimes of the renegade frontier settlers and gamblers."[23] Describing the various treacheries played out with bowie knives and the massacres then taking place across the borderlands, Capron expressed sympathy for the Indians, who were frequently caught in the middle of conflicts between Mexicans and Americans. Capron did not oppose the dispossession of Indian lands, just the harsh methods which he thought would only fuel continued resistance. The long, hot days stretched out over the summer, broken by brief bursts of action and news from the East Coast. Capron spent his leisure time reading and studying Spanish as a constant flow of wagon trains carrying men and supplies arrived from the US government. The federal government's support made possible the celebrated myth of rugged individualism in the American West.[24]

The Texas borderlands was a far cry from Oneida County in New York State, where Capron grew up, the descendant of French Huguenots who first arrived in the Americas around 1656. His father fought in the Revolutionary War with General Washington and had built the first cotton factory in New York State, later opening the first woolen factory in the United States. In 1836, through his wife, Capron inherited farmland in Maryland, midway between Baltimore and Washington, DC, in Prince George's County. In the following years, he launched a campaign of improvement on the land. Capron experimented with new agricultural technologies on his lands, seeking to improve the red clay soil of the area through the rotation of crops. He supervised the construction of drainage to reclaim swampy areas on the land. Capron's management of his estate earned him a reputation as an authority on agriculture.[25] He kept a prized herd of 100 thoroughbred North Devon cattle. The cattle would eventually move west with him to Illinois. All the while, Capron kept abreast of the latest agricultural innovations by subscribing to various pioneer agricultural journals.[26] He wrote letters to these journals describing his latest efforts and was also frequently mentioned in their pages, lauded for his industrious efforts. In a letter dated December 21, 1848, Capron advocated for the Southern states to diversify their employment with mixed agriculture and manufacturing, as he was doing on his Maryland estate and much like what was already taking place in the Northeast and mid-Atlantic states. He wrote that "there is no obstacle, either in climate, soil, or population, but what would yield to the march of improvement."[27]

Capron's efforts on his farm undermined the dichotomy that has since set in place between industry and agriculture. The original title of *American Agriculturist*, *The Plough, the Loom and the Anvil*, as well as the name of Capron's estate, *Laurel Factory*, reveal the close connection between agricultural and industrial innovation. For a time, the farm contained both. One visitor waxed poetic on the fruits of Capron's (and his workers') labor, "There you behold industry guided by knowledge. There it is that visible improvement and increased productiveness vindicated the cause of Agriculture and assert its claim to be ranked among intellectual professions."[28] These improvements showed the fruit of industry, the florid praise implied, in contrast to the perceived passivity of American Indians, who wasted the bounties of nature. In July 1849, President Taylor spent some days on Capron's farm, meandering on the grounds and in the stables and enjoying the rural idyll. In his memoirs Capron recalled with pride the president's visit, which he managed to pull off in secrecy.

Early American leaders from Washington, Jefferson, and Madison to John Adams were deeply interested in the exchange of agricultural knowledge and in implementing the latest technologies and farming practices from Europe. They all paid close attention to new knowledge that could improve their lands. The earliest American organizations for science were agricultural societies in each state. Based in Philadelphia and founded by Benjamin Franklin in 1743, the American Philosophical Society is the oldest learned society in the United States. Discussions at the society during its early years focused on the introduction and dissemination of economically valuable plants. During the Constitutional Convention in 1787, the interests that united delegates from states large and small, North and South, were botany and agriculture.[29] As in Europe, the applications in the management of one's estate attracted elite interest in science. In turn, agriculture served as a bridge to modern science.

In the United States, as elsewhere, agricultural knowledge predated modern science and served as an essential link connecting elite interest to gradually professionalizing scientific disciplines. Early nineteenth-century farmers like Capron often undertook their own experiments with seed varieties and published the results of their trials in publica-

tions like the *American Farmer*—multiple states published such agricultural journals with slight variations on the name. A separate Department
of Agriculture was not established until 1862, described by President
Abraham Lincoln as "The People's Department."[30] Even before the official
founding of the United States Department of Agriculture (USDA), however, farmers could avail themselves of numerous resources provided by
the federal and local government. From the turn of the century, farmers could display their prized crops and livestock at agricultural fairs
and learn about the latest farming techniques and equipment.[31] They
could write to the Patent Office and later the USDA for seeds collected
on government-sponsored overseas expeditions and seen as particularly
promising in commercial appeal. On larger homesteads, they could also
branch out into light manufacturing as Capron did.

The days of this picturesque idyll were numbered. By the mid-
nineteenth century, the United States was straining under the growing
pains of industrialization in pockets of the country, particularly in New
England and the mid-Atlantic regions, rapid territorial expansion along
the frontiers, and a railway and transportation boom. Some farmers adopted new practices like crop rotation to restore soil fertility, and others
began to pay attention to new developments in chemistry that explained
the nitrogen cycle. For most farmers, however, the depletion of soil fertility after several years of planting tobacco was a problem best solved by
abandoning the land and moving to clear new fields out of woodlands.

Fortunately for Anglo settlers, over the nineteenth century the frontier was on the move and new lands steadily became available. The
prosperity of the nation was built on the promise of what seemed to be
limitless frontiers of land and resources. Capron notched some success as
a commercial farmer, but ultimately could not hold out against the wave
of changes sweeping across the country as the expansion of capitalist
practices also made itself felt on the farm. Unlike most of his wealthy
neighbors in Maryland, Capron employed tenants rather than slaves. Despite pioneering mixed manufacturing and agricultural use of the land,
the financial turbulence of the 1840s bankrupted Capron. This difficult
period also saw the death of his wife, the mother of his five children.[32]

In 1854 Capron headed west, following his mother, who had earlier
moved to Illinois. His formative experiences in Maryland, where his
children were born, left a lifelong fondness for the region. As an old
man writing his memoirs just months before his death in February 1885,

Capron recalled the genteel hospitality of antebellum Maryland. Wealthy plantation owners thought nothing of daily setting the table for fifteen or twenty unannounced guests. He recalled fondly how a Mr. Contee—related by marriage to Capron's wife and who owned 400 negroes and six large tobacco plantations—always kept a full house of guests.[33] The pretty image of rolling hills, well-tended farmlands, and warm hospitality covered up the harsh economic reality of the slave labor which made possible the wealth and gentility of plantation life in the American South. In the pastoral paradise of Capron's memory, slavery lurked as the snake that would eventually lead to the Civil War. Capron fought for the Union. The conflict cost him his oldest son and namesake, Horace Capron Jr. In his absence during the war, he complained bitterly, a charlatan managed his farm and allowed his prized purebred Devon cattle to run wild. The war would deplete Capron's fortunes yet again.

In 1852, however, the immediate concern was the redrawing of boundaries in the Southwest. In the aftermath of the Mexican-American War, Congress authorized $25,000 for the new state of Texas to remove its Indian tribes, without designating areas where they might be removed to or endorsing any concrete plans. Left with no instructions, militia men set loose along the border executed people wholesale, killing the Lipan Apache tribe indiscriminately and even confiscating as trophies of war presents of blankets previously given them by federal Indian agents.[34] The surviving Indians were cast into the wilderness without any provisions or clothing. As a result of this escalating conflict, Chief Geronimo joined forces with other Apache bands to raid against American forces in a series of skirmishes that continued until the 1880s. Violence suffused the advancing frontier and the dispossession of land from the Indian tribes in the way.[35] In 1852, it was still several decades before Chief Joseph of the Nez Perce uttered the famous words, "I will fight no more forever," marking the last of the Indian resistance to the relentless advance of settlers and the US military, but their fate already looked bleak.[36]

Years later, when Capron met the Ainu tribe in Hokkaido, he would be reminded of his experience in Texas, writing that "I have been struck with many peculiar customs of these Ainos, so similar are they in many ways to those of our North American Indians, although there can be but one opinion that they are a very superior race of beings in every respect, having none of their savage brutality."[37] Despite their docility,

Capron was pessimistic of the Japanese effort to transform and civilize Hokkaido. It would be easy for American pioneers, but the Japanese, "their race physically and mentally dwarfed by their meager diet and circumscribed employment," lacked the hardiness necessary for the effort.[38] These comments fed into stereotypes of the Ainu as Japan's Indians, viewed by social scientists as examples of primitive peoples unsuited for the modern world and destined for extinction. By century's end, they could point to the example of American Indians, impoverished and made listless in their forced enclosure on barren reservations in the American West.

Atlantic and Pacific Crossings

But we're getting ahead of ourselves. In the early 1850s Capron still had no inkling of the forces set in motion which would one day take him to Japan. As he made his way to one frontier between the US and Mexico, another American was taking a very different route to Hokkaido by way of crossing the Atlantic. On March 7, 1851, a young American from New England studying abroad at Georgia August University in Germany wrote a letter home to his father filled with descriptions of his life and studies in a foreign country.

The young man, William S. Clark, was born in 1826. He had grown up exploring the countryside in Massachusetts and showed an early interest in mineralogy. Coming out of an upbringing steeped in the puritanical traditions of the New England region, he was deeply religious. That influence showed in his letter, in which Clark noted the superiority of German sciences and European facilities for higher education, while staunchly defending New England as the "home of true spiritual religion."[39]

Ambitious young Americans in the nineteenth century often looked to German universities and other European institutions of higher learning for the latest developments in the sciences while bemoaning the inadequacy of higher education in the United States. Among the most exciting scientific advances of the century, the chemist Justus Liebig (1803–1873) discovered the importance of nitrogen to plant growth, which led to the founding of agricultural chemistry.[40] His laboratory attracted American students eager to improve American education and agriculture by importing his scientific methods, including the linking of the

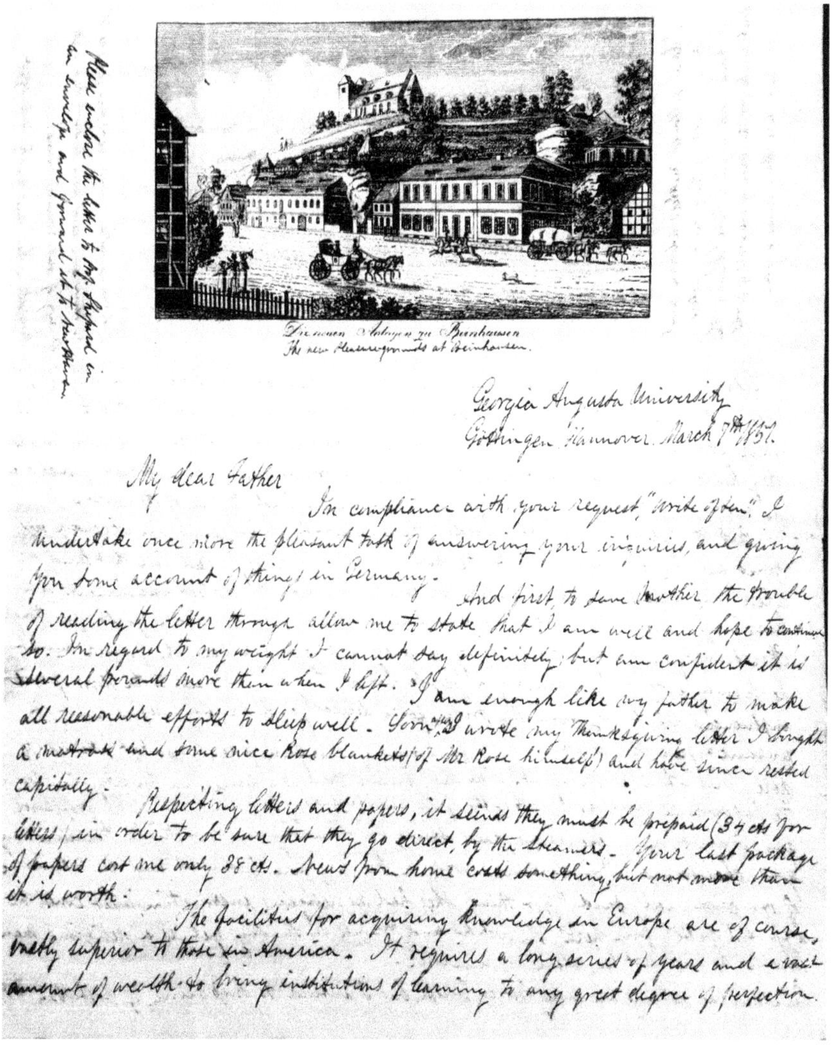

FIGURE 1.3: Letter from William Clark to his father. In the nineteenth century, young Americans looked to Europe for models of higher education. With permission from William S. Clark papers, Special Collections, University of Massachusetts, Amherst.

previously separate spheres of the chemistry laboratory, the agricultural experimental station, and the farm.

In other areas of technical expertise Americans also acknowledged the superiority of European institutions. The young American Raphael Pumpelly (1837–1923) decided against attending Yale University and instead traveled to Europe, where he studied at the Freiberg Mining Academy in the 1850s.[41] Upon his arrival, Pumpelly immediately bemoaned the inadequacy of his mathematical training in the US. The famous Freiberg Academy (founded in 1765) was the oldest such academy in Europe. A century earlier the Prussian polymath naturalist Alexander von Humboldt had also attended the academy and worked as a mining inspector before he established himself as a naturalist through expeditions in the Americas. Humboldt emerged out of a strong Central European tradition in the applied and technical fields, particularly in mining. In turn, Humboldt's renown later attracted American students to Germany. Humboldt's travels in the Americas at the turn of the nineteenth century had made him a household name on both sides of the Atlantic. In 1858, US Secretary of War John Floyd wrote to Humboldt of the many places in the US, including three counties and seven cities, named after him. Humboldt also held honorary membership in nine American learned societies.[42]

The westward push of the American frontier and the rise of higher education and the sciences in the United States were closely intertwined. In January 1848, James Wilson Marshall discovered gold at Sutter's Mill in California. When news of his find filtered out, tens of thousands of gold seekers from across the world descended upon California, transforming San Francisco into a boomtown. A decade later, the discovery of gold in the Rockies attracted 100,000 people to the Great Plains, twice as many as those who rushed to California in 1849, transforming the ecology and landscape of the West.[43] At the same time, the new science of geology promised to make prospecting more than an inexact combination of miners' lore and luck. A degree from Freiberg Mining Academy carried special weight, even in the wild and unregulated mining industry in the American West. American schools struggled to catch up. The first mining and metallurgy school in the US, the School of Mines of Columbia University, was not founded until 1864. Similar efforts to start mining schools at Yale and Harvard stalled and never came to fruition.

For the first decades in the nineteenth century, American students who wished to earn degrees in new sciences and applied fields from chemistry to mining had to travel to Europe. In turn, these eager American students went on to leading positions in the American academy and helped to proselytize the scientific method overseas. America was at a crucial turning point of development, and a growing number of people recognized the importance of education and science in a new age. A member of this new generation, Clark went to Germany to study chemistry and botany. He explained to his father, "The facilities for acquiring knowledge in Europe are of course, vastly superior to those in America. It requires a long series of years and a vast amount of wealth to bring institutions of learning to any great degree of perfection."[44]

The rise of science and institutions of higher learning helped to make Europe a hub for knowledge from around the world. These developments built upon an existing framework and infrastructure for the transfer and exchange of knowledge in the early modern world. The Age of Discovery and the demands of running global empires set the stage for this framework. In turn, people like Clark helped to transmit knowledge to North America and the rest of the world.

In contrast to the French and the British, the Germans did not have an empire and the possession of tropical islands to test out new climate theories. Nevertheless, German writers, like Baron Otto von Münchhausen, published works on estate management and used such works, which recorded their accomplishments in agricultural improvement on their estates, to establish their reputation as natural philosophers to their peers. Like Zuo Zongtang, Münchhausen experimented with farming techniques on his land. Figures such as Münchhausen demonstrate the looser definition of experimentation in the eighteenth century, before the professionalization of the sciences.[45] These connections underscore the European-wide exchange of ideas and intellectual networks that extended across imperial boundaries.

Figures like Münchhausen, Zuo, and Capron run counter to the traditional narrative of modern science. Agricultural knowledge is dependent on soil and weather, making many such "experiments" impossible to replicate. As the definition of science changed to require the systematic study of nature, the need for verification and replication of results became increasingly important to establish new theories. At the same time, the position of agricultural knowledge in relation to the new sciences was precarious. In similar ways, geography, which also long predated the rise of science, underwent a period of intense scrutiny in the nineteenth century as the discipline attempted to reposition itself as a science.[46] In the eighteenth century, Münchhausen's claims of accomplishment as a natural philosopher based on his estate management were not exceptional. Nor did Zuo's devotion to agricultural studies mark him as eccentric. Münchhausen and Zuo Zongtang were respected elites in their communities and part of networks of scholars but a far cry from our current conception of the scientist, which is revealing of the distance that science has traveled in the two centuries since.

Historians have traced modern science to men like Copernicus and Galileo, who looked to the heavens in the Age of Discovery and others with more earthly pursuits like Robert Boyle and Robert Hooke, who began to experiment in distinct spaces marked off as laboratories.[47] For all its recognized importance to the state, agriculture remained largely overlooked among the sciences. Each year, new crops grew, ripened, and reached harvest. Drought, or other extreme weather like storms and flooding, could quickly ruin a year's work; untimely frosts or pests could easily decimate the harvest. The specter of famine haunted those who depended for their livelihoods on the vagaries of weather, soil, and the environment. Aside from some gentlemen farmers and officials, most agriculturists carried knowledge of their experience in their memories and bodies rather than in texts that could circulate and be collected in libraries. Yet, peppers and potatoes made their way from the New World to supplement the diets of the poor in Europe and Asia; horses and pigs crossed the Atlantic and ran feral across the Americas. Plant hunters trekked across jungles and deserts in search of exotic blooms and economically valuable floras.

From the time before it became an independent country, the United States had joined this global circulation, initially as a source of exotic new plants and animal species along with other global outposts of European empires from Tahiti to the Bahamas. In the nineteenth century, the country gradually became a global economic and trading power. In this transitional period, figures like Capron and Clark played an important role as the conduits of change, both in their personal lives and in the larger context of this period of American history that saw the nation's territorial expanse reach across the continent and then extend across the Pacific.

The frontiers played an essential role in these transformations. Not only did westward expansion provide an outlet for settlers from New England and the mid-Atlantic states, including people like Horace Capron who migrated westward for new opportunities, but these lands, dispossessed from Indian tribes, went on to fund American higher education. The creation of the land-grant university system, established by the Morrill Act of 1862, brought the research university model to the United States.[48] Funding for the land-grant universities came from the allotment and sale of western lands, taken by force from Indian tribes, who were then removed to distant reservations. The development of agriculture, higher education, and the frontier were entangled from the beginning. In 1863, the Massachusetts State legislature took advantage of the Morrill Act to fund the Massachusetts Agriculture College. New England was known for its picturesque homesteads. By the mid-nineteenth century, however, more and more people were lured west by cheap or free frontier lands. New England farms, after generations of farming and the exhaustion of the soil, saw decreasing yields. At the same time, industrialization was changing the landscape. These developments fueled the sense of crisis for farming communities. The creation of the land-grant university sought to alleviate this crisis by bringing science to agriculture and providing the means for farmers to increase yields.

From Berlin on May 2, 1852, Clark wrote to tell his parents that he had finished his studies.[49] He bid farewell to Göttingen. With his PhD in hand, Clark returned to the US for a professorship at Amherst College in analytical and applied chemistry. He also promoted agricultural education from his position. A decade and a half later, in 1867, Clark became one of the first presidents of the newly established Massachusetts Agricultural College, which was later renamed the University of Massachusetts, Amherst. Clark was concomitantly appointed professor of botany and horticulture. In the meantime, on the other side of the world, forces were at work that would bring him briefly to Japan.

Scientific Exploration and Empire

In 1852, the final ingredient that would eventually bring both Capron and Clark to the northern frontiers of Japan in the 1870s steamed across the Atlantic onboard the coal steamer *Mississippi*. As Capron embarked upon his adventures in Texas, another veteran of the Mexican-American

War, Commodore Matthew Perry, was on his way to reach Asia via Cape Town, Ceylon, and Hong Kong. If the Mexican-American War marked an attempt by the American government to push the extent of its frontiers, the Perry mission offered an alternative to continental expansion. On their way around the world, Perry's ships helped to redefine the spheres of American influence across the Pacific.

Starting in the eighteenth century, large-scale expeditions circumnavigated the world with both military and scientific aims. The best-known example of such joint military-scientific ventures was Captain Cook's expeditions on behalf of the British Royal Navy, ostensibly to track the transit of Venus across the Southern Hemisphere, but also with an eye to claim new territories. The British Empire was not alone in deploying such missions. Cook's French counterpart, Louis Antoine de Bougainville, circumnavigated the globe on scientific expeditions in the 1760s, which led to French claims to the Falkland Islands in South America and to Tahiti in the South Pacific. From 1777 to 1816, multiple expeditions crisscrossed the Spanish Empire to survey the flora of the Americas, the Caribbean, and the Philippines. These expeditions supplied specimens to Madrid's Royal Botanical Garden and the Royal Natural History Cabinet, while also producing more than 12,000 botanical illustrations.[50]

By the early decades of the nineteenth century, the relatively young American republic began to send out joint military-scientific expeditions, much as the British Empire, the Spanish, and the French had sponsored in the previous century. In 1843, Secretary of War John M. Porter recommended keeping a pine box on all outgoing vessels to allow officers the ability to collect specimens in their spare time. The following years saw a number of joint missions, including the Wilkes Expedition to the Pacific (1838–1842), expeditions to the Dead Sea and the River Jordan (1847–1849), the Herndon-Gibbon Expedition to the Amazon (1851–1852), the Naval Astronomical Expedition to the Southern Hemisphere (1846–1852), and the Page Expedition to Rio Paraguay and Rio de la Plata (1853–1856).[51] These expeditions followed the scientific practices of the times and included onboard naturalists, who often played key roles in the collection and assembly of specimens and the subsequent publication of the records of the expeditions. These reports often included large numbers of illustrations, preserving an essential botanical record of the time.

American foreign interests turned to the Pacific decades before the

Spanish-American War and the acquisition of Philippines as a colony at century's end. Of the various expeditions sponsored by the US government in the nineteenth century, the Perry expedition was arguably the most consequential. The agriculturist and physician James Morrow from South Carolina was charged with collecting seeds and surveying agricultural practices on the expedition.[52] Morrow took charge of the seeds and agricultural implements that formed part of the official gift to the Japanese. At every port stop in the ship's circumnavigation, Morrow set out to procure local seeds and plants. His upbringing on a slave-owning plantation in the American South attuned Morrow particularly to the varieties of crops and plants with economic potential, including an assortment of beans and rice varieties, which served as staple foods for slaves on plantations.

Although President Fillmore charged Perry with a diplomatic mission, Perry himself was mostly interested in locating coaling stations for the navy and a burgeoning American trade in the Pacific.[53] Securing an adequate supply of coal was a major logistical concern for the navy and shipping companies as they transitioned to steam power. These concerns underlined the material and geographical constraints of new technologies that sped up travel and made possible the global migration of millions of people in the nineteenth century. The fuel needs of these new transportation technologies depended on fixed infrastructure networks. Steamships needed ports where they could take on new supplies of coal; trains required railways laid out not too far from coal mines. Industries needed to be located within easy transport distance of raw materials and energy sources, which tied them to canal systems, riverways, and railroads. These infrastructural networks in turn created their own spatial hierarchies and altered the path of development.[54]

The leisurely pace of the Perry expedition, spread out over three years from 1852 to 1854, followed the pattern of similar state-funded missions with both scientific and diplomatic goals dating from Captain Cook's famous explorations in the eighteenth century. The length of time—measured in years—mattered. The various fueling and supply stops on the Perry expedition, including on Madeira, St. Helena, and Madagascar, replicated the imperial island circuits in Richard Grove's work, which helped to create a modern ecological understanding of forests and their role in regulating climates. Each stop provided an opportunity for the transfer of knowledge and the exchange of information about new vari-

eties of economically valuable plants and animals, innovations in agriculture, and experiences from the settlement of these islands.

Perry and members of his mission became intensely interested
in the Ryukyu Islands (the spelling in the published account is "Lew
Chew") to the south of Japan. Bayard Taylor, an American who joined the
Perry mission on the *Susquehanna* in Shanghai, described their time in
Ryukyu in detail. Beyond his role in the Perry mission, Taylor led a life
that exemplified the global possibilities of the nineteenth century for an
adventurous American. Taylor was born in the village of Kennet Square
in Pennsylvania, a small hamlet about forty miles west of Philadelphia.
From these rural roots, Taylor went on to live an epic life of global travel,
which saw him trek across Europe, Mexico, Egypt, and Asia. His travels in Africa and Asia landed him in Shanghai when the Perry mission
docked. In addition to the sections from the Perry expedition records,
Taylor also penned a book on his travels in Asia, *A Visit to India, China,
and Japan in the Year 1853,* based on his diary entries from the time.

While in Shanghai, Taylor was with the American consul when news
arrived of the siege and eventual fall of Nanjing to the Taiping rebels in
April 1853. At the nadir of the rebellion, refugees from the surrounding
provinces flooded into Shanghai, including scholars who had previously
regularly convened to discuss Jesuit writings on mathematics. The Taiping Rebellion brought this group to Shanghai, where they were suddenly
exposed to all manner of new imports from horse-pulled carriages and
kerosene lights, to works written by Protestant missionaries about science and technologies in the West.[55] For the moment, however, the city
faced the imminent threat posed by the rebels. Taylor noted the atmo-
sphere of fear and terrible uncertainty in the treaty port. Chinese merchants in the city pulled together $340,000 for the possible ransom of the
city, should Shanghai fall to the rebels. American and British expatriates
gathered at their respective consulates to adopt defensive measures and
build barricades. To reconnoiter the situation for himself, the British diplomat and interpreter (later Sinologist) Thomas Taylor Meadows dressed
as a Chinese to travel to the rebel camp, bringing with him Western-style
clothing to change into upon his arrival.[56]

Living through these adventurous times apparently did not instill
any fondness in Bayard Taylor for Asian people and cultures. He found
the Chinese countryside "disgusting" upon close inspection—perhaps he

noted the human excrement used as fertilizer. During his time in China, Taylor took long walks around Shanghai and saw a horticultural exhibition in an old temple, where he noted some pretty peonies and lotuses. But the Chinese, he wrote, were "morally the most debased people on the face of the earth."[57] After Taylor's return to the US, he achieved some fame as a novelist and continued to travel but never returned to Asia. He died in 1878 in Berlin, where he had taken up the position of the United States Minister to Prussia.

American merchants had eagerly joined in the lucrative East Asian trade, although for many years they were greatly outnumbered by the British presence and overshadowed by the monopoly on the China trade enjoyed by the British East India Company. After the Opium War (1839–1842), the balance of power rapidly shifted and the Chinese were forced to cede concessions, including Hong Kong, and the opening of treaty ports including Shanghai and Hankou (Wuhan today) to the British. Other European powers quickly joined in the scramble for a piece of the action. Americans benefited from the new arrangement without having to go to war. Unlike the mostly merchant British presence, however, Americans included among their numbers many missionaries who were drawn to China by the promise of its vast populations of souls awaiting salvation. The evangelical roots of the US-China relationship shaped the two countries' interactions for the next century.

The British led the governance of the treaty ports in China, as well as entrepôts like Singapore, which connected East Asia to their colonial holdings in Southeast Asia. From across the Pacific and second fiddle in Asia, the Americans saw untapped potential in Japan and the nearby islands. The Americans recognized claims from both China and Japan on the Ryukyu Islands and were keen to explore its culture and environment in part because its exact sovereign status was open to debate.[58] The mission spent considerable time on the islands, surveyed the coasts, and collected animal, mineral, and plant specimens on the islands, as well as extensive interactions with the island rulers. Far more space in the official narrative was devoted to the Ryukyu Islands than any other stop. The extensive focus of the Perry mission on the Ryukyus indicated a burgeoning social science and natural scientific interest in the islands. Gunboat diplomacy enabled scientific survey; in turn, science paved the way for the development of newly acquired territories. The lesson was not lost on Japanese reformers eager to modernize the country in the subsequent decades.

Upon joining Perry in Shanghai, Taylor became the mission's unofficial record keeper. Taylor kept a diary and carefully recorded his experiences on the Ryukyus, parts of which were then incorporated into the official narrative of the mission. Taylor's anthropological interest in the islanders and curiosity led him to repeatedly barge into native inhabitants' huts to catch "the natives" unawares. In most cases, however, Taylor's curiosity was frustrated by encountering deserted huts during the day.[59]

The reason for the intense American interest in these islands became clear in July 1853, when Perry went beyond his official instructions to demand that the Ryukyu king provide land for a coal depot under the threat of a military occupation of the royal palace. The following year, in July 1854, Perry negotiated a treaty between the United States and the Ryukyu Kingdom allowing for "unrestricted travel and free trade for American citizens throughout all Ryukyu."[60] These harsh conditions, far more stringent than the agreement signed with the shogunate in Japan, exposed the risks the European international order posed for countries that operated outside of its standards for independent states.

Recognizing the threat posed by these conditions and ongoing disputes with Russia over outlying islands, Japan moved to formalize their claims over the Ryukyus. In 1872 the Japanese government designated the archipelago the Ryukyu Domain, incorporating the islands into the formal territories of Japan. The islands had previously operated in an East Asian order that left room for ambiguity, allowing all parties to look the other way and maintain fictive cover while the Ryukyu king both offered tribute to Qing China and affirmed its subject status to Japan.[61] The Ryukyus became one of the first East Asian test cases for the shift to an international law system, which did not accommodate the kind of dual relations that island rulers maintained with both Qing China and Tokugawa Japan. Japan, realizing the vulnerabilities of their underdeveloped borderlands, turned their attention to the northern island of Ezo.

Perry's gunboat diplomacy and the signing of the Treaty of Kanagawa set off a chain of reactions, ultimately leading to the Meiji Restoration in 1868 and bringing an end to two and a half centuries of Tokugawa rule. The loosely defined idea of sovereignty and subjectivity in the Sinocentric system long in place in East Asia came under challenge from the European-based system of international law, which left no leeway for the ambiguity of states such as Korea or the Ryukyus.[62] Despite their inclusion as part of the Japanese nation-state, the Ryukyus, subsequently known as Okinawa, continued to occupy a liminal space between the inner and outer territories of the Japanese Empire. In the Japanese colonies the Okinawans were identified as the "other Japanese." In the coming decades, thousands of Okinawans migrated in search of job opportunities. By 1940, 10 percent of residents from the islands lived abroad, many as the essential workers of empire—shopkeepers, servants, and low-level bureaucrats.[63]

The global circulation of knowledge was not a new phenomenon in the nineteenth century. Trade connected the far corners of the world since the rise of civilizations, and ideas and technologies moved along with goods.[64] Scientific knowledge flowed both ways between Europe and Asia in the early modern period and created meaningful dialogues around the world. In China, the seemingly cataclysmic rebellions of the nineteenth century forced officials to look to imported technologies and cash crop alternatives to opium to aid in the country's recovery. The ecological crises of the nineteenth century were exacerbated by a drug epidemic that drained the country's silver in exchange for a drug-induced haze. In turn, the association of opium smoking with the Chinese fed into the cultural stereotypes in the West of an inscrutable people populating seedy opium dens.

The year 1852 would not make it into a timeline of major nineteenth-century events. In an era of revolutions, rebellions, and natural disasters, the year 1852 saw the aftermath of failed revolutions and foreshadowed the developments that would lead to the global conflicts of the 1860s. People were clearly on the move, and the global connections were tightening as industrialization picked up speed. We may see the farm as the opposite of smokestacks and working-class slums, but in a world that was still predominantly agrarian, interest in agriculture crossed state boundaries and was equally prominent in industrializing countries. From the American West to Asia, this common interest in the cultivation of land and agrarian development became a central node of multiple nineteenth-century currents: the rise of science, revisions of empire and imperial territory, and the spreading influence of an international order that valued clearly demarcated borders and relations of power. Increasingly, attention turned to the frontiers and borderlands, both real and imagined, as the experimental zones for the modern state. The world was changing and people were on the move; at the same time, the familiar paved the way for the new.

TWO

The Experimental Grounds of New Imperialism

> Ours has been a task without precedent, and amidst novel sur-
> roundings, where most undertakings were, necessarily, only
> experimental.
>
> *Horace Capron*[1]

When we left them in 1852, our various protagonists were each rushing headlong in different directions to meet their fates. Within two decades some of their paths would cross again on the northern Japanese island of Hokkaido. How they got there is illustrative of the seemingly random intersections of networks, with particular people and places becoming hubs of activity at certain points in time. In the nineteenth century, the United States, particularly the American West, attracted travelers from around the world. Hokkaido and Japan similarly served as a hub from the 1870s. From these pivots, people and the ideas they carried with them fanned out across the globe. Whether they were conscious of it or not, the protagonists of the first chapter, Zuo, Capron, and Clark, became the human vehicles in the knowledge network for important ideas about agricultural development, technology, and science. Through the process of imperial expansion, the knowledge they carried took root in other parts of the world.

Experimental Stations of Empire

Contrary to the stereotype of an insular society closed to the outside world, Japan took part in the early modern global circulation of goods and knowledge. After the Tokugawa shogunate enacted the isolationist policy called *sakoku* in the seventeenth century, they continued to allow for extensive trade with China through the port of Nagasaki on the western coast and with Europeans via the Dutch East India Company on the small island of Dejima. Although restricted, Western knowledge filtered into the country through exchange between those Europeans employed by the Dutch and a few interested Japanese scholars. This scientific, technical, and medical knowledge became known as *Rangaku* ("Dutch learning").

Japanese scholars recognized the difference in emphasis between Chinese and Western works of natural history, cartography, and *materia medica*. Illustrations of flora and fauna in foreign works helped to transform Japanese representations of reality in the nineteenth century, in turn paving the way for the adoption of science through visual images.[2] In the more realistic depictions of medicinal plants and animals from fish to insects, Japanese scholars adapted knowledge from the West for their own uses while classical Chinese works continued to maintain their prestige in Japan into the second half of the nineteenth century.[3] Through various means, ideas about science and the natural world simmered in Japan beneath the tranquil surface of *sakoku*.

A chain of actions and reactions brought Japan into the modern world order. The shogunate's dithering response to Perry's arrival seriously undermined its prestige and led a group of samurai to act in alliance to topple the regime. These samurai restored to power a largely symbolic emperor from Kyoto. With the Meiji Restoration, as the events of 1868 came to be called, Japan sought to adopt those practices which would affirm its status as an equal in the international order defined by European states. Like Germany, Japan began to explore that marker of modernity and power in the new world order—the acquisition of overseas empire—and ways to use science to achieve that status. Japan lacked the imperial experience of its larger continental neighbor, China, but quickly pivoted to new global norms. Initially the Western powers imposed the same unequal treaties and terms as in China. As the country turned towards modernization, the urgent issue of empire (or how to acquire an empire) focused the attention of the new Meiji government on its frontiers.

Americans and Europeans, particularly the Russians, had long expressed interest in the island of Ezo and its main port city of Hakodate, which could potentially serve as a refueling stop for fishing vessels and ships plying the north Pacific trading routes. For Japan, the northern frontier became the perfect experimental station for empire. Like the Ryukyu Islands, Japan's colonization of Ezo and its indigenous residents predate the arrival of Western gunboats. Just as over time native Americans in North America overextended hunting and exhausted other natural resources on increasingly limited territories and came to rely on Europeans for their survival, the Ainu became dependent on trade to fulfill burgeoning commercial demand in Japan in the early modern period.[4] What started in the seventeenth century with growing Japanese demand for precious metals accelerated in the nineteenth century. In 1802, the shogunate established a magistracy, administered in Edo (present day Tokyo), to oversee affairs on the island.

Over the next decades, the administration of the colony took on "modern" forms with the central government participating in the planning of economic policy and overseeing the assimilation of the Ainu people. Direct rule by the shogunate eventually included everything from the building of infrastructure, including roads and more elaborate trading posts, to forms of state-sponsored medicine such as smallpox vaccination campaigns in 1857.[5] Shortly after the Meiji Restoration, the new government formed the Hokkaido Development Agency (Kaitakushi) to oversee the continued colonization of the island. Like the Okinawans, the Ainu discovered that they had become the first colonial subjects of a newly expanding Japanese Empire.

The flat landscape and black soil of the northern island provided the ideal conditions for Japan to reproduce a colony of their own at a time when colonial possessions represented the ultimate marker of civilization and status. The Meiji state renamed the island Hokkaido in 1869 (北海道 "northern sea circuit"), the adoption of the ordinal marker effectively orienting it to Japan proper. Meiji officials consciously framed their efforts in the same language and adopted the superficial appearance of Western imperialism. These elaborate efforts have led historians to coin the term *mimetic imperialism* to describe early Japanese colonization efforts.[6] A closer examination reveals the shallowness of the mimesis; instead, in the last decades of the nineteenth century Japan adroitly switched from the careful study of the Chinese imperial example to Western models, adapting those aspects of empire which they found useful.

In 1871, Kuroda Kyotaka, the official then in charge of the colonial office on Hokkaido, traveled to the United States in search of capable experts in colonial settlements. After consulting the Japanese minister in Washington, DC, Mori Arinori, and several days of discussions with Agricultural Commissioner Horace Capron, the Japanese government offered Capron a consulting position at a salary of $10,000 a year, in addition to covering all his travel, living, and other expenses in Japan. At the time, members of Congress made $5,000 per year, and the president $25,000, which included the considerable entertaining costs at the White House.[7] Capron also negotiated for a team of American assistants, including A. G. Warfield, a civil engineer with the Baltimore and Ohio Railroad, Dr. Thomas Antisell, a chemist with the United States Bureau of Agriculture, and Stewart Eldridge, a Washington physician.[8]

From Washington, DC, as he had done two decades earlier, Capron once again set off on a journey. In his lifetime, Capron traversed the spectrum of the American nineteenth-century experience. From his childhood in New York State, his experimental plantation in Maryland as a young adult, to the homestead in Illinois, Capron's life followed the arc of American history. When he trekked to the Mexico-Texas borderlands in 1852, sections of railroads were scattered across the US, with significant gaps in between. In 1871, he could travel on the rail, the mountainous westerns sections of which were painstakingly blasted out of solid rock by Chinese laborers, straight across the continent before taking a steamer from San Francisco to cross the Pacific.[9]

Capron would spend the next four years in Japan as a foreign consultant to the country's halting first steps towards acquiring an empire. These years were attended by considerable controversy. Although he had hired his own team, Capron did not get along well with his American underlings. The disparity in pay between Capron's salary and those of his subordinates created rancor. Rumors and complaints by his American employees circulated of his limited competency in his job. Already close to age seventy upon his arrival in Japan, Capron spent his winters and most of his time in Japan in Tokyo rather than enduring the harsh winters in Hokkaido and the rigors of fieldwork. As one of the first foreign advisors hired by the Meiji government, Capron was accorded great respect in the Japanese capital and granted an audience with the emperor upon his arrival. Capron appeared captivated by the elaborate rituals and social etiquette of Japanese culture, which further fueled scorn and gossip from his American underlings that he preferred to socialize over hard work in the field.

Countries around the world eager to adopt the latest technologies and sciences provided lucrative opportunities for engineers and other technically skilled workers. The new Meiji government employed numerous foreign experts in key industries, continuing and greatly expanding efforts that had begun in the last Tokugawa years. In the 1860s, the Tokugawa shogunate directly engaged William Blake and Raphael Pumpelly, both mining engineers, to conduct geological surveys of mineral resources in the country. The two men arrived in Yokohama after sailing across the Pacific in ninety days aboard the sail ship *Carrington* (a decade later, the steamship *SS Japan* that Capron had taken would have made the journey in a month. The world was getting measurably smaller as new technologies of transportation sped up travel.).[10] After their arrival, another three months passed while the government tried to figure out their assignment. Finally, the shogunate instructed them to proceed to Ezo to conduct their survey. In February of 1863, the Japanese government terminated Pumpelly's service after political turmoil ended many of the ongoing reforms at the time.[11] Pumpelly then went to China, where the Qing government, at the time in negotiations to purchase a fleet of gunboats, engaged his services to assess some coalfields outside of Beijing that might supply fuel for these vessels. After the Meiji Restoration, the hiring of foreign experts dramatically increased. Eager to build a modern navy, the Meiji government hired a team of French engineers at the shipyard at Yokusuka Dockyards in the early 1870s. The French team was subsequently replaced by British engineers after 1878.[12]

From Tokyo, Capron supervised a group of American experts who provided substantive reports on conditions in Hokkaido. The engineer-in-chief Capron hired on behalf of the Japanese, A. G. Warfield, conducted a ground topographical study of the island in the winter of 1871. Warfield recommended the construction of the city of Sapporo along the lines of American cities, with a gridded design. Warfield suggested paving the streets and constructing more bridges over an existing canal to allow for the introduction of wagons as the local means of transportation. These reports helped to inform Capron's recommendations to Kuroda. As with subsequent efforts over the course of the twentieth century, American efforts abroad sought to promote development in the mold of the American frontier experience. Before he had even stepped foot in Hokkaido, Capron drew parallels between its northern climes with the American Northeast. Oak, beech, and ash trees grew equally well in New York, Pennsylvania, and Ohio, he noted, as they would in Hokkaido.[13] Even after he traveled to Hokkaido in 1872 to see the island for himself, Capron remained largely inflexible in his ideas and continued to promote American-style mechanized agriculture. Capron introduced American plants, animals, and technology to Japan to remake Hokkaido into a version of the American frontier.

Capron advocated for developing the mineral resources of the island, improvement of roads and transportation to the city of Sapporo, and the cultivation of fruit trees and wheat and the introduction of machines to replace human labor. Capron wanted to transform Hokkaido into a version of the American West with tractors plowing endless flat fields of wheat, never mind that most Japanese settlers had far more experience with rice. Japanese settlers had very limited experience with the kind of crops Capron recommended for Hokkaido in his efforts to recreate American farms on the northern Japanese island. The enormous cost of these recommendations, which he estimated could be accomplished in five years for $5,947,500, or equal to the total budget for the region for twelve years, made them both impractical and unrealizable in the foreseeable future.[14] Yet, his views were not unusual for the time. Anglo settlers aimed to transform the natural environment of North America, South Africa, and Australia into new versions of the countries they had left behind.[15] By wresting lands from indigenous peoples who wasted its full potential, they would transform New Worlds into plentiful new Edens.

The limited financial resources of the Japanese state forestalled the complete overhaul of the agricultural economy on Hokkaido. Photos taken from the time, however, illustrate at least the superficial adoption of some of these ambitions. More importantly, American-style large-scale agriculture became an aspirational goal for the nascent Japanese Empire. For leading Japanese advocates of overseas emigration, the American West remained an ideal frontier to which they aimed their efforts, first in the transformation of Hokkaido, then in overseas settlements, including in the United States, and finally, on the Asian continent. The expansive fields of wheat may not have been fully realized but the language of "virgin" lands took root in Hokkaido and across Eastern Europe to Siberia, crossed the Amur River, and reached China by the 1930s.

Some of Capron's American underlings, as well as subsequent American assessment of his tenure in Hokkaido, judged him harshly as a querulous and incompetent old man more concerned about social appearances than the actual work of developing Hokkaido. These views overlook what the Japanese got out of the deal. Whether he in fact contributed anything concrete, the Japanese government acclaimed his role, in the process also placing themselves in the same category as the Americans civilizing the lawless and wild frontiers. Decades later in the 1940s, when Japan controlled the puppet government in Manchukuo on the Asian mainland, Japanese administrators continued to advocate for Hokkaido-style continental farming and the deployment of the "Capron plan" in the image of American agricultural settlement of the West.[16] The employment of prominent Americans in the early Meiji years reveal a self-conscious effort to join the international community as an equal. As for Capron, shortly before his death, in 1884 Capron was awarded the Order of the Rising Sun for his work in transforming Hokkaido. Proud of this achievement, he devoted a great deal of space in his memoirs to discussing the award.

Growing Empire

In the 1870s, as the president of the Massachusetts Agricultural College, William Clark corresponded with Japanese government officials regarding his efforts to promote education and agricultural development in Massachusetts through the public university. Clark offered suggestions for its counterpart in Hokkaido, the Sapporo Agricultural College. In a September 8, 1871, letter to Kuroda Kyotaka, head of the colonial office in charge of Hokkaido, Clark detailed suggestions for the hiring of foreign faculty, the adoption of "the most rational and approved system of farm economy . . . experiments with new crops," and establishment of manufacturing plants for silk, sugar, beer, and vinegar," to be conducted "in the outset upon a moderate scale."[17] In 1876 the Japanese government formally issued an invitation to Clark to oversee the organization of the Sapporo Agricultural College, including the purchase of books and equipment and the hiring of faculty, offering for his services for one year 7,200 gold yen.[18]

Although Clark spent less than a year in Hokkaido, he helped mold the curriculum and strategic vision of Sapporo Agricultural College just as he did for the Massachusetts Agricultural College. At a time when American land-grant universities sought to bring science to the farm while also emulating the European universities as research centers, Clark helped

Uncultivated Lands

Surveying Party

Surveying Virgin Lands

Cultivating

FIGURE 2.1: Capron advocated for the mechanization of farming on Hokkaido. Decades later Japanese colonial administrators in Manchuria still referred to a "Capron plan." Image from *American Influence upon the Agriculture of Hokkaido, Japan* (Sapporo, Japan: College of Agriculture, Tohoku Imperial University, 1915).

to bring Sapporo into a global network of research and learning. He also brought his New England brand of earnest religiosity and missionary zeal, which helped to convert some of the first students he trained during his brief time in Japan. The lasting fondness for his memory is reflected in the statue of Clark that still graces the campus of Hokkaido University today, inscribed with his parting words to his Japanese students, "Boys, be ambitious." Clark returned the affection. Writing to his sister Belle from Sapporo during his brief sojourn to Japan, Clark described with awe the vast undertaking on the Japanese frontier. A farm near the city of Hakodate encompassed 15,000 acres, worked by 430 men and their families at an annual expense of $40,000. Clearly impressed, he asked his sister in a rhetorical flourish, how does the Connecticut experimental station at Middletown fare in comparison?[19]

The American influence on the globalization of scientific knowledge is further discernible in the 1877 catalog of the Sapporo College library—in addition to 500 books in Japanese and Chinese, the library boasted ten copies of mineralogy textbooks written by the prominent Yale geologist James Dwight Dana, as well as a copy of Charles Darwin's *On the Origin of Species*. Western missionaries in China had been hesitant to touch upon Darwin's controversial ideas, and a systematic translation of Darwin did not appear until the end of the century. In Japan, a visiting professor of zoology at Tokyo University, American Edward Sylvester Morse (1837–1925), lectured on Darwinism in 1877.[20] The presence of *On the Origin of Species* in the Sapporo College library meant that even before Morse's lectures in Tokyo, ideas about evolutionary biology were already available on the northern frontiers. Instruction at Sapporo was in English, and Japanese students could plausibly read Darwin on their own.

Capron and Clark were part of a wave of 2,500 American advisors who were hired by the Meiji government to aid in the modernization of Japan, along what they viewed as the Western standards of civilization, wealth, and power. Complaints about the exorbitant pay granted these advisors overlook the larger Meiji strategy. Perry had deployed gunboat diplomacy in the opening of Japan, and the resulting Treaty of Kanagawa contained unequal clauses. The unequal treaties codified Japan's inferior status to the West. Diplomats such as Mori Arinori, the first Japanese ambassador to the US from 1871 to 1873, spent years vainly attempting to renegotiate the terms of these unequal treaties with Western powers. Both Capron and Clark occupied a stratum of American society which gave their appeals on behalf of the Meiji government far more weight than any Japanese diplomat might achieve in these lobbying efforts. On his return to the United States, Clark hosted events on behalf of the Japanese embassy.

As they sought to achieve equal status with Western countries, in addition to hiring foreign experts, the Japanese actively turned to the sciences to attain wealth and power. By the second half of the nineteenth century, both China and Japan had recognized the need to import Western expertise. In the 1870s and 1880s, Japan instituted programs for importing foreign teachers (*oyatoi*) while at the same time sending talented students (*ryūgakusei*) abroad for further study.[21] In addition to the early hiring of American experts, the Japanese government selected certain "target" nations as the most advanced in specific fields.[22] The hiring of foreign experts was part of a calculated effort to adopt such practices as would enable Japan to attain equal status with Western powers.

Along with the global circulation of personnel, ideas about the frontier traveled from the US to Japan and then beyond, bound up with newly created disciplines in agricultural science and geology and existing fields such as geography and chemistry. As an ascendant empire in the late nineteenth century, Japan became a crucial hub of knowledge transfer from the West to other parts of Asia, the Middle East, and South America. In each case, Japanese settlers benefited from circulating ideas about agriculture, economic development, and settlements and, in turn, helped to spread these ideas to other corners of the world. A new global network was opening in the nineteenth century in the sciences and social sciences, and people like Clark and Capron were active agents in its creation. At the same time, the interest Zuo Zongtang and other Qing officials and literati showed in agriculture demonstrates why this new knowledge found such a receptive audience around the world—in many places it was not considered new nor foreign but part of a long running tradition in statecraft that valued knowledge in agriculture and geography as important tools of governing.

Continental Empires

In one of the mass population movements of the nineteenth century, millions of ethnic Germans migrated to the Americas to escape population pressures and land scarcity at home. The population loss alarmed both political and academic advocates of empire in Germany. To combat this perceived loss of population barriers to the East, the Prussian *Landesökonomiekollegium* (Agrarian economic council) and the Prussian Ministry of Agriculture funded a fact-finding mission. In 1883, a twenty-six-year-old German agronomist named Max Sering, a student of the economist Gustav Schmoller, toured North American homesteads on behalf of the Prussian government.

In the late nineteenth century, the economist Gustav Schmoller presided over an extended academic network that stretched across the Atlantic and included many of the founding figures of American social sciences. As historian Daniel Rodgers has noted, many figures in the American Progressive movement were deeply influenced by parallel movements in Europe, particularly Germany.[23] From his academic perch in Strasbourg and Berlin, Schmoller promoted the empirical studies of social conditions that informed a liberal politics in Germany. Social scientific investigations provided the evidential basis for progressive policies, including worker rights in urban areas and the rationalization of agriculture in rural regions. Fieldwork and fact-finding missions such as the one Sering embarked upon in 1883 informed these policies. Upon his return to Germany, Sering published *Agricultural Competition in North America: Present and Future* (*Die landswirtschaftliche Konkurrenz Nordamerikas in Gegenwart und Zukunft*) by examining land management, transportation, and colonization as the different facets of economic development.[24] A few years later, he applied the same analytical lens to the issue of inner colonization in East Prussia.[25]

In Germany, the liberal democratic efforts in the nineteenth century and the Holocaust in the twentieth century both cut through the borderlands in Eastern Europe. The point is not so much that one led to the other. Other countries around the world, from the United States to Britain, France, and Japan escaped the scrutiny bestowed on Germany and its "special" history. Progressives in the United States, liberal democrats in Europe, and reformers in Asia shared an interest in frontier development which often came at a human cost to those who had to carry out settlement on the ground and those who were dispossessed in the process. People like Schmoller, Sering, and figures who will come up later in this work, including Japanese and Chinese agronomists like Nitobe Inazo, Takaoka Kumao, and Tang Qiyu, helped to craft policy but never experienced the hardships and challenges of colonizing new territories themselves nor bloodied their hands with the violent eviction of indigenous populations.

In North America, Sering encountered German settlers who showed little interest in returning to the old country or to take up opportunities in eastern Prussia as human bulwarks against Slavic fertility. On the contrary, they encouraged Sering to spread the word of America's bounties and to urge even more people from the old country to emigrate.[26] In North America the German settlers had found lands cleared of indigenous peoples and the promise of limitless opportunity for White settlers. In the boundless wheat fields of Manitoba, Sering experienced an epiphany about the importance of frontiers and rural development. The journey itself was a formative experience that shaped his subsequent intellectual growth. After his return to Germany, Sering embarked on a long and fruitful academic career and co-founded the Society for Inner Colonization in 1902 to promote German settlement of the East. Along with his teacher Gustav Schmoller, Sering became a leading member of a liberal intelligentsia who advocated for the settlement of the Prussian East to break the monopoly on power of the landed aristocratic Junker class.

Max Sering's work in the social sciences was backed by a Prussian state eager to support the inner colonization project to push back against the encroachment of Polish populations in the East. From 1886 until 1918, the Prussian government sponsored the purchase of lands in the East and the recruitment of ethnic Germans to settle in these areas. Over the course of these decades, the Prussian state spent over nine hundred million marks on land purchases in the East.[27] By deploying the new social sciences, the money was targeted at districts with large ethnic German minorities, where the extra support from the state could potentially tip the German populations to a majority. The state offered ethnic Germans essentially interest-free loans and other perks to acquire lands and farm in the East. A detailed trail of schematics and plans bound in heavy leather volumes remain in the Prussian archives.[28]

These plans looked oddly familiar when I first encountered them in the Prussian archives. I had examined similar plans before, but for the German colony in China. In my own moment of epiphany, the division between the "blue-water" (overseas) empires and the continental variety melted away in the common appearance of development plans from the Chinese northeastern coast to the Prussian East. By the 1890s Germany had transformed from the backwaters of Europe to a leading economic and scientific power. Political ambitions and the longing for empire followed Germany's economic rise. On December 6, 1897, the new Prussian State Secretary and Minister, Bernhard von Bülow, made his first appearance before the Reichstag and in unmistakable terms demanded for Germany a "place in the sun," that is, a colonial empire.[29] Bülow's speech made explicit the connection between a colonial empire and control of the seas with the building of a viable navy. In 1898, Germany took a significant step towards that place in the sun by acquiring a leasehold in China in Shandong province, strong-arming the Qing for the concession as recompense for the murder of a German missionary.[30] What happened in China had global ramifications. The German actions led to an arms race with the British Empire as each sought to dominate the seas and to extend their influence around the world. The Great Game included competition for the building of a railroad through the Ottoman Empire.[31] The Versailles Peace Treaty two decades later would trace to this aggressive expansion in China one of the root causes of World War I.

By the early 1900s, liberal politicians like Bernhard Dernburg, who served as state secretary from 1907 to 1910, crafted a colonial administration with ostensibly progressive economic policies that aimed to improve indigenous cultivation and make the colonies attractive locations for German investment. Dernburg argued for the rule of experts, emphasizing the "important role played in this new form of colonialism by science and technology, hydrology, and electrical technology as well as by geologists, chemists, geographers, botanists, zoologists, and land economists, and not least, by ethnologists, anthropologists, legal scholars, economists, historians, and statisticians."[32] This was the heart of New Imperialism, with scientific expertise reigning supreme.

In adopting science as the foundation of empire, the Germans aimed to depart from British and French precedents. The turn to scientific colonization, however, also exposed the tension between the universalist claims of science and the incorporation of indigenous and local knowledge. The subsequent decades would show the possibility of accommodation—not by the German colonial government, but by the local elites who recognized the potent power of science as a tool of modernization and a means to push back against foreign encroachment. Chinese nationalists adapted science for the purposes of maintaining the Qing imperial territories in the age of the nation-state while Japanese experts used the same methods to administer their growing continental empire.

Over the course of its less than two-decade long occupation, the German Reich invested around 200 million marks in building the city of Tsingtao (Qingdao), the crown jewel of their China leasehold in Shandong province. The amount far exceeded the government's investment in its other colonies, including Germany's much larger holdings in Africa. The harbor alone cost 26 million marks.[33] Neatly laid out streets and plans of development placed Qingdao amongst the ranks of scientifically administered colonies. The city's gridded design and, less visibly, its taxation scheme, won over Chinese admirers, including the founding father of Chinese nationalism, Sun Yat-sen. Planned development spelled the future of empire. Yet, even what seemed an exorbitant investment in its overseas colonies was ultimately dwarfed by the inner colonization program. Side by side comparisons of plans for the city of Qingdao in the Kiautschou leasehold and villages in East Prussia reveal the overlapping intellectual foundations for both the overseas and continental empires. Both featured the latest ideas on planned development. The inner colonization program deployed the latest tools coming out of developing fields in the social sciences to draw up land surveys, tax registers, ethnographic studies, and architectural plans for settlements. Extensive plans sketched out details down to the height of livestock stalls.

In Qingdao, similarly detailed plans called for segregated European and Chinese living quarters and provided regulations down to the inch of height requirements for doorways and ceilings. Segregation allowed the colonial government to quickly quarantine the Chinese population during the Manchurian plague outbreak in 1910.[34] The synchronous nature of these plans offers up a chicken-and-egg conundrum—did Germany influence China or did China influence Germany? In the end the most plausible answer is that the same experts (or experts trained in the same disciplines) drew up plans for both the blue-water empire and the inner colonization efforts. People and ideas traveled around the world, exposing the futility of national boundaries even as countries eagerly sought to ascertain and define them to beat back competing claims from bordering and rival powers.

The appeal of these development schemes crossed national boundaries and the specificity of place. They aimed to turn settlement into a science, with universal and rationalized laws equally applicable in eastern Europe, Asia, Africa, and the Americas. The visual similarities of rural development plans around the world mirror the similarities in the ap-

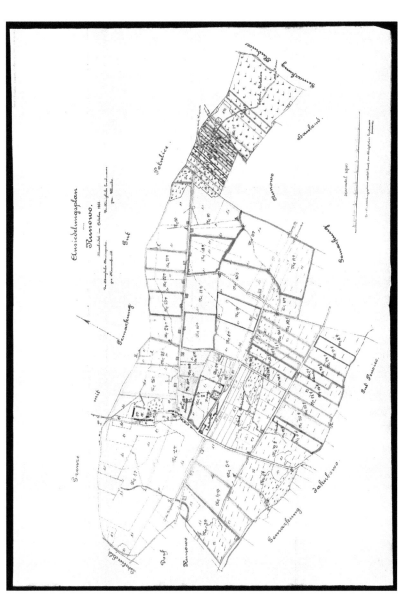

FIGURE 2.2: Inner colonization plans in East Prussia, 1886–1920. Geheimes Staatsarchiv Preußischer Kulturbesitz, HA I. 212 Nr. 801.

pearance of mass politics in the twentieth century. The Soviet Union and
Nazi Germany stood on opposing ideological ends, yet both deployed
parades and mass gatherings to further their consolidation of power.
Images of endless fields of grain could be taken in the United States or
the Soviet Union.[35] For countries like Germany, Japan, and China, these
images had an aspirational appeal. Social scientists promoted the mechanization and industrialization of agriculture as the most efficient, productive, and rational use of space.

In this sense, the movement of frontier discourse follows a similar
path as ideologies like fascism.[36] Efforts to create a synthesis of fascism
have foundered on its slippery core set of ideas, the inconvenient exceptions to the rule, along with the personal animosity and individual foi-
bles that shaped movements. Ideological differences concealed certain
underlying similarities. Both conservative and leftist movements embraced the frontier as a malleable concept open to interpretation. It could
be the place of untrammeled freedom or a place of exile beyond the pale
of civilization; it could be the atavistic origin place of the modern state or
the birthplace of its future glory. The relationship of the frontiers to the
state was easily refashioned through historical revision, which turned
borderlands into either primitive wilderness or the vanguard of an inevitable modernization, depending on the context. Not coincidentally,
during the same period movements to fashion new national histories
took place around the world.[37] People around the world rewrote their
histories and created new national identities. What brought factions
from across the political spectrum together was the political chaos in
the transition between empire and the nation-state. What lubricated the
discussion was the backing of the new social sciences, with an emphasis
on data and social survey and a rush to embrace geo-modernity.

It was not a coincidence that a global interest in inner colonization
peaked during the transitional period from empire to nation-state, particularly in countries where imperial concerns needed to adapt to the
new mode of state formation. Nor should we be deceived by various
appellations of "new" to overlook the various ways that pre- and early
modern areas of knowledge shaped their successors. The administration
of empires used a limited set of tools—clearly visible in the similarities
between continental empires and the various established dynasties
around the world. The rise of mass politics and modern science altered
the calculation. New technologies created a new range of possibilities in

areas previously made off-limits by climate and geographical conditions. Nevertheless, countries as varied as the United States, China, and Germany continued to operate in the shadows of imperial precedents.

Settler Colonists of Asia

In 1877, after Clark left his mark on Sapporo Agricultural College and returned to the US, a young man named Nitobe Inazo enrolled in the school to study agriculture. Clark left academia to open a mining company out West that ultimately ruined him financially and destroyed his reputation among family and friends who invested in the scheme. He died a broken man in 1886, a victim of the dark flip side to the much-touted untrammeled freedom of the American West. For Nitobe, on the other hand, Hokkaido was the start of a global journey that would take him to the United States, where he studied briefly at Johns Hopkins University, and to Germany, where he received his PhD in agricultural economics at Halle, before returning to teach at Sapporo. Nitobe spent so much of his adult life abroad that he became more comfortable writing in English than Japanese. This was no bad thing for intellectuals of his generation, some of whom seriously entertained replacing the Japanese language and its unwieldy combination of Chinese characters and Japanese script with English.

Born in 1862 to a wealthy family in Nambu domain, a precocious Nitobe enrolled at Sapporo Agricultural College at age fifteen and converted to Christianity at the school. He later became a prominent Japanese Quaker and served as the Under Secretary General in the League of Nations. His career thrived in parallel with the Japanese Empire. Like a number of other leading Meiji era intellectuals, Nitobe advocated for empire in the context of broadly internationalist and pacifist views. In 1900, during a three-year stay in the United States, Nitobe published his most famous work in English, *Bushido: The Soul of Japan*, which more than any other work of the era constructed the myth of Japan and its samurai code of ethics for audiences in the West. American and European readers eager for Orientalist accounts to satisfy their appetites for the exotic made the book a global bestseller.[38]

In Asia, it was in his role as an agronomist and advisor to the colonial administration of Hokkaido, as well as an avid promoter of Japanese emigration, where Nitobe made his lasting impact. From the late

nineteenth century, Japanese social scientists and geographers began
to construct new disciplines of colonial science and to conduct extensive fieldwork and surveys on the Asian mainland. After initially relying heavily on Western consultants, Japan developed its own corps of
technically skilled scientists and social scientists. Men like Capron and
Clark served their purpose at a time when Japan was at a particularly
vulnerable stage of transition between regimes and looked for allies in
the West. The arrangements they made with the Japanese government
were mutually beneficial. But the exorbitant salaries they negotiated
made these appointments too expensive to maintain. In the brief periods
of their service in Japan, the Western consultants were limited in what
they could contribute to the building of the Japanese Empire. Not so for
the Japanese experts who followed in their wake. Borrowing heavily
from the German model, geographers, reformers, and colonial officials
like Shiga Shigetaka (1863–1927), Fukuzawa Yukichi (1835–1901), and
Goto Shimpei (1857–1929) promoted the use of the sciences and social
sciences in the administration of empire.[39]

In the Meiji era, many Japanese students studied in US and Europe
and brought back the latest agronomic theories. Among them, Nitobe
Inazo helped to create a new vocabulary of colonization and empire and
served as a vocal advocate of Japanese emigration. As the country underwent rapid social and political changes in the early Meiji years, the
samurai class lost their traditional privileges and stipends from their
lords. Encouraging these declassed samurai (*shizoku*) to take up "free"
land in Hokkaido appeared to solve multiple problems. In 1869, the Meiji
government formed the Hokkaido Development Agency (Kaitakushi).
Shortly thereafter, in 1871, Kuroda Kyotaka took charge of the agency
and became the main contact person for the assorted Western experts
hired to aid in the colonization, including Horace Capron and William
Clark. The Development Agency launched two flagship programs to encourage migration from the home islands. The farmer-soldier program
(Jp. *tondenhei* 屯田兵) was based on the imperial Chinese precedent of
military frontier settlements and recruited volunteer *shizoku* to settle in
Hokkaido by providing free land, housing, and farming facilities, while
also conducting military training. A second program recruited nonmili-
tary *shizoku* and provided free lease of land.[40]

The term *shokumin* 殖民 dates from the early 1870s, when it was used
as an alternative to the classical Chinese name for military-run agri-

cultural settlements (Jp. *tonden*, Ch. *tuntian* 屯田) to describe the colonization efforts on Hokkaido. From the beginning, however, linguistic slippage occurred in the application of *shokumin.* There are two characters, both with the same pronunciation in Chinese and Japanese, which was used interchangeably in the neologism of *shokumin.* The word 殖民 was far more prevalent in Meiji period documents and intellectuals' writings. The character 殖 means to reproduce and clearly connects the settlement of Hokkaido with population concerns and the aim of accumulating capital. By the beginning of the twentieth century, however, 植民, "planting people," became increasingly popular. In a 1916 article, Nitobe Inazo explicated the difference in meaning between the two written terms and then intentionally used 植民 throughout the article, highlighting the renewed focus on agriculture as the central purpose of migration for advocates of Japanese overseas expansion.[41] The linguistic question would come up again for the Chinese for land reclamation, *tunken* 屯墾—which was not extensively in use before the twentieth century but combines two well-known characters which had appeared in documents since antiquity. What makes a word or a concept modern? What role did the historical antecedents play in how people understood these neologisms? These linguistic issues underscore the various continuities that cross over between empire and the age of the nation-state and the contradictions at the heart of geo-modernity.

The interchangeable use of homonym characters denoting colonization indicated the changing ideals of empire for Japanese colonial advocates like Nitobe. Like the fungal tendrils connecting trees in a forest, certain common knowledge coursed through global networks in the nineteenth century. Where such knowledge appeared above ground, however, they were cloaked in culturally and historically specific language. Through the invention of its own language of colonization, Japan formally cast away China's imperial precedent to craft its own identity as a colonial empire, as befitting the rising power in Asia. But part of what intellectuals like Nitobe adapted for use in Japan's expansion was a central European concept of inner colonization, which grew out Germany's unique history. In the great age of global travel, flora and fauna circulated and adapted to new environments. Ideas, too, and language dispersed, transformed, and took root in new places and in time became indistinguishable from what had flourished before their arrival.

The Japan historian Sidney Lu has traced how the intellectual justification that he terms *Malthusian expansionism* underlay both Japanese colonization of areas of its empire, starting with Hokkaido, then expanding to Taiwan, Korea, the Asian mainland, and the South Pacific, as well as emigration of Japanese laborers to North and South America. Like other industrializing countries around the world, Japan in the late nineteenth century experienced "statistics fever," based on the adoption of new disciplines of social sciences. Spurred by early adherents, including students of Dutch Learning (*Rangaku*), the Japanese government began to conduct population surveys and to manage the country through the collection of data, using the household registration system, but also reorganizing the population through classification based on gender and age rather than familial units.[42] The rise of the social sciences reinforced the interventionist power of the state. To some extent, land and population surveys were always essential functions of the state in imperial China, as well as Japan, and undergirded the state's basic taxation abilities.[43] But now under the umbrella of scientifically oriented disciplines like geography and agricultural economics, this data gave weight to new arguments for the importance of empire. The specter of overpopulation and the limits of natural resources gave added urgency to the need to expand the frontiers of settlement, be it in Brazil or Manchuria. The concept of Malthusian expansionism connects Japanese settler colonialism in the various parts of its empire with overseas emigration, with various intellectual connections and overlapping figures in both movements.[44]

From the 1860s, ideas about settler colonialism and frontiers circulated in Japan and became the intellectual foundation for the empire. The Meiji era intellectual Fukuzawa Yukichi (1835–1901), a member of the Japanese embassy to the United States in the 1860s, wrote a bestselling geography book for children in 1869, *Sekai Kunizukushi* 世界國盡, which popularized the concept of "frontier" in catchy verse form.[45] In the 1880s transpacific agricultural colonization societies first attempted to carve a "New Japan" in the Lake Washington area near Seattle, Washington; in 1901, a separate group attempted to bring working-class Japanese to the US-Mexico borderlands. Japanese intellectuals and members of the diaspora in the US together built these transpacific and transnational connections. They also helped to spread the idea of American-style "continental farming" and agricultural experimental stations, taking the same concepts from these failed ventures in North America to Manchuria and other Asian outposts of the Japanese Empire.[46]

From the Meiji period the Japanese government sponsored programs aimed at encouraging settlers to take up agricultural development at the forefront of the empire. Early interest in immigration to North America had waned by the late nineteenth century as the Japanese awoke to the racism and legal curbs in the United States and Canada, particularly the Chinese Exclusion Act of 1882. By the 1920s and 1930s, Japanese immigration to Brazil became part of an internationalist claim of co-prosperity and coexistence which predated the World War II use of the same terms for the idealistic goals of empire.[47] As the Japanese Empire expanded from the late nineteenth century, the Japanese interpretation of colonial science spread with it. By the 1930s, the Japanese colonial empire had expanded from Hokkaido to Taiwan, Korea, and Northeast China. Japan's continental ambitions entered a new phase in Manchuria, where the colonial administration established collective farms at the same time that the Japanese home government promoted the region as an industrial and modern Eden.[48] Notably, the language of coexistence and co-prosperity was already part of an agrarian discourse in Japan during the 1920s and 1930s and played a key role in Japanese emigration to Brazil even more so than the subsequent Manchukuo campaigns on the Asian mainland. The idea of the frontier was malleable enough to be easily adapted to new historical and environmental contexts. In these new contexts, and long after American experts returned home, only faint echoes of the American West remained.

Lives and careers did not neatly follow national borders. The internationalization of science easily crossed newly consolidating national boundaries and temporal divisions based on the changing of political regimes. Contributors to the series on scientific colonization published by Schmoller and Sering included a volume written by Takaoka Kumao (1871–1961) on the inner colonization of Japan.[49] Takaoka dedicated his 1904 work to his brother, the director of the colonial government in Hokkaido. The extensive use of charts, census, and surveys in the work makes it an early example of the Japanese Empire's reliance on social science methods to control its population and territory.

The mobility of figures like Takaoka or Nitobe Inazo, who crisscrossed the globe in their educations and subsequently in their advocacy of the Japanese Empire, made them the human agents of global networks. The science of settlement and administration connected inner and external colonization, Qingdao and East Prussia, the American West and Hokkaido. Takaoka went on to a distinguished career in agricultural economics. In the 1910s, he participated in the meetings of the conservative Social Policy Association (Shakai Seisaku Gakkai) and delivered reports on the plight of Japan's small family farmers.[50] The society identified rural overpopulation and the underutilization of household labor as the causes of Japan's rural problems. Emigration was seen as a solution. In the 1920s Takaoka was commissioned by the Japanese Ministry of Foreign Affairs to study the condition of Japanese settlers in Brazil.[51] His life stretched from the start of the Meiji era to the peak of Japanese emigration to South America in the postwar period. Supported by several generations of reformers and experts, the idea that Japan's population was unevenly distributed and overcrowded on the home islands helped to propel these successive movements from the early Meiji period in the 1870s to a brief postwar period of emigration to Brazil and other parts of South America that peaked in the 1950s.

Experimental Grounds of Empire

Empires and would-be empires around the world deployed a toolbox of similar state apparatuses in securing contested areas. These included the expansion of state bureaucracy, infrastructure building, and knowledge production, billed as "modern," although historians like Laura Hostetler have shown a remarkably similar set of responses in the eighteenth-century Qing expansion into the Southwest and in other early modern empires.[52]

Before it became a science, in both Asia and Europe, elites and scholars studied agriculture improvement and viewed it as an important field. The first uses of the term *experiment* in Japan and subsequently in China was in the context of chemistry and agriculture. *Shiyan* 試驗, the Chinese term for experiment, already existed in the Song dynasty (960–1279), although the meaning in classical Chinese differed from modern usage. The first modern use of the term *experiment* (Jp. *shiken* 試驗) in Japan appeared in the 1847 *Rangaku* work *Introduction to Chemistry* (*Seimi Kaiso* 舍密開宗) by Udagawa Yōan (1798–1846). The work contained illustrations of various experiments, including a description of an electric battery. The *shiyanchang* 試驗場 (Jp. *shikenjō*) or 実験所 (Jp. *jikkensho*), the neologism for the laboratory, was first coined in Japan in the 1870s. The term evolved to denote a distinct space for science before circulating back to China as a neologism.[53] In the harsh climate and remote corner between Korea and China, the first Meiji era Japanese colonization efforts included the opening of plant experimental stations. The establishment of these stations took place in the vanguard of colonial administration and particularly in contested zones as models of modernization. The historian Nianshen Song, in his study of the northeastern borderlands at the intersection of Qing, Korean, and Japanese interests, described the experimental station established by the Japanese Empire in the region as a veritable cornucopia of greenhouses and gardens. Along with cutting-edge cultivation methods and trial plots of rice, fruit, and vegetable varieties, the Kanto experimental station that Japan established in 1907 actively promoted education and hygienic projects.[54]

Neither the location of the experimental station nor the timing of its construction is coincidental. Japan's astonishing victory in the Russo-Japanese War (1904–1905) reverberated around the world, giving hope to non-Western countries for the possibilities of modernization to lead to triumph over European countries. The victory also allowed Japan to supplant Russian influence in Northeast China. In 1910, Japan formally announced the inclusion of Korea as part of its colonial orbit. At the same time, across the Chinese borderlands, the agricultural experimental station became a favored tool of the state, both the Qing and its successors, to bring modernizing forces to the peoples widely viewed as backward and even further down the scale of civilization. For these modernizers, the experimental station represented modern science and progress. As a traditional field of knowledge and area for statecraft, agricultural experimental stations won the backing of conservatives, as well as reformers. Despite the adverse political conditions and rumblings of a coming revolution, the Qing state and individual officials around the country displayed great interest in new agricultural technology and sciences.

Both the neologism *shiyanchang* and the actual opening of agricultural experimental stations quickly spread throughout China, bridging traditional interest in agriculture with the new concept of the laboratory. In 1906, the newly established Ministry of Agriculture opened the first national agricultural experiment station on land outside of the Xizhi Gate, near the northwest corner of Beijing's city walls. The station is now part of the Beijing Zoo, with a plaque to commemorate its previous history. In the same period, provincial officials established agricultural experiment stations in all the provinces, with some provinces operat-

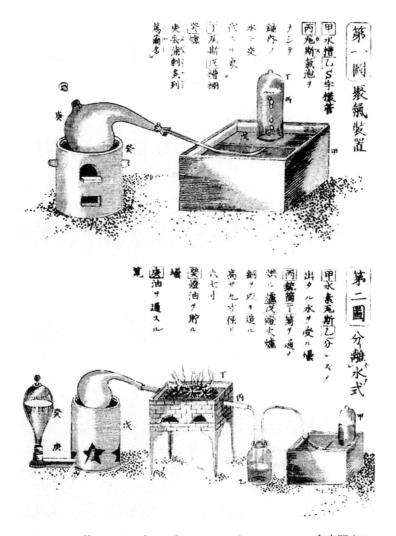

FIGURE 2.3: Illustration from the 1847 work *Seimi Kaiso* 舎密開宗 by Udagawa Yōan (1798–1846). Image from Wikimedia Commons.

ing multiple stations, like Guangdong, which opened seven stations by 1911, as well as launching additional sericulture and forestry stations.[55] Agricultural stations survived the collapse of the Qing dynasty. More important than the actual physical stations, the language of scientific agriculture and experimental stations proliferated in the subsequent decades and into the People's Republic of China after its founding in 1949.

From the late nineteenth century onward, Qing officials and later

Republican-era reformers alike were open to new solutions to age-old problems and promoted the importation of agricultural studies. Agricultural science and agronomic studies linked empire, republic, and the communist state across political watersheds. Qing officials who practiced statecraft beliefs had long encouraged agricultural experimentation on their own lands and in the areas under their jurisdiction. The end of the dynasty saw growing interest in new media from newspapers to pictorial magazines. Many such publications featured science and technology, including foreign agricultural practices.[56]

This new agricultural knowledge and technologies fit easily into existing intellectual frameworks, particularly the local gazetteer. For the past thousand years, from approximately the tenth century through the twentieth century, local officials and elites in China have produced gazetteers, which contain copious information on the local administration, economies, environment, flora and fauna, cultural and religious practices, and in many cases, maps and illustrations of the locality.[57] Gazetteers particularly flourished during the Qing dynasty, so much so that the state attempted to make uniform their content and regulate their production across the empire.[58] These (not entirely successful) regulations indicate the gazetteer's peculiar cultural niche as a product of an ambiguous gray area between official and commercial publication. Gazetteer production and the number of maps included considerably expanded in the last decades of the Qing dynasty.

A set of maps and images from the *Dali County Gazetteer* (*Dali Xianzhi Gao* 大理縣志稿, 1917) provide an interesting example of the way agricultural experimental stations found their way across the country.[59] Yunnan province lies in the southwest corner of China, bordering Burma and Vietnam. Much of the province is mountainous and difficult for outsiders to access. In the eighteenth century, mines from the province supplied silver and copper for use in the currency. As the capital of the province, Dali shares a name with the kingdom (937–1253) that ruled the region before it was conquered and incorporated into the Chinese Empire during the Ming dynasty (1368–1644). In the late nineteenth century, French explorers traveled through the region and looked to exploit the province's mineral wealth. In the early twentieth century, the Republican Chinese government disputed the Burma border with the British Empire. The matter was handed to the League of Nations international courts in the 1930s. During the negotiations, both sides conducted surveys of the region and dispatched researchers to investigate the local climate, political, economic, and transportation conditions.[60] None of these details would seem to place Dali at the forefront of scientific development in China.

Yet, the 1917 gazetteer features a sophisticated contour map of Dali port, as well as a city map. The city map clearly shows the location of schools and what appears to be an extensive agricultural and forestry experimental zone. Both the editor-in-chief and the compiler were prominent revolutionaries in the events which brought about the collapse of the Qing dynasty. The editor-chief, Zhang Peijue, was an early member of Sun Yat-sen's Revolutionary Alliance, the Tongmenghui. Zhang was executed in 1915 and died a martyr of the revolution. The chief compiler, Zhou Zonglin, was an educator and principal of a high school and teacher's college in Dali. The biographies of the two men and the contents of the *Dali County Gazetteer* suggest that the spread of the sciences accompanied a variety of advocates, from officials to educators, to their hometowns and villages far from the major treaty port cities. By the late Qing and early Republican period, local elites from Yunnan in the Southwest to Jinan in the Northeast had embraced reforms and established schools as the bases to spread their ideas.[61]

The presence of agricultural experimental stations across China, in interior and frontier provinces, maps the spread of modern science in China from below—through agricultural experimental stations. As early as the 1870s, provincial gazetteers of borderlands such as Gansu in the Northwest and Mongolia featured the latest mapping technologies and contained information about potential mineral resources and infrastructure, as well as more traditional content about agricultural products and local religious institutions. Officials and local gentry involved in these projects were often the first to adopt new agricultural technologies from abroad and open schools that featured instruction in science and applied skills instead of the traditional focus on the classics. From the nineteenth century disciplines like geography, agricultural science, economics, and even histories of the nation were linked in international professional and academic networks.

In addition to local gazetteers, new kinds of publications appeared in the late nineteenth century catering to elite interest in agriculture and technologies. The *Journal of Agriculture* (*Nongxue Bao* 農學報), founded in 1897, featured a cosmopolitan variety of articles on the latest farming implements, seed varieties, and chemical fertilizer production in the

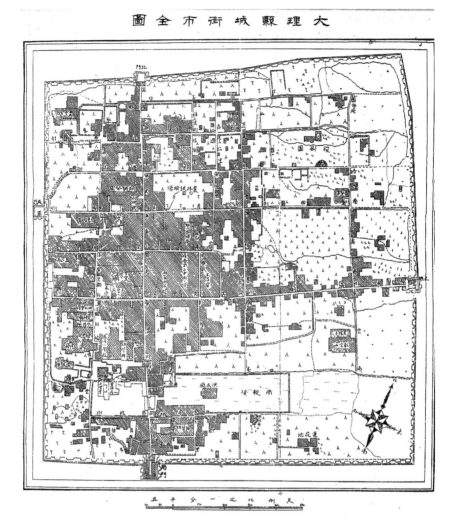

圖全市街城縣理大

FIGURE 2.4: City map included in the *Dali County Gazetteer* (Zhang Peijue and Zhou Zongluo, eds., *Dali Xian zhi gao* 大理縣志稿, 1917). The Agricultural and Forestry Experimental Zone is prominently featured in the top left corner of the map. Courtesy of Harvard University Libraries.

United States, Europe, and Japan, most of which were translated in their entirety from Japanese works.[62] In many cases, the Japanese "originals" were also translations. Illustrations often accompanied the articles. Of the first eighteen works translated, eleven pieces were from Japan and another work, on beet farming in Germany, was translated into Chinese from a Japanese translation. As ideas circulated, the process of transmission obfuscated what was original and what translated. The Japanese work *Introductions to Agricultural Studies* (*Nongxue Rumen* 農學入門, originally by Inagaki Otohei 稻垣 乙丙), for example, included a chapter encouraging the farmer to use a diary to record the yields of various crops. Another chapter promoted careful accounting on the farm. Such advice clearly came from Western agricultural science texts. The works included in the *Journal of Agriculture* covered an esoteric range of topics including food science, mushroom farming, wine-making, sugarcane farming and the sugar-making process, botany, ways to improve rice varieties, and gooseberry farming.

The establishment of agricultural experimental zones took place extensively throughout China, in the borderlands as well as interior provinces, in coastal cities and remote inland areas. Increasing numbers of Chinese students headed overseas to study sciences and social sciences by the end of the nineteenth and in the first decades of the twentieth century. They brought back new concepts and terminologies, but also adapted this knowledge for China. This circulation of knowledge and personnel was far more widespread than previous scholarship has acknowledged. Like Dali in Yunnan province, Guilin in the neighboring southwestern province of Guangxi is an unexpected location for the vanguard of scientific development. Yet, the *Linggui County Gazetteer* 臨桂縣志 (1905) has one the earliest mentions of the establishment of an agricultural experimental station in China.[63] According to the gazetteer, the Guangxi higher school was located outside the city walls in Guilin, in the location of the old machine shop. In 1900, the governor general Huang Huaisen 黃槐森 memorialized the throne to open a technical school in the province. Three years later, a new governor general renamed the school Guangxi University. The school recruited poor students to study agricultural sciences, including in disciplines like chemistry, with practical applications for the manufacturing of fertilizer and in grafting and other botanical techniques. Local officials, working with the school, dispatched people to Japan to investigate the purchase of new agricultural machinery, entirely bypassing cities like Guangzhou, Shanghai, and Beijing to connect directly to the outside world.

At the same time, on the frontiers of the Qing Empire, late Qing expansion and development plans followed the individual ambitions of expansionist provincial leaders and imperial precedent and varied ac-

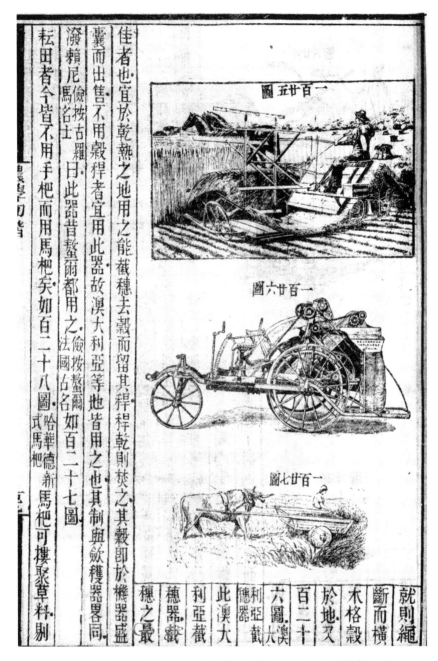

佳者也宜於乾熱之地用之能截穗去穀而留其稈得乾則焚之其穀即於機器盛

囊而出售不用穀稈者宜用此器故澳大利亞等地皆用之也其制與斂穫器畧同 儉按鰲爾如百二十七圖

潑賴尼馬按古羅日此器昔鰲爾都用之法國古名如百二十七圖 哈華德新馬杷

耘田者今皆不用手杷而用馬杷矣如百二十八圖式馬杷可摟聚草料別

就則繩 斷而橫 木格穀 於地又 百二十 六圖澳 利亞大 此澳大 利亞截 德器 穗器截 穗之最

圖五廿百一

圖六廿百一

圖七廿百一

FIGURE 2.5: From the *Journal of Agriculture* (*Nongxue bao* 農學報), which included an esoteric range of articles on new farming techniques and crops from the West from 1897. *Nong xue bao* (Shanghai: Nong xue bao guan, 1897), 1309.

cording to local conditions. The push for inner colonization of Mongolia, Chahar, and other border regions, for example, built upon existing trends that had begun during the late Qing, when the faltering central government opened borderlands to migrants from the interior. Regional officials in the borderlands often supported the opening of agricultural settlement zones intended for Han Chinese farmers in response to international pressures and incursions from neighboring states.

To conquer China, the Manchus organized its military according to a banner system, in companies of 300 men each. After conquest, the Qing retained the banner system, distinguished by different colored flags, with some banners composed entirely of a particular ethnicity, like Mongolian or Han Chinese. To support themselves, the banner men were granted land. As the military declined, the sale of Mongolian lands by impoverished bannermen and nobles to development by Han Chinese merchants began long before such projects took on undertones of nationalism and race in the twentieth century.[64] Ironically, in the 1930s Japanese social scientists attributed the decline of Mongolian populations in the borderlands to the encroachment of Han Chinese settlers while largely silent about their own complicity with Japanese imperialism.[65]

In broad outlines, Mongolia, Xinjiang, and the southwestern frontiers in China followed a similar process of development as Hokkaido. Merchant- and state-sponsored development plans started long before the arrival of Western imperialism, driven by the growing tendrils of global markets and demand for goods from ginseng to precious metals and furs. Trade linked frontiers to the heartlands and altered cultural practices and consumption, from the wearing of fur, which before the Qing was viewed as barbaric, to the use of medicinal ginseng growing exclusively in the mountains of the Northeast.[66] Western imperialism in the late nineteenth century added new dimensions and, in some cases, accelerated the ongoing process of integration into global systems.

Several trends played into this continued imperial discourse even after the collapse of the Qing Empire. During the Qing, distance from Beijing and the time it took for missives to travel from the capital to the borderlands allowed frontier governors considerable leeway to pursue their own agenda. The most important of these was regional interest in maintaining control over the borderlands. For example, because of its geographical location in the southwestern borderlands, Sichuan province was used by the Qing state as a launching pad for military operations in Tibet. Viewed as a strategically important area, the province was given considerable tax breaks by the central government.[67] Towards the end of Qing rule in the late nineteenth century, both the central government and provincial officials recognized the risks posed by the British Empire in neighboring India and worked to contain potential trouble spots.[68] To counter these threats, late Qing governors pursued active campaigns into eastern Tibet, even against misgivings from the Qing emperors.

Activist governors at times pursued their own agenda of expansion, going beyond central directives to support development schemes in contested areas including land reclamation, the opening of agricultural experimental zones, and encouraging industry and mining. Another effort which enjoyed broad support was the founding of schools, which promoted "New Learning." Topics under the heading of New Learning included agricultural science, geography, and other newly introduced sciences from the West. After military reforms in 1904 and the termination of the civil examinations the following year, the most promising students in the Southwest region were instead sent to military academies in Japan. Provincial leaders also founded the Sichuan Military Academy, based on the model of New Schools, which offered courses in the sciences.[69]

After the collapse of the empire in 1912, the weak central state during the Republican period allowed local strongmen to emerge. Some regions fell under the control of warlords. Many educational and land reclamation efforts stalled from lack of funding. The weak state and decentralization during this period, however, obscure the strong centrifugal forces in China. The Japanese invasion in the 1930s and retreat of the central government to the southwestern region redoubled efforts to spur development and bolster defenses in the borderlands. Inner Mongolia and Northeast and Southwest China all experienced a variety of development schemes from the late Qing to after 1949, when the country once again consolidated centralized control. Once we step back from the minutiae of local interactions, the pattern becomes clearly visible—China in the late nineteenth and early twentieth centuries experienced a brief interlude of reassessing the possibilities of empire, or at least maintaining the territorial expanse of empire while adopting the trappings of a nation-state. In the wake of this interlude, the rhetoric of nationalism provided a superficial but effective screen for the retention of imperial territories. The historian Xu Guoqi has coined the term *international na-tionalism* to describe a process that began in the last years of the Qing dynasty of building nationalism with efforts to cooperate and participate in the international community to demand equal treatment.[70] Domesti-cally, agricultural development and the opening of experimental sta-tions became key tools of empire in the guise of the modern nation-state.

The Qing official Zuo Zongtang's interest in agriculture and new technologies was not unique. The trajectory of his career demonstrated some of the ways that concerns over foreign encroachment and new knowledge from the West intersected on the frontiers. The cataclysmic turmoil China experienced in the nineteenth century was brought about by a perfect storm of domestic social conflict, compounded by environ-mental issues and escalating demands by Western empires backed by steam power and new weapons. How to address this tidal wave of prob-lems consumed late Qing officials. The adoption of agricultural science allowed for engagement in an area that was acceptable and valued by re-formers and conservatives alike. On the frontiers from the Northeast to the Southwest, land reclamation projects enjoyed broad official support and continued after the fall of the Qing dynasty.

The spread of agricultural experimental zones bridged the transition from empire to nation and introduced modern science, but also created an opportunity for the state to experiment with new forms of governance and social control. The agricultural experimental zone proliferated in writings about the frontier—in China, in Japan, in Germany, in Russia, and in the United States. It parallels discussions of national security and the concept of the "buffer zone." It also crosses the artificial divide between inner colonization and overseas colonialism. The Germans viewed both arenas of "colonial space [as] an experimental field, a some-what utopian laboratory where vast social experiments can take place."[71] Inner and external colonization efforts connected in the experimental zone.

———

The late nineteenth century brought about three significant develop-ments. First, the rise of the social sciences created a global network of knowledge that at the same time was geared towards the specific politi-cal and economic interests of countries and their stage of development. From the mid-nineteenth century, the US began to look overseas for further arenas of expansion while undergoing vast changes in agriculture and industrialization which both elevated the importance of cities over the countryside and turned farms into factories.[72] In Germany, liberal advocates of empire viewed the settlement and development of the East as the means to counter the power of the landed aristocracy and ameliorate conditions for landless tenants and proletariats. A new generation of Japanese academics trained abroad brought these ideas about frontier settlement and agricultural development to assist in building the Japanese Empire. In China, scholar-official interest in statecraft fed early interest in translations of scientific texts, particularly in fields with a clear practical application, such as geology/mining, geography, and agriculture.

Second, while the open frontiers of the world were seen as closed, international law made clear the importance of clearly demarcated borders and instituted the values of agricultural settlement and the exploration and exploitation of natural resources as a means of asserting sovereignty over contested lands. These development schemes created value out of loosely defined "wastelands," including wetlands and grasslands that environmentalists have subsequently recognized as essential to maintaining balance in delicate ecosystems. The word *wasteland*, like *frontier*, appeared frequently in popular works with the assumption that everyone shared a common understanding of their meaning. Yet, considerable linguistic slippage occurred in the process of translation and global circulation, leaving room for imported ideas to become nativized through historical revision.[73] Nationalists and colonial administrators alike used the term *frontier* strategically to bolster territorial claims without acknowledging the highly contested meaning of the word.

Finally, the nineteenth century brought about New Imperialism and a reassessment of empire. Where the British, Dutch, and French had acquired territories through the initiative of private trading companies, the later modernizers, the Germans and Japanese, consciously sought out colonial expansion. The Americans, as former colonists themselves, were deeply ambivalent about empire, or at least the formal acknowledgement of empire, while at the same time eagerly taking part in a global search for new resources. In the last decades of the Qing dynasty, officials actively sought ways to bolster the dynasty's control over borderlands using a hybrid mixture of age-old imperial tools and newly imported technologies, sciences, and ideas about race and knowledge of Western colonization efforts. By the end of the nineteenth century, the nation-state gained traction. The revision of empire and rise of the nation-state overlapped to a significant degree and in multiple instances built upon each other. In the same way, colonialisms possessed modular qualities that compounded over time, allowing different colonial regimes to "build projects with blocks of one earlier model and then another."[74] The frontier became the locus of these efforts, the place where one could see the convergence of these multiple and sometimes conflicting trends.

THREE

In Search of New Frontiers

No government can afford to ignore the development of its resources. . . . vacant land can be a source of political danger . . . It
is the business of government leaders not to permit any land that
they may control to be politically passive.

Isaiah Bowman[1]

What does the frontier mean to different people? To Qing officials in
the nineteenth century, China's various frontiers signified the growing
risks and challenges from the British Empire to the West in Tibet, the
French in the Southeast, the Russians in the Northwest and, by century's end, the Japanese in the Northeast. In the United States, the frontier
became entangled with Manifest Destiny and the push across the continent, evolving into the embodiment of American exceptionalism. For
the Germans, the eastern frontiers displayed Slavic mismanagement and
the potential for ethnic Germans to carve out agriculturally productive
zones from wastelands. In Japan, the search for new frontiers overseas
represented an opportunity and outlet for the overpopulated and impoverished countryside.

These national differences in interpreting the frontier have long obscured how a relatively small, select group of geographers and agronomists provided the ideological underpinnings for territorial claims
in both domestic regions resistant to centralized control and colonies
overseas. Beneath seemingly considerable differences, up-and-coming

nations around the world like the United States, Japan, and Germany, and Eurasian empires like the Russian and the Qing, shared certain common concerns as the rhetoric of the frontier assumed growing importance around the world. Ideas about territory, natural resources, and development took shape in the context of the tightening connections of a globalizing world. Whereas the previous chapter examined agricultural science, this one traces these connections through the lives of geographers who strived to remake their discipline into a science and indispensable tool of the modern state.

The Golden Age of Global Travel

As European opinions on China gradually hardened in the years leading up to the Opium War (1839–1842), the allure of the Orient faded while the American West rose in cultural cachet. For the German writer Karl May (1842–1912), the fifth child of a desperately poor small-town weaver in Ernsttal, in Saxony, the American West served as the backdrop for rousing tales of adventure, conjured entirely out of his imagination. His most popular work, *Winnetou*, featured a gentlemanly Apache hero. May himself never stepped foot in the United States. On his one extended global journey, a trip that took him from Egypt and over the Suez Canal to Ceylon and Sumatra, he suffered multiple mental breakdowns. The actual Orient, the tropical climes, the tastes and smells of spiced foods, the narrow, twisting streets, the strange sounds and thronging crowds—all of it frightened rather than exhilarated May. His readers, however, were not deterred by the fact that May had never actually seen the American West. A series of popular films based on the Winnetou books in the 1960s cemented his appeal for a new generation. Into the twenty-first century, German and Eastern European fans of May's work still travel to the United States in search of the "authentic" West, the land of cowboys and Indians.[2]

In the German press and in fictional works, writers juxtaposed the American West and the Polish East, creating a discursive bridge between two otherwise disparate frontiers. The enormously popular mid-nineteenth-century German novel, *Soll und Haben*, by Gustav Freytag, featured two protagonists who respectively sought their fortunes in the American West and the Prussian East. While the hero Anton Wohlfart discovers his middle-class identity through his experiences in the Prussian East, his aristocratic friend von Frink becomes embroiled in shady mining enterprises in the American West. It was only by extricating himself from North America and arriving unexpectedly at the Polish estate where Anton was employed that Fink finds happiness and a productive outlet for his energies.[3] Other popular writings in the German press similarly refashioned the Prussian East into empty prairie landscapes replete with nomadic Polish "Indians." Buried beneath the surface of these adventure tales was a more serious assessment of the factors important to national wealth and power.

Karl May's unusual life, from a small-time thief and con man born in extreme poverty to best-selling author, was exceptional. Global travel was not. The mass movement of peoples in the nineteenth century left little trace outside of shipping logs, secondhand accounts, and the occasional treasured family letter. In contrast, the global circulation of a much smaller group of educated elites produced voluminous correspondences, diaries, and published works that have survived into the present. Between 1830 and 1900, close to 2,000 travel books were published in the United States, with an even higher number in Europe.[4] Travelers from Asia soon joined the international ranks of these authors, producing works that described in vivid detail for domestic audiences the technological wonders and political and cultural workings of Western societies. Late Qing writers like Wang Tao and Li Gui published engaging accounts of their world travels, describing in close detail their experiences in the West, visiting museums, theaters, foreign mints (factories that make money!), and landmarks like the White House in Washington, DC.[5]

The world travelers included those who subsequently achieved renown in academic circles, like the geographer Friedrich Ratzel and agronomist Max Sering; consultants in the colonial ambitions of ascendant powers like William S. Clark and Horace Capron; and eager observers of the West and the roots of its wealth and power, like Xu Jianyin (1845–1901) and Nitobe Inazo. Xu had accompanied his father, the mathematician Xu Shou, to the newly established Jiangnan Arsenal in Shanghai in 1866; served as an attaché of the Chinese legation to Germany in the 1870s; and advocated for civil and military reforms in the 1890s. In 1901 Xu was killed in an explosion of the gunpowder factory he managed, a devastating accident from which rescuers only managed to recover his foot. Despite the lack of physical remains, Xu left behind diaries describing in detail his experiences in Europe.[6] This cosmopolitan and highly mobile group of people were geographers, agronomists, economists, and sociologists; they promoted reform of higher education and the adoption of new statistical and "scientific" analysis of modernizing societies. As members of an educated elite from Europe, the United States, or Asia, the majority were also men.

Educated elites from around the world looked eagerly to learn from the experiments and trials of other countries in the rush to modernize. Alexander von Humboldt's expedition to the Americas at the turn of the nineteenth century became a model for scientific exploration and writings of the period. By the end of the nineteenth century, global travel had become essential to establishing one's scientific credentials. On his travels in Europe, Xu Jianyin eagerly noted German manufacturing and industrial practices as a member of the Chinese legation to Germany. Americans traveled to Europe; Japanese students studied in the US and Europe; and Europeans spread out in their various colonial holdings, but also turned to the United States and the rest of the Americas. For travelers with an interest in education, German technical institutions became a mandatory stop on their tour of Europe. Japanese visitors, whether they were engineers or professors in institutions in Japan or employed by the South Manchurian Railroad on the Asian mainland, regularly wrote to the German Foreign Ministry to request tours of laboratories and schools. At times the sterling reputation of German technical education worked against the instructors at these institutions. So many foreign visitors "dropped by" without making an appointment that it caused considerable grumbling among the teachers, who saw the steady stream of visitors as a source of disruption during instructional time.[7]

In the 1870s, before he became one of the first named chairs of geography at a German university, Friedrich Ratzel (1844–1904) undertook an extended journey around the United States, Mexico, and Cuba as a correspondent for the newspaper the *Kölnische Zeitung.* After his return to Germany, in 1876 Ratzel published his travel writing pieces in one volume, *Sketches of Urban and Cultural Life in North America.*[8] Ratzel would later become best known for his contributions to the fields of geography and anthropology and for coining the term *Lebensraum.* In his interpretation, nations took on an organic life of their own and thrived or declined. To prosper, they required space. The search for *Lebensraum* or "living space" became a central tenet for the twentieth-century formulation of the field of geopolitics. In his 1897 work *Politische Geogra-*

phie, Ratzel analyzed the relationship between politics, the structure of the state, and geography.[9] The analysis then led to a separate 1901 work, *Der Lebensraum,* in which Ratzel defined the concept of *Lebensraum* as the "area necessary for a state to enjoy security in its independence."[10] Through his writings and his network of students, Ratzel influenced a generation of geographers by expounding on the historical and environmental concerns in geography. His ideas directly shaped the development of geopolitics as its own distinct field of analysis in the twentieth century, which emphasized the territorial control of natural resources and strategic infrastructure, particularly in borderlands.

In his travels in North America, Ratzel paid particular attention to the institutional and economic factors necessary for industrialization, the importance of an expansive frontier, and the educational institutions underpinning developments in science and the social sciences. Even with the power of hindsight, few have paid much attention to Ratzel's early writings as a twenty-eight-year-old journalist traveling in America. Yet, it's clear that the trip was a formative experience. Ratzel recognized the US as a country undergoing rapid urbanization and changes that presaged the future of Europe and the rest of the world. These changes created a new spatial hierarchy, with vast rural hinterlands supplying ever-growing cities and highlighted the importance of expansive territories with plentiful resources. Earlier in the century, the German economist and aristocrat Johann Heinrich von Thünen (1783–1850) had formulated an influential theory of economic geography based on the efficient use of agricultural lands that supplied a central city. Industrialization and new technologies changed the calculation. Ratzel pointed out that "better transportation facilities make it possible for countries with many cities or completely organized areas to import their grain and meat products from predominantly agricultural regions which lack urban development. . . . Agriculture through mechanization is beginning to resemble industry. . . . all this contributes to bringing the small cities and villages closer together."[11]

Through his travels Ratzel had recognized how new transportation technologies were transforming the economic and spatial organization of countries and creating advantages for countries with large, continental territories like the United States. New technologies like the railroad altered the balance between territory size, resources, and the logistical difficulties of transport. Urban hubs like Chicago ballooned in size and import, growing from a handful of settlers in the early years of the nineteenth century to a teeming metropolis with over a million residents by century's end. Railroads brought logs from ever more distant forests, while refrigeration allowed butchered meat to journey across the country quickly and easily.[12] On the other side of the world, in the Ottoman Empire, new coaling depots sprang up on the Mediterranean on shipping routes connecting Australia to London. A host of new technologies that used coal were transforming all facets of life from the consumption in coaling depots of desalinated water, a byproduct of steam engines, to the increased intake of meat made possible by refrigeration, which made Somalia into "Aden's butcher shop."[13] New technologies—steam engines, refrigeration, concrete construction methods—shaped the city's development and expanded the reach of its hinterlands. Travel opened Ratzel's eyes to the significance of these changes under way around the world.

This was a golden age for American cities. At the time of Ratzel's travels in the 1870s, 4 million people in the US lived in cities with over 100,000 inhabitants, compared to 2.1 million Germans and 3.1 million French. Most of these new American cities adopted gridded designs, wide avenues with room for trolleys, and were supplied by a large hinterland. These innovations foretold the future economic organization of modern states and underscored the importance of sufficient territorial expanse to supply these hubs. One could easily glean from these writings the prescient understanding of urbanization as a marker of modernization and the insights leading to Ratzel's later ideas on the *Lebensraum*. In connecting geography to history and using a variety of data, including environmental conditions, Ratzel's ideas displayed more nuance than some later adherents to environmental determinism, which became especially prominent in early twentieth-century American geography. Empire and territory clearly impacted Ratzel's thinking. For Germans, an identity as a modern European country and up-and-coming world power necessitated the possession of a colonial empire. The United States, with its seemingly endless frontiers and contiguous continental territories, presented an alternative to the acquisition of overseas empire (referred to as blue-water empire).

The developments that Ratzel wrote about approvingly in his reporting for the *Kölnische Zeitung* had in fact begun to alarm Americans. From the 1870s, American writers began to express anxieties about the closing of the frontiers and fears about the apparent exhaustion of new arable lands. Richard T. Ely, an economist and colleague of the historian Frederick Jackson Turner, wrote about Malthusian fears of the closed frontiers in his 1893 work *Outlines of Economics* and introduced to Americans the ideas of Italian economist Achille Loria on sustainable land-to-man ratios.[14] Such concerns led the geologist John Wesley Powell, the director of the US Geological Survey in the 1880s, to advocate for federally sponsored irrigation projects and study of semiarid western lands in order to bring more acreage under cultivation.[15] In turn, the USDA sent employees around the world to geographically similar regions, such as the Chinese Northwest and the Russian steppes, in search of trees and crops that might easily adapt to conditions in the Midwest and help fight soil erosion and other deleterious effects of agricultural development.

Ratzel's astute observations on some aspects of the modern world, as reflected in the US, contrasted with gaping blind spots regarding the issue of race. Ratzel casually adopted the racist views of the German immigrants he encountered in the American South, agreeing with them on the unsuitability of Black men as politicians and independent landowners during the Reconstruction period after the American Civil War. He adopted the denigrating language used by German immigrants to describe the former slaves who now held political power. In his travels, Ratzel met several émigrés who had lost their fortunes during the war—one man in Richmond showed him wads of worthless Confederate bills that were the bulk of his savings and ruefully observed that he would have been better off returning to Germany.[16] In Charleston, in contrast, he encountered a particularly prosperous German community composed mostly of middle-class and a few very wealthy immigrants that formed a close-knit and cohesive community.[17] A decade later, Max Sering similarly discovered pockets of German settlers who were fully satisfied with their improved lots in the New World as the beneficiaries of a racial order that privileged incentives for White settlers at the cost of the Black and indigenous populations.

In the years following his return to Germany, Friedrich Ratzel's ideas on the relationship between geography, environment, and history matured. By the 1890s, Friedrich Ratzel's thinking had evolved into a synthesis of history, geography, and the study of human civilization. Ratzel's larger body of works drew heavily upon the connections between history and geography and contributed to the nascent field of anthropology by demanding that all societies be studied historically.[18] Consider, for example, his influential 1894 work *Völkerkunde,* which was subsequently translated into English and published as *The History of Mankind* in 1896. Of Chinese civilization, Ratzel wrote that,

> The creation of science, therefore, forms one of the greatest epochs in the life of humanity, and among civilized nations the deepest cleavages result from the lack or possession of it. . . . When we find in Chinese tradition one and the same prince inventing or regulating the calendar, music, and the system of weights and measures . . . we see in this close connection of science with State power a proof of the purely practical estimate of science, or one would rather say, of knowledge and skill. For this very reason the most modern scientific works of the Chinese look to us like a survival from the Middle Ages.[19]

Ratzel made the same connection that the Japanese did—that the adoption of modern science predicated membership as an equal in an international community of nations. The racial underpinnings of Ratzel's hierarchy of civilizations should not distract from the way that non-White intellectuals, where they could, also eagerly adopted these ideas and adapted them for use in their own countries.

Ideas, like subterranean mycelial networks, circulate in mysterious ways. Ratzel's works, which broadly linked geography, history, and the social sciences, began to push geography from the example par excellence of the natural sciences to a social science. Paradoxically, as the nation-state became the dominant state form around the world, empire and the benefits of large territorial possessions became an overarching concern for social scientists. As European empires extended their reach across the globe, the prevalence of scientific metaphors expressed optimism and a belief in the progress of societies that, for all of their social ills, stood on the brink of conquering nature. In Germany, Hermann von Helmholz (1821–1894) formulated his theories on the conservation of energy in 1847. Across the European continent, scientists and social reformers, led by Helmholz himself, envisioned a society powered by universal energy.[20] Ultimately, Ratzel's formulation of *Lebensraum* and an organic understanding of the state built upon these broader scientific trends while placing geography at the heart of the melee. His early writings made explicit the racism that informed his later ideas, cloaked in more subtle forms. In his travels as a young man Ratzel recognized, as did many of his time, that the prosperity of one people required the dispossession of others.

Global travel became an essential rite of passage for geographers at the same time that truly unknown territories disappeared. In 1887, the British geographer Halford Mackinder declared that all but the polar regions had been explored. A new age had dawned, where the imperative to expand clashed with the fact that most regions were already claimed.[21] Six years later, Turner gave his famous frontier address at the Columbian Exposition, with essentially the same insight on the closing of the frontiers. Yet, despite the diminishing returns, geographers continued their expeditions to regions near and far. American geographer Ellsworth Huntington kept detailed notes of observations on his trips to Africa and Asia; Halford Mackinder's diaries reflect a similar interest in recording every observation made during his travels.[22] On his trip to Egypt and Africa in 1899, as Mackinder traveled through the Suez Canal and down the Arabian coast, he noted the temperature (97 degrees at midday in the shade) and the exact shade of blue of the sky and the water.[23] He did not note whether he used a cyanometer, an instrument for measuring "blueness" invented by Alexander von Humboldt and used by him in his exploration of South America at the dawn of the nineteenth century.

Territory and Power

American geography underwent a critical period in the late nineteenth century, as the country evolved into an international economic and scientific power. Geography became key to this evolution by teaching generations of schoolchildren how to conceptualize the world, its resources, and the American place in the global order. From his perch at the country's leading center of higher education, the Harvard University geographer William Morris Davis trained some of the most important early twentieth-century American geographers, including Ellsworth Huntington (1876–1947), who shaped his generation's understanding of the relationship between geography and climate, and Isaiah Bowman, who became the most influential and powerful American academic of the first half of the twentieth century. The nineteenth-century founding of natural science disciplines at Harvard and Yale was strongly influenced by figures like the Swiss geologist and comparative anatomist

Louis Agassiz (1807–1893), who taught at the Lawrence Scientific School at Harvard for many years and built up an impressive collection of skulls and early photographs of indigenous peoples in the pursuit of phrenological studies.

Another center of American geography developed in Baltimore, where Daniel Coit Gilman, the country's most influential geographer, was appointed the first president of Johns Hopkins University in 1876. Gilman was born in 1831 and graduated from Yale University in 1852. He then proceeded to graduate studies at Harvard University. As a student at Harvard, he lived in the home of the Swiss-born geologist and geographer Arnold Guyot. Guyot encouraged his interest in geography, which Gilman subsequently pursued in Germany. Gilman adopted the ideas of Carl Ritter and the wholistic approach to geography as the study of everything on earth, an approach that connected geography and historical development. He became familiar with the European university model and, like William S. Clark before him, saw it as the future of American higher education.[24] Back in the United States, Gilman corresponded widely with politicians and academics alike. By the time he became the president of Johns Hopkins University, Gilman embodied the two seemingly contradictory impulses of the nineteenth century—a geographer whose work was an essential tool of promoting nationalism and an educator in the global ascendance of science.[25]

The kind of geography advanced by Davis, Huntington, Bowman, and Gilman was solidly based in physical geography and fieldwork. Ellsworth Huntington's training illustrates how this type of training depended on global travel. In 1903, Huntington embarked on a trip to Russia, Central Asia, and China. Leaving from New York, he made his way to Asia by way of Vienna, Bagdad, Baku, Samarkand, and Tashkent. In a letter to his father from Vienna, he described meeting Albert Penck, the doyen of German geography and friend of Davis, his professor at Harvard. Huntington flirtatiously tried out his German on Penck's daughter at dinner.[26] Over the course of his long career, Huntington continued to travel around the world, going to India and Tibet and the Himalayan mountains in 1905, noting their structural similarities to the Tianshan plateau in Northwest China, which he examined on the 1903 trip. He went on multiple trips to Africa. Each expedition resulted in multiple volumes of field notes. He dabbled in all manner of experiments, some of which bordered on the bizarre. His interest in eugenics, for example, led to a study of birth control and twin births. He also conducted studies on the relationship between humidity and health. Huntington built on the empirical evidence collected from these assorted experiments a theory of environmental geography.

A generation earlier, Americans like William S. Clark and Raphael Pumpelly had headed to German universities in search of the latest developments in the sciences before taking this knowledge back to the US and then further afield to Asia. In the founding era of American universities and land-grant schools, German universities served as a model. Even after American views of Germany began to sour in the 1880s in response to its aggressive foreign policy, the German-American intellectual network continued to expand through a steady stream of graduate student and professorial exchanges until the eve of World War I. German influence on American social sciences fostered an unshakeable faith in the survey and statistical analysis of data to shape policy. A similar attention to data and numbers carried over to the administration of colonies and borderlands. Borders around the world were beginning to harden into solid black lines separating nation-states, but the growth of the social sciences cut across these artificial divides. It was the grand age of science and modern state formation in Europe, the Americas, and Asia. Around the world countries aspired to develop their borderlands according to the latest innovations in transportation, communication, and agricultural and mining sciences, with geography providing the intellectual framework.

After Ratzel's return to Germany, his student Ellen Semple helped to popularize his ideas on anthropogeography to the nascent American geographical community. Ellen Churchill Semple (1863–1932) was a founding member of the Association of American Geographers in 1904 and elected its first female president in 1921. Semple taught for years at the University of Chicago and Clark University. Over the course of her career, Semple pioneered the study of human geography in the United States and played a key role in the prominence of environmentalism in the development of the discipline in early twentieth century. At first glance, her biography seems to challenge the male dominance of the field of geography.

Born in Louisville, Kentucky, in 1863 to a wealthy family, Semple attended Vassar College, where she received a BA and MA in history. After she became interested in geography, Semple went to Leipzig in Germany to study with Friedrich Ratzel, who in 1886 had taken over the famed geographer and China expert Ferdinand von Richthofen's chair in geography. Semple was the only woman among 500 students attending Ratzel's lectures and the first woman admitted to the seminar on economics and geography. During his journey in the United States in the 1870s, Ratzel wrote approvingly of visiting women's schools. Now he had an American woman as his student. Since the University of Leipzig did not officially enroll women, however, Semple never received a formal doctoral degree. An incident from her time in Germany reveals some of the ways that wealth paved the way for her pioneering studies. Ratzel expressed an interest in an American journal which was not available in Germany. Semple had the entire run shipped to Germany. To Ratzel, it appears that Semple was not "a woman" in the generic sense, but a wealthy White American woman with the financial means to fashion her own life.

By the late nineteenth century, independently wealthy White women, particularly if they, like Semple, chose not to marry, enjoyed considerable freedom of movement and the latitude to pursue their passions. Upon her return to the US, Semple spent summers living in a tent in the Catskills while writing her most important work, *The Influences of Geographic Environment on the Basis of Ratzel's System of Anthropo-Geography.* She rode 350 miles around the Appalachia Mountains. In June 1911, she embarked on her longest journey—an eighteen-month world tour with two women companions. She spent three months in Japan studying agriculture, trekked 200 miles around the mountain districts of Hondo, and in China traveled west to the Kalgan mountains to study desert conditions. In all her travels around the world, Semple was treated with respect and deference by local officials. In the Kalgan mountains, she was escorted by a security detail of Japanese soldiers.[27]

Network science has a concept called "preferential attachment"—the observation that nodes and social connections are not randomly or evenly distributed; instead, networks tend to grow fastest from more connected nodes.[28] Preferential attachment, like the Matthew effect, a term coined by the pioneering sociologist of science Robert Merton, helps to explain why "the rich get richer and the poor get poorer" and also why gender disparities get amplified. Social networks benefited men and women, but not equally. Semple's Vassar connections eased her travels—her classmates included the first Japanese woman to receive a college degree, Yamakawa Sakiko, who later married the commander-in-chief in Manchuria during the Russo-Japanese War, Field Marshal Prince Oyama.[29] Semple's time in Japan was the highlight of the world trip and a productive influence on her later work. Not only did she conduct many field trips throughout the Japanese Empire, Semple commissioned a series of exquisite lantern slides that she used in a subsequent lecture tour. On the same trip, she also traveled around the Middle East, including in Egypt and Lebanon, and in India. At the height of European imperialism and power, the infrastructures created by empire allowed Semple and her female companions to safely journey to the most remote outposts while the intangible infrastructures created by educational and professional networks shaped the field of geography.

Nevertheless, Semple was limited by her gender, and her reputation and impact on geography depended on the sponsorship of her male mentor. Semple's most important work names Ratzel in the title, firmly defining herself as acolyte and apostle rather than pioneer of new research. Like Ratzel, Semple was attuned to the way geography and environment shaped a country or region's development. But Semple pushed the connection between territory, environment, and national prosperity further than he had done and adapted anthropogeography to American conditions. Semple argued in *Influences of Geographic Environment*, "A broad territorial base and security of possession are the central guarantees of national survival."[30] This point presaged later geopolitical writings in the twentieth century, which similarly connected territory with social Darwinian concerns about national survival in a ruthless international order. The winners accrued new lands; losers lost their countries to become colonial subjects. Semple, more forcefully than Ratzel, connected territorial expanse to national power.

With *Influences*, Semple placed herself at the leading edge of the prevailing fashion in early twentieth-century US geography. Semple falls into a group of thinkers in the late nineteenth and early twentieth centuries from across the social sciences and on both sides of the Atlantic who sought causal links between the environment, history, and the development of civilizations. A wide range of intellectuals including *Annales* historians like Lucien Febvre and Marc Bloch, writers Thomas Henry Huxley, Ellsworth Huntington, Oswald Spengler, and Karl August Wittfogel shared with Semple a common interest in crossing disciplinary boundaries to find universal laws of historical development.[31] Like Ratzel and Ellsworth Huntington, who opposed immigration to the US over eugenics fears, many of these figures expressed overt racism in their works.[32] But the underlying idea of a grand explanation for civilization has continued to exert influence in the social sciences well into the twenty-first century. In the preface to Samuel Huntington's 1996 book, for instance, he rather humorously referred to the unprecedented amount of public interest that accompanied the publication of his original essay, "Clash of Civilizations," in *Foreign Affairs* in 1993.[33] What he didn't mention was his place in the unbroken intellectual lineage from the late nineteenth century of social scientists in pursuit of a theory of civilization.[34]

The intellectual networks that constituted the infrastructure of the global social sciences are far more difficult to visualize than the physical infrastructure of modern states, from underwater network cables, to canals, to railroads.[35] Yet, ideas, too, tend to grow and transform in existing knowledge frameworks that establish patterns of development that become increasingly difficult to overcome for areas left out of these connections. Where trade had connected the world in earlier eras, from the nineteenth century, science and empire both served as the frameworks for the international transfer of ideas. Agricultural economists, geographers, and agricultural scientists held conferences for the exchange of ideas. Geography and agricultural texts were broadly translated and circulated. Empire created the infrastructure for the movement of personnel and, along with the people, the circulation of ideas. American geographers, German social scientists looking to the East, Japanese officials in Hokkaido and the Asian mainland, and Chinese intellectuals proposing development plans for the Northeast and Northwest each existed in and of themselves in unique historical, geographical, and environmental contexts. But through the intellectual scaffolding created by empire and science, ideas of frontier development circulated until they found their targets—the kind of political and military leader in positions of power to transform them into reality.

Translating Geographical Knowledge

In China and Japan, a highly cosmopolitan local elite adapted these global trends in the social sciences by accommodating for the variables of history, geography, and climate. This was not a global flattening of knowledge, but rather a phenomenon in which modernization efforts followed certain intellectual pathways, even as it was shaped by local culture. Indigenous knowledge was not erased, but rather absorbed and adapted to newly defined social science disciplines, which touted their superiority over traditional sources of knowledge by dint of their basis in science. Far from being swept away by modern science, traditional areas of knowledge shaped how societies nativized science. Geo-modernity took on the distinctive characteristics of specific places and cultural fixations. *Nongxue* 農學, the study of agriculture, and *dixue* 地學, the study of Earth, occupied such an important vanguard role in the rise of modern science in China because both areas of knowledge were already valued in Chinese imperial statecraft.

Leading intellectuals in Asia viewed geography as essential knowledge for modern nations. A strong geographical tradition in China dates to the fourth century BCE when the "Tributes of Yu" ("*Yugong*") section of *The Book of History* (*Shang Shu*) divided the country into nine provinces and carefully documented the topographical geography of each province, as well as their natural fauna and mineral production. From the time of the earliest polities, the Shang (ca. 1700–ca. 1100 BCE) and Zhou (ca. 1100–256 BCE), states expressed authority over their domain as the "central lands" or *zhongtu*.[36] From the Warring States period (475 BC–221 BC), rulers saw maps as the expression of their authority over territory.[37] These visual representations of territorial control worked alongside the deployment of soldiers and settlers to the borderlands to assert authority. The first emperor of the Qin dynasty, who unified and created the first Chinese Empire, ordered half a million soldiers to the southern region and in 214 BCE created three commanderies to establish control over the southern borderlands. The Han dynasty and subsequent dynasties each developed their own fraught relationships with border peoples, although the tenor of that relationship differed according to the Northwest, Northeast, Southwest, or Southeast borderlands, with the Xiongnu peoples in the north enjoying a particularly fearsome reputation.

By the Ming dynasty (1368–1644), an extraordinary flourishing of commercial activity and trade led to widespread interest in geography. Ming officials participated in the ethnological gathering of information about the peoples who lived in border regions. In conjunction with changes then occurring also in medicine and other fields, the literati took part in this trend by writing down their firsthand observations of peoples as well as descriptive accounts of their travels. The Ming set the precedence for the Qing in frontier settlements and dealings with the southern neighboring states and border tribes. As the last dynasty ruled by Han Chinese, Ming officials established complex relationships with minority border peoples. During this period many of the categories of ethnicity we now use to classify minority populations of China first appeared.[38] Ming merchants as well as literati sponsored the making of maritime and land maps of the empire.[39] In addition to commodities from South American silver to rare ostrich eggs, Jesuits arrived and brought with them the latest geography and cartographic methods from Europe. These innovations made their way into coastal maps paid for by merchants who plied the waters connecting Chinese ports to Southeast Asian trading hubs.

Geographical knowledge came in many forms: thousands of administrative gazetteers, primarily compiled and used by officials; route works, which were written for itinerant merchants as guidebooks during their travels; a growing body of travel accounts, or sometimes travel diaries written by literati for circulation among their social circles as the written records of their travels and impressions—all these sources fed an increasing appetite for geographical knowledge. The late-Ming writings directly influenced early-Qing scholars, who traveled to collect empirical knowledge, with a preference for practical knowledge.[40] One area of geographical studies examined the historical evolution of localities and place names. This scholarship, *yange dili* 沿革地理, roughly translates to historical geography in English and methodologically combined linguistic and historical analysis in a uniquely Chinese textual geographical tradition.

Over the course of the Qing dynasty, change began to sweep in from abroad. The turn to empiricism flourished with the expansion of empire. During the Qing, the needs of empire building channeled geographical research into the empirical study of border peoples and their customs.[41] These sources used in the governing of frontier territories served analogous purposes as European geographical compendiums in the nineteenth century. Impressed by the mapmaking techniques of the Jesuits, the Kangxi Emperor undertook to learn this new knowledge and techniques himself. Kangxi ordered an empire-wide geographic survey with astronomical observations and trigonometric measurements, which required the triangulations of measurements by multiple observers and was deemed more accurate. The project was headed by Jesuits over the course of multiple expeditions from 1708 to 1715 and resulted in the *Kangxi Atlas*, formally known as the *Imperially Commissioned Maps of All Surveyed* (*Huangyu quanlantu*), the most advanced and scientific atlas anywhere in the world at the time.[42]

By the early eighteenth century, select geographers in the Qing Empire had mastered longitude and latitude, triangulation, and projection cartography. At the same time, Chinese cartographers continued to use more traditional methods, including the grid, particularly in local gazetteers, well into the twentieth century. The coexistence of both old and new, imported technologies alongside indigenous methods, indicates the complex nature of how knowledge changes over time.[43] As with their rule of border and frontier areas, Qing cartography showed the flexibility of mapmakers' approach, depending on the specifics of the situation. Traditional and new techniques served different purposes; what was useful in negotiations with the Russian empire did not necessarily apply in the contested areas with Korea.[44] We can see significant differences in the late nineteenth century gazetteers of Mongolia to the Northwest and other borderland gazetteers.[45] The Mongolia gazetteer featured maps using the latest cartographic techniques. Other borderland gazetteers from equally strategically important regions in the Northeast still employed traditional maps. In other words, the divide between traditional scholarship and modern science was porous; both could and did coexist and were deployed depending on specific local circumstances and individuals involved.

Beyond the incorporation of new cartographic technologies, the Qing applied different policy approaches to different regions of the empire. In the dispute with the kingdom of Chosan over the demarcations of the Qing/Korean border, for example, the Qing deployed the principle of "let them do whatever is convenient" (*zan cong ge bian*), which allowed local legal and social norms to be used in carrying out local affairs, at the same time emphasizing the ultimate authority of the state.[46] In the southwestern Tibetan area, in contrast, local officials based in Sichuan pursued a much more aggressive policy of "administrative regularization of native chieftains" (*gai tu gui liu*), in part because of their recognition of the far greater threat posed by the British Empire, as well as the much more tenuous relationship with Tibet.

In the nineteenth century, Asian countries with their own long history of both cartographic and geographical knowledge eagerly turned to geographical works from the West for sources of information about the encroaching threat from overseas. The Opium War (1839–1842) saw the mighty Qing Empire defeated by British gunboats. Domestic rebellions over the course of the nineteenth century covered as much as a third of the empire. In this rapidly changing and disorienting world, many turned with great interest to science and technology from the West. The loss particularly spurred Chinese interest in compendiums of geographical and other information about Western countries. In the 1840s the Qing official Xu Jiyu (1795–1873) became interested in world geography while serving in Fujian province. He spent five years collecting foreign maps and information. In 1848, Xu published a geography of the world titled *Brief Account of the World* (*Ying huan zhi lue*). The work was printed in China in 1850 and reprinted in 1855. From China, the work arrived in Japan in 1859 and was reprinted in 1861.

Lin Zexu (1785–1850), the Qing official disgraced in the fallout of the Opium War, collected and translated information for over thirty countries around the world in the *Gazetteer of the Four Continents* (*Si zhou zhi*). The material he compiled then became a major source for Wei Yuan's *Treatise on the Maritime Countries* (*Hai guo tu zhi*), which first appeared in 1844.[47] These compilations predated the founding of the translation bureaus attached to the arsenals established in the wake of the Taiping Rebellion, the location for the earliest state-sponsored translations of Western science texts. Geography served as the vanguard of the encounter with the West. When the scholar-official Wei Yuan took up the problem of geography to compile a comprehensive vision of the world, he also placed China into a global context.[48]

In the period after the Meiji Restoration, Japan, too, turned to modern science as the key to its campaign to join the world order as an equal. In seeking wealth and power, the Meiji government imported science from Europe as one might import a commodity, along with the "correct" research methodology which centered on a mechanical worldview and empiricism.[49] Along with the sciences, Japan developed the social sciences, including history, geography, and agricultural science with the same basis in empiricism and scientific methodology. At the same time, the state took to rewriting the country's own past in an idealized time and space, while reorienting its geographical relationship to China and Inner Asia.[50] Just as in the United States, the discipline of geography became a key part of Japan's engagement with the world.

At the same time, Japan became the source of assorted geographical texts that flooded into turn-of-the century China. One might be tempted to see in the huge number of "translations" a wholesale adoption of Western geography as already previously filtered through Japan and its modernization efforts. A closer look, however, reveals that this was far from what happened. In fact, various Chinese "translators" recognized in the Japanese promotion of geography the discipline's central role in the formation of the modern state. But at various points of slippage, Chinese "translators" also recognized the racial hierarchy inherent in this new geography. Even when they did not hesitate to apply its language of scientific racism to the various ethnic minorities within the Chinese Empire, the Chinese recognized its less-than-desirable implications for the place of Han Chinese within the Japanese spatial and racial hierarchy.

As Japan pulled away from Asia, Chinese intellectuals themselves began to see geography and more importantly, science, as an integral part of what qualified a people as civilized, even as Chinese learning lost its once central place in the Japanese discourse of civilization.[51] The newspaper *Hubei Student News* (*Hubei xue bao*), published by Chinese students who had studied in Japan, contained numerous translations of Japanese writings on geography. A piece in 1903 pointed out that "of the matters of importance to the country, not one is not related to political geography."[52] Another piece in 1903 highlighted geography's expansive boundaries bridging the humanities and the sciences.[53] Most of these writers mentioned the broad areas of knowledge included in geography and that, as a discipline, it bridged the natural and social sciences. A 1903 essay translated from Japanese in the *Hubei Student News* pointed out the ancient origins of geography as a means to record and organize natural phenomena. Nowadays, the article argued, geography had expanded to include everything from the relationship between the earth and heavenly bodies, to explanations of life and the development of humankind, to the relationship between animals, minerals, and humans, industry and its political organization, to diplomatic relations.[54]

Geographical and agricultural knowledge had long been widely accepted as the most important areas of applied learning for Chinese imperial officials, easing the way for newly imported ideas to take nativist cover. By the last decades of the Qing, various literati turned to the collection of geographical material to bridge traditional learning with new knowledge from the West. The Qing official Tu Ji 屠寄 (1856–1921) is one such example. Tu Ji had followed the traditional path of civil examination and entry to officialdom and used his spare time to pursue his interests in both history and geography. He compiled a history of the Yuan dynasty, Mongol history, and collected maps and geographical information about the northeastern frontier in the Heilongjiang region.[55] In the twentieth century, late Qing literati like Tu Ji gave way to a new generation of intellectuals and foreign-trained scientists. Certain aspects of the imperial ideology underpinning Chinese geography, however, never fully disappeared, instead taking on the guise of scientific geography, agricultural science, and geopolitical thinking. Nor was Tu's career path an exceptional case. The steady production of local gazetteers in this period, often helmed by local gentry or officials with similar types of backgrounds to Tu, displays a remarkable continuity in the production of knowledge from the late Qing into the Republican period.

Imperial Thinking in the Age of Nation-States

The popularity of geography in Asian countries owed much to its importance as a conduit of Western conceptions of borders and nations. Other scholars have focused on the use of international law as a measure of civilization. Recognizing its importance, the Qing sponsored the first translations of works on international law, which subsequently circulated in both Japan and Korea.[56] Japan deployed international law and the concepts of *terra nullius,* first developed in the New World context, to justify its acquisition of Hokkaido and Taiwan and the dispossession of indigenous populations.[57] Land made empty on the map was free for the taking.

In the age of imperialism and the politically turbulent transitional period between empire and the rise of the nation-state, geography began to be conflated with new notions of race, historical progress, and civilization across Asia.[58] The prominent intellectual and promoter of westernization of Meiji Japan, Fukuzawa Yukichi, published his most famous essay in 1885, "Escape from Asia" ("Datsu-A-Ron"), which ruthlessly criticized Korea and China as the backward elements of East Asia. Fukuzawa went on to develop these early ideas into a theory of civilization.[59] For Fukuzawa, the advanced West stood at the top of the pyramid of civilizations, while in Asia, backward Korea and China did not qualify as civilized. Geography played a prominent role in the Meiji educational reforms, as well as discussions about civilization and social classifica-tion.[60] *Bunmei Kaika* (civilization and enlightenment) became the catch phrase of the era.

When word of Japan's victory in the Sino-Japanese War reached Bei-jing in 1895, the best and brightest young men in the country were in the capital for the pinnacle of the vaunted civil examinations. Among their numbers was a precocious young man named Liang Qichao (1873–1929). China's loss to its smaller neighbor caused ripples of consterna-tion among the assembled young men, some of whom began to call for dismantling the status quo and instituting changes to the Qing bureau-cracy. For his role in advocating for these reforms, Liang had to flee to Japan when a conservative faction led by the Empress Dowager Cixi staged a palace coup and placed a sympathetic young emperor under house arrest for the rest of his life.

Japan became for Liang both a refuge and a model for the kind of reforms that he wanted to see enacted in China. From exile Liang wrote extensively on history and geography, linking the two fields together with the development of civilization. He adopted this approach, in part, in response to the problem of the Qing Empire's territorial expanse. How did this vast, multiethnic land expanse fit into a discourse of the nation? Liang tied geography to new ideas about the nation-state by linking China to the newly coined geographical concept of "Asia."[61] In recent years, Liang has become a magnet for scholarship precisely because his work reflected so many of the broad intellectual trends of his times—from social Darwinism, to new ideas on race and ethnicity, to national-ism and empire.

In his writings, as in earlier Chinese compendiums of knowledge, Liang placed geography under the general heading of history. He sepa-rated China into two geographical components: the eighteen provinces of the traditional heartland and the dependent regions (*shubu*) in the borderlands, including Manchuria, Mongolia, and Tibet.[62] Liang Qichao took it as a given that the geographical differences within China, divided along three main river systems and different climate zones, also reflected the racial characteristics of the ethnicities populating these regions. For Liang, the "people of Asia" with whom the Chinese had interaction in-cluded only those successfully incorporated into the Qing Empire (the Tibetans, Mongols, Tongus, Xiongnu, Manchu, and the Han), a concept that corresponded to the territorial extent and constituency of what he

was configuring as the modern Chinese nation.[63] As the reification of culture and civilization, geography played a leading role in these accounts.
Liang Qichao did not reject empire in favor of nationalism so much as
advocate for the retention of empire under the umbrella of Chinese nationalism.[64] He openly acknowledged the influence of earlier Qing scholarship on his ideas, which many intellectuals who wrote on geography
in the subsequent decades often did not.

In turn-of-the-century China, with the threat of imperialism looming
over political crisis, and a pervasive sense of gloom among the gentry
elite of the country, the promotion of geography was seen as a way to
inculcate patriotism among the young and educate the general populace.
References to geography invariably took on social Darwinian undertones. In 1902, the progressive paper *New Citizens News* (*Xin min cong
bao*) published an article entitled, "The Relationship between Geography
and Civilization."[65] The article discussed among other things why people
in tropical regions did not develop civilization and promoted the idea
that human evolution depended not only on material conditions but also
on the triumph of the spirit. World civilizations, including China, the
author pointed out, only developed on relatively flat terrain, mostly on
plains. Such writings echoed geo-determinist concepts then in circulation around the world.

The following year, in 1903, the *New Citizens* ran a series on geography, stating that "the biggest question of the twentieth century is the
future existence of China as a country."[66] The writer defined imperialism
geographically. The author saw the expansion of European empires as
the direct result of political stasis on the European continent itself. Since
Europe by and large was already settled politically, expansion by neces-
sity must come at the margins of the world in relation to Europe. For the
writer, European territorial ambitions posed a keen danger for countries
like China, which stood to lose to the overwhelming wealth and power
of the West. The dangers of annihilation and the destruction of the country loomed large in these articles. Such writings circulated in China
leading to the rise of an entire genre envisioning imminent demise of the
country as a sovereign nation.[67] The proliferation of this particular genre
of writing had its roots in the previous decades of reforms and the sense
of futility and failure following the Sino-Japanese War. The very coinage
of the concept of Asia was related to the social Darwinian dynamic of

the era and the way that both Chinese and Japanese intellectuals saw the world as aligned between colonized and the colonizers.

In China, the transition from empire to nation-state was hardly a clean break: empire continued to influence how intellectuals thought about the modern Chinese state long after its supposed obsolescence. In the decades between the collapse of the Qing in 1912 and the emergence of a communist regime in 1949, the borderland regions in the Northeast, Northwest, and Southwest operated largely outside of centralized control. Even areas controlled by warlords who paid lip service to a national government retained considerable autonomy under a series of weak regimes that lacked the means to enforce centralized rule and extract taxes or intervene in local government. Although their ideas were as yet unenforceable, aided by imported knowledge and the professionalization of new disciplines of social sciences, geographers, anthropologists, economists, archaeologists, and historians worked to craft the ideas that informed political and military leaders to adapt the best aspects of empire for the age of the nation-state. The language of nationalism took root in parallel with efforts to replace classical Chinese, which had undergirded for many centuries the civil service examinations, with vernacular. Phrases such as "science saving the nation" became part of the popular discourse in the 1920s. Yet, the empire also continued to exert an inexorable force in shaping the new nation-state. Nationalist leaders like Sun Yat-sen embraced China's imperial territorial expanse, even when such views conflicted with their stated political stance on self-determination. When they deemed it necessary, they deployed the Western imperialists' language of civilization against those peoples, including Mongolians, Tibetans, and Uighurs, as insufficiently mature for true independence. The Han people would once again lead the way. But in the new world order, the Han people would lead by modernization and science.

After the collapse of the Qing dynasty, geography continued to enjoy enormous popularity during the Republican period. The publishing industry churned out a wide variety of geographical works, encompassing everything from textbooks for all educational levels to atlases and books for general interest readers, many of which featured copious numbers of maps that highlighted in both obvious and subtle ways the conception of the nation's territorial expanse.[68] The broad range of sources, from textbooks to popular atlases, contributed to the construction of a China with a coherent national territory (and at odds with the messy political reality of the time).[69] Beyond the texts themselves, this rhetoric of geo-modernity inculcated new ideas of the nation and perpetuated a geography of China's empire in the age of nationalism.

Textbooks from the late Qing into the People's Republic of China period after 1949, for example, used mnemonic rhymes and simple visual analogies to stake claims to contested territories. A page from a 1908 children's geography book compares the shape of Chinese territory to the leaf of a crabapple tree. Below the image is a simple rhyme that extolled the territorial expanse of the country.[70] At the time of the book's publication, the borderland areas, including Mongolia and Xinjiang, had largely moved away from the Qing government in Beijing. Yet, on the page these areas remain part of the Chinese crabapple leaf. The continuity of this form of geographical education can be seen in a 1960s geography rhyme book.[71] In the 1963 work, each province and autonomous zone has a textual counterpart in a matching couplet with a listing of local products, echoing not only the 1908 book but also the content of imperial era geographical gazetteers.

Around the turn of the century, most geographical works published in China were translations from the Japanese. Of these, the majority were Japanese interpretations of Western geography. At the same time, the Chinese themselves were actively constructing a geographical imagination that liberally adapted foreign ideas into a very material concept of what Chinese territory should look like—in this case, a complete leaf that includes all the frontier territories, much of which had been brought under the empire by the Manchus. Anti-Manchu sentiment at the end of the dynasty, then, did not extend to the territory of the Qing Empire.

In recent years, the topic of geography has become increasingly censored by the Chinese government as it has aggressively moved to assert claims in the South China Sea. Many of the works from the early twentieth century have been resurrected as historical evidence, taken out of context, to bolster the People's Republic of China's current territorial claims. The use of these early twentieth-century works to fortify claims of contemporary, twenty-first-century Chinese nationalism obscures their original engagement with questions about retaining the territory of the Qing Empire. In a metaphorical transformation, an empire becomes a leaf and then turns into a nation. That nation assumes the shape of something immutable and fixed in time and space. Yet, we know that to not be true. All things change.

Chicago and a New World Geography

Parallel and sometimes competing discussions on the relationship between geography, history, and civilization took place around the world at the turn of the twentieth century, connected by geographers as the human agents of a global intellectual infrastructure. These networks intersected not only in the abstract realms of print publications, but occasionally also at physical or temporal junctures. Chicago in 1893 became one such juncture. On the evening of July 12, 1893, Frederick Jackson Turner (1861–1932), an assistant professor at the University of Wisconsin, gave the last of five addresses to an audience of two hundred or so historians gathered in Chicago, the ballooning industrial hub of the Midwest. The historians had gathered for a conference of the American Historical Association, that year held in conjunction with the Columbian World Exposition.[72] The historians were tired from a day spent touring the fairgrounds and all its many wonders. Some had attended Buffalo Bill Cody's Wild West Show, conveniently located just outside the fairgrounds. Indians, now pacified and corralled on reservations, no longer posed a threat to the lives of Anglo settlers and could safely perform alongside cowboys and sharpshooter Annie Oakley for the entertainment of audiences around the country.

The muted reaction to Turner's address on "The Significance of the Frontier on American History" gave no hint of its subsequent impact on the American historical and geographical professions. The 1890 US Census had declared the end of a steady line of frontier in the US, but it was Turner who in his address made the frontier the defining feature of a new national history, in the process setting in motion the myth of the American West as an example of American exceptionalism, rugged individualism, and the triumph of civilization over barbarism. In this effort, Turner was deeply influenced by the country's geographers, including Francis Amasa Walker and Daniel Coit Gilman, who promoted thematic and statistical cartography as the essential tools of an expanding nation. Turner relied on *Scribner's Statistical Atlas of the United States* (1883) in making his argument, which was executed according to

Walker's agenda of mapping the geography of the nation's census data. As an indication of the impact of these maps, Turner sent his frontier essay directly to Walker, who immediately recognized the cartographic basis of its argument.[73]

Turner's remarks came at a moment when history and the social sciences were still in their professional infancy in the United States. In the first decades of the twentieth century, disciplines from history and geography to agricultural science defined their professional boundaries and bars for entry within an increasingly national context. Proselytized by Turner as the apostle at the center of an emerging, national academic network of historians, the frontier shaped the narrative of American history, assuming a near mythical status as the forge of American democracy and freedom. Historian Susan Schulten has mapped out how the late nineteenth century also became a formative period for American geography, writing that "the growth of university disciplines in the 1880s and 1890s, together with symbolic declarations of the exhaustion of spatial frontiers, demanded a reconceptualization of geography as a modern analytic, scientific body of knowledge."[74] The geographers, like the historians, embraced the concept of the frontier. A geographical concept, the frontier, became the founding principle of American history. Rebuttals during Turner's lifetime, subsequent revisions, and the rise of New Western history in the 1990s failed to dim, at least in the popular imagination, the allure of Manifest Destiny and the boundless freedom of the American frontier.[75]

The central tension of these related developments in history and geography was that the frontier became nationalized at the same time that it globalized. Preoccupied with institutional legitimacy, American geographers eagerly provided their services to the American government, both its domestic agenda and expansionary efforts overseas. Natural resources and commerce dominated the content of late-nineteenth-century American atlases.[76] The National Geographic Society planned a popular lecture series on an eclectic range of topics from the exploration of Alaska to Venezuelan boundary disputes, conflicts in the Transvaal and Manchuria, progress in the Philippines, Arctic exploration, and the prospect of a canal in Nicaragua.[77] The world was made legible to Americans on maps and through public lectures.

The Columbian Exposition celebrated the 400th anniversary of Christopher Columbus's arrival in the New World. Chicago won the bid in part because of its ascendant status as a railway and commodities hub of a nation on the move. In 1830, Chicago had a population of somewhere around 50 to 100 settlers, mostly military men. This group had a grand total of fourteen taxpayers. By 1890, its population had ballooned to over a million, an example of the kind of hyper or explosive colonization that historian James Belich argues exemplified the settler revolution in regions of the world led by the British colonies.[78] At century's end, by hosting the World's Fair, Chicago further cemented its place as a world city, joining the ranks of London, Paris, and Vienna. Its meteoric rise symbolized the vast economic possibilities of new frontiers and the wealth of natural resources of its hinterlands.

By the end of the nineteenth century, multiple developments worked to tighten global connections. These included the flow of millions of migrants in search of free and open lands; the industrialization of agriculture, leading to increasing size of farms; and the transformation of agriculture from the realm of farmers who depended on their experience and hard work to a field of professionals, from managers, engineers, to agricultural scientists, all of whom were incredibly mobile in their study and collection of seeds and the spread of the newest innovations. These same conditions contributed to experts' interest in the relationship between frontiers and economic growth. The American frontier—with or without the Turner thesis—became a model for other countries aiming to replicate the expansive farms of the Midwest or the explosive growth of cities like Chicago. Countries like Canada and Argentina studied the American frontier.[79] The Germans had, of course, been thinking about settler colonialism for a long time, having started a process of internal colonialization of the eastern frontier in Polish and Baltic territories in the Middle Ages.[80] Nevertheless, the American frontier loomed large in the German imagination, from novelists, to scholars, to politicians. In fact, as the German historian Robert Nelson has observed, German accounts of the American West—a utopian fantasy of a government organizing citizen resettlement from a dirty and overcrowded East to the free and productive West—bore all the hallmarks of a romanticized fiction with little basis in reality.[81]

In World's Fairs, perhaps nowhere more clearly than Chicago in 1893, we see the tension between internationalism and nationalism on open display. The fair allowed for the physical intersection of people, ideas, and conflicting historical forces, an intellectual hub for propagating new ideas and technologies. Adventurers and academics alike were drawn to the World's Fair. The Columbian Exposition itself became a turning point in American history. Turner's claim that the 1890 Census had signaled the end of the frontier was shared by many others drawn to the fair for its displays of the latest technological marvels. Some of these visitors, having absorbed the idea that the American West and the Australia were filling up, turned their attention to the possibility of expanding new frontiers in Africa, Asia, and Latin America. Cultural affinities and ties between the US and the British Empire brought American missionaries and Boer fighters to settle parts of northern Mexico. The physician Nathan Boyd left Chicago by rail for southern New Mexico in search of new frontiers to settle; the inveterate adventurer Frederick Russell Burnham's journey to Chicago took him from a childhood in Minnesota to the American Southwest, Southern Rhodesia, and finally the Mexican North. [82] In Chicago, Japan constructed a Buddhist pavilion on a wooded island in the central lagoon. Soon, following the example of human zoos pioneered at the Columbian Exposition, from 1877 to 1903, Japan hosted a series of national industrial exhibitions intended to provide a meeting place for foreign technologies and Japanese industries. Alongside the machinery and agricultural displays, human exhibits showcased the colonization of Ainu, the Ryukyuans, the Taiwanese, and Koreans. [83] At the same time, in the 1900s, Japanese colonization societies sent thousands of working-class settlers to Mexico. Faced with harsh working conditions, some immigrants returned to Japan, others moved to more hospitable lands in northern Mexico, and still others joined the Mexican Revolution. [84] World's Fairs and the social sciences both provided the conduits for ideas about settlement projects and frontiers.

The frontiers were closing, while the race to secure the frontiers took on added urgency. The end of the frontier signaled the beginning of a new struggle to reconceptualize empire. In the following decades, the United States, Germany, Japan, and China, all late industrializers, all sought to redefine empire in a modern age that was ostensibly billed as the age of the nation-state. From the sixteenth through the nineteenth century, the expansion of the British Empire—in Australia, South Africa, and New Zealand—proceeded in parallel with the American vision of Manifest Destiny. Anglo pioneers in North America moved the line of settlement ever westward until it reached the Pacific. [85] The British, Dutch, and Americans, like the Spanish Empire before them, created a legal framework which cast the frontiers, land already in use by indigenous peoples, as *terra nullius,* emptied of indigenous populations on paper if not in actuality.[86] Surveys and maps and the technology of creating gridded spaces from irregular and varied landscapes played an important role in the creation of a moving line of frontiers.

The great land grab closed at the end of the nineteenth century, when the US Census declared the closure of the frontier and when Frederick Jackson Turner first posited the frontier thesis. This end point was also a new beginning. The geographer John Weaver described the continuation of the frontier this way: "The panoply of improvements to land—individualizing title, surveying, registration, reallocation, irrigation—had arrived to stay. Throughout the twentieth century, missionaries of improvement—this time not land hunters or irrigation engineers but economists, bankers, and the governments of developed countries—promoted it in other regions of the world."[87] The technocrats inherited the legacy of the pioneers.

The close and closely intertwined relationship between the intellectuals from the United States, Germany, Japan, and China allowed for the circulation and development of various views reenvisioning empire for the modern age. Collectively, they ushered in the age of geo-modernity. The German economist Gustav Schmoller oversaw a transatlantic and global network of social scientists; his student Max Sering similarly maintained an international network of correspondents up to his death in the 1930s. In his various roles as the president of the American Geographical Society, founding member of the Council on Foreign Relations, and president of Johns Hopkins University, American geographer Isaiah Bowman corresponded with geographers and scientists around the world (including a polite exchange with the German geographer Karl Haushofer). Chinese geographers and agronomists like Zhang Qiyun and Tang Qiyu were similarly conversant with the language of inner colonization and part of international networks of their disciplines.

The Columbian World's Fair was not, of course, the only hub where these intellectual networks converged. Conferences like the International Congress of Geographers and the International Conference of Agricultural Economics highlighted these networks of scholarship and knowledge, at the same time bringing out the implicit tensions of their international claims in the age of the nation-state. When the students who attended returned to their home countries, they carried with them new ideas about the importance of the frontier to national development. Ideas about the frontiers did not remain static as they circulated. From the nineteenth through the twentieth centuries, the discourse of endless frontiers stretched from Eastern Europe, Soviet Central Asia, and Siberia to Inner Mongolia and Western China, in each case becoming absorbed into long-running historical concerns about territory and identity.[88] These disparate places shared a centrally planned vision of turning the frontiers into fertile agricultural heartlands.

Picture to yourself the transportation map of the United States. Across the vast middle of the country, a single line—a road—connects some towns. In contrast, major hubs like Chicago, New York, and Los Angeles are surrounded by a dense web of transportation links, including roads, railroads, ferries, and flight paths. Follow these lines on the map, and you may find yourself in Shanghai or across the Suez Canal, in London or Singapore. The limitations of nation-based histories have forestalled the creation of an analogous map of the intellectual connections across the nineteenth and twentieth centuries. Yet, such connections are there and they, too, centered around certain hubs: Turner and the frontier thesis, but also the lesser-known figures who converged on the Columbian Exposition in 1893 and from Chicago made their way to the global frontiers.

The turn of the twentieth century was an era marked by the unprecedented movement of peoples. This movement was aided by technological advances in transportation and networks of infrastructure. The example of academics, however, also demonstrates the existence of invisible intellectual networks alongside the physical infrastructure of trains, steamships, telegraphs, and electricity. The gridded organization of cities enabled the construction of sanitation as well as transport systems. New railway systems gave rise to new cities at the center of transportation hubs. Maritime entrepôts enabled the transfer of knowledge in the early modern world; in the nineteenth and twentieth centuries, new cities like Chicago, St. Louis, Hankou (present day Wuhan), and Frankfurt in turn became the new hubs of finance and commodities. New knowledge networks connected countries in ways that crossed borders. In this revision of empire enabled by the social sciences, science, and new technologies, the frontier played a powerful role. German historians Erik Grimmer-Solem, along with Adam Tooze, Timothy Snyder, and Carroll Kakel, have highlighted how, by World War II, German war aims echoed earlier calls for both inner and external colonies in order to provide "a vast, resource-rich eastern frontier to deliver American-style material prosperity and food security in the metropole while serving as an outlet for settlers to seek freedom and opportunity in the lands and on the backs of colonial others."[89]

In actuality, the motivation to settle the German East, Hokkaido, Manchuria, the Chinese Northwest, and so on, as well the conditions and environment in each region, differed widely. As a metaphor, however, the American frontier served a powerful purpose in attracting the interest of both bureaucrats and intellectuals. The liberal imperialist fantasy of frontier was the product of a generation of intellectuals trained in the social sciences, who themselves became faithful acolytes of their own fantasy. This belief in the limitless possibilities of frontiers persisted despite the repeated failures of actual settlements and various efforts by colonization societies. In the real world, faced with harsh climates, poor soil, and endemic diseases, settlers quickly retreated from paper plans. The academics who crafted those plans seldom ventured into the breach. Globalization and internationalization created their own vicious cycles of nationalist frenzy. The way that these different strands of thought have since been obscured in national histories, a reimagining of the past based on idealized notions of the nation and how it came into being, is itself the damning result of the inequitable distribution of blame for the great twentieth-century conflagrations.

FOUR

Versailles and the Birth of the Geopolitical Age

> The Europeans have dreamed a great dream of the omnipotence
> of science, but today they cry that this science is bankrupt.
>
> *Liang Qichao*[1]

It was no coincidence that geopolitics as a science distinct from geography emerged in the early twentieth century, during the same period that saw rapid colonial expansion by European powers, the United States, and Japan as well as widespread discussions about the relationship between science and the modern state. The social and natural sciences allowed for the circulation of ideas across borders, where they could be adapted to specific historical and geographical conditions. Such connections were secured not only by an educated elite but also by a new technological infrastructure based on the rapid development of networks of railways, steamships, and telegraphs. A human network overlay these transportation and communication networks, both of which allowed for an unprecedented economic integration of territories. For the Germans, looking to Russia to the east and to the United States to the west, these developments foretold the emergence of new world powers based on continental territories rather than the old school of maritime empires like the British, then at the zenith of its power.[2] These broader trends arrived in China at a time of exceptional political and cultural upheaval as the country fractured following the collapse of the Qing dynasty in 1912. For Chinese intellectuals, this combination of external encroachment from imperialist powers and internal problems further underscored the importance of retaining territorial possession of the empire as China entered the age of the nation-state.

The last chapter focused on the points of contact within global networks in the discipline of geography, exploring how ideas about territory and frontiers transformed through translation and political passage. This chapter examines the influence and fate of one offshoot from these encounters, geopolitics. World War I created unprecedented logistical demands on the combatants, bolstering interest in achieving national autarky and further emphasizing the advantages of possessing empires or extensive territories, preferably endowed with the natural resources essential for industries.[3] The last chapter traced the intellectual genealogy of geographical ideas about territory, environment, and economic development. World War I further reinforced the importance of access and control over natural resources. In Asia, social Darwinian fears about weak states succumbing to the strong underlay the same concerns from the turn of the century, fostering an interest in geopolitics when it was introduced in the 1920s. In the years between World War I and World War II, geopolitics, despite being vaguely defined in its distinction from existing fields in geography, enjoyed a surge of popularity as a new science to facilitate strategic planning for national development in peace and war. Such loose distinctions aside, this chapter shows how geopolitics had sprung from a global movement to geo-modernity.

World War I sped up the disintegration of multiple empires, but also created the conditions for the ascendance of geopolitics as the new science of the state. The peace negotiations created a hub, physically located at Versailles, France, and intellectually focused on the frontiers, which brought together geographers who served as territorial experts for major delegations. Through the geopolitical lens, territorial experts recalibrated the relationship between state power, science, and territory and brought about a renewed focus on borderlands and the creation of territorial boundaries. Much scholarly attention has focused on the role the peace treaty and the failure of the Wilsonian calls for self-determination played in creating the conditions that led to a second global war barely two decades later. Yet, for Germany, as well as for non-Western countries like Japan and China, the decisions made at Versailles merely reinforced the importance of retaining imperial territories. The popularity of geopolitics in these countries provided a scientific veneer for national claims to borderlands. The internal contradictions of these views are particularly evident in China, long seen as a victim of Western imperialism at Versailles, which over the interwar years asserted claims over its own borderlands using the language of the civilizing mission.

The Mirage of Self-Determination

On January 8, 1918, American President Woodrow Wilson delivered his famous Fourteen Points speech before the US Congress. In his speech Wilson called for the freedom of navigation, armament reduction, the adjustment of colonial claims, and the reassessment of territorial claims from the Ottoman Empire to Poland and Russia. Wilson's speech seemingly ushered in a new post-imperial era of national self-determination—seemingly, because it's not quite clear the extent to which he thought through the issue to its logical end. He certainly did not intend for non-White peoples to claim independence from European empires. Versailles appeared to provide an ideal opportunity for Wilson to advocate for the international adoption of his vision of a new democratic world order. However, the lack of a coherent and comprehensive vision regarding the territorial fallout of the war quickly became apparent when negotiators arrived in France.

In December 1918, Wilson and a large American delegation sailed across the Atlantic onboard the *USS George Washington*. Upon their arrival, the Americans joined diplomats from thirty-two other countries. The Americans settled into the Hotel du Crillon and prepared for the long haul. The war had brought about the collapse of multiple empires, including the Ottoman, Austro-Hungary, Russian, and German Empires. The territories formerly under their control had splintered into multiple nationalities, each with their own claims to sovereign independence. The decisions made at Versailles would establish the new boundaries of these nations. The French, led by Georges Clemenceau, were eager to punish the Germans; the British, led by David Lloyd George, had no desire to give grounds to colonial nationalists.

As negotiations began, Korean, Indian, and Egyptian nationalists looked to Wilson with high hopes.[4] The Chinese delegation, led by foreign minister and veteran diplomat Lu Zhengxiang, Sao-ke Alfred Sze (Shi Zhaoji), V. K. Wellington Koo (Gu Weijun), and Chengting Thomas

Wang (Wang Zhengting), was even more optimistic. Lu, who spoke fluent French, had graduated from the new schools that emerged in China after the Taiping Rebellion that taught foreign languages and science. Shi had graduated from Cornell, Koo from Columbia, and Wang from Yale. The group was as cosmopolitan as any in France and, they thought, had an easier task than the stateless petitioners. Not only did China possess unquestionable national sovereignty, but the country had also entered the war on the Allied side. During the war, China provided over 100,000 laborers who mostly helped dig trenches on the Western Front.

Like hopes of endless scientific progress, self-determination turned out to be a mirage. The Wilsonian vision collapsed ignominiously in the harsh reality of postwar France. The agreements that emerged from the intense rounds of negotiations profoundly discouraged colonial participants whose hopes had been buoyed by Wilson's Fourteen Points. Despite the caliber of its delegation, China received less representation than the Japanese and was excluded altogether from discussions concerning Chinese territory. Early in the war in 1914, the Japanese army had captured the German leasehold in Northeast China in Kiautschou in Shandong province.[5] Instead of being returned to China, the German holdings in Shandong were handed over to Japan as part of a secret agreement signed during the war with the British and French. When news of this betrayal reached Beijing on May 4, 1919, protesters, led by students in the university quarter, took to the streets and set off a massive anti-imperialism movement in the country.[6] The League of Nations created a Permanent Mandate Commission (PMC) to oversee the former colonial holdings of the German and Ottoman Empires. In practice, the historian Susan Pedersen has argued, the PMC reinforced the message that imperial powers were needed to carry out the civilizing mission in these former colonies.

The Versailles negotiations served as a last hurrah for a peculiarly nineteenth-century form of high diplomacy, performed in palatial surroundings by White men of an elite class, while non-White men, many from equally elite backgrounds in their home countries, looked on from outside the room as their fates were determined. Alongside the memoirs published in its wake and letters exchanged among participants, elaborate menus and place settings testify to a highly ritualized niche of European culture. Granted a seat among the great powers and allowed to claim the spoils of war, Japan nevertheless fit awkwardly into this scheme. Meiji-era intellectuals like Fukuzawa and Nitobe idolized the West; the following generation recognized the racism and hypocrisy at the heart of European imperial ideology.[7]

With the exit of the Americans from the League of Nations, the Permanent Mandate Commission soon steered power back to the European empires. Crises began to bubble up in various corners of the world almost immediately. In the territories Germany had formerly occupied in Southwest Africa, for instance, the treaty had transferred control to the British. The Bondelswarts people accordingly eagerly participated in the removal of the German colonial administration and their harsh policies. To their dismay, however, their new British masters reinstituted the land claims of the German settlers, their fellow Whites. In 1922, the Bondelswarts, impoverished by policies designed to force the men into lowly paid wage labor, rose in rebellion. A few years later, Arab nationalists led an uprising in Syria. The French responded by bombing Damascus and its civilian populations. Although Egypt declared independence in 1922, significant control resided with the British Empire, including on matters involving national defense. In the former German Samoa, the administration installed by New Zealand met with broad resistance and open defiance. In each case, the PMC tamped down the fires and reinforced the racialized order of European empires.[8]

At Versailles, the Chinese were eager to throw off the yoke of Western and Japanese imperialism by invoking their right to self-determination. Yet, they simultaneously refused to relinquish their own claims to the territories of frontier peoples in Tibet, Mongolia, and Xinjiang, who desired to establish their own sovereign states. Instead, Chinese nationalist leaders cast these peoples as hopelessly backward. From their perspective, any efforts at independence were the result of imperialist meddling, particularly from the British and the Russians. In the longer transitional period from empire to the nation-state, broadly conceived from the mid-nineteenth to the mid-twentieth centuries, the Wilsonian vision fades in importance. Resentment at the jarring disparity between the Wilsonian vision of self-determination and the reality of the Versailles Peace Treaty, however, had a far longer afterlife. In the various colonies around the world and in the heart of Europe in the vanquished German Empire, lingering resentment against Versailles held long-term consequences and sowed the seeds of the next global conflagration. For one American geographer, however, Versailles opened the door to the world.

American Empire in the New World

The search for new frontiers and a science of settlement imbued the career of the most prominent American geographer of the twentieth century. Isaiah Bowman (1878–1950) grew up on the northern Michigan frontiers, one of eight children in a Mennonite family that had moved from Ontario to Michigan when he was eight weeks old. As it turned out, Bowman's greatest contributions to the field of geography would echo his own family's history of frontier settlement as a form of border development. In the late eighteenth century, groups of German Mennonites answered Catherine the Great's call for settlers to colonize land in southern Russia. These Mennonite settlers, who enjoyed a reputation in Russia as fine agriculturalists, eventually moved into new territories along the Molochna River in Ukraine and newly acquired lands in the Crimea that Russia had pried from the Ottoman Empire.[9] These territories, called New Russia, were incorporated into an expanding Russian Empire by the first half of the nineteenth century. Once settled, Mennonite farmers supplemented their existing agricultural knowledge, which included extensive libraries on agronomy and records of experimentation on new climate and soil conditions, with local knowledge and cultivated crop varieties already farmed by Nogai and Crimean Tatar populations. By the 1870s, groups of Mennonites looked to Canada and the American Midwest as the next frontier, arriving by the thousands on the Red Star Line and newly built railroad connections.[10]

The Mennonites helped to shape the expansion of early modern empires like Russia. In the twentieth century, geographers, agronomists, and other experts constructed new kinds of empires, although they might eschew the use of the term *empire building* to describe their actions. As a boy, Bowman attended a one-room rural school. He went to Michigan State Normal College in Ypsilanti, where his sharp intellect drew the attention of his professor, Mark Jefferson, who recommended Bowman to his old teacher at Harvard College, William Morris Davis. The boy from the Michigan frontiers fit awkwardly in among his Harvard classmates, some with the last names of past presidents and who could trace their lineage to the first pilgrims on the Mayflower. That unease stayed with him for the rest of his life, dulled over time by his meteoric rise to become the most powerful academic in the country. After graduating from Harvard, in 1905, Bowman received certification from the United

States Civil Service Commission on geology, geology of oil, gas, and underground water. Subsequently the Department of Interior appointed him to the Geological Survey at the salary of four dollars per diem. He had just started work on the survey when an offer came through to teach summer school at Yale.

The Yale job became a turning point for Bowman. While at Yale, Bowman participated in three expeditions, in 1907, 1911, and 1913, to South America and the central Andes region. These expeditions provided the materials for his PhD dissertation and a series of published articles that became the basis for his career. This research came at a time when research on South America was still novel for American scientists. Bowman's interest in South America continued under his leadership of the American Geographical Society, where his signal achievement was the sponsorship of the million-scale map of Hispanic America.[11] By the mid 1910s, although he didn't know it, Bowman's career was about to take off.

In 1915 Bowman was named the director of the American Geographical Society, a position he served in until 1935, when he was named president of Johns Hopkins University. Many of the larger delegations at Versailles, including the American delegation, brought along their own geographers. Their involvement in the negotiations and proximity to political leaders and diplomats in turn opened doors and made careers. In addition to Bowman, the group of geographers who contributed to the American delegation included Ellen Semple and Bowman's old teacher in Michigan, Mark Jefferson.[12] The American delegation discouraged women from traveling to Europe due to their weak constitutions. Although Semple had organized her own global travels in 1911, she now had to remain in the US to complete her study of the principles for partition in the Mediterranean and Mesopotamian regions.[13] Bowman, armed with reams of maps and assistants, oversaw the inquiry as the chief territorial specialist for the American contingent. On his return to New York, Bowman found elite social circles in the city suddenly receptive to his ideas.

In Versailles, experts in the American delegation often felt frustrated by Wilson's unilateral decision making. Having brought a large contingent of experts to France, Wilson then proceeded to ignore their advice. Stewing in their impotence, these men were nevertheless free to socialize and network with the contingents from other countries around the world. Informal meetings in France between British and American delegates led to the formation of the British branch of the Institute of International Affairs. A planned American sister organization failed to come together. Instead, in 1921, Bowman became the founding director of the Council on Foreign Relations in New York City, combining academics and moneyed elites in an organization intended to provide a forum for "men of influence" to shape American foreign policy.[14] In its first years before acquiring its own headquarters, the council met at the Harvard Club in midtown Manhattan.

The following year, Bowman published the most popular book of his career, *The New World: Problems in Political Geography*, which also doubled as the summary of his views on geography's role in American claims to global power. On the cover, the book advertised its 215 maps and 65 engravings from photographs. The abundance of images and maps helped to illustrate the places mentioned in the book, from the boundary disputes in South America to the Albanian mountains and the Caucasus region of Central Asia. *The New World* addressed the territorial reordering that occurred in the wake of the war and Versailles. In explaining the reasons for writing the book, Bowman took a page straight from German geographer Friedrich Ratzel, acknowledging the ways that geography, history, and economics were entangled forces in a society's development. The book went into considerable detail about regions of the world that had undergone significant change because of the war, particularly the places with ongoing boundary disputes. Even as Bowman explicitly endorsed democracy as a form of government, the book displays his grudging respect for empire, in particular the structural underpinning of the conditions for trade and commerce.

The New World begins with the largest and most important empire in the world: the British Empire. Bowman immediately acknowledges the need for natural resources as a strong motivation for the acquisition of colonies.[15] This attention to a country's agricultural and mineral resources is present throughout the book's analysis. On the Austro-Hungarian Empire, for example, Bowman describes a splintering of the three "great eastward-reaching prongs of German population . . . part of the general process of expansion of the higher civilization of western Europe eastward against the lower oriental civilization that long threatened to overwhelm it."[16] The breakup of the empire excluded large populations of Germans outside Germany, particularly in the territories formerly part of the Austro-Hungarian Empire. It also left Austria and Hungary landlocked and lacking the essential raw materials for industries. Austria, in the aftermath of the war and the collapse of the Austro-Hungarian Empire, now depended on Hungary, Bohemia, Russia, and Romania for food crops and needed to import nearly all her coal and rubber. Hungary became one of the smallest states of central Europe. Bowman pointed out that "even with a loan with which to start her industries and import raw materials, it would be difficult for Hungary to avoid anarchy."[17] The breakup of empire, he argued, doomed its components to economic irrelevance.

The significance of imperial collapse on its remnants was not lost on the social scientists from these countries. In 1926 the Laura Spelman Rockefeller Memorial Fund approved $100,000 for five years of support for the Geneva Institute, which was established as a hub for social scientific and economic research. The institute attracted a core group of Austrian economists who were then contemplating questions about the role of tariffs, labor costs, and, in the wake of the Habsburg Empire's collapse, how small countries like Austria might fend for themselves in a world economy. Members of this loosely affiliated group in the "Geneva School" included William Röpke, Ludwig von Mises, and Michael Heilperin. In the politically chaotic interwar period, they nostalgically idealized the Hapsburg Empire and its accommodation of economic life across diverse political and national boundaries. In the crucial interwar years, these economists had already begun to dream of establishing a new global order after the collapse of empire. Their discussions generated the basis of neoliberalism around the central idea of an "economic constitution" that transcends the nation.[18] Like Bowman's views on global frontiers and settlements, however, this transcendence clearly privileged White populations of European origins. Other economists were occasionally made uncomfortable by the open expression of racism but chose to look the other way. Röpke, for instance, later openly supported Apartheid in South Africa.[19]

Bowman's views on race appear throughout his work. Across the Eastern European countries from Romania, to Hungary, to Poland, he describes the Jews as dominating commercial and financial activity, enjoying power out of proportion with their numbers as a percentage of the population—a claim at odds with the various laws and restrictions, as well as history of persecution, targeting Jews in Eastern Europe. Nor was this the only indication of anti-Semitism in Bowman's book. On the Jewish population in Poland, for instance, he repeats a well-worn anti-Semitic trope, claiming that Polish Jews had "worked rather for racial rights than for national revolutionary aims."[20] His account portrays Jews as at once a powerful political bloc and an internationalist force that betrayed national interests. This portrayal of Jews contrasted against his largely positive account of German colonization, both in Eastern Europe and in the prewar overseas colonies. In Bowman's telling, these large-scale movements of European people in search of fertile and open lands took place under the auspices of empires, which encouraged the settlement of agriculturists on contested borderlands and deployed the language of improvement as justification for seizing indigenous lands.

In *The New World,* Bowman provided a political geography of the world that accounted for both the geographical strengths and weaknesses of the newly reordered world. In essence, he broached the same question as the group of Austrian economists who formed the core of the Geneva School—how could nation-states retain the benefits provided by an imperial infrastructure? *The New World* was popular for the same reason that Rudolph Kjellén's turn-of-the-century coinage of the term *geopolitics* suddenly came into vogue—the interwar period exacerbated global anxieties about the collapse of the previous spatial order. *The New World* represented Bowman's geopolitical vision and his answer to the question of what comes after empires. He presented a more accessible version of Ratzelian geography by examining the world through the geographical lens. This perspective incorporated in equal parts a historical and environmental analysis of various world regions, their geographical advantages and constraints. The perspective is distinctly American, despite North America's absence in the book.

After the publication of *The New World*, Bowman's intellectual focus shifted to the uses of science and technology in developing frontier lands that had previously been off-limits because of their extreme climate or geographical conditions. As the leader of the discipline of geography, Bowman sought to adapt the field for a new age, or as he put it in a *Foreign Affairs* article in 1927, "the stage of a five-dimension world. To the three classical dimensions of space we now add a fourth dimension of time and a fifth dimension of quality."[21] The locus of his attention for

making this new, five-dimensional world was the pioneer fringe, the remaining undeveloped edges of the world. Bowman was not just interested in the science of settlement applied broadly, but also in creating
the conditions for White settlement. In this race for the last open lands
on Earth, the non-White peoples of the world, including the "Chinaman,"
had the advantage of their fecundity. Against this specter of rapidly
multiplying non-White hordes, Bowman argued, governments needed
to back up their settlers with policy, aid, and new technologies. Just as
Ratzel had accepted as a fundamental truth the hierarchy of races (and
the unsuitability of American Black populations for governing), so Bowman's foreign policy vision sought to reinforce the dominance of Western civilization rooted in White power.

Bowman provided a broad overview of all these ideas in a 1927 article in *Foreign Affairs.* In "The Pioneer Fringe," Bowman made the case
for a globalized reconceptualization of space. Just as worldwide cities
experienced rapid growth, on the frontiers across the world, mankind
challenged nature in settlements from the Canadian Northwest, Rhodesia, West Australia, and Eastern Europe. Bowman wrote that, in this new
age of technological advances, "no government can afford to ignore the
development of its resources. . . . vacant land can be a source of political
danger . . . It is the business of government leaders not to permit any land
that they may control to be politically passive."[22]

In this analysis of the relationship between state power and territory,
Bowman was influenced by Friedrich Ratzel and his ideas about the relationship between geography, economic development, and state power.
They differed in the importance each assigned to physical territory, re-
flecting in part the different autarkic capabilities of the United States and
Germany. The geographer Neil Smith teased out the differences between
Ratzel and Bowman, pointing out that, "According to Ratzel, a state's political control of territory is vital for its economic and cultural survival,
whereas for Bowman economic control of resources, workforces, and
markets is the much more direct key to national economic survival and
growth."[23] Isaiah Bowman claimed a clear demarcation between geopolitics and political geography, and he vehemently denied involvement in
the former, particularly after the German school of Geopolitik became
so closely associated with the Nazi regime.[24] His own words, however,
reveal a more complicated story. In *The New World* (1921), he wrote about
Manchuria:

Manchuria offers Japan a highly strategic position on the continent. It enables her to secure preferential terms for her manufactured goods; and what is of greatest importance, it enables her to control agricultural and mineral resources capable of large exploitation. The coal mines are in Japanese hands. Not only is it a strategic hinterland to Korea (now definitely annexed to Japan); it was here that Japan learned how important was the possession of Manchuria if the Chinese Eastern Railway and the South Manchurian Railway were not to invite armed hosts to the western shores of the Sea of Japan. China cannot control the region, though sovereignty nominally resides in the Chinese government today.[25]

Bowman's explanation for Japan's interest in annexing Manchuria demonstrates his close attention to the control of natural resources as the foundation of state power, the same concerns various geopolitical writers in Europe and Asia similarly showed.

For Bowman, the study of geography, including the survey of resources and population needs, turned settlement policies into a science. Bowman strongly disagreed with Turner over the closure of the frontier, but he acknowledged that beyond the Antarctic, the idea of "free and unclaimed" land no longer existed. The search for new outlets for surplus populations must turn to science and technology to make possible the settlement of territories long considered inhospitable to development. In a publication presented to the Council on Foreign Relations in 1937, on "Population Outlets in Overseas Territories," Bowman argued that "Population capacity, under given conditions, is the question we aim at in a study of the world's pioneer fringes. Geographers were once called 'environmentalists.' They are better described today as 'capacitators' . . . . The course of empire now follows all compass directions. The earth's tolerance and man's resistance and endurance have been vastly widened by modern science."[26]

The politicization of frontier settlements was already evident in the 1920s, while Bowman was busy promoting geography's role in the new science of settlements. A February 25, 1930, letter from Senior Agricultural Economist O. E. Baker to Bowman discussed the importance of frontier agriculture to the development of countries from the USSR to Australia and Argentina. Baker was in broad agreement with Bowman on the continuation and expansion of the frontier across the globe with the aid of technology that industrialized agricultural production, writing,

> There are vast areas of land in the southern U.S.S.R., in Australia, in Argentina, and in other semi-arid regions of the world which the tractor and the combine appear likely to render available for wheat production. It appears that there is now developing a new type of pioneer agriculture quite different from that in the past. The old pioneer was generally a man with only a little capital; whereas the new pioneer is a man bringing large amounts of capital in the form of power machinery. It is probable, therefore, that similar problems exist in other pioneer belts of the world, and the methods of study worked out in our Northern Plains may be helpful to students in these other areas.[27]

The stereotype of the rugged and independent settler of the American West (made possible by violent campaigns of dispossession led by federal troops and public investment in the building of railroads and other infrastructure) in the nineteenth century gave way to state-sponsored settlements in the twentieth. Instead of just playing a behind-the-scenes role in building infrastructure, the state brought in tractors and combines, planned communities, and enforced the voluntary and involuntary settlement of frontiers.

For the rest of his life, Bowman's geographical writings would focus on this idea of frontier development. For Bowman, the frontier had not closed, but rather lived on in pockets around the United States. Technological advances further opened new frontiers by allowing for human habitation and development in regions formerly closed because of inhospitable climate conditions. From the Arctic to the depth of the oceans, science created new frontiers and new possibilities for the discovery of natural resources. Bowman effectively extended the concept of the frontier beyond a purely geographical concept and internationalized American territorial expanse through science, commerce, and capital. Just as the Geneva School of economists attempted to navigate the global economy in the post-imperial era of the nation-state, Bowman worked to create a new territorial order at once based on but separate from national roots.

As the first non-European president of the International Geographical Union, Bowman oversaw the organization of the 1934 International Geographical Congress in Warsaw. As the world lurched into crisis in the interwar years, these international congresses continued as the simulacrum of global amity, taking place in Cambridge in 1928, Paris in 1931, and on the eve of World War II in Amsterdam in 1938. Geographers from around the world enacted amiable collegiality and underlined the internationalism of the discipline. Writing to the Assistant Secretary of State George Messersmith, who headed the American consulate in Germany during the rise of the National Socialist Party in 1930–1934, Bowman described the 1938 Amsterdam International Congress of Geography as a resounding success: "No congress that I have attended since the world war was marked by arrangements so elaborate as the congress at Amsterdam for the proper representation of all divisions of geography . . . . There was a large German delegation, an Italian delegation, and two groups of representatives from Spain . . . I may add that personal relations so far as I could judge were pleasant among the representatives and that everyone left the Congress feeling that it had been a success."[28] Less than six months later, the German Wehrmacht invaded Poland, setting off World War II in Europe. The jarring discordance between the collegial tone of Bowman's various correspondences and real-world events expose the tensions between nationalism and internationalism in geography and in academia in general. Geographers' eager proffer of their services to the state politicized the field in ways that in time would prove extremely detrimental on its claims to the universality of science.

Birth of Geopolitik

When Bowman contrasted political geography with geopolitics, he was referring to a specific school of geographical thought that had become increasingly popular in interwar Europe. As coined by the Swedish political scientist and amateur geographer Rudolf Kjellén, the concept of geopolitics invoked a world with clear winners and losers. The winners expanded the territories and resources under their control, and the losers lost their homelands. Such was social Darwinism carried out in territorial form. Kjellén viewed geopolitics as distinct from geography or political geography by its emphasis on the nation as a living organism. Like all living organisms, its survival depended on having sufficient space and resources. In this organic conception, states were "conscious and reasoning beings" that "hold congresses or fight on the field of battle."[29] This

combative assertion of national rights to territory and resources simmered in intellectual circles in Europe in the years leading up to World
War I before finally boiling over during the interwar period.

In Germany, the de facto leader of the German Geopolitik school
was Karl Haushofer (1869–1946), whose lack of formal training in geography proved no barrier to his influence. As a young military officer
stationed in Japan in 1909–1910, Haushofer filed extensive reports on
Japanese military maneuvers.[30] The experience left a deep impression
on Haushofer, and the brief interlude became the basis of his interest
in Japan and the Far East.[31] It was also the start of extensive correspondences with Japanese colleagues and Germans who worked in Asia and
shared his interest in geography and political analysis. In the interwar
years, Haushofer maintained cordial relationships with Japanese con-
tacts, exchanging letters, for example, with the military attaché from the
Japanese embassy in Berlin. Members of the Japanese legation returned
the favor and regularly invited Haushofer to official events, from holiday
celebrations to receptions for visiting dignitaries from Japan.[32] Between
1913 and 1938, Haushofer wrote a total of six books on Japan.[33] He regularly contributed a column on the political situation in the "Indo-Pacific"
region, which included Japan and China, to the *Journal for Geopolitics*
(*Zeitschrift für Geopolitiks*). Throughout his career, Haushofer's "scientific" theories on the connection between geography and politics would
remain vaguely defined. As an analyst of international relations and the
situation in the Far East, however, Haushofer often wrote very astute
political commentaries.

During World War I, severe food and material shortages in Germany
made tangible the importance of autarky. In that sense, it was hardly surprising that geopolitics, which emphasized the importance of geography,
territorial size, and control over natural resources, gained in popularity. In 1924, influenced by Bowman's publication of *The New World,* Karl
Haushofer founded the *Journal for Geopolitics.* Despite the later demoni-
zation of geopolitics as the ideological underpinnings of Nazi expansionist war aims, the anodyne content of the journal in its early years largely
focused on political analysis of events around the world. In 1925, for
example, the journal published a photograph of the Chinese leader Sun
Yat-sen's (1866–1925) death mask, along with a discussion by Haushofer
on the implications of his death for the political situation in China and
Sun's views on China's future development.[34]

Haushofer was friendly and made himself available to the German government, as well as anyone who contacted him, a personality trait (or strategy) that contributed in no small part to his growing prominence in the 1920s both in Germany and internationally. From Buenos Aires, a former foreman at Pingxiang Coalmines in China wrote him reminiscing about their meeting before World War I; an officer from Teheran wrote to discuss the importance of air routes over Persia; the American journalist Agnes Smedley wrote to consult about the possibility of her attending a German university to study India. In 1928, the director of IG Farben industries wrote him about Sun Fo's (Sun Fo was the Chinese leader Sun Yat-sen's son) visit.[35] And Haushofer returned these favors and requests: in 1933, in his capacity as the general secretary of the Berlin Geographical Society (Gesellschaft für Erdkunde zu Berlin), Haushofer sent Bowman a polite letter regarding a celebratory event for the society's founding and the 100th birthday of longtime board member Ferdinand von Richthofen (1835–1905). [36]

During the interwar years, Haushofer gained renown in German geographic circles and became known as the leader of the Geopolitik school. Haushofer had long expressed admiration for Bowman's work, in particular *The New World*. During World War II this influence became quite inconvenient for Bowman, especially because Haushofer was portrayed in the American press as the mastermind behind Hitler's wartime aggressions. This one correspondence, however, spoke more to the professional networks that connected scientists and social scientists around the world. In an address on political geography at Cornell University in 1936, Bowman emphasized the importance for geographers to go beyond a purely quantitative analysis to encompass the relationships more broadly between people and the environment. In an address given before the Institute of Public Affairs at the University of Georgia on May 13, 1937, entitled "Is There a Logic in the International Situation?" Bowman reiterated the point,

Geopolitik, a world of power in Germany since the World War, is neither the invention nor the dispensation of God though it is all but worshiped by Nazi elements. One has only to read the works of any or all of the writers in political geography, myself included, to realise how desperately if not fatally hard it is to free oneself from the restraints that national affiliation impose. . . .

The collective actions of men are not based on tonnages, topographic profiles, packages of industrial and trade statistics, conceptual "frameworks" of systematists, nice distinctions of landscapes, or the "musts" of the nationalistic expounders of scholastic doctrine. . . . Never was science so debased as when it was consciously invoked to prove the national case.

Bowman underlined a point which he repeatedly made in various public addresses, that "Geopolitik is not science but rather an underprivileged child of the World War."[37] While Bowman publicly denounced any association with the German school of Geopolitik, both men drew from similar underlying ideas about territory, natural resources, and autarky that gained purchase during World War I. British, American, and German geopolitical thought all addressed essentially the same anxiety about empire.

Geopolitics in China

In the second half of the nineteenth century, the accumulated effect of a gradual change in geographical thinking had begun to crescendo to a reformulation of the global order. Geographers around the world cultivated an interest in theories of civilization, even as geopolitical events challenged their understanding of their individual country's place in a new world order. Shortly after the Columbian Exposition, the Sino-Japanese War (1894–1895) and a decade later, the Russo-Japanese War, thrust Japan into the unfamiliar position of the dominant power in East Asia. Japan's victory in the conflict announced to the world its rapid ascendance as the first non-Western state to reach the front ranks of industrializing powers, while China's loss cemented the decline of the Qing Empire and ushered in an extraordinarily turbulent twentieth century.

The term *geopolitics* was coined around the same time, borrowing heavily from popular discussion over the previous decades that equated countries with biological organisms competing for resources and survival. In England, Darwin published *On the Origin of Species* in 1859. Through a series of highly influential translations/adaptations of social Darwinism, sociology, and Western philosophy in the 1890s and 1900s, Yan Fu (1853–1921) brought China into the global discussion about evolution. From Benjamin Schwartz's classic study of Yan Fu in 1964, historians have pointed out Yan Fu's primary concerns with political economy and philosophy rather than with the consistent and accurate translation of natural science.[38] Instead, as it circulated in both Japan and China around the turn of the century, social Darwinism foreshadowed the geopolitical concerns articulated later in the interwar period—how a country's territorial expanse and possession of natural resources could ensure its survival as an independent state. Countries either became global powers by adopting science and technology, like Japan, or were devoured by more powerful neighbors, like Poland.[39]

The rapid spread of geopolitics in 1930s China was testament to the popularity of its underlying ideas as a territorial form of social Darwinism from the turn of the century. Chinese academics, led by a generation of geographers, social scientists, and scientists who were trained abroad, brought back the language of inner colonization and development and ultimately adapted these ideas into a uniquely Chinese framework of frontier/borderland settlement, rooted in Chinese history and understanding of empire. These ideas began to percolate in Chinese geographical works long before the arrival of geopolitics. The 1905 work *Political Geography* (*Zhengzhi dili* 政治地理) by Liu Hongdiao 劉鴻釣 and Huang An 黃安 is one such example of the complex global circulation taking place at the turn of the twentieth century. According to the preface, the book is a compilation and translation of a Japanese work, also entitled *Political Geography*. The translators / editors acknowledged that, because they worked from abroad, they were unable to consult their old collection of books and therefore provided at best a loose translation.[40] The work begins with a discussion of the relationship between mankind and geography and the organization of the different countries of the world. The primary concern for the two editors revolves around the issue of what constitutes a nation, or *guo* 國, and in turn, the question of discrete borders, both on land and in the seas.[41] But it is in the section on imperialism that one can already see the connections to geopolitical ideas. For the authors of the work, the world has reached a stage of development when no unclaimed land remained. Therefore, in order to attain the status of a strong nation, territorial expansion must come at a cost to other countries.[42] In this respect, the Japanese merely followed the relentless logic of a geographical / biological imperative of the survival of the fittest. This new spatial construct idealized empire with access to the natural resources as necessary for economic development and industrialization.

The amorphous and inclusive nature of geography made difficult the building of a cohesive community of geographers in China. Some common ideas, however, underlay these successive generations of geographers. The search for mineral resources, including coal, oil, and precious metals, drove Chinese state building in the twentieth century. This desire to locate and control natural resources paralleled similar efforts around the world, including in the United States, and formed the foundation of geopolitical thought as it developed in the early twentieth century. Concurrently, from the late Qing through the Republican period and the founding of the People's Republic in 1949, geological surveys bolstered Han Chinese claims to resources in frontier areas. Both traditional forms of knowledge that continued to be disseminated in the twentieth century, like local gazetteers, and modern scientific reports, such as the geological survey, heavily featured discussions about coal and other mineral resources. The need to increase arable land acreage to feed a growing population, one of the driving forces in environmental change in the imperial era, continued to motivate the conquest of nature in the twentieth century, but the fuel needs of industrialization became an essential part of the rallying cry for the modern Chinese state to extend its control over borderlands occupied by non-Han peoples. This process helped to create resource hinterlands, areas that supplied the fuel needs of Chinese industries but enjoyed little of the benefits. Instead, they bore the environmental costs of heavily polluting extractive industries.[43]

By the 1920s professional geologists and mining engineers alike had embraced natural resource mapping as a crucial way for China to take part in a global ranking of nations. In 1928, the director of the China Geological Survey, Weng Wenhao, contributed a preface to Boris Torgasheff's survey of the mineral industry in East Asia. He pointed to the dearth of knowledge about mines in China and the changing relationship between mining and national boundaries as the industry became increasingly international in nature and integrated into the global commodities markets.[44] Weng portrayed Torgasheff's work as the valuable contribution of a knowledgeable expert on mining. Indeed, the *Mineral Industry of the Far East* featured 320 statistical tables, 14 maps, and an impressive coverage of metals and nonmetals, as well as coal, iron, and oil. Torgasheff discussed market conditions in Asia and the various uses of these mined products. Torgasheff saw as immaterial the fluid power dynamics in contested territories. His map of coalfields in Manchuria, for example, drew from both Chinese and Japanese geological surveys of the area.[45] What mattered to him was the value of these mines in metric tons and US dollars.

While Torgasheff appeared indifferent to nationalist concerns, subsequent Chinese writers viewed the country's mineral resources, particularly its coal production, as a point of pride. The writer Hu Rongquan (1886–1972) served on the editorial staff of the popular Commercial Press in Shanghai and wrote several works on the Chinese mining industry in the 1930s. For the 1935 book *Chinese Coal Mining* (*Zhongguo meikuang*), Hu surveyed geological and mining industry journals.[46] Hu was quick to point out the importance of the mining industry to the nation. In the first section of the book, Hu examined the geographical spread of coal mines in the country; estimated of the size of coal reserves; and assessed the transportation infrastructure and the market for coal production. He then turned to brief overviews of the largest coal mines in the major coal-producing provinces in the country. Hu's book contains numerous charts of various mines around the country and their production levels. Hu and others who followed in Torgasheff's footsteps similarly used extensive charts and statistical analysis of coal production, but, unlike Torgasheff, also painted the extraction of coal deposits as a positive reflection on the industrial development of the nation.

By the 1930s, the growing prominence of geopolitics in the West increasingly attracted the attention of Chinese intellectuals. In addition to German works, the British geographer and geopolitician James Fairgrieve (1870–1953) and his 1915 work *Geography and World Power* was also highly influential in China, along with translations of Ellen Semple's book, *The Influences of Geographic Environment on the Basis of Ratzel's System of Anthropo-Geography.*[47] Sidelined by her gender in the US, in China Semple's book was a popular translation that promoted the relationship between territory and power. For his part, Fairgrieve belonged to a coterie of British geographers whose works became particularly fashionable within military circles on both sides of the Atlantic.[48] He was a discipline of Halford Mackinder, one of the progenitors of the British geopolitics school, whose works argued for the importance of geography at the intersection of science and the humanities and as essential to understanding the strategic concerns of the British Empire. Fairgrieve's work had been translated into Chinese in 1938, with a second edition coming out in 1939. Although the work showed a shallow understanding of China's history and geographical situation, it was popular with Chinese readers, with a new edition coming out in Taiwan as late as 1967. In the section on China, Fairgrieve asked the question, "How is it that China was, and is, so homogeneous?"[49] To this question, Fairgrieve unequivocally answered: geography. According to Fairgrieve, Chinese geography determined that Beijing and Xian were the two key entries into China from the Northeast and the Northwest. These cities should become the terminus of future railway lines across northwestern China. Using Mackinder's concepts of heartland and periphery, Fairgrieve argued that the northwestern plateau, at the nexus of China, the Soviet Union and Mongolia, formed the core of Central Asia and the Eurasian continent.

The Japanese invasion further spurred geographers' interest in the geographical study of vulnerable borderlands, including their potential for resource extraction. In his efforts to promote the study of geography, in 1939 geographer Bai Meichu 白眉初 (1876–1940) petitioned the government to support the incorporation of geography in school curriculums. In his missive, Bai promoted the field's contribution to vital national defensive efforts.[50] Bai pointed out that China had done little to counter the efforts of foreigners who had been coming to China to survey its lands and resources for more than thirty years. In the absence of comprehensive surveys and government support, Chinese geography lacked a firm scientific foundation. Bai then went on to list the various areas which still required study, including surveys of the country's endemic diseases, ethnic composition, transportation, forestry, and natural resources. Bai called for geography students to make fieldwork an essential part of their education and for students to study the soil conditions, flora and fauna, and mineral deposits in their localities to familiarize themselves with their own country.

Bai, along with other late Qing intellectuals like Zhang Xiangwen, had founded the first geographical association in China in 1909 in Tianjin. The following year, in 1910, the association published the inaugural issue of the flagship journal for the discipline of geography, the *Journal of Geography* (*Dixue Zazhi* 地學雜誌). Over the course of the Republican years, Bai increasingly viewed geography through a nationalist lens. In 1936, Bai published the *New Atlas of China's Construction* (*Zhonghua jianshe xintu* 中華建設新圖), a work which has returned him to prominence in recent years because of its purported support of China's territorial claims on islands in the South China Sea. Along with a series of "national humiliation" maps published throughout the Republican period, maps that highlighted Korea, Mongolia, Tibet, Taiwan and sometimes even Vietnam as Chinese territories lost to Western and Japanese imperialism, Bai's work served a rhetorical purpose of stirring outrage and mobilizing the population against foreign encroachment. As such, the maps included in these works served an important function but were not based on historical evidence. Bai Meichu brought geographical skills from the imperial period into the reconceptualization of the field in the twentieth century, serving as the editor-in-chief of the *Journal of Geography* for twenty-five years.

China's desperate war of resistance against Japanese invasion radicalized geographers, who threw their full support into the war effort.[51] Hu Huanyong, a frequent contributor to scientific publications and chair of the geography department at Central (Zhongyang) University, in collaboration with the political department of the Nationalist or Guomindang (GMD) Military Affairs Committee, penned a work of military geography to be used in GMD party training schools. The work, *Geography of National Defense* (*Guofang dili*), explicitly connected geography, national defense, and the need for resource management.[52] Such works were very popular during the war, but what distinguished Hu's work is the section on border defense. Hu cataloged Korea as a former *shuguo*, or dependency. Hu also listed both Burma and Vietnam as *fanshu*, or outer dependencies, before their occupation by the British and the French respectively.[53] In the desperate struggle for survival, geographers like Hu staked the claims of the Chinese Empire to bordering states, as well as to the ethnic minorities living within what they considered the rightful borders of a Greater China.

Other geographers and geologists contributed to the war effort through their expertise. In the space of one year in 1938, Xu Zhuoshan's *Geography of the Chinese Resistance* (*Zhongguo kangzhan dili*) went through four printings and three editions in February, April, May, and September. Another work with the same title, *Geography of the Chinese Resistance*, by Wang Weiping was published in 1940 and included seven maps. The impact of the war and material shortages is visibly apparent in the poor quality of paper used for these books. Both the 1938 and the 1940 works emphasized the importance of strategic resources such as coal, oil, and metals essential to weaponry and armaments. The geolo-

gist Weng Wenhao joined the wartime government as director of the Industrial and Mining Adjustment Administration and put into action his
views on the relationship between science and industry by overseeing
the evacuation and relocation of Chinese industries.[54] GMD official Zhu
Jiahua 朱家驊 (1893–1963), a geologist by training who entered politics
in the 1930s, encouraged and supported the research emphasis on the
frontier regions of the Institute of Geography and the Geological Survey
of China, which had relocated to Sichuan with the retreating Nationalist
government. Zhu not only funded the scientific study of the frontiers but
also attempted to foster the building of a Nationalist party structure in
the Northwest, including in Xinjiang.[55]

Geopolitical writings fully bloomed in China during World War II.
In April 1940, the political scientist Lin Tongji (1906–1980), historian
Lei Haizong (1902–1962), and writer and literature professor Chen
Quan (1905–1965), along with a motley group of twenty-six of China's
leading humanists, joined together to found the journal *Warring States
Policies* (*Zhan Guo Ce* 戰國策) in Kunming in the southwestern province
of Yunnan. Facing dire wartime shortages, the semimonthly journal appeared sporadically in Kunming and the wartime capital of Chongqing
until July 1942.[56] Most of the intellectuals involved had studied abroad
in the United States or Germany and were interested in German philosophy, Arthur Schopenhauer and Friedrich Nietzsche in particular, along
with a geopolitical outlook on the world in a state of war. During its brief
existence, the journal published articles on the concept of Li 力 or *Macht*,
the Faustian spirit, Nietzsche, and updates on the progress of the war in
Europe. The loosely connected founders of the journal soon garnered the
moniker "Warring States Clique."[57] Under siege from Japanese invaders,
Chinese intellectuals turned to geopolitics as both an explanation for
and a solution to China's wartime dilemma. This select group of Chinese
intellectuals mined German philosophy and literature for analogies to
the Chinese situation. Like the scientists and social scientists discussed
in other parts of the book, this group of intellectuals represent the entangled intellectual networks of the twentieth century.

In the journal's inaugural issue, political scientist Lin Tongji published a defining essay titled, "The Replay of the Warring States Era." He
opened the essay with a bold call that "we must understand the meaning
of our era." Only two options remained open to China, Lin went on to
argue. Either the Chinese people learned to understand the significance

of the era and actively moved forward to become masters of the times, or they would become victims of the times. In 1940, Lin contended, the world had once again returned to a period of warring states, much as China had experienced from the fifth century BCE until unification through Qin conquest in 221 BC. During this earlier period, the smaller of the seven warring states sought alliances and maneuvered for survival while the larger and militarily powerful states aimed to expand their territorial possessions. This relentless competition between states, Lin argued, pitted strong against weak, large against small, and ultimately proceeded amorally, following only the logic of military might: "This is what we must clearly acknowledge: the era of warring states has arrived. No country can avoid wars of annihilation . . . It is a ruthless era, filled with slaughter and cruelty. But it is also a grand era, and there are great possibilities everywhere."[58]

Lin's analysis focused on competition between states, with the mighty swallowing the weak. Social Darwinism suffused the subtext in his proclamation of a new era of warring states. At the same time, the strident tones of the essay also served as a rallying cry for his countrymen. Just a month before the publication of the first issue of the *Warring States Policies*, in March 1940, former GMD leader Wang Jingwei formed the Reorganized National Government of China in Nanjing under the protection of the Japanese Empire. Widely derided as a puppet regime, the newly formed government never gained traction as a legitimate rival to Chiang Kai-shek's wartime government in Chongqing. Lin's essay left no doubt of his sympathies—if the state of war was the cruel essence of the age, it also entailed a fight to the bitter end, a struggle for either victory or annihilation that left no room for compromise.

Aside from various pieces introducing literary and political theory, the *Warring States Policies* carried articles analyzing events on the European battlefronts from a geopolitical perspective. In the third issue, for example, Hong Siqi examined the battle for Norway and the effect of topography on war; in the fourth, he discussed Italy and the relationship between a country's geopolitical position and diplomatic strategy.[59] Contributors to the *Warring States Policies* came from a broad spectrum of backgrounds, including literature, law, political science, history, and economics. Across these disciplines writers for the journal shared a common concern with the nature of power in the modern world: whether in diplomacy or on the battleground, land-based or ocean power, in theory or in practice, and in remote history or fresh from the news. The rumination on power ran as a theme through discussions of how countries or civilizations could survive in ruthless periods of warfare, as well as in seemingly unrelated essays on Faust, Schopenhauer, and Nietzsche.

The clear German influence on many of the writers continued even after Germany formally severed relations with the GMD regime. Officially, the Germans were allied with the Japanese enemies, yet writers for the *Warring States Policies* continued to tout German military and scientific superiority. Contributors to the *Warring State Policies*, like many other leading Chinese intellectuals of the first half of the twentieth century, received their training overseas, primarily in Japan, Europe, and the United States. Scientists and intellectuals with foreign degrees, especially from Europe and the United States, leapfrogged ahead of the competition for academic positions. Meanwhile, their Japanese enemies also produced a geopolitical journal, the innocuously titled the *Journal of Geography* (Jp. *Chigaku Zasshi*), that echoed similar themes colored by Japanese, rather than Chinese, nationalism.[60]

Chinese academics, commentators, and scientists operated in an interconnected world in which ideas and people moved, both directly and indirectly, in overlapping networks of common educational backgrounds and intellectual influences. Rather than associating geopolitics with aggressive imperial expansion, 1940s Chinese writers linked geopolitics to national defense. The war appeared to have bolstered the case for the importance of geopolitics. In 1943, the Chinese geographer Sha Xuejun (1907–1998) published *New Concepts in National Defensive Geography* (*Guofang dili xinlun*). Sha had studied abroad in the United States and Germany and shared a similar educational background and outlook as many of the Warring State Clique's more prominent members.[61] In his 1943 work, Sha placed the Sino-Japanese War as a conflict between industrialized Japan and agricultural China.[62] The war, therefore, was fought not only on the battlefield, but also as a race to industrialize. Moreover, Sha argued, in the age of great oceans only a seafaring state could attain the status of a great power. The key to China's future, therefore, depended on ocean rights as well as land power.[63] From 1939, the Department of Education had mandated all universities offer to their student bodies the choice of classes on national defensive geography and the history of the war of resistance. All GMD Party training schools also offered classes on these two subjects.

A direct translation of Haushofer's geopolitical work did not appear until April 1945.[64] Geographer and former Fudan University professor Zhou Guangda translated Haushofer's *National Defensive Geography* (*Guofang dilixue*). According to the preface, Zhou had studied historical geography at Berlin University. His preface for the translation described geopolitics as becoming a fashionable term in recent years. While Germany's defeat in World War II less than a month later permanently discredited the German school of Geopolitik, in China the very same concepts were adapted to local concerns and came into popular use in addressing the boundaries of the nation. In August 1947, an article from the magazine *The Core* (*Zhongjian*) used geopolitics to consider the question of Northwest China. Using the familiar language of geopolitics to discuss the importance of holding onto the Xinjiang region, the writer opined that "after our country makes progress in science and technology, this region will become the necessary *Lebensraum* [the author translates the term as *fuyang kongjian* 扶養空間] for our race."[65] In a 1948 issue of *Military Affairs* (*Junshi Zazhi*), an article on geopolitics defined its ideal goal as the determination of the concept of *guojie* 國界 (national boundaries).[66] In 1947, one of the Warring States Clique's members, He Yongji, published an article in the magazine *Observations* (*Guancha*) titled "From All-Under-the-Heaven to the Geopolitical State," in which he argued that China must grasp the importance of becoming a geopolitical state if it was to continue as an independent nation-state.[67] As such geopolitical writings proliferated in the 1930s and 40s, it was clear that geo-modernity had arrived in China.

In 1947, the German geographer Carl Troll published an apologia for all that the field of geopolitics had wrought in the previous decade. He depicted geopolitics as an intellectual aberration and a departure from the hallowed tradition of German geography as represented by figures like Alexander von Humboldt, Carl Ritter, and Ferdinand von Richthofen.[68] But Troll based his essay on a false premise. Neither ideas nor people exist in a vacuum. We are all connected and part of personal and professional networks. Some connections are obvious: nationalities, gender, or professional groups. Other connections less so, because they cut across divides in space or time. And because modern historical practice has been to follow these boundaries, the connections are lost or overlooked, hidden in musty archives and in letters crumbling with time.

The central ideas of geopolitics—from the connections between historical development and geography, to the organic nature of the state, to its social Darwinian undercurrents—were both influenced by and influential in mainstream geography. As geographical writings circulated globally, the underlying forces that encouraged the development of geopolitics, including the rise of modern science and new technologies of transportation and communication, informed the arrival of geo-modernity while accommodating for differences in history and geography of specific countries. From its birth in the late nineteenth century, geopolitics would go on to have a long afterlife into contemporary discourse in twenty-first-century China, but from the period before it had acquired a new name, *diyuan zhengzhi xue* (地緣政治學) in the 1920s and 1930s, geopolitics in China was already concerned with the fraught transition from empire to nation-state. The question that intellectuals from around the world engaged with was how to retain the advantages of empire in other forms. In the interwar years Americans and Chinese both saw science and technology as providing a solution to seemingly intractable problems of rural impoverishment, as the next chapter will show.

FIVE

Rural Development and Its Discontents

Pioneering today does not conform to the American frontier traditions of the nineteenth century. . . . The pioneer belts of the
world are regions of experiment—"experimental zones" we might
call them.

Isaiah Bowman[1]

In the last few years, talk of a new Cold War has once again begun to
bubble up in Washington, DC, and in think tanks in the US. Instead of
the Soviet Union, the new nemesis and rival is seen as China. Congressional leaders have offered up new legislation, including the Endless
Frontier Act of 2021, to address China's challenge to American scientific
and technological leadership by expanding funding for the National Science Foundation and for maintaining American dominance in strategic
technologies. The United States' role in establishing science in China is
often overlooked in these discussions. Nor have commentators sought to
learn the lessons of American policy failures in China before 1949 and
the founding of the People's Republic. There are no easy answers to this
central tension of the twentieth and twenty-first centuries, but there's
a precedent for the fraught Sino-US relations of today in the 1930s and
1940s, when both American philanthropic organizations and Chinese
leaders sought to deploy science to achieve their political agendas. This
history demonstrates the difficulties of controlling and confining science within national boundaries.

The interwar years saw extraordinary outbursts of political foment from Berlin to Shanghai, mixing in a toxic brew the rise of mass culture and calls for revolution. In furious backlash, right-wing movements around the world promised a restoration of national glory and agrarian idyll. Yet, beneath the polarization of the political discourse, both left- and right-leaning governments and nongovernmental agencies like the Rockefeller Foundation promoted agricultural science as a solution to rural problems. The Green Revolution is typically associated with the scientific breakthroughs in the 1960s and 1970s, but the research which led to the breakthrough occurred during the interwar period. In the wake of the Wilsonian debacle, the United States officially adopted an isolationist foreign policy. Leading social scientists like Isaiah Bowman took on the mantle of international leadership and spearheaded research into the scientific settlement of remote frontiers around the world. China lost its claims for the return of German colonial holdings to Japan. During this period, both self-proclaimed anti-imperialists in the Nationalist government and regional warlords actively adopted the civilizing mission in the borderlands, recruiting Han Chinese settlers to encroach into territories inhabited by minority populations. One of the purported winners coming out of Versailles, Japan increasingly turned against what they viewed as the hypocritical racist stance of Western countries. The grudge fed a growing resentment against the perceived curbing of Japan's imperial ambitions. Ultimately, the military seized control of the empire from a civilian government in Tokyo and led the nation into a disastrous continental war in Asia.

As Japan extended its influence in Manchuria and eventually launched into an all-out invasion of China in 1937, a new fervor for frontier settlement crossed the Japanese / Chinese divide. While heralding themselves as anti-imperialists, Chinese military officers, affiliated both with the Nationalist government in Nanjing and regional warlords, launched the scientific colonization of border regions, for which they claimed a precedence dating to antiquity. Indeed, the image of happy peasants turning apparently unpopulated wasteland into productive agricultural tracts turned up everywhere from the Nazi push into Eastern Europe, the Japanese-controlled puppet state of Manchukuo, Soviet Siberia, to the largely unrealized Nationalist Party (GMD) Chinese settlement plans for the frontiers.[2]

During this period of political and cultural transition, the frontier came to be seen as a laboratory for the accumulation of new knowledge about agricultural modernization and the exploitation of natural resources. Science as a universal form of knowledge interacted with specifically Chinese historical and epistemological constructs to create a distinctive new discourse that blended both the global and the local. What happened on the frontiers in the crucial decades from the 1920s to the 1940s helped to shape a distinctly Chinese territoriality, mode of state building, and conceptualization of nature. It was also very much part of a global wave of reconciling imperial ambitions with the seemingly conflicting goals of nationalism. Examples of frontier discourse around the world in the first half of the twentieth century displayed the power of science and the social sciences as an international and common language of state power. Such discussions built upon a rising consciousness of natural resources and environmental dependency. In the Chinese case, the rhetoric of opening and development became deeply entangled with a politically charged discourse of the frontier.

Exporting the American Heartland

The 1930s saw a growing interest in rural reforms around the world. If global forces, including dramatic swings in commodity prices, helped fuel widespread crises of rural impoverishment, the rise of the social sciences as a global phenomenon now aimed to provide a solution. In the United States, President Roosevelt pitched the New Deal as a way out of the country's economic depression while promoting infrastructural improvements and development of isolated regions in an American version of inner colonization. The Tennessee Valley Authority (TVA), for example, not only constructed dams and promoted electrification, but also put in place conservation programs to combat soil erosion and depletion in Appalachia and the South. Planners envisioned the hydroelectric projects turning the Appalachian region into a new Ruhr valley. In turn, the TVA became a model for other efforts around the world. The New Deal, born of international influences, then exported and reinforced the connection between modernization and agricultural development, particularly of borderland and interior regions previously classified as wastelands.[3]

American global influence coincided with the period when philanthropic organizations like the Rockefeller Foundation looked to expand their footprint abroad. The Rockefeller Foundation (RF) was a key non-governmental agency in the early twentieth century, which helped to propagate developmental ideas based on science and the social sciences around the world. During the Progressive Era, philanthropic foundations in the United States played a significant role in reform movements that advocated for issues ranging from temperance, poverty alleviation through social assistance, to educational reforms, all directed at a vaguely defined "public" good. Progressives looked abroad for solutions to social issues—how to deal with poor White populations and promote eugenics policies, for example—and in turn, promoted American programs abroad.[4] What began with domestic programs and the involvement of private citizens during the Progressive Era led to similar efforts overseas during the interwar years and continuing during the Cold War. These overseas ventures frequently bolstered elite networks in support of repressive but staunchly anti-Communist regimes—evident during the Cold War in Indonesia, Chile, and Nigeria, three of the favored foreign recipients of aid in Asia, Latin America, and Africa from American philanthropic foundations.

By the 1930s, the Rockefeller Foundation had already expanded into several areas which required international collaboration. At a time of severe economic contraction after the 1929 stock market crash, the RF devoted close to $18 million to research in the social sciences, providing a lifeline to these disciplines and placing an enormous bet on the power of knowledge to solve problems with global ramifications.[5] These international engagements built upon the work that the RF had supported domestically in the American South.[6] At the same time, the Rockefeller Foundations helped to fund university programs in international affairs, including a grant of $100,000 to be disbursed over five years to the Yale Institute of International Studies (YIIS).[7] The YIIS produced books that helped to define the US security policy, including Nicholas Spykman's most influential work, *American Strategy in World Politics* (1942), which argued for the need for military preparedness on a global scale. Spykman argued that "no region of the globe is too distant to be without strategic significance, too remote to be neglected in the calculations of power politics." Spykman's views laid the foundations for American international policy for the subsequent decades.

The American experience in pre-1949 China marred the successes of the "Big Three" American foundations—Rockefeller, Carnegie, and

Ford—in setting the policy agenda of the American Century. Building on a strong American missionary tradition dating to the nineteenth century, China was one of the first places where the Rockefeller Foundation invested considerable resources. In 1906, the RF funded what was widely considered to be the finest hospital and medical school in China, the Peking Union Medical College Hospital. The luxurious facilities vividly contrasted with conditions in other parts of the country experiencing devastating poverty and going through a period rife with both man-made and natural disasters. As Chinese nationalism developed in the early twentieth century, many increasingly saw the Peking Union Medical College Hospital as a potent symbol of well-intentioned foreign aid that was out of touch with the reality of Chinese society.[8] Chinese critics charged that the state-of-the art facilities barely made a dent in a society in crisis.

In the 1920s, in part as a response to this criticism, the RF broadened the scope of its support and issued funding to help existing research networks in countries like India and Mexico, as well as China.[9] Through both institutional support and individual scholarships, the RF advanced the cause of science. The scientific agenda worked in parallel with pilot programs to promote democratic practices. On one side, the RF funded research into plant improvement under a cooperative agreement between the College of Agriculture and Forestry at the University of Nanking, the International Education Board, and Cornell University. On the other side, RF funded programs to monitor rural elections to foster democratization. Agricultural science and rural elections were effectively two sides of the same coin in the political worldview underlying the RF mission overseas. For the RF, the turn to agricultural programs was a calculated bet on the continued importance of the social and natural sciences. By the mid 1930s, two major centers of agricultural research had emerged in China, in Nanjing and Guangzhou.[10] Both locations benefited from transnational ties and funding from abroad. By 1935 at least fifteen locations around China experimented with rural reconstruction programs, several of which were funded directly or indirectly by American philanthropic institutions like the RF.[11] These efforts made significant inroads because of the collaboration of local elites. In China, RF funding further reinforced missionary efforts dating to the nineteenth century to remake Asia modeled on the American model of a progressive democracy.[12]

The RF helped to lay the foundations for Chinese science through these rural reconstruction programs and scholarships for students to study in the United States. During a trip to China in 1932, the foundation's long time vice president, Selskar Gunn, wrote to the American scientist Warren Weaver describing the organization's goals: "I am convinced that the fellowship program in the natural sciences, as a whole, has been a good piece of work and a considerable number of the outstanding Chinese scientists are our returned fellows."[13] These Rockefeller programs helped to train a key cohort of Chinese scientists. These efforts shaped the sciences in China, including after 1949 and the communist rise to power. Time proved Gunn right. Geneticists Li Ruqi and Tan Jiazhen, for example, both received Rockefeller research fellowships. In the US, they worked with T. H. Morgan's group at Caltech. They returned to China to start their careers at Yanjing University, a missionary-affiliated college in Beijing.[14] After 1949, Li taught in Beijing University's biology department until 1980, while Tan was a leading proponent of modern genetics and a member of the biology faculty at Fudan University in Shanghai. These two careers illustrate the transnational ties that connected Chinese scientists to the international scientific community, even over decades with no diplomatic relations and exchange between the US and China.

In addition to larger grants to rural reconstruction projects, the RF oversaw multiple small one-time grants to programs around the country. For example, the RF approved a $3,000 grant to the Department of Agriculture at Lingnan University, under the direction of Professor G. W. Groff, to continue the development of its Plant Receiving Station. Over two decades, the Lingnan program had carried on fundamental plant science work in botany and agriculture, focusing on the cultivation of undeveloped hilly areas. This work was particularly important given significant deforestation and soil erosion issues in many parts of the country, due in large part to rapid population growth in the previous centuries and the expansion of agricultural development into environmentally fragile areas. Groff, who held the position as professor of horticulture for thirty-five years at Lingnan, was particularly interested in plants with economic potential. He helped to establish an exchange station on the west coast of Florida and experimented with transplanting various semi-tropical and tropical plants between Florida and South China.[15]

In another example of the research the RF sponsored, in 1935, the RF made a grant of $17,300 to the College of Agriculture at National Central

University in Nanjing to support its veterinary sciences program and research in animal husbandry and veterinary preventive medicine.[16] When Japan invaded two years later, the program relocated to Sichuan with the wartime government and sought to reestablish the animal husbandry department. Under the leadership of T. Y. Hsu, the group continued research on swine, comparing gestation period and litter size of various pig varieties both foreign and native. Hsu eventually published his wartime research, "Chinese Swine and Their Performance Compared with Modern and Crosses between Chinese and Modern Breeds," in the *Journal of Heredity*, in a collaboration with Ralph W. Phillips from the United States Department of Agriculture and the Chinese Ministry of Agriculture.[17]

Another of the RF's major sponsored projects was headed by the Yale-educated reformer James Yen (Yan Yangchu 晏陽初, 1893–1990). Yen was a highly charismatic figure, who in many ways represented the cosmopolitanism of Chinese intellectuals in this period. Born in rural Sichuan, Yen belonged to a tight-knit network of Chinese Christians. His involvement with the Chinese YMCA led him to the United States in the summer of 1916, armed with sixteen letters of introduction to Oberlin College in Ohio. On the way, however, Yen met a teacher from Yale-in-China and decided to attend Yale instead.[18] The impulsive shipboard decision changed his life. At Yale, Yen met and married Alice Huie, daughter of Huie Chin, the pastor at the First Chinse Presbyterian Church in New York's Chinatown. Yen found himself by religion, marriage, and education plugged into an influential transpacific network. From this fortuitous convergence of networks, Yen found the backing for his life's work. James Yen had started his efforts of moral and educational uplift by taking on illiteracy during World War I, when he provided assistance to the Chinese laborers recruited to work for the Allies. Over 100,000 "coolies" eventually traveled to Europe and worked mostly to dig trenches on the Western Front. The sizable contingent of Chinese workers experienced the outside world for the first time, an exposure that made them ideal targets of progressive efforts.

In the interwar years, Yen's program quickly grew into the Mass Education Movement (MEM). The National Association of the Mass Education Movement eventually established its headquarters in Peking in 1923 and rapidly expanded a network of People's Schools for Illiterates. By 1930, the movement had reached approximately five million people, taught by about 100,000 volunteer teachers. The basic literacy textbook that Yen wrote for classroom use, *The Thousand Character Books*, sold twelve million copies. The program had all the components of a wildly successful feel-good story coming out of a country that did not have many such triumphs in the early twentieth century. The vision also proved attractive to big American funders—both Henry Ford and John D. Rockefeller personally cut checks for Yen to support the MEM. In 1932, James Yen, Liang Shuming, and others interested in progressive programs began to meet and coordinate their efforts to transform rural society in China, eventually forming the Rural Reconstruction Movement.[19]

The Ding County experimental zone (referred to as Ting Hsien in contemporary documents) developed from the Mass Education Movement and became the most prominent showcase of the Rural Reconstruction Movement, along with Zouping in Shandong province run by Liang Shuming.[20] The Ding County Experimental Zone was based in a county 170 miles south of Beijing, along the Peking-Hankow railroad, with a population of around 400,000 scattered over an area that included 400 villages. Within this zone, the program featured intensive citizenship and civic training and showcased modern agricultural sciences such as plant breeding, seed selection, animal husbandry, beekeeping, horticulture, improvement of fertilizers and agricultural implements, and control of plant diseases.[21] In short, this was precisely the kind of project which appealed to the RF philosophy of promoting science and democratic practices.

The idealism of the movement attracted the same educated elites who traveled in large numbers to the northwestern and the northeastern borderlands to carry out and oversee the settlement of these regions during the interwar years. One such figure, Rui Feng, headed agriculture studies for MEM. Feng received his BSc in agriculture from Nanking University. He then went to Cornell University for graduate training in plant breeding and seed selection and received his PhD in agricultural economics. From Cornell he proceeded to Europe and studied at the International Institute of Agriculture at Rome, where he also learned about cooperative movements in Germany and Denmark. After some years in Europe, Feng returned to America and spent half a year in the US Department of Agriculture. When he returned to China, he taught at Canton Christian College and later at National Southeastern University in Nanjing. In 1923, Feng learned about MEM and its education work with farmers. The program so strongly appealed to his idealism that he resigned from his professorship and joined the movement. Agricultural science in China was at the time usually confined within the walls of a college, but Dr. Feng saw that through the Mass Education Movement, science could be put within the reach of every Chinese farmer.[22]

James Yen's funding requests to the RF repeatedly emphasized the role of social survey in these projects. A summary report in 1934 pointed out that "survey work in Ting Hsien is not conducted for survey's sake but with two specific objectives, 1) to collect facts about the district so that upon them an intelligent and scientific program of education for reconstruction may be formulated; 2) to evolve through actual experience a Chinese technique of conducting social investigation under the existing conditions in rural China."[23] A subsequent report from 1936 couched the Ding County project specifically as a "laboratory" and the first of many other "stations" in other parts of the country.[24] A statement of policy on July 1, 1936, listed three key functions for the MEM: rural reconstruction, research and experimentation, demonstration and training.

The idealism of the Ding County Experimental Zone and Yen's astutely framed appeals for foreign funding glossed over significant structural issues with the Chinese rural economy. Science and literacy classes could only go so far in addressing issues with global commodity prices, onerous tenancy and taxation policies, and deteriorating soil conditions. Had it not been for World War II, however, the assessment of the program might have been very different. The eventual collapse of the program began with the Japanese invasion in 1937. Within two months of the Marco Polo Bridge incident in July 1937, which set off open warfare between Japanese and Nationalist Chinese troops stationed in the vicinity and led to the rapid expansion of the war to the rest of the country, the Ding County "laboratory" fell to the invaders, and several thousand youths were massacred by the advancing Japanese army. That winter, Japanese troops captured the national capital, Nanjing, and went on a binge of rape and killing. In the larger tragedy of the war, the Mass Education Movement became an afterthought. The MEM limped on through the war. Yen continued to request funding for the construction of experimental stations in the Free China zones. These included experimental zones in Guangxi, Hunan, Guangdong (which would incorporate rural reconstruction with civil and military training), and a rural normal school in Henan province.

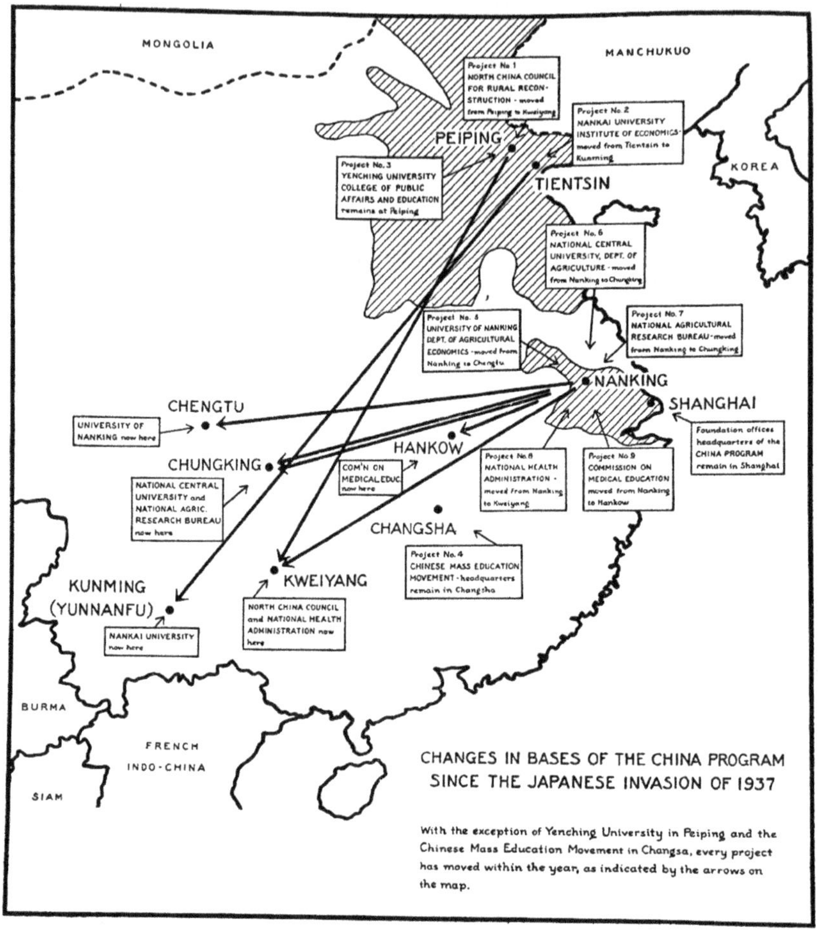
MONGOLIA
MANCHUKUO
Project No. 1
NORTH CHINA COUNCIL
FOR RURAL RECON-
STRUCTION - moved
from Peiping to Kweiyang
Project No. 2
NANKAI UNIVERSITY
INSTITUTE OF ECONOMICS -
moved from Tientsin to
Kunming
PEIPING
Project No. 3
YENCHING UNIVERSITY
COLLEGE OF PUBLIC
AFFAIRS AND EDUCATION
remains at Peiping
TIENTSIN
KOREA
Project No. 6
NATIONAL CENTRAL
UNIVERSITY, DEPT. OF
AGRICULTURE - moved
from Nanking to Chungking
Project No. 5
UNIVERSITY OF NANKING
DEPT. OF AGRICULTURAL
ECONOMICS - moved from
Nanking to Chengtu
Project No. 7
NATIONAL AGRICULTURAL
RESEARCH BUREAU - moved
from Nanking to Chungking
NANKING
SHANGHAI
CHENGTU
UNIVERSITY OF
NANKING now here
HANKOW
CHUNGKING
COM'N ON
MEDICAL EDUC.
now here
Project No. 8
NATIONAL HEALTH
ADMINISTRATION -
moved from Nanking
to Kweiyang
Project No. 9
COMMISSION ON
MEDICAL EDUCATION
moved from Nanking
to Hankow
Foundation offices
headquarters of the
CHINA PROGRAM
remain in Shanghai
NATIONAL CENTRAL
UNIVERSITY and
NATIONAL AGRIC.
RESEARCH BUREAU
now here
CHANGSHA
Project No. 4
CHINESE MASS EDUCATION
MOVEMENT - headquarters
remain in Changsha
KUNMING
(YUNNANFU)
KWEIYANG
NANKAI UNIVERSITY
now here
NORTH CHINA COUNCIL
and NATIONAL HEALTH
ADMINISTRATION now
here
BURMA
FRENCH
INDO-CHINA
SIAM
CHANGES IN BASES OF THE CHINA PROGRAM
SINCE THE JAPANESE INVASION OF 1937
With the exception of Yenching University in Peiping and the Chinese Mass Education Movement in Changsa, every project has moved within the year, as indicated by the arrows on the map.

THE GEOGRAPHY OF THE CHINA PROGRAM

The shaded areas in the north and along the eastern coast indicate the invaded regions as they were at the end of April. Since then a region north of Nanking has been taken, joining the two war zones.

FIGURE 5.1: A map of the locations of the RF-sponsored crop programs in China and their relocation during the war. RG I, Series 601, Box 12, Folder 126.

As the war proceeded on its relentless course and left devastation in its wake, as well as difficult conditions for survival let alone any sort of research, the RF grew increasingly dissatisfied with Yen and his loose accounting of RF funds. The American foundation had long supplied the bulk of Yen's funding. In a series of letters from 1940, RF staff member Marshall Balfour, who had joined the foundation in 1926 and participated in malaria control programs in the US, Greece, China, and India, expressed his increasing frustration with Yen.[25] Balfour voiced his dissatisfaction in no uncertain terms, "Since we are indulging in frankness, it is well enough to talk of going forward and considering the Foundation as a partner in the MEM but additional and substantial assistance has got to be met by other sources of support."[26] By September 1940, Selskar Gunn informed Balfour that "as far as I can gather the feeling here has not changed and the idea is that the China Program, so-called, is to be liquidated over a period of years."[27] A memorandum written by Balfour on April 3, 1944, acridly noted that "the MEM and Dr. James Yen represent both idealism and a tradition in mass education and rural reconstruction. But, to put matters frankly, the MEM does not occupy a very important place or influence in education or government reconstruction in China today."[28]

In the fall of 1945, interoffice correspondence at the RF noted that the greatest enthusiasm for the Dingxian experiment and Yen's work was on the part of those he met in the US and more a measure of his considerable personal charisma than on account of his actual influence and results in China. Nevertheless, over a decade from 1935 to 1945, RF continued to provide funding to the MEM, totaling the not insignificant amount of $242,000. Yen made further requests for a capital contribution of $500,000, and annual contributions of $250,000 per year for another decade while Balfour was recommending the liquidation of the China program and cutting the foundation's ties to the MEM.[29] After the end of the war, Yen returned to the global circuit of invited talks and conferences on alleviating rural poverty and illiteracy.

While the RF soured on Yen's MEM, through various hardships and the retreat of coastal institutions to the Southwest during the war, the foundation continued support of Chinese agricultural research. The Yenching Field Station in Yunnan province, for example, carried on work on the intensive sampling studies of selected areas in the frontier provinces. The war, the flight to the interior of the country, and other hardships created by the war led to innumerable hurdles for research. In some instances, RF funding reinforced existing relationships between American colleges and Chinese programs. In Shanxi in 1937, the Oberlin Shansi Memorial Schools featured an Agricultural Department headed by Raymond T. Moyer to improve the quality of wool produced in the province by crossbreeding local sheep with Western breeds like the Rambouillet. RF support of the North China Council for Rural Reconstruction (NCCRR) aided in the continuation of county fairs during the war.

The reports on these county fairs are perhaps more revealing than intended. According to the report submitted to the RF, one such county fair in the Sichuan countryside, in the Free China zone, was held from October 9 to 13, 1939. The county fair was held at the extension center and featured 1,170 exhibits, arranged in 75 groups. Professor Y. W. Chang was appointed director in charge of all preparations. Of the total number of exhibits, 872 pieces were provided by the Ministry of Agriculture and 298 pieces by individual farmers. Out of these, 212 pieces or 71 percent of the farmers' exhibits were rewarded prizes. The fair was originally planned for three days, but on request from the participating villages, it was extended to six days. In addition to the fair, the program also organized the "five-petaled" or Agricultural Youth Club, modeled on the American 4-H programs. According to the report, fourteen such youth clubs were organized in the region. During the county fair, the club members had a club day with its own full-fledged program.[30] For the RF, these numbers and reports of enthusiastic participation made the fair an unqualified success.

In the larger context of wartime events in China, however, the rosy report, with its careful accounting of ribbons and prizes awarded, appears wholly out of touch with reality. The NCCRR had retreated with the Nationalist government to Chongqing in Sichuan province. By the summer of 1938, Japanese troops controlled all North China. To stop their further advance, Chiang Kai-shek made the fateful decision to intentionally destroy the dikes along the Yellow River. The resulting floods inundated thousands of square miles of farmlands and killed upwards of 800,000 people trapped in the flood zone.[31] Millions of survivors became refugees. No hint of the disaster and its fallout appears anywhere in the report on agricultural fairs.

The RF arrived in China with a particular vision that emphasized science, technology, and the importance of data. The ideology of the

American Progressive Movement, itself heavily influenced by European center-left politics and the professionalization of the social sciences, underpinned this vision. Idealism about the possibilities of scientific development turned out to have been a blinkered view of the situation on the ground in China. Chinese researchers in search of funding, many of whom had studied at US institutions, provided what the RF looked for in the grant process, creating a self-perpetuating feedback loop. American-trained Chinese scientists used their familiarity with the culture of American institutions and fluency in grant-writing language to apply for funding to carry out American-style reform in China, with an emphasis on technical rather than structural solutions to rural problems.[32] The war exposed the fallacy of the RF's assumptions and led directly to the failure of these programs, but also let the RF leadership off the hook since any issues could plausibly be attributed to the widespread disruptions of the war. Their subsequent work in Mexico, for example, showed little evidence that they had learned from the China experience.[33]

What happened in Mexico has become a cautionary tale on the limits of science without broader political change. RF-funded research on hybrid wheat in Mexico in the 1940s led to the American agronomist Norman Borlaug's 1970 Nobel Peace Prize. Borlaug's research resulted in substantial wheat production increases. But without accompanying land reforms and government policies in place, these advances notably failed to alleviate rural poverty and malnutrition in Mexico. The benefits of increased wheat production went almost entirely to large landholders, further exacerbating social inequalities.[34] These glaring issues left Mexico sidelined in the triumphal narrative of the Green Revolution. Today the gains in agricultural productivity of the Green Revolution are more commonly associated with widely touted programs in Asia from the 1960s, leaving obscured the local dynamics in place in Mexico before Borlaug's arrival and the contribution of the Mexican seeds to the cultivation of hybrid wheat in India.

The Rockefeller Foundation and other American-based funding agencies subscribed to the view that educational programs, the promotion of farm machinery, mechanization, and agricultural science were sufficient measures to combat entrenched rural impoverishment and tenancy problems in China. This is part of a larger perspective on international relations and American involvement in the world that colored the efforts of all three large American philanthropic organizations of the twenti-

eth century. Not until 1948, when Communist forces were on the verge
of decisively winning the civil war on the mainland did the US Congress authorize $40 million for a rural reconstruction plan in China that
addressed land reform and the structural aspects of the agrarian problem.[35] By 1946–1947, even the Mass Education Movement had shifted left
and started a pilot program on cooperative farming.[36] American experts
sent to China, including Wolf Ladejinsky, a Ukrainian-born agronomist
working for the USDA, concluded that land reform was the best and only
means to prevent a Communist takeover by improving conditions for the
peasant masses.[37] After retreating to Taiwan in 1949, Nationalist leader
Chiang Kai-shek also instituted land reform to carry out Taiwan's highly
successful Green Revolution.[38]

Over the long term, the Rockefeller vision ultimately bore fruit for
Chinese science. Leading Chinese scientists who received scholarships
to study in the US on their return to China helped to establish genetics
and nuclear physics, among other fields. The globalized nature of science helped to seed the accomplishments of Chinese national science
during its period of greatest isolation in the 1950s through the 1970s. The
Rockefeller Foundation saw as its most coherent historical mission "the
development of institutions to train professional people, scientists and
scholars in the applied disciplines, who in turn will train succeeding
generations of students, advance the state of knowledge in their fields."[39]
The approach favors investment in elite institutions and networks over
mass education. For a brief window in the 1930s and 1940s, the Rockefeller program in China explored alternatives to the elite approach by
supporting James Yen's efforts in rural education.

Although touted as a Mass Education Movement, however, Yen in fact
did not broach the third rail of Nationalist policy. The Nationalist Party's
staunch anti-Communism stance and dependance on the rural gentry
as a power base made land reform politically impossible. This failure
became evident during the Japanese invasion. The "loss of China," however, became so entangled with other political considerations that the
Rockefeller Foundation never had to fully confront the real reasons why
the China program failed and the limits to deploying science for political ends. Just as China embarked on its own Green Revolution and path
to modern science, the country escaped the internal logic of American
philanthropy.[40] For the RF, the ignominious demise of their extensive
China programs freed up funding to promote science and democracy in

other parts of the world, which were then beginning to pick sides in the Cold War.

This was a generation in US history rich with China Hands, experts on the country, many of whom grew up or lived in China for many years as part of the evangelical missionary movement. The *Times* publisher Henry Luce, who coined the phrase the "American Century," was born in China to missionary parents. The writer Pearl S. Buck came out of this tradition, as did her husband, the agronomist John Lossing Buck. John Buck had graduated from Cornell University with both his undergraduate and graduate degrees. In the early years of their marriage, the couple traveled around the country to conduct statistical surveys on the Chinese farm economy.[41] Later, as head of the Department of Agricultural Economics at Nanking University, John Buck led efforts to conduct the most comprehensive analysis of the Chinese rural economy in the Republican period, *Land Utilization in China,* which was published by the University of Chicago press in 1937.[42] Among members of the American political leadership, Franklin Delano Roosevelt always expressed great sympathy for and interest in China born out of his family background: on his mother's side, the Delanos had made their fortune in the China trade.

In the end, however, this wealth of expertise led to one grave miscalculation: that the US, through both individual, church, and government intervention, could strategically deploy science to "save" China. The Chinese themselves had already coined the phrase *kexue jiuguo*, "science saves the nation."[43] The global forces underlying the emergence of geo-modernity crossed national and political boundaries. These events of the previous century prefigure the current debates about China and a twenty-first century Cold War, with science and technology as the fields of battle. But does science have borders and what country could claim proprietary ownership of science?

Geo-modernity on the Frontiers

While the RF worked to solve the problems of rural impoverishment through science and technology, both the Nationalist government and regional warlords sponsored military land reclamation efforts on the Chinese frontiers. These borderland experiments embraced forms of collectivization and the extensive use of science and technology far earlier than reconstruction efforts in the interior provinces, where the entrenched gentry class vociferously opposed land reform. Mongolians and other ethnic minorities on the frontiers, their land use rights in many cases already weakened by late Qing land sales to raise funds, offered little resistance to Han Chinese settler colonialism.[44] The biggest obstacle to these efforts was the adverse environmental conditions and lack of infrastructure in the border regions.

From the late Qing, a series of efforts to develop frontier lands, introduce new crops, and open small industries and mines to tap into local natural resources had met with limited success. Sichuan provincial officials who sought to develop strategically important regions in eastern Tibet had difficulty recruiting Han Chinese settlers willing to farm in harsh and unfamiliar terrain. The few recruits they scrounged up either never turned up in the first place, absconded immediately upon seeing the remoteness of the area and the harsh climate, or abandoned the land after some months of making little or no progress.[45] Other regions faced similar challenges in sustaining development. Private enterprises quickly failed in the absence of substantial state investment in infrastructure. In 1925, there were ten private reclamation companies in Linhe alone in the northern province of Suiyuan, on the border with inner Mongolia, with a capital investment of Ch$260,000.[46] A few years later, all but one or two had gone bankrupt.

Despite the failure of private enterprise in these areas, the central government in Nanjing periodically proposed reclamation plans. In the imperial period, soldier colonization of the frontiers was viewed as a sound solution to the logistical issues of supplying troops in the borderlands. Reclamation (*kaiken* 開墾) was not limited to borderlands and frontiers, but any area with potential for agricultural development. The Taiping Rebellion, for example, had laid to waste significant acreage of prime farmland. To reclaim these areas, officials offered financial incentives, agricultural implements, and tax breaks for peasants to return to the land.[47] In the Republican period, the Forestry Ministry oversaw efforts to reclaim domestic territories. The ministry regularly issued calls to reconnoiter any region with potential for development, looking to investigate the geography, climate, soil, transportation, and other local conditions.[48] Despite various proposed incentives, however, few recruits took up offers to reclaim these so-called wastelands. In 1936, the government issued guidance on the use of criminals in reclamation, limiting recruitment to those with life sentences who had served five years or more, or those who had served at least 20 percent of their sentences of three years or more.[49]

Bureaucrats in the Nanjing government were not alone in viewing reclamation efforts as a panacea for all woes. In November 1928, the Han-Chinese military commander Zou Zuohua (1893–1973), who was closely affiliated with the Manchurian warlord Zhang Xueliang, gave a speech "On the Brief History of *Tunken*" to the men under his leadership in the Xing An Military Land Reclamation Zone in a corner of Northeast China bordering the Soviet Union and Mongolia.[50] Zou shared with a number of Chinese warlords and leading military men of his generation a cosmopolitan education overseas and had graduated from the Imperial Japanese Military Academy. His address, however, gave little hint of this international background. His speech appealed to Chinese nationalism placed in the context of an unbroken imperial history.

According to Zou, during the Han dynasty, the general Zhao Chong-guo (137–52 BCE) came up with the brilliant idea of allowing troops stationed on the frontier to farm or *tuntian* 屯田 (the character *tun* denotes a military garrison, while *tian* means agricultural fields). This simple strategy solved the logistical difficulties of supplying troops stationed in the distant frontiers and turned steppes and wastelands into agriculturally productive lands. Now in the 1920s, besieged by Soviet and Japanese aggression, Zou headed a newly formed Military Land Reclamation Bureau of the Xing An region to carry out a modern form of *tuntian–tunken* 屯墾–which similarly involved the use of troops to reclaim "wastelands" on the frontiers. Instead of pacifying barbarian tribes as in the Han dynasty, Zou asserted that Chinese *tunken* efforts were a means to extend a modernizing and helping hand to their Mongolian compatriots, one of the five recognized ethnic groups in the Republic of China, each primarily populating a frontier area to the provinces of China Proper. This narrative had the advantage of dating Chinese settlements on the frontiers significantly before Japanese imperial ambitions. Efforts over the next two decades by Zou and others like him from across the political spectrum to bolster the Chinese frontiers from the Northeast to the Northwest and the Southwest would define the territorial extent of the modern Chinese state.

As a native of Jilin in the Northeast, Zou Zuohua would have been intensely aware of the complex and often conflicting military, political, and economic alliances in the region, which had once been considered the Manchu homeland and closed to Han Chinese settlers. Chinese settlers in search of fertile land trickled in, nevertheless. Starting in the late nineteenth century, the sale of land became a source of income for the ailing dynasty and increasing numbers of Han Chinese settlers flooded in to both the Northeast and Northwest from China Proper, escalating tensions with Mongols and other indigenous people in these regions.[51] In the waning days of the Qing, the true flood of Chinese settlers began. Roughly 25 million workers poured into the region from the 1890s to World War II.[52]

The chief attraction of Manchuria for Zou and other military men, however, lay in its strategic and economic potential. In his 1935 book, Owen Lattimore put forward his "reservoir" theory of Manchuria. The territories on the other side of the Great Wall, he asserted, served as a reservoir ground for the successive waves of foreign invaders who eventually conquered China. Significant Japanese presence in Manchuria dates from the Russo-Japanese War in 1904–1905, when Japanese victory garnered the prize of railways that soon became the backbone of the Southern Manchurian Railway Company, a semiofficial corporation modeled after the British East India Company.[53] The Japanese Empire prioritized the development of the region and aimed to create an industrial base.[54] At the same time, the Japanese also encouraged settler colonialism from the home islands and opened plant experimental stations in the Northeast.[55]

Japanese troops stationed in the empire acted independently of the civilian government on the home islands. On the ground in Northeast China, the situation steadily deteriorated. In June 1928, officers in the Kwantung Army conspired to assassinate the Manchurian warlord Zhang Zuolin, who had attempted a dangerous game of playing Soviet and Japanese interests against one another, using one as leverage for demands for more weapons and aid from the other. An already tense political situation threatened to further spin out of control after Zhang's assassination, which rogue Japanese officers had initially attempted to pass off as the work of Chinese bandits. The timing was hardly coincidental, then, that in the fall of 1928, Gao Renfu (1897–1966), an officer affiliated with Zhang Zuolin's son, Zhang Xueliang, led three units of men to carry out a *tunken* project in the Xing An region. Zou Zuohua headed the official Xing An Military Land Reclamation (*tunken*) Bureau.

Located in today's Inner Mongolia, along the reaches of Tao'er River, in the 1920s the region was thinly populated with Mongolian tribes. In the flat plans of the region, nomadic peoples pursued a living through herding livestock. An extremely short growing season started in May; by the second half of August, the first frost of winter descended. Snow and extreme cold swept the region in the winter. Limited rains frequently led to drought conditions. In years without drought, sudden bursts of rainfall frequently caused flooding and landslides.[56] Yet precisely in this harsh and unforgiving clime, modernizing officers now attempted to control banditry, build an outpost, and farm corn, soybeans, wheat, millet, sorghum, and buckwheat.[57] The official report on the reclamation zone reiterated the ethnic policy of the GMD, which viewed China as a multiethnic nation made up of Han, Manchu, Hui, Mongolian, and Tibetan peoples. The geopolitical reasons for the settlement effort trumped the idealistic goals of bringing economic security and development to the frontiers and the more implausible proffer of aid to Mongolians in the region.[58] In order to ensure the military goals of occupation, survey teams for the settlement district prioritized points of military importance: transportation hubs, roads, and existing villages.[59]

Pressed on one side by the Soviet Union and the suspicion that Soviet machination lay behind calls for Mongolian independence and on the other side by the continued expansion of Japanese military presence in Manchuria, the reclamation troops turned to a neo-traditional term, *tunken,* with its historical and imperial connotations of frontier pacification and added touches of science and modernity. According to those spearheading the reclamation effort, the Mongolians enjoyed a glorious past but, by following a nomadic lifestyle, had fallen behind not only the Han peoples but also the rest of the world. Instead of making steady progress towards civilization and adopting the accoutrements of the modern world, Mongolians, at least according to ethnic Han officers, stubbornly clung to their traditional nomadic lifestyles. As a result, these officers argued, the Mongolians remained mired in backwardness in agriculture, public health, and education.[60] In contrast, the Xing An Tunken Bureau claimed to serve as the vanguard of a technological modernity on the frontiers. The bureau immediately went about overseeing the building of a wireless radio station, long distance telephone connections, and extending tracts of road to connect remote reclamation outposts to the nearest towns.[61] The Chinese officers equated civilization and scientific progress with the newest technologies of communication, including a rapturous belief in the possibilities presented by the shortwave radio.[62] In this fascination with technology, Chinese officers shared the views of their Japanese counterparts.[63]

Following the example of social scientists, the Xing An Tunken Bureau issued hundreds of pages of reports detailing the progress of colonization, none of which made any mention of the Mongolian perspective and whether they asked for "aid" from Han Chinese troops. These reports, of course, also served another purpose as a form of propaganda. From a practical standpoint, sending out hundreds of men to the area right before the onset of severe winter weather made no sense; neither did the conveyance of a printing press to an agricultural settlement before the arrival of farming tools. The American scholar and Inner Asian specialist Owen Lattimore traveled to Xing An during an extended trip in 1929–1930 and painted a considerably different picture, writing that, "This colonization was brutally carried out: the Mongols were evicted at the point of a bayonet and Chinese colonists planted on their land. If any Mongols resisted, they were dealt with as 'bandits.'"[64] In effect, Chinese settlers carried out on the Mongolians the same process that Japanese colonists enacted on Chinese populations in the Northeast.

The Japanese adapted their colonialism from previous examples in the United States of the removal and decimation of indigenous populations. In each case—White pioneers in the US, Japanese colonists in Hokkaido and subsequently the Asian mainland, and Chinese military officers taking part in frontier reclamation—the incoming settlers portrayed themselves as bringing agricultural productivity and realizing the potential of lands the indigenous populations wasted. From the mid-nineteenth century German writers compared Poles to American Indians and made the case for German settlers to create order out of the "wilderness" on the eastern borderlands. The similarity of the language used by bureaucrats overseeing frontier settlement resulted from an international infrastructure of knowledge created by the rise of the social sciences. This intellectual network undergirded the physical infrastructure, from roads to irrigation projects and dams, that reformers around the world, from both the left and right end of the political spectrum, advocated for in the mid-twentieth century. It is emblematic of the uniquely public and modern nature of the project that the military officers in charge of the reclamation effort went about establishing the zone as one might roll out a public relations event. Before a single crop was harvested, any roadways laid, or mines opened, the Reclamation Bureau had publicized their efforts in national newspapers. They kept a photographic record of the progress on the frontiers and a printing press for their reports and Zou's speech to his troops. As a counterimperialism effort against the Japanese, the battle was fought in the press for the benefit of the Chinese public.

Three units of men left for the military colony in late October of 1928, missing the entire growing season. Upon arrival they had to immediately begin to construct housing by digging holes in the ground (also known as "ground nests" or *diwou*) to endure the harsh winter on the steppes.[65] Once they arrived in the zone, the soldiers were told to rise at 5 a.m. every day for a morning jog. During the day they dug out ground dwellings. The real work of settlement began with the coming of the spring. At that time, approximately 4,800 refugees, including women, children, and the elderly from Shandong and Henan, joined the troops in the settlement zone.

Beginning in 1927, a severe famine in North China had forced millions from their land, and some of the refugees now arrived on the Xing An frontier.[66] Despite its geopolitical importance at the juncture between Soviet and Japanese claims, Xing An lay outside infrastructure networks connecting the region to larger populations centers and the interior provinces of China. The successful development of the region required enormous capital and resource investments at a time when growing Japanese

整 裝 待 向 興 安 區 進 發 之 屯 墾 軍

FIGURE 5.2: Officers before their departure for the Xing An Tunken zone and their encampment en route. *Xing An Qu Tunken Jun di er tuan gong zuo bao gao shu* (Xing An Tunken Ju, 1928), 1.

encroachment in the Northeast made large scale infrastructural projects nearly impossible to fund. A few tractors made for good photo opportunities but did not essentially alter the balance between an unrelenting environment and the ill-coordinated efforts of a few military units and several thousand refugees. Yet, for those who spearheaded the Xing An Resettlement Zone, the photo opportunities may have been enough. In publicizing their efforts, their audience was the Japanese military as much as the Chinese public.

For Japanese officers in the Kwantung Army, Zhang Zuolin's assassination did not lead to the desired outcome, but the situation in Manchuria did not diffuse with Chinese appeasement. In 1931, another instigation, the Mukden Incident, would lead to the formation of the Japanese puppet state of Manchukuo. The Xing An Land Reclamation Bureau was not wrong about the importance of the region nor about the Japanese interest. Within a year of the publication of the first Xing An Tunken Report, the research section of the Japanese-run South Manchurian Railroad had translated the report, minus the political rhetoric of Chinese nationalism but including two maps, including a rough geological survey of the region, which needed no translation.[67]

In the Northwest a similar development project unfolded. The Suiyuan region in the Northwest bordering Shanxi province and Mongolia underwent waves of development and settlement schemes from the late nineteenth century. Both the Qing and the subsequent Republican government attempted to develop agriculture in the arid Suiyuan region by constructing irrigation networks.[68] Nevertheless, in the 1930s, the region was still widely known as an impoverished backwater, although it became a fashionable cause for academics, social scientists, and politicians promoting border security and economic development of the frontiers.[69] Chinese quasi-academic / political societies promoting the settlement and development of the Northwest proliferated, as did publications with titles like *New Northwest* (*Xin Xibei*), *Developing the Northwest* (*Xibei Kaifa*), and *Northwest Monthly* (*Xibei Yuekan*). Various colonization schemes inevitably focused on the need to develop the region's mineral resources and touted the availability of free land, rich potential natural resources, and unlimited possibilities for the enterprising settler.

The Northwest Society, based in Xi'an Zhongshan University, published one of the multiple magazines entitled *New Northwest* (*Xin Xibei*).

In the inaugural 1929 issue, multiple congratulatory prefaces praised the Northwest as the birthplace of Chinese civilization.[70] According to the various authors, despite the early flourishing of Chinese civilization, by the twentieth century the Northwest had fallen far behind the coastal regions in economic and material development. Various environmental constraints in the region hardly deterred these champions of frontier development. Writer after writer pointed to the vastness of the land in the Northwest and the wealth of natural resources, including coal, oil, and precious metals, along with a sparse population.

The Malthusian expansionism that became one of the key underpinnings of the Japanese Empire similarly motivated Chinese intellectuals and propagandists of inner colonization. Indeed, one Yang Lisan wrote that the region could solve China's population problem and described a three-phase plan to encourage the westward migration of Han Chinese from the surrounding overpopulated provinces, starting with the establishment of tourism bureaus and exploratory missions.[71] These proposals all entirely overlooked the inconvenient presence of peoples already living in these frontier areas and the environmental conditions of an arid zone ill-suited to large-scale agriculture without the construction of extensive irrigation networks. The German historian Robert Nelson describes this paradox this way, "The realization that land was both empty and full at the same time, empty for colonizers, but full of 'problem' populations, was at the heart of inner colonization."[72] In fact, by the 1920s the influx of Han settlers led to fears that the growing flood of Han Chinese migrants could further provoke Mongolian resistance and calls for independence.[73]

In a publication by the Society for the Study of the Northwest in 1932, National Tongji University director of education and Nationalist (GMD) party cadre Guo Weiping made clear that the call to develop the Northwest was the direct result of imperialist encroachment on the Northeast, which left only the far west open for development.[74] He argued that the Northwest, which he broadly defined as including Shanxi, Gansu, Ningxia, Qinghai, Xinjiang, and Mongolia, contained the greatest resources in the country, including coal and oil. Guo called for greater control over the Northwest to bolster border defenses and protect the country from the imperialist threat from both the Soviet Union and Great Britain. In Suiyuan, local notables and modernizers from neighboring Shanxi began compiling a local gazetteer in 1931 to document the history and development of the region. A first draft of the gazetteer was completed in 1937, just in time for the Japanese invasion.[75] Chinese ideas about building mineral industries on the frontiers responded to both perceived and real threats of foreign encroachment.

Interest in agricultural knowledge and development schemes that promoted land reclamation bridged the various political regimes from the Qing dynasty to the communist regime that triumphed in 1949. Agricultural experimental zones were one of the first innovations adopted by late Qing reformers—in fact, officials didn't necessarily recognize these as a foreign import, given the wide circulation of agricultural texts among the literati of previous periods and the generally acknowledged importance of agriculture as the central pillar of statecraft. In this sense, agricultural science was an ideal gateway science, because cultural conservatives and modernizers alike agreed on the importance of agriculture for a predominantly agrarian society. The adoption of cash crops like cotton in the Northwest integrated China into a global commodities market and in one measure signaled the advance of capitalism into the interior and frontier regions of China.

The term *warlord* conjures up images of semiliterate men wielding power through force and violence. While some early twentieth-century Chinese warlords fit this stereotype, others, including Yan Xishan and Zhang Xueliang, viewed themselves as modernizers and saviors of a nation in turmoil. The warlords were a colorful bunch. Zhang Xueliang had been a playboy and drug addict before his father's 1928 assassination by Japanese officers unceremoniously thrust him into a position of power and responsibility. The northwestern warlord Feng Yuxiang was also known as the Christian general and trained his men to sing hymns, which endeared him to the Americans. The warlord of Shandong province, Zhang Zongchang's claim to internationalism was his large harem of women of all nationalities—Chinese, Japanese, Korean, Russian, and one American—whom he hauled around the country to battles in two personalized luxury train cars. Zhang was pilloried in the press as the "three not knowns:" no one knew how much money he had accumulated, how many soldiers he controlled, or how many concubines he had.

These sorts of salacious depictions in the popular press belied the cosmopolitan backgrounds of many military men in the early twentieth century. A number had attended Japanese military academies, including Yan. Upon establishing authority over Shanxi province in 1917, Yan

Xishan had progressively launched a series of reforms and industrializing plans.[76] In the 1920s, he launched the Society for the Promotion of Forestation, established a Bureau of Water Control, and aimed to transform Shanxi's agricultural products from cereal grains to cotton aimed at a world market.[77] Yan had great ambitions and showcased them in the rebuilding of Taiyuan, the capital of his base of power in Shanxi province, including an airstrip that in the years since has turned into the broad and straight main drag, Yingze Road, running through the city today.

What paid for many of these schemes was Yan's control over the province's mineral resources and railway network. To establish a monopoly over coal mines in the region, Yan used a full range of unsavory practices, including cutting off the rail connection to his competition and essentially kidnapping rival mine owners by inviting them to "meetings" in the provincial capital Taiyuan. At the same time, Yan created the conditions in his power base for scientists and social scientists to draw up ambitious plans for the development of Shanxi and bordering frontier areas.[78] He also regularly invited leading intellectuals for extended visits to Shanxi, although given his reputation, at least some had second thoughts about accepting his offers.

Yan's modernization efforts drew inspiration from Chinese historical precedents as well as from frontier and borderland development proposals from around the world. Ideas traveled through the international professional networks laid by disciplines like geography, agricultural science, and economics. In 1932, Yan Xishan launched one of the most ambitious (on paper, at least) *tunken* plans in China in the Suiyuan region.[79] For the next five years, until the full-out Japanese invasion of the Chinese mainland in 1937, Yan invested resources and manpower to create a new rural modernity in the Northwest.[80] Despite his ideological differences from reformers like James Yen and Liang Shuming, Yan's *tunken* plans in Suiyuan joined the ranks of the rural reconstruction efforts taking place around China. Yan claimed that 4,000 acres in western Suiyuan had been brought under cultivation under the leadership of ex-soldiers and retired army officers.[81] Detailed reports of the *tunken* efforts stated that the establishment of the settlement zone was a means to counter growing international turmoil, which led to widespread rural impoverishment. For these reasons of "jiuguo" or saving the nation, Yan recruited experts to form committees on transportation and hydraulic engineering to develop the Suiyuan region. As the troops in Xing An had quickly realized, the long-term economic development of a region required major infrastructural improvements.

In the semiarid climate of the Suiyuan region, agricultural development necessitated the construction of extensive irrigation and water control networks. Yan designated the Suiyuan settlements as "New Villages" and recruited engineering and survey expertise to the region. In turn, these engineers and experts delineated a long-term development plan, broken into multiple stages, like Soviet central-state planning of settlements in Central Asia and Siberia. The Suiyuan land reclamation zone spatially integrated agricultural and industrial production. The use of the latest technological expertise and scientific planning placed Suiyuan in line with model frontier settlements from around the world.[82]

Carefully laid plans mapped out uniform, gridded village space, with provisions for hospital and recreational facilities, schools and factories, all surrounded by wide, straight streets.[83] Detailed regulations guided the lives of inhabitants. Smoking of opium was strictly forbidden; efforts would be made to improve the drinking water, to rid the area of mosquitos, build bathing facilities, and garbage and sewage disposal; and in an effort to elevate cultural content, also to establish a wireless radio station, music and martial arts clubs, and schools (not only for children but also continuing education for adults).[84] A weather station was outfitted with the latest models of instruments, including barometers and thermometers imported from Germany.[85] In addition, each town also made space for an agricultural experimental area and a livestock husbandry laboratory. The New Villages would integrate military and civilian lives and bring science to the people. Agricultural experimental stations tested various varieties of seeds and used these experimental plots to work on methods to prevent blight and other plant diseases.[86]

According to the report writers, from the nineteenth century, the Chinese countryside suffered disproportionately from the country's incorporation into the global commodities markets and its turbulent ups and downs.[87] By the 1930s, the Nanjing regime had recognized the seriousness of the problem. Yan from his fiefdom in Shanxi also tried to address these issues of rural impoverishment even as he tried to forcibly convert peasants in his province to cash crops such as cotton. Seen in this context, the New Village plan in Suiyuan was envisioned to deploy the latest science and technology to improve rural life without enacting

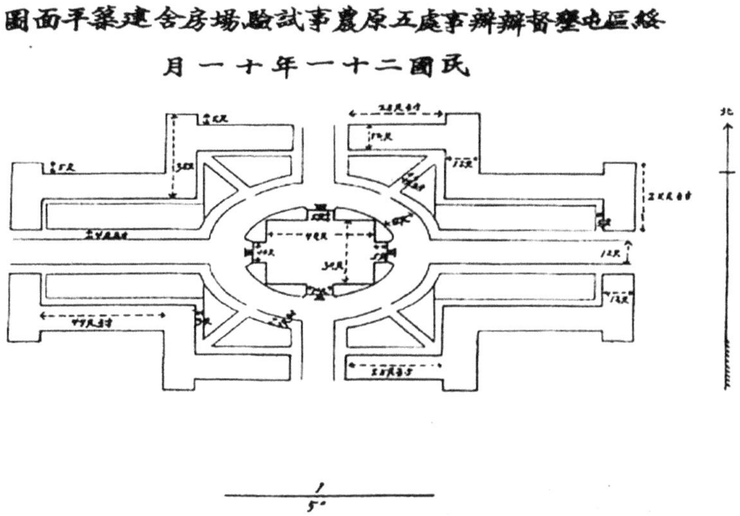

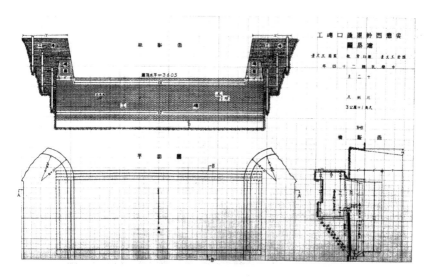

綏屯墾督辦辦事處五原農事試驗場房舍建築平面圖
民國二十一年十一月

FIGURE 5.3: Plans for a livestock husbandry laboratory in the Suiyuan tunken zone. *Sui qu tunken di er nian gong zuo bao* (1933), 215.

FIGURE 5.4: Plans for irrigation networks in the Suiyuan tunken zone. *Sui qu tunken di si nian gong zuo bao* (1935), 191.

the land reform that was anathema to the staunchly anti-Communist political right.[88]

Planners believed the careful design of the New Village would reduce the death rate, and improve food, living conditions, and hygiene.[89] No expense was spared to bring in personnel and equipment to help with the construction of new agricultural experimental stations.[90] The Wuyuan experimental station, for example, planted twenty *mu* of land (1 *mu* = 0.165 acres) with varieties of grass, including Kentucky Blue grass, to see which would be most appropriate for grazing.[91] Other farms experimented with varieties of corn, sheep, and fowl in the region.[92] Experimental farms across the Suiyuan region set up controlled fields of corn, oats, peas, soybeans, winter wheat, rice, and peanuts.[93]

Yan's son-in-law, Wang Jingguo, explicitly connected *tunken* to the glories of China's imperial past and positioned *tunken* as an essential part of establishing a modern nation.[94] He argued that although China's entry into the modern world order and global commodities markets had bankrupted its countryside, science and technology would provide the salvation. Over the course of four years from 1932 to 1936, fifteen New Villages were constructed in the *tunken* zone.[95] As with previous efforts, ambitious plans encountered various natural and man-made obstacles, from drought and flooding to invasive pests. To counter these problems, the Suiyuan *Tunken* Bureau deployed the tools of social science and technology, using charts, statistics, and visual representation to conquer the natural environment. The statistical analysis extended to the selection of saplings in forestation efforts.[96] The latest scientific methods did not forestall natural disasters, including flooding, early frosts, or insects.[97] They did, however, allow for the collection of raw data invaluable to scientists and social scientists. The agricultural experimental stations collaborated with Beiping University Agricultural Institute to analyze the chemical composition of beets.[98] Long-term goals for the *tunken* zone included the improvement of local varieties of livestock and crops through improved education of farmers, better equipment, more extensive use of fertilizers, and scientific weeding practices.[99]

Yan's promotion of science and technology and agricultural reform was by no means an isolated instance during the Republican period; rural reform enjoyed broad support across the political spectrum. In 1933, reformers in Shanxi founded a journal named *New Village Life* (*Xin nongcun*), which addressed issues such as rural education, educational

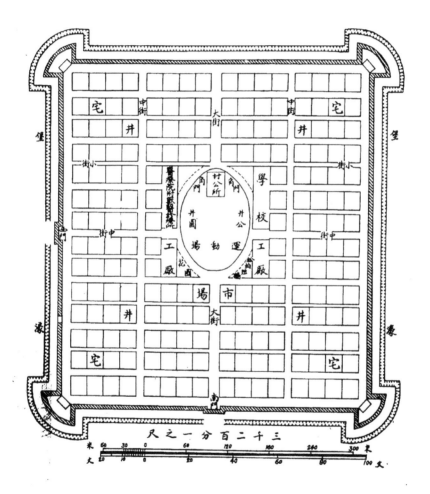

FIGURE 5.5: One of the New Villages designed for the Suiyuan tunken zone. *Sui qu tunken di yi nian gong zuo bao gao shu* (1932), 235.

development in the American countryside, and agriculture in the Soviet Five-Year Plan.[100] Another journal with the same name came out the same year from Zhejiang province; yet a third *New Village Life*, affiliated with Communist Party efforts to train cadres on rural reforms, started publication in 1949 from Shenyang in the Northeast. These efforts to reimagine rural development came from different and sometimes opposing ideological perspectives. In practical terms, however, they advocated some of the same methods of rural reconstruction, including grassroots outreach to promote new scientific farming methods and crops.

———

In the interwar years American philanthropic groups such as the Rockefeller Foundation promoted building an international infrastructure for the social and natural sciences. They achieved notable successes in targeted programs around the world but miscalculated the potential for science to bring about democratization. Instead, ideas about frontier development displayed remarkable ideological flexibility, adopted and adapted in the Japanese Empire, as well as the Chinese Nationalist regime, by the communist forces, as well as staunchly conservative military leaders. Under the patronage of regional warlords like Yan Xishan and Feng Yuxiang and bureaucrats in the Nanjing government, the frontier became identified not only as an experimental space for the latest innovations in technology, agricultural science, and social management, but also as a fashionable marker of one's patriotism. China was not unique. Supporters of inner colonization in Germany leaned right but the political affiliations of the social scientists whose work contributed to the discourse ran the gamut. In the United States, New Dealers, including Vice President Henry Wallace, were often sympathetic to agricultural reforms overseas developed by Socialist governments. Countries around the world raced to embrace geo-modernity, both as part of rural revitalization efforts to counter the global swings of commodities markets and the expansion of capitalism and as a measure of national defense.

The outbreak of World War II interrupted these efforts at rural reconstruction in China but also gave lie to the notion that science alone could save the nation. For the better part of three decades Yan Xishan astutely navigated between rival warlords, the GMD, and the Japanese without committing to any single ideology except for anti-Communism and self-preservation. At the same time, he oversaw one of the most aggressive modernization efforts in the country. When the Japanese army rolled over Shanxi in 1937, they continued Yan's industrial push and invested a further $62.5 million to develop coal mines in the province.[101] Yan, however, finally had to make a choice—and he picked the side of the Nationalists. His political duplicity made him an untrustworthy partner to Chiang Kai-shek. In exile in Taiwan after 1949, Yan lived out the rest of his years under house arrest. As Japanese tanks rolled through China in 1937, a new age of Warring States dawned in Asia and proceeded to take over the world.

SIX

The Devil's Handwriting

Alle Gegenwart is ein Folgezustand von dem, was vorher war,
und alle Zukunft is eine Frucht von dem, was heute geschieht.
[The present is the result of what had been, and the future the
fruit of what happens today.]

Paul Rohrbach[1]

During World War I, the German government considered plans to settle
wounded soldiers in the East, where they would gradually recover or
adjust to their injuries. Once returned to productivity, they would reclaim lands where, according to the Germans, the native Polish populations had failed to realize their full potential. A similar plan came to
fruition in southwestern China during World War II. This was no acci-
dental resonance, but rather an illustration of the hidden global intellectual pathways established over the previous decades. The resettlement
efforts across China, Eastern Europe, and other parts of the world took
place in a new age of warring states. Starting in 1937, the Japanese invasion had driven the Nationalist Chinese government on a harrowing retreat to the mountainous Southwest of the country. In the Soviet Union,
the harsh winter of 1941–1942 brought the German advance to a stall
within sight of Moscow. As the siege of Leningrad dragged on, German
victory receded from view. Yet, remarkably, on both the Allied and Axis
sides of the war, planning continued in Berlin and Chongqing for the
remaking of the agrarian order.

For these two regimes on the opposite sides of the war, frontier development plans grew out of unresolved tensions in the transition from
empire to the nation-state, between the nationalism and internationalism underlying the sciences both countries adopted to aid in their efforts
in securing the borderlands. What the German historian Jeffrey Herf
termed *reactionary modernism* to describe the Third Reich's avid enthusiasm for modern technology along with the rejection of Enlightenment
values, in the Chinese case entailed the dubious revision of history to
justify the absorption of Qing imperial territorial into a Han-dominated
nation-state.[2] German and Chinese efforts drew inspiration from prewar
inner colonization movements discussed in previous chapters. In both
cases, the academic apparatus of science and the social sciences, including geography and agricultural science, geared towards supporting the
aims of their respective regimes.

The various examples discussed in this chapter showcase the global
nature of geo-modernity. Despite this convergence between Germany
and China, the individual fates of the scientists and social scientists involved in the war effort diverged widely in the postwar period: some
faced war crimes tribunals or were persecuted during political campaigns in the 1950s while others continued to build illustrious careers.

Inner Colonization without Borders

At the turn of the twentieth century, German-speaking social scientists
and agronomists began to formalize their knowledge about the administration of empire into something resembling a scholarly discipline. Starting in 1908, the Prussian journal *Archives of Inner Colonization* (*Archiv
für Innere Kolonisation*) brought together the professional and academic
advocates of empire. A related Society for the Advancement of Inner Colonization (Gesellschaft zur Förderung der inneren Kolonisation or GFK)
formed in 1912. Unlike the American geographers at the *National Geographic*, the publishers of the *Archives* made no effort to appeal to the
broader public. Instead, in hundreds of dense pages per issue, the journal
published analysis, mostly by academics and bureaucrats, on land usage
and the progress of settlement efforts around the world. Some issues
printed lengthy settlement regulations verbatim.

Backed by the science of settlement, inner colonization advocates promoted policies that would increase ethnic German populations in East-

ern Europe through targeted loan programs and tax deductions. Despite
the Prussian state's considerable expenditure of funds, the inner colonization plan was never very successful because the idea failed to appeal to
an urbanizing German population, particularly young women, who rejected the idea of returning to an agrarian life in new settlements in the
East. Over the course of four decades, considerable financial incentives
and tax breaks netted only 400,000 settlers, compared to the millions of
Germans who voluntarily headed to North and South America.[3]

Nevertheless, inner colonization plans drew considerable political
interest. During World War I, in 1916, the *Archives of Inner Colonization* published a piece on "Inner Colonization and Soldier Homes," detailing plans to settle invalided veterans in the East, where they would
find plentiful "free" land while securing the borderlands.[4] Chancellor
Bethmann-Hollweg contacted several experts on Eastern Europe associated with the journal and the inner colonization society to solicit their
ideas about the creation of a *Grenzstreifen,* or "frontier strip," cleansed
of undesirable populations and ready to be filled with ethnic Germans.
German defeat put those plans on indefinite pause; but the ideas that
would later take on the mantle of geopolitics were already being floated—
that frontiers could be emptied of indigenous populations and refilled
with settlers, who would also serve as humans buffers essential for national defense.

The Versailles Peace Treaty gave life to a right-wing resurgence in
Germany in the interwar period. Despite the fact that Germany had lost
all its overseas territories, the German Colonial Association, led by two
former governors of German East and West Africa, Heinrich Schnee and
Theodor Seitz respectively, continued to enjoy a robust membership of
30,000 and the support of the German Foreign Ministry. Both the Colonial Association and the Foreign Ministry lobbied for the rights of
German settlers and angled for Germany's return to the League of Nation's Permanent Mandate Commission. Throughout the Weimar period,
the colonial movement staged exhibits, lectures, and wrote articles for
the press to make their case for the German people that the colonies had
been unjustly stolen from them.

In making the case for the importance of empire, both the inner and
overseas colonization advocates availed themselves of academics and
the international infrastructure of knowledge. German political scientists, for example, eagerly participated in the biannual conferences of the

League of Nations Institute for Intellectual Cooperation, which sought to create a framework for the new field of international relations.[5] From the University of Cologne, the conservative law professor Carl Schmitt articulated a new framework for understanding the transformation of the world order, one which accounted for the United States' ascendance in the global order, based not on the possession of colonies but a hemispheric hegemony over client states.[6] Hjalmar Schacht, later the Nazi Minister of Economics in the 1930s, reoriented the division of the world from empires and colonies into protectionist trade blocs.[7]

As the liberal democratic adherents of the inner colonization movement lost their moorings after the disastrous outcome of World War I, their ideology metastasized during the interwar period in much more explicitly racialized and radical directions. Yet, the simple assignation of political affiliation fails to encompass the complexities and individual variables of the people involved. The agronomist Max Sering's career in academia and in politics stretched well into the 1930s, when he was still actively collaborating with agronomists not only in Germany but also in the United States, Asia, and other parts of the world. Supporters of inner colonization responded in a variety of ways to the National Socialist takeover of Germany. Max Sering remained deeply wary of the National Socialists to his death in 1939. Throughout the 1930s, Sering continued to maintain extensive correspondences with international agronomist associations and kept politics separate from his academic activities. Extensive letter exchanges from 1930 to 1938 document his involvement with the International Conference of Agricultural Economists. Cornell University hosted the organization's conference in August 1930. Plans to host a second conference in Berlin in 1932, however, were delayed by the deteriorating economic and political situation in Germany. Among those in attendance at the eventual meeting in 1933 were the Japanese agronomist Shiroshi Nasu from the Department of Agriculture at Tokyo Imperial University and C. C. Chang from the University of Nanking School of Agriculture.[8]

Many of his fellow advocates of inner colonization did not share Sering's reluctance to embrace the extreme right and viewed the National Socialist regime as offering an opportunity to restore Germany to its rightful place amongst imperial powers. One of the founders of the *Archives,* Heinrich Sohnrey, immediately embraced National Socialism and joined the party. For some inner and overseas colonial advocates, the initial excitement over the National Socialists' rise quickly faded as they discovered, to their chagrin, that the Nazis had their own agenda. Heinrich Schnee, having led the charge for years for the restoration of German imperial territories, cast his lot with the Nazis in 1932. Once in power, though, the Nazis forced Schnee out of the leadership. The Nazis established their own Colonial Bureau, led by Ritter von Epp, former Freikorps leader and veteran of the German suppression of the Herero Rebellion.[9]

The colonial advocates argued that Germany's economic future depended on the restoration of its former colonies. Even before World War I, American economic rise had caused considerable anxiety to Europeans, particularly the Germans, who feared missing out on the benefits of possessing an empire and an associated economic bloc.[10] Over the course of the 1930s, as a global economic depression pushed governments worldwide into protectionist policies, Germany's former political enemies grew more sympathetic to these arguments. Like the Japanese and the Italians, the Germans' loss of their colonies forced them into the cohort of "have-nots" of world powers. Many of the colonial advocates believed that the National Socialists would be the vehicle for this restoration. Yet, for all the sound and fury of the colonial movement in the Weimar period, these self-proclaimed experts on empire merely fooled themselves (and the British) into believing their indispensability. From 1936 to 1938, the British, led by Austen Chamberlain, came around to bargaining for German reconciliation with the international order by proffering the possible return of its African holdings in Togo and Cameroon.[11] But Hitler was never interested in Africa. He looked instead to the East.

World War II–era Nazi plans to settle ethnic Germans in Ukraine and other parts of occupied Eastern Europe clearly fed on ideology and infrastructure put in place by these earlier movements. In the winter of 1942, as the fearsome German Wehrmacht advanced east, planning had already begun in Berlin to create a settlement zone for 15 to 20 million ethnic Germans in the allegedly free and open lands of Eastern Europe and the Soviet Union. The remaking of Eastern Europe would be a massive undertaking that would entail the creation of a new agrarian order. Long before the German military occupied these territories and created an opportunity for social scientists to realize their visions of development, domestic institutions and think tanks such the Deutsches Ausland

Institut (German Overseas Institute) in Stuttgart published studies on ethnic Germans in the Soviet Union and the fate of German farmers in the East.[12] The rapid advance of German troops in the fall of 1941 brought a new optimism and urgency to the planning. At this turning point of European history, Reich ministers approached resettlement plans from the perspective of transport, economic development, and settlement.[13] They also had to account for the social scientific problem of rural reconstruction. At stake was the reputation of the Reich, which had prioritized the settlement of ethnic Germans.

From the field in Ukraine, the agronomist Dr. Hans Rempel reported on the rural issues of German settlement in December 1942.[14] He provided a case study of the village of Marienburg (Orloff), originally settled by German Mennonites at the invitation of Catherine the Great in the eighteenth century. In 1942, the village had 132 families, with 143 males over the age of 15. The village encompassed 1,700 hectares of farmland and 300 hectares of pasturelands grazed and worked by 135 horses, 150 cows, an assortment of ploughs, and 30 wagons. According to the study, the German village differed from surrounding Ukrainian villages in that it featured broad, straight streets, stone fencing, and sturdier housing. As settlement progressed, Rempel provided further studies on the progress of development.[15] In 1942 and 1943, as the German army invaded Russia, letters between experts and the SS (the paramilitary organization Schutzstaffel) once again discussed practical and theoretical details regarding the settlement of ethnic Germans in the region.[16] From Ukraine, in October 1942, as the siege of Stalingrad continued and the German offensive stalled against heavy Russian resistance, the question that preoccupied Berlin bureaucrat Dr. Metzer was the shortage of good cement and lumber that would be needed to build a reservoir dam in the region. Perhaps, he speculated, cement could be made in Croatia and then transported on the Danube and other waterways. As he worked to resolve the transport of construction materials, a more pressing issue loomed—6,000 ethnic Germans were ready and awaiting transport to the newly occupied territories. Even as the war effort on the Eastern Front floundered, the settlement of ethnic Germans enjoyed precedence over the transport of war material and soldiers.

These settlement plans drew on expertise developed by social scientists affiliated with the field of *Ostforschung*, the study of Eastern Europe. *Ostforschung* grew out of the politicization of agricultural studies in the 1920s, having roots in Wilhelmine-era reclamation efforts in which agronomists like Max Sering and his teacher, the economist Gustav Schmoller, played key roles.[17] In the intervening years, as agrarian policy in Germany shifted steadily right, it continued to draw on the same underlying ideas about the development of the borderlands. In the drive to design settlement and economic development in the East, social scientists took charge. Agronomists, anthropologists, statisticians, and population experts all provided their expertise in the SS planning for the reordering of Europe.[18] Some well-known figures aided in the construction of this new order, but for the most part, its architects were technically skilled cogs in the bureaucratic machinery of empire.

The social scientists of empire participated in international networks at the same time that they eagerly contributed to German nationalism. Sebastian Conrad described these disciplines so essential to the project of modernization as part of a "colonial globality." They were, he has argued, modern forms of knowledge that served "not just [as] an instrument and a weapon but, at a more fundamental level, themselves the product of a context that had been shaped by the colonial order."[19] As part of these global interactions, the geographer Ferdinand von Richthofen traveled in China in the 1860s and 1870s and brought to Asia new ideas about mineral resources and industrialization. Robert Koch conducted experiments in East Africa in 1906 that were only possible in the colonies. Prussian military advisors like Otto Liman von Sanders made their services available to the Ottoman Empire; Jacob Meckel advised the Japanese on the restructuring of their army; and Karl Haushofer built his career starting from a brief stint as a military observer in Japan. These men (women participated in the larger migration movements, albeit in smaller numbers relative to the men; the much smaller group of academic and military consultants, however, was composed entirely of men) helped the global circulation of certain ideas, even when politically they were marginal.

The Nazi Party's rise to power in 1933 brought to the fore the political undercurrents of geography and agricultural science. Prominent members of the scientific community faced a choice about whether to embrace the new regime. Erwin Baur, the leading German geneticist and director of Kaiser Wilhelm Institute for Breeding Research, personally loathed Richard Darre, the Reich Minister of Food and Agriculture and ideologue of the "blood and soil" movement. Despite this personal antipathy, Baur was interested in National Socialist agrarian policy and visited party headquarters to learn more about them. Nor did personal conflicts affect the new regime's recognition of the importance of the plant sciences. After Baur's death from a heart attack in 1933, the new regime continued to support research at the institute. Like Baur, many fellow scientists at the research institute were interested in National Socialist agrarian policy and joined the party in the early 1930s.[20] As Jewish scientists and academics were forced out from their positions, the German academy increasingly reflected the political orientation of the party in charge. The universal and borderless ideals of science encountered the harsh reality of partisan nationalism.

The geographer Walter Christaller's career encapsulated the complex nature of the relationship between the state and the social sciences. In 1932, Walter Christaller (1893–1969), at the time a member of the Social Democratic Party (SPD), defended his dissertation in geography at the University of Erlangen. Published a year later, *Central Places in Southern Germany* (*Die zentralen Orte in Süddeutschland*) became Christaller's most famous work.[21] In the book he first proposed central place theory as the spatial organization underpinning rural development by illustrating how certain "central places," such as villages, towns, or cities, control a market area determined by population density and purchasing power. When the Nazi Party first ascended to power, a key office the party established in 1935 and figuratively headed by Hitler himself was the Reich's Office for Spatial Planning, encompassing the centralization of all planning and research on the spatial reorganization of a new German Empire. Despite his previous affiliation with the social democrats, Christaller would join the National Socialist Party and work in Himmler's Planning and Soil Office as part of *Generalplan Ost.*[22] At the end of the war, in 1945 Christaller joined the German Communist Party (KPD), before returning once again to the Social Democratic Party in 1959. Christaller became one of the most prominent geographers in postwar West Germany.

During the Nuremberg Trials, Christaller's boss at the Planning and Soil Office, the renowned agronomist Konrad Meyer, cited the fact that he had hired left-leaning researchers like Christaller as part of his defense. Meyer argued that, as a scientist and agriculture expert, he was only a part-time worker in the regime. He had, after all, retained his professorship at the University of Berlin. Most importantly, Meyer emphasized that the planning done by his office was never carried out. In issuing a not guilty verdict, the International Military Tribunal acknowledged Meyer's international reputation as an agronomist and found that there was "no proof" to support the idea that any of the horrific activities conducted by German officials and troops in the East had their origin in Meyer's planning.[23] Of all the charges he faced, Meyer was found guilty only of being a member of the SS, which the tribunal categorized as a criminal organization. After his acquittal, Meyer finished a distinguished career in Hannover.

In the postwar years, central place theory gained broad acceptance in both geographical and historical analysis. In 1964, the Sinologist G. William Skinner published a landmark series of articles in the *Journal of Asian Studies* on the marketing and social structure of rural China, based on his fieldwork in the 1940s.[24] The essay became the basis of his later advocacy for a spatial understanding of China, which he detailed in his 1984 presidential address to the Association of Asian Studies.[25] In the introductory pages of his 1964 essay, there's a reference to a German geographer Walter Christaller. Today, central place theory explains the rise of Chicago as much as the spatial organization of rural China and Bavaria.

The postwar careers of both Meyer and Christaller stand in stark contrast to that of the man most identified with German geopolitics, Karl Haushofer. Following his testimony at the Nuremburg Trials, Haushofer committed suicide in March 1946. At age seventy-seven, Haushofer died heartbroken over the death of his eldest son in the last days of the war and the discrediting of his life's work. He had suffered a stroke shortly before his death. In a letter to an American professor, riven with typing mistakes, he revealed his wife's despondency over the death of their son. She had long helped him with typing, he wrote, but was now sunk in depression. His son Albrecht, also a geographer, had been imprisoned for his involvement with a plot to overthrow Hitler in 1944. Albrecht was executed by the Gestapo on April 23, 1945, as the Allied troops were closing in on Berlin. In the period after his imprisonment, Karl desperately attempted to use his professional networks to help his son. He wrote a letter to the Führer which was never delivered, and to his old friends at the Japanese embassy, pleading for any aid possible.[26] These desperate letters underscore the extent of Haushofer's powerlessness. And now that the Americans had arrived, they ransacked his house and confiscated all his issues of the *Journal for Geopolitics* as well as Albrecht's writings.

In Haushofer's last publication, he argued that the Nazis had distorted geopolitics to suit their own agenda. If intended as a strategy to preserve his historical legacy, the publication proved moderately successful. Already by 1947, when the German geographer Carl Troll first published his apologia and critique of German geography, the general opinion of Karl Haushofer had begun to change from that of a Nazi mastermind to that of a genial man with questionable scientific credentials whose ideas were used by the Nazis for their own purposes. In his essay, Troll devoted an entire section to the development of geopolitics and Karl Haushofer's role, concluding that Haushofer "was, to be sure, neither a genuine scholar nor in the proper sense a professor of scholarship; he was, however, a personality of distinguished education and capability, who in another position could have accomplished something better."[27] At the same time, Troll invoked the glories of German geography in the past and the contribution of geographers outside the circle of geopolitics to the field. It was an introspective account born out of the "consummation of the general German catastrophe," but also a remarkably blinkered view of the relationship between the discipline of geography and state agenda.[28]

From the Baltics to Africa

The career of the colonial propagandist Paul Rohrbach is yet another example of the ways that global networks of science and the social sciences aided in perpetuating public interest in empire. Paul Rohrbach was born on June 29, 1869, in Irgen, Livland (what is today Latvia) to an ethnic German family that had first immigrated to the Baltics in 1764.[29] In 1890, Rohrbach traveled to Berlin to continue his study of medieval history. The occasion was a momentous one for him; as the train rolled over the German border, he felt a sense of belonging and the "most intense emotions of his life up to that point: now [he] was in Germany, the spiritual home of us of Balts!"[30] In addition to studying medieval history, Rohrbach also found time to attend the geography colloquiums of Ferdinand von Richthofen, the famous explorer of China. Among Richthofen's other accomplishments, he coined the term *Silk Road* to describe the trade connections leading westward from China across Central Asia to Europe.[31] From von Richthofen, Rohrbach learned "to think geographically, not only in the sense of putting together a picture of the landscape geographically but seeing also the interrelation between landscape and history."[32] On his end, Richthofen recognized in Rohrbach the gaze of the natural-born geographer and encouraged Rohrbach in his early expeditions through the Mesopotamia.[33]

Rohrbach's understanding of the connection between history and geography, informed by Richthofen, would remain a key element of his views throughout his life. He subscribed to the view that Germany's historical destiny lay in its geographical location, arguing, "Our destiny lies in our geographical location in the heart of Europe, with open borders against strong nations that achieved national unity long before us and that seek the extension of their political power."[34] This geopolitical approach similarly informed Rohrbach's views on Russia and Eastern Europe. His extensive travels and knowledge of the region separated him from the more radical and extremist polemicists of his time.

With a PhD in hand in 1891, Rohrbach returned to Dorpat, only to find out that, with the onset of Russification campaigns in the 1890s, he could no longer hope for an academic position in the Russian Empire. He returned to Germany to seek his fortunes. Rohrbach's experience reflects a greater trend in the 1890s, when Russification campaigns and narrowing career options led a wave of ethnic Germans to return to the their homeland.[35] For Rohrbach, his forced return to Germany left a bitter taste, marking a key turning point in his thinking. Even before he became a naturalized German citizen, Rohrbach began to publish anti-Russian articles. During World War I, Rohrbach, along with his fellow repatriated German historians Theodor Schiemann and Johannes Haller, would incorporate his background in the Baltic into his policy views on Russia and the annexation of the Baltic provinces. But not all ethnic Germans in the Russian Empire followed Rohrbach's footsteps. His brother was a decorated office in the Russian army who served in the Russo-Japanese War (1905–1906) in Manchuria and in World War I. While Paul Rohrbach lobbied the German government to break apart the Russian Empire, his brother served as a Russian reserve officer in Galicia.[36]

During Rohrbach's Berlin years and thereafter, he located a new mentor in the conservative historian Hans Delbrück. It was Delbrück who first involved Rohrbach in the *Prussian Yearbooks*, where he became its Russia and Eastern Europe expert. Under its aegis, Rohrbach traveled extensively in the outlying regions of the Russian Empire. Rohrbach attended the 1896 All Russian Exhibition in Novgorod to study Russian industry and agriculture. His itinerary took him by train from Tiflis to

Baku, over the Caspian Sea by steamboat, then via the Trans-Caspian rail to Samarkand.[37] These early trips convinced him of the "absolute backwardness of [Russian] agricultural and the general lack of spirituality [*allgemeiner geistiger Unkultur*]."[38] Moreover, these trips allowed him to visualize the far-flung and essentially disparate nature of the Russian Empire, a realization which helped to formulate his later wartime views. It was also Delbrück who advised Rohrbach to take up a colonial appointment in German Southwest Africa. Convinced that the colonial experience would add to his marketable skills, Rohrbach set off for German Southwest Africa in 1903 as a colonial administrator (settlement commissar *Ansiedlungskommissar*).

Rohrbach quickly found himself a firsthand witness to the Herero Rebellion. The Germans arrived to the scramble for Africa late, when the most lucrative lands had already been grabbed by the British and French. German Southwest Africa, established in 1884, covered territory that today is Namibia. In the late nineteenth and early twentieth centuries, German colonial rule featured policies designed to encourage ethnic German settlers while limiting the freedom of movement of Africans in the colony, thereby forcing the men into low-paying wage work. These policies created escalating tensions with the tribes already living on these lands. In 1904, the Herero leader Samuel Maharero declared war against White settlers. The death of a few hundred settlers in the early months of the conflict led the German colonial government to a wholesale genocide against the entire Herero people.[39]

For historians of the rebellion, Rohrbach's book *Difficult Days in Southwest Africa* (*Aus Schweren Tages in Südwestafrika*) provides an important primary document of the uprising and the German response.[40] Although Rohrbach served on a punitive expedition during the uprising, he was critical of the military handling of the matter. To put down the rebellion, Kaiser Wilhelm replaced the civilian leadership in the colony with General Lothar von Trotha, a veteran of the Boxer Rebellion. In 1900, a group of Chinese rebels with strong xenophobic beliefs laid siege to the foreign legation quarters in Beijing. In response, eight countries, including Germany, sent in troops to rescue their besieged citizens. Before their departure for China, on July 27, 1900, the Kaiser infamously exhorted the German expeditionary force to be merciless as Huns in battle. His men did not disappoint. The German forces were particularly brutal in their conduct in China, summarily executing anyone they suspected of aiding the rebels. They terrorized civilian populations and demanded decimated villages pay for statues to commemorate German missionaries killed in the uprising.[41] From China von Trotha took the scorched-earth strategy of counterinsurgency to Africa.

Rohrbach viewed the military campaign as a misstep. He voiced the opinion that "it was a mistake to take the matter from Leutwein's hands and send to the Southwest a general who had experience in China [in the Boxer Rebellion] but did not understand that in a colony such as Southwest Africa it was in no ways useful to 'annihilate' the natives as enemies. It would have been better to collect their livestock animals, keep them alive, and give them as punishment a sharp lecture. Southwest Africa is worth more to us with its natives than without."[42] The statement is more remarkable for its chilling calculation than as a condemnation of the German handling of the matter; it underlines the fact that, for Rohrbach, the economic viability of the colony and its German settlers caused more concern than the fate of the "natives," of whom over 20,000 died of starvation after being driven into the desert. Horrific contemporary photographs showed the skeletal forms of those who survived the desert only to die in large numbers in prison camps run by the German colonial government. To Rohrbach's dismay, large numbers of livestock were left unattended and died during the uprising, making it impossible to bring more German settlers to Southwest Africa.[43]

Further clarification of Rohrbach's views on the fiasco in Southwest Africa comes in his 1934 work *Germany's Colonial Demands* (*Deutschlands koloniale Forderung*). In the book, Rohrbach expounded at length on the "colonial guilt lie" and the "robbery" of German colonies. Rather than defend German actions in Africa, Rohrbach instead pointed to the British conquest and subjugation of India, Belgian brutality in the Congo, and atrocities committed in the French colonial empire.[44] For Rohrbach, the history of White enslavement of Africans served as irrefutable proof of the inherent inferiority of the Black race. Although he by no means advocated their extermination to clear the land for German settlement, as had occurred with indigenous populations in the Americas, neither did he concern himself with their fate above and beyond their impact on the success of German colonization. The historian Isabel Hull has argued that the German military's violent suppression of the Boxer Rebellion in China, the Herero Rebellion in Southwest Africa, and its actions during World War I in Europe were all symptoms of a military culture that valued above all the "logic of technology, science and planning," to the point of excessive violence beyond any possible military or strategic value.[45] As I have shown, however, the "logic of technology, science and planning" was not limited to the German military. In the course of settling the global frontiers, various countries around the world took part in the global and compounding nature of violence against indigenous populations. From the Indian wars to the Japanese puppet state in Manchuria, Germany in Southwest Africa to Belgium in Congo, civilian deaths resulted from the escalating costs of empire. As the frontiers closed and the so-called free lands disappeared, the costs of removal to accommodate new settlers increased until they reached their logical conclusion: a final solution of genocide. Rohrbach observed that the Germans were hardly alone among the colonial powers in conducting violent extermination campaigns against their colonial subjects, and he was not wrong about that.

Following the rebellion, Rohrbach served as a member of the Compensation Committee in the colony (*Entschädigungkommission*). In this role he tirelessly lobbied the Reichstag to provide adequate funding to reimburse the German settlers for their losses in property and livestock during the uprising.[46] While Rohrbach was still in Africa, the philosophy department at Berlin University was approached by government ministries with the proposition of establishing a chair in "colonial management" (*Kolonialwirtschaft*). Rohrbach's mentor, Hans Delbrück, immediately lobbied for Rohrbach to take up the position. Had Delbrück succeeded, Rohrbach would have had the distinction of becoming the first chair of colonial science in Germany. Instead, the firm opposition of the geography chair, Albrecht Penck, sank Rohrbach's chances.[47] Finally accepting that an academic career was not in the stars for him, Rohrbach turned to full-time journalism and writing.

The press welcomed Rohrbach as an expert capable of crafting concise and compelling accounts of far-flung regions of the world. During this period, Rohrbach published accounts of his travels, his experiences in Africa, and discussions of geopolitical issues. In these works, Rohrbach argued that, as Germany entered the first rungs of world powers, she needed colonies to maintain her status. As the German population grew, its territories would prove inadequate to accommodate the needs of its rapidly increasing population.[48] Even if it were possible to annex Austria and the western parts of Russia, this would only alleviate, rather than resolve, the problem of Germany's encirclement by enemy powers. These additional lands would not fundamentally settle problems of food production and trade. To accommodate the increased population, Rohrbach saw overseas expansion as essential. The ultimate goal for Germans, Rohrbach maintained, was to become a people who could create world history in the twentieth century. To become a great power, Germany needed to increase its population and expand its territorial possessions.

Rohrbach reached the pinnacle of his writing career with his 1912 work *German Thought in the World* (*Deutsche Gedanke in der Welt*). The book sold 75,000 copies and was translated into numerous languages, including English. To become a world power of the first rung, Germany needed a sizable population and territorial possessions, whatever the costs to indigenous groups: "We cannot grant that the preservation of some small and insignificant nationality as a political unit is as important for the development of mankind as the growth of those world nations who are the standard bearers of culture."[49] Rohrbach shared the view of many would-be imperialists who viewed empire as providing a necessary infrastructure for economic activities. Foreshadowing ideas in geopolitics, Rohrbach viewed territory in social Darwinian terms. Size mattered, and as a continental power, Germany needed to reinforce its borderlands to achieve world power status. Using the language in vogue at the time among geographers, including American Ellen Semple, Rohrbach wrote, "No strong national existence is possible without a sufficiently broad territorial basis. During the first years of their known history the Germans occupied a much greater part of Europe than they did later."[50] The American frontier, the gridded and endless stretches of flat and fertile land, loomed as the unspoken subtext for Rohrbach's territorial aspirations for Germany.

On the eve of World War I, Rohrbach and his friend Ernst Jäckh started the publication *The Greater Germany* (*Das Grössere Deutschland.*) The publication provided a forum for colonial lobbyists, historians, and intellectuals, including the likes of the historian Friedrich Meinecke, to express their views on the colonial possessions and German war policy. In the publication, Rohrbach not only developed his views on agricultural methods in Africa, but also reiterated the Russian threat and delineated Germany's goals in Weltpolitik. Rohrbach proposed that the only way to handle the Russian threat was to curtail its territory in the East, namely, Finland, and the eastern provinces, Ukraine, the Caucasuses, and Turkestan.[51] *Greater Germany* became a public extension of the "Delbrück evenings," an informal salon of politically minded intellectuals who gathered to discuss current events, amongst whom Rohrbach served as the Russia expert. As the German army marched over Eastern Europe, succeeding beyond anyone's anticipation, for a moment Rohrbach experienced the euphoria of dreams fulfilled. With the signing of the treaty of Brest-Litovsk and German acquisition of a vast stretch of Eastern Europe, Rohrbach gleefully participated in the "fall of a world empire," which "is only comparable to the fall of the Roman empire."[52]

Germany's defeat in the war changed Rohrbach's career trajectory. "As a matter of fact R. died politically with the German Republic," Ernst Jäckh said of his friend Paul Rohrbach.[53] He continued to agitate for colonies to waning public interest and diminishing fame. Instead of big publications in Berlin, Frankfurt, and the other large cities, Rohrbach turned to the smaller provincial presses, which offered the advantage of addressing a nonpartisan, local readership. Rohrbach supported the new republic, but he never relinquished aspirations for German colonial expansion and grew increasingly disillusioned with Weimar policies. Rohrbach started the Weimar years in the German Democratic Party (DDP) before moving right to the German Volks Party (DVP). The parties welcomed his involvement on account of his solid journalistic credentials. He pushed for the establishment of German libraries and cultural propaganda through German films, literature, and exhibitions.

The interwar years may have been a particularly humbling period for Paul Rohrbach, but he remained embedded in international professional networks. In 1925, Rohrbach was offered a position in the German Academy in Munich, a spot previously occupied by the geopolitician Karl Haushofer.[54] It was not the only point of intersection between Rohrbach and Haushofer. German universities had few academic chairs, then as now, and these were highly competitive; instead, many of those with advanced degrees in such fields as geography ended up as members of a highly mobile, globe-trotting contingent of writers and consultants. By his own account, Rohrbach's time at the German Academy was unhappy and beset by political intrigues and frustrations. In the meantime, Rohrbach continued his global travels and made extended trips to South America, North America, and around the world, during which he lectured at numerous stops, including extensively in Japan. His talk on population growth and emigration overseas apparently found a receptive audience in that ascendant colonial power, where, Rohrbach noted, the trains ran on time, like in Germany.[55]

Rohrbach was a rare carry-over in German intellectual and political circles—a man who lived through both world wars and combined interest in Eastern Europe with a lifelong belief in the need for colonies, whose life spanned the Wilhelmine colonial empire and the Hitler continental empire. Rohrbach continued to publish extensively during the interwar years, including a large, handsome volume published in 1926, *Germandom in Need: The Fate of Germans in Europe outside the Reich* (*Deuschtum in Not, die Schicksale der Deutschen in Europa außerhalb des Reiches.*) The four-hundred-odd page book discusses at length ethnic Germans from Austria to the Baltic provinces, Romania, and Russia, and includes 191 plates and black-and-white glossy inserts of photographs, mainly of German-style buildings located throughout Eastern Europe.[56] Rohrbach was certainly not alone in his concern for ethnic Germans, and the phrase he used in the book, "home to the Reich," later became the name of a Nazi resettlement program during World War II.[57]

Although Rohrbach continued to write and publish after the National Socialists came to power, he never supported Hitler and actively campaigned against his election. Traveling through Southwest Africa in 1933 on another one of his extended trips, he considered permanently relocating there. Hitler, for Rohrbach, represented the "Idea-Surrogate," a false prophet carried to power in the power vacuum then in Germany.[58] Once the National Socialists came to power, however, Rohrbach did not resist. For their part, the Nazis tolerated Rohrbach's work, especially with regard to the return of the colonies and such matters as coincided with their own agenda. In what must have seemed like a replay of his role in World War I, in the years 1941–1942 Rohrbach was frequently invited by the German army to give educational talks to the troops. He spoke about Russia, the Baltics, and his experiences in Africa, Japan, and America. Rohrbach never acknowledged at any point the mass murder then proceeding in the conquered territories.

Writing in 1947 to the American historian Henry Cord Meyer, who had served in the US intelligence agency, the Office of Strategic Services, during World War II, Rohrbach remained reticent over the convergence of his own Eastern European / Baltic geopolitical views with Nazi war aims. He was far more effusive in his thanks for the care packages the sympathetic Meyer sent. It was not easy, Rohrbach wrote, to keep up one's strength on the postwar rations of 1,550 calories per day.[59] The belligerent prose of Rohrbach's 1912 work, *German Thought in the World,* which advocated territorial expansion in Africa and cultural imperialism elsewhere, appeared painfully out of place in the aftermath of World War II. To the end of his life, Rohrbach maintained a remarkably blinkered view of his own role in the larger historical trends—the title of his memoir, *The Devil's Handwriting,* refers not to his and his fellow social scientists' complicity in the Nazi regime, but to the terms of the Versailles Peace Treaty, which Rohrbach viewed as causing the right-wing ascension of the National Socialists in Germany.[60]

In the postwar period, Henry Cord Meyer pressed the point in his letters to Rohrbach—surely Rohrbach must acknowledge the similarities between his promotion of German settlement in Eastern Europe and Nazi actions during the war? Rohrbach's response is not in the archived records. To the end, Rohrbach claimed to be a peaceful imperialist. He recognized no qualitative difference between what the German army accomplished in World War I and World War II. He summarized his final views in his memoirs, "Today when I think back over the years, I say to myself: the world lies open for our nation to conduct a generous and non-imperialistic policy."[61] For Rohrbach, the idea of a greater Germany both incorporated and extended beyond the colonies and cultural and territorial imperialism. Rohrbach worked his whole life to advance the cause of those ethnic Germans living on the edges of the empire, whether in Africa or the Lettland. But he was not alone. On the other side of the world, Chinese geographers and agronomists also made the same argument about the indispensability of empire.

Reclaiming Wastelands for the Nation

After the collapse of the Qing Empire in 1912, a weak Chinese republic sprung up in its place. Nominally, the Nationalist Party (GMD) managed to reunite the country and establish a central government based in Nanjing in 1927. Regional power holders like Yan Xishan in Shanxi and Zhang Xueliang in Manchuria controlled their own military forces. Despite offering lip service to the Nanjing Nationalist government, these regional leaders maintained considerable latitude to pursue their own policies, including the frontier reclamation projects discussed in the previous chapter. During the war, Chiang Kai-shek maintained limited control over military forces held by these regional power holders. He had lost some of his best, German-trained troops in the battle of Shanghai at the start of the war in 1937. Cut off from the coastal port cities, the Nationalist forces relied on a tenuous supply line from British-controlled Burma. The last German and Italian military advisors had withdrawn in 1938; Soviet aid slowed down and then ended altogether as it faced its own bitter war of attrition. American assistance, in the form of "volunteer" fighter pilots, provided a morale boost. Increasingly, however, the Chinese position teetered on the edge of defeat.

Just as the regional warlords had done in the Northeast and the Northwest, the wartime GMD Ministry of Agriculture and Forestry worked with the Ministry of Defense and the military to formulate detailed plans for land reclamation, or *tunken* (in this context I use both terms interchangeably). The wartime government also established local bureaus and model farms over the course of the war, efforts which continued in the postwar period up to the eve of communist victory in 1949.[62] As a war for the very survival of a free China raged on the mainland, the GMD regime established at least seventeen experimental collectives, or *tunken* zones, in areas under their control, explicitly designated as experimental areas for future agricultural and rural renewal.[63] More such zones sprang up around the country on local initiative. The GMD issued lengthy handbooks of regulations for these *tunken* experimental zones that betrayed a state concerned with details at once quotidian and banal, yet also deeply revealing of the ways that the state, even a wartime one with severely limited resources, increasingly surveilled and intervened in individual lives.[64]

As the military situation deteriorated, the wartime Chinese Nationalist government nevertheless formally established the East West Mountain Experimental Reclamation Zone (四川東西山屯墾實驗區) in Sichuan province on November 11, 1941, as a resettlement zone for veterans.[65] From its founding in the 1920s, the Nationalist government had limited control over the borderlands, instead relying on the Jiangnan region around Nanjing for its bureaucracy and on Shanghai as its financial base. Ironically, the Japanese invasion and the wartime government's retreat to Chongqing in Sichuan had finally brought the central government to the frontiers. Of the first group of around 200 soldiers to arrive at East West Mountain zone, around half were illiterate, and the majority came from agricultural backgrounds. Nevertheless, the soldiers were encouraged to keep diaries, repurpose old temples, and build new dwellings to expand the reclamation area. Finally, because the East West Mountain was known to be a bandit redoubt, the reclamation zone maintained its own security force. The East West Mountain Experimental Reclamation Zone became one of at least seventeen such zones established during the war years for both veterans and civilian refugees.

In the first year after its founding, the East West Mountain zone created six separate reclamation farms totaling 23,920 *mu* (1 *mu* = 0.165 acres). In 1942, 787 people in 312 family units worked at five farms. Each farm built at least 30 *li* (about 15 kilometers) of roadways. The collective leased a coal mine from locals, with plans to open two to four additional coal mines, two to four limekilns, and a papermaking site in the coming year. The farm had also opened a cooperative society and credit union. The administration of the East West Mountain zone opened a medical facility in the zone staffed with one doctor and a nurse. News of the medical facility spread quickly in the region. In the first year of operation, the medical facility treated 373 workers, 758 soldiers and their families, and 386 poor villagers from the surrounding areas. The veterans appear to have been more interested in farming and mining than politics; administrators floated plans to provide an additional stipend as incentive for attendance at mandatory, but apparently poorly attended, political indoctrination sessions.

For party bureaucrats, these collective farms would accomplish the dual goal of providing employment for demobilized soldiers and reinforcing Chinese sovereignty on the frontiers.[66] On paper at least, proposals for these *tunken* districts featured utopian plans for hospitals, manufacturing plants, recreational facilities, movie theaters, and theater troupes. Not surprisingly, the reality at such *tunken* farms differed dramatically from the paper proposals. Taken in conjunction with the scientific agenda of major research institutes, these plans offered a vision for rural renewal by setting up laboratories for social engineering. In the ideal world, such frontier farms would become the experimental zones for agrarian renewal and postwar reconstruction.

In the *tunken* experimental zones, the state, weakened by war and corruption, nevertheless attempted to keep track, enumerate, and evaluate. In the East West Mountain zone in Sichuan province, officials filled out detailed evaluations of settlers. In one of the more effusive evaluations, we learn that the secretary Ren Gongan orchestrated the filing of documents, working steadily and fast, that his behavior was sober and grave, that he observed the regulations, and that he was constantly on the lookout for ways to improve his productivity. Not everyone proved equally capable.[67] Some were criticized for carelessness; others merely fulfilled the bare minimum of their job requirements. The state kept salary charts of employees and collected forms which tracked the employees, their ages, province and town of origin, and graded them on a 100-point scale.[68] Each *tunken* location accounted for their existence with detailed expenditure and intake charts. In 1941, East West Mountain zone boasted the possession of one world map (valued at 17 yuan), two maps of China (17 yuan each), two maps of Sichuan province, and one poster for the New Life Movement (30 yuan).[69] By 1944, the East West Mountain zone aimed to expand to a total of six farms, add to the acreage under cultivation, and open coal mines, charcoal manufacturing, and other small industries. The *tunken* zone also sought to expand the recruitment of veterans, hold workshops for making farm tools and furniture, and to add to the medical facilities in the zone.[70]

The ideas for scientific development and frontier settlement did not originate with warlords or political leaders, but rather from a cosmopolitan educated elite. The late Qing and early Republican years witnessed political turmoil, but also provided opportunities for the first generation of Chinese scientists to receive training abroad. Part of the funds from the American portion of the Chinese Boxer Indemnity went towards scholarships for Chinese students to study in the United States.[71] Among the students who received the Boxer scholarships were Zhu Kezhen, who studied agriculture at the University of Illinois; and Hu Mingfu, Zhao Yuanren, Hu Shi, and Zhou Ren, who attended Cornell to study the sciences, including physics, mathematics, and engineering. Zhu later became the vice president of the Chinese Academy of Sciences after 1949. These and other Chinese students in the United States went on to establish the Science Society of China in 1914–1915. The Science Society returned to China with many of these students in 1918 and would go on to shape the development of science in the country until its dissolution in 1950.

Cornell University became one of the global hubs for agronomic research. Chinese students founded the Science Society of China not in China, but at Cornell. The career of one of the Chinese students who trained at Cornell, the agricultural economist Tang Qiyu, illustrates one of the intellectual pathways for ideas about frontier settlement. In 1924, Tang received his PhD in agricultural economics with a thesis on "An Economic Study of Chinese Agriculture."[72] Already in his dissertation, one could clearly trace the influence of widely circulating ideas about excess population and land scarcity. Tang argued that inner colonization provided the one legitimate solution to surplus populations in China's densely populated core regions. The state should encourage large-scale migration to the sparsely populated peripheries: Gansu, Yunnan, Xinjiang, Mongolia, and Manchuria.[73] Such migration would be beneficial on multiple counts, increasing the food supply, raising the standard of living, and producing the raw materials for the nation's industrial progress.

Tang posited that racism dimmed prospects for Chinese migrants overseas, as Australia, South Africa, and the United States respectively closed their borders and erected various legal barriers to Chinese settlers. When Japanese colonization societies came to the same conclusion, they turned to Brazil. For Tang, inner colonization of China's own frontiers provided the next-best alternative. Tang wrote, "China needs her millions to develop her natural resources and to construct her transportation system rather than send them to work for wages in other countries."[74] Some of Tang's fellow Chinese students at Cornell experienced American racism firsthand. These incidents spurred their nationalism and desire to return to China, where they established scientific disciplines in their home country.

Upon his return to China, Tang Qiyu found a ready audience for his ideas. In early 1925, the warlord Feng Yuxiang established a "Northwest Reclamation Planning Society" to draw up large-scale plans for development. Ambitious plans were reduced to modest levels when promised funds failed to come through from the central government, but the society did arrange a visit from a survey team headed by Tang Qiyu to Inner Mongolia.[75] With his return to China, Tang returned to writing and publishing in Chinese. What he described in English as "inner colonization," he translated as *tunken* in Chinese, resituating inner colonization as part of an unbroken Chinese historical tradition dating back to the first empire.

During the Japanese invasion that began in 1937, Tang Qiyu continued to actively promote inner colonization. In 1938 he authored a pamphlet on refugees and reclamation, which was published by the Jiangxi

Provincial Reclamation Bureau. Tang listed various examples from China's history in which imperial authorities deployed refugees to cultivate
and reclaim wastelands. Refugees would become a fount of labor and a
lifeline for the survival of the Han nationality. The nation needed not
only warriors who shed their blood on the battlefield, but also farmers
who would transform the wilds into farmlands through their sweat and
labor. Science and technology would aid the work of reclamation.[76] The
florid language of the pamphlet, painting a heroic image of settlers transforming wastelands with their sweat and toil, contrasted vividly with
conditions on the ground. Jiangxi did open a reclamation zone in June
of 1938. However, from the beginning its operation stalled because of a
lack of funding. Out of a planned budget of 19,000 yuan, only a third,
or 6,500 yuan, was dispensed. As a result, the planned construction of
irrigation, roads, and buildings failed to materialize.[77] Such discrepan-
cies between paper and real budgets were pervasive for these wartime
projects, and they corroborate the accusations of widespread corruption
in the Nationalist regime made by contemporary observers. But another
way of looking at these documents is to see the perseverance of these bureaucratic dreams of Chinese territorial expanse and the transformation
of the borderlands, even as invaders occupied most of the country.

In 1943, Tang participated in one of the wartime Nationalist government's signature scientific research programs: the Northwest Expedition
to Xinjiang. Sponsored by the Chongqing government and headed by Academia Sinica, the Northwest Expedition sought to lay the foundation
for the future growth of the region. In addition to exploring and surveying the natural resources in the Northwest, various wartime government
agencies came up with the first plans for the postwar development of
the Northwest, which they forwarded to Chiang Kai-shek for comment.
Among the proposals was a plan for the Ministry of Forestry, the department overseeing reclamation, to move headquarters to the Northwest.
Plans called for the construction of a national agricultural experimental
station in the region. The government would additionally establish an
industrial experiments department within the Ministry of Finance and
a branch of the national geological survey in the Northwest. Finally, the
Social Science Institute of Academia Sinica would be moved to Jiuquan,
in Gansu province in the Northwest.

By the war's end in 1945, the language of *tunken* pervaded the military, bureaucratic, and the social scientific circles. In a 1945 work, Tang

Qiyu investigated *tunken* practices from the Han dynasty through the Qing.[78] Whereas in 1928 the military officer Zou Zuohua of the Northeast saw a need to differentiate *tuntian* in the earlier dynasties from modern *tunken*, by 1945 Tang conflated the two terms in his book by examining practices at military colonies throughout Chinese history. Tang continued to advocate for the inner colonization of the Chinese frontier in the subsequent decades, including after the Communists came to power in 1949. The political leaders changed; plans for inner colonization of the frontiers continued.

Soldier land reclamation drew broad support across the political spectrum. Communist forces that had survived Chiang Kai-shek's multiple extermination campaigns formed a *tunken* zone in Nanniwan, a remote area 45 kilometers to the southeast of their main base in Yan'an in Shanxi province.[79] When the GMD official Wang Jingwei went over to the Japanese, his collaborationist government similarly set up *tunken* bureaus for rural areas, touted as a vital contribution to the Greater East Asian Co-Prosperity Sphere. For all their ideological differences, both the Nationalist and the Communist Party viewed the peripheral regions from the same Han Chinese–based perspective. Both parties offered frontier minorities political and cultural autonomy in exchange for their incorporation into a multiethnic yet unitary nation.[80] Frontier policy was a central part of Marxist discourse—which accounts for why the changing of regimes in 1949 did not fundamentally alter the Chinese state's stance on borderland minorities.

Archival documents reveal a yawning divide between the rhetoric of patriotism and the reality of hardship on the ground. For educated elites like Tang Qiyu and members of the bureaucracy, *tunken* was a panacea for the country's many troubles and pointed the way to the future development and securitization of the borderlands after the war. For the refugees who arrived in these resettlement zones, however, paper budgets and plans made little difference to their plight. Established in October of 1937, the Jiangxi Wenshan Reclamation Zone was one of the earlier efforts. It was opened to refugees fleeing the advancing Japanese army.[81] Officials acknowledged the difficulties of transforming urban refugees to competent farmers. In the remote location in the Jiangxi mountains, poor hygienic conditions contributed to rampant disease and waves of epidemics. To ameliorate conditions, government officials attempted to fix the roads in the area in the spring of 1939. As the war ground on, the summer of 1939 saw the arrival of three groups of refugee settlers. A group of 1,060 settlers were assigned to farm 3,000 *mu* of land. In addition to agriculture, officials promoted local industries in paper, soap, and glass manufacturing, and saw further potential in developing mineral resources and mining. A map of the reclamation zone also displayed light industries such as a brick factory, a textile mill, and an oil press.

As the central government had limited control outside of Chongqing, it frequently worked with provincial and local officials to administer these reclamation zones. In 1940, the government-run Liping Reclamation Zone in Shaanxi was to receive a budget of 185,000 yuan to accommodate a first group of 2,000 refugees, including 90,000 yuan for food and living stipends for the refugee settlers.[82] The zone had a monthly budget of over 40,000 yuan earmarked for construction, animal feed, seed, equipment, and additional funds to aid refugees. Actual received funding that could be used to pay for construction and stipends was an altogether different story. In many cases, these reclamation zones eked by on a fraction of their proposed budgets.

In 1942, the Ministry of Forestry issued a set of five recommendations for the Chinese Wartime Reclamation Society.[83] The Reclamation Society had initially been formed to carry out reclamation efforts and resettle refugees in Mabian County, some 300 kilometers southwest of Chengdu, in Sichuan province. The area encompassed a large population of Yi minority peoples. The Reclamation Society aimed to erect large-scale experimental farms to improve agricultural production, develop borderlands and forests, and promote public health and hygiene. The Reclamation Society listed as their first target the recruitment of settlers. They also sought to build roads and telephone lines, expand industry, education, medical facilities, aluminum mines, and conduct ethnographic study of border tribes.[84] By the start of 1940, county official Song Jilong estimated that approximately twelve collectives operated in the county. However, due to the lack of technical expertise, these groups found it difficult to fully exploit mineral deposits in the area.[85]

Outside of Sichuan and the immediate vicinity of the GMD government, settlement zones faced even more dismal odds. Further west in the Ningxia, bordering Tibet, the vastness of the territory and restive tribal populations led to considerably more difficulties for settlers. In language reminiscent of late Qing officials, the bureaucratic report on *tunken* efforts described a troubled history of the region. In the past, entire villages of settlers had been slaughtered by bandits, and residents had been kidnapped and human trafficked.[86] A few years later, in 1943, the local Committee on Tunken stated that, in the four years since the formation of the committee, they had managed to educate six groups of frontier residents, totaling 1,500 people, including over a hundred members of the local tribal population.[87] Faced with a multitude of challenges regarding the allocation of scarce resources, funding, and property and land disputes, the GMD retreated to printing more regulations. New rules required settlers who planned on undertaking reclamation to submit yearly reports on their progress.[88] The government also set time limits for settlers to begin farming. For grasslands under 1,000 *mu,* settlers had to begin farming within a year, with up to eight years for 10,000 *mu* of land; work on wooded areas needed to start within two years; marshlands could take up to four years. The number of regulations increased as the odds of enforcing them decreased.

In 1943, the Guizhou Six Dragon Mountain zone surveyed its collected properties, revealing a pitiful inventory of a piece of blackboard, one kitchen knife, one foot basin, a couple of wooden barrels, and one iron pot.[89] That September, the farm's management reported severe insect damage, resulting in the loss of over 50 percent of the harvest. Administrators advocated four methods of insect control: manual (using hands to catch the insects), wooden clapboards, oil, or finally, pesticide.[90] Listed last, pesticide was likely not actually available. Under these difficult circumstances, the Guizhou Six Dragon zone had trouble attracting settlers. The Six Dragon Mountain Tunken Bureau advertised for refugees from Zhejiang and the northern provinces, promoting Guizhou as sparsely populated, with abundant free land.[91] Despite such efforts and the steady expansion of farms to five locations by December of 1943, altogether the *tunken* zone only attracted 146 people.[92] Officials acknowledged that the *tunken* site lay on remote and mountainous grounds with special climate conditions and late harvest times. The first two farm locations only managed to retain two people when both farms required twenty workers to be fully staffed.[93]

In a series of reports to the Chongqing government from 1940, the leaders of another refugee reclamation zone in Guizhou painted a grim picture of appalling conditions and low morale.[94] In the fall of 1938, when Anhui became a war zone, a group of refugees from the province, including women, children, and the elderly, fled to Hankou. From there,

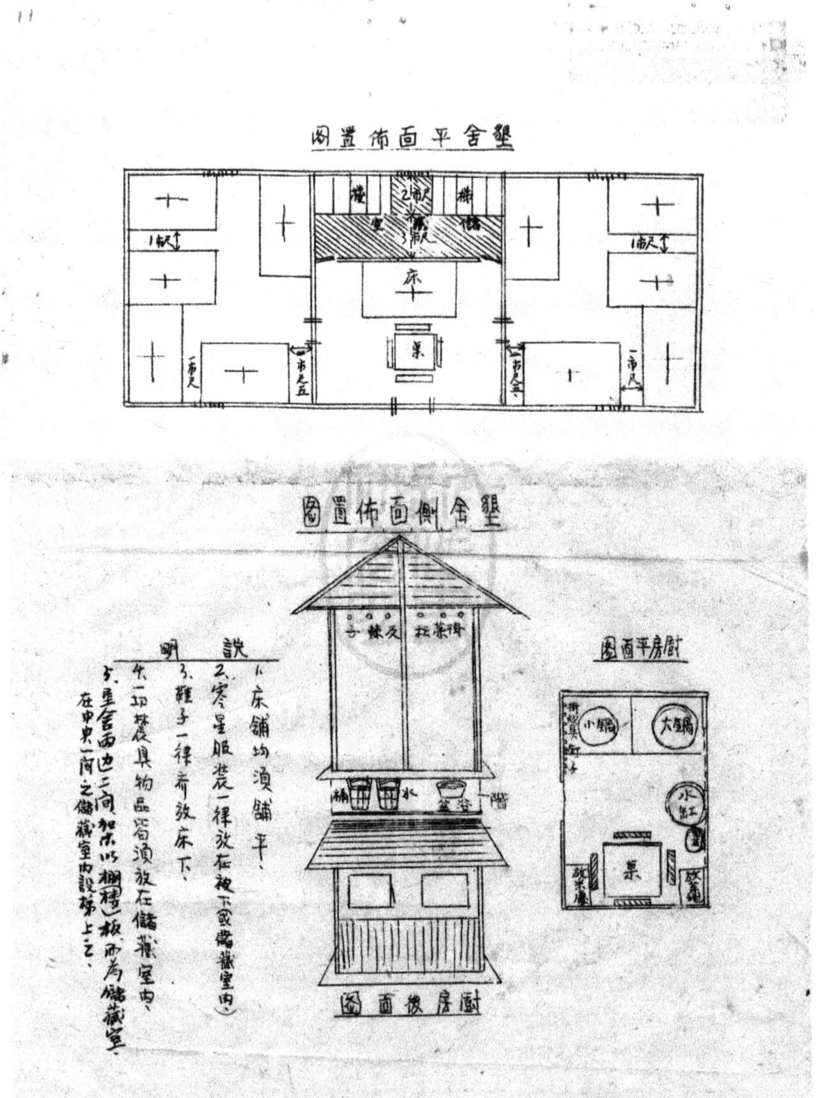

FIGURE 6.1: Schematic of living quarters from the progress report for the Guizhou Six Dragons Tunken Bureau, 1943. With permission from the Institute of Modern History Archives, Academia Sinica, Taipei, Taiwan. IMH 20-87-206-07.

7

農林部貴州六龍山屯墾實驗區管理局
内　務　規　則
(附轄部第一墾區福山鎮佛區圖)

福山鎮形勢圖

農林部貴州六龍山屯墾實驗區管理局第三課

中華民國三十二年十一月編訂

FIGURE 6.2: The front cover of the report on progress at the Guizhou Six Dragons Tunken Experimental Zone, 1943. With permission from the Institute of Modern History Archives, Academia Sinica, Taipei, Taiwan. IMH 20-87-206-07.

over 600 refugees formed a reclamation group and continued onward to
Guizhou in the Southwest, where they were told that Lingui County had
several thousand *mu* of wasteland free for the taking. They were additionally told that they could obtain temporary housing in one of the more
than ten villages in the vicinity. The group of refugee settlers who had
arrived from Anhui were mostly illiterate. Of the 600 people in the group
at the start of their journey to the borderlands, only around ten people
had an elementary school education. Nevertheless, in keeping with the
central government's vision, the reclamation zone established two elementary schools and found seven people with some level of education to
serve as teachers. Instruction began outdoors before the expenditure of
500 yuan converted an abandoned temple into a simple school building.
But because the zone could not afford to pay the teachers' salaries, all
seven eventually abandoned the school.

The high point of the venture came in December 1938, when the
group reached Guizhou. Immediately upon arrival, the refugees discovered that local officials had painted far too rosy a picture of the area and
its potential for development. The reclamation zone was remote, about
30 *li* (1 *li* = 0.31 miles) from the nearest village. The soil in the area was
rocky and not suitable for agriculture. Before long, settlers abandoned
any further reclamation efforts. Instead, members of the group relied
entirely on the 0.2 yuan per person per day subsistence stipend provided
by the central government. Faced with harsh conditions, able-bodied
members quickly abandoned the group. In short order, only 271 people
remained in the reclamation zone, 101 of these children under the age
of ten. Another 67 were elderly and disabled individuals, and the rest
women—in other words, all able-bodied males had fled the zone. As order
and morale deteriorated, group leader Zhang Dexuan threatened to personally go to Chongqing to petition for his group of destitute refugees.
His letters to the Chongqing government dripped with growing despera-
tion as he detailed the dire conditions they faced in Guizhou. The grand
language of patriotism and utopian paper plans of resettlement zones
played well in Chongqing, in meetings of bureaucrats and political leaders. On the ground, these fantasies crashed into the reality of remote
locations, poor conditions, and helpless groups of elderly people, women,
and children who found themselves stranded with little government aid.

The wartime resurgence of interest in frontier development led to the
formation of reclamation zones across areas controlled by the GMD, all

based on the idea that these zones would serve the double purpose of increasing wartime food production and providing a refuge for those dislocated by war. The vision proved to be a mirage. Across the war-torn countryside, reclamation farms had trouble recruiting settlers. In Xichang in western Sichuan, such farms recruited refugees and settlers to concentrate on growing grain. As with other reclamation zones across GMD-controlled areas in Guizhou, Sichuan, and Jiangxi, the Xichang zone found it difficult to meet the government's lofty aspirations. Instead, most people on these farms survived on meager daily stipends provided by the government. Most who arrived at the farms left again soon there-after. The Xichang farm appeared to have at no point managed to attract even half of their 600-settler recruiting target.[95] Yet, even as the dream of agricultural revitalization encountered the harsh reality of inhospitable terrain and lack of funding, the wartime government simultaneously sponsored twenty-seven geological expeditions in the Southwest as well as road-building projects in the region.[96] At times, government engineers and workers vastly outnumbered actual settlers.

Faced with only a limited number of refugees willing to move to the experimental settlement zones, the GMD followed the path of Weimar Germany in generating plans to send wounded soldiers to military-run reclamation zones. One proposal circulated by the Ministry of Defense specified the basic standards that should govern the use of veterans in reclamation projects. They should have experience with farming and be interested in reclamation; their physical condition should be adequate to carry out farming tasks; they should be hardworking; they should have skills in metallurgy, masonry, or carpentry, and have other skills for rural industries. In additions, these veterans should carry out experimental work on soil, fertilizer, or other agriculturally useful topics. The likelihood of finding enough men who met all these requirements in late 1944, after years of war and when the military had resorted to conscripting young boys and old men as cannon fodder, was next to zero.[97]

By 1943, the wartime Chongqing government had begun to plan for the postwar future. The government plans sent for Chiang Kai-shek's review included sending 20,000 people to Xinjiang. The planned mass migration would allow refugees to take up farming and increase food production, but it would also redistribute excess populations to the borderlands to bolster national defense. Given the various challenges and infrastructure issues in the region, government bureaucrats allowed

that settlers would need to be transported in the warmer months, between April and October.[98] The regime issued clear guidance on the land
and support that would be provided for each settler, including rations of
grain and at least 7 yuan per month per person. They also issued guide-
lines on the construction of dwellings, assuming at least 1,000 refugees
would necessitate the construction of 200 houses, on average each with
three rooms.

For all the disastrous realities of these reclamation zones, they were
not entirely a top-down creation. The benefits of reclamation had circulated in both government documents and in popular discourse. Local
officials lobbied the central government for permission to open these settlement zones. In 1940, Yang Chunhua wrote to Chongqing to promote
the possibilities of reclamation in Cangyuan County, Yunnan province.
Yang described how an influx of settlers would benefit the region and its
population. Bringing in settlers, he claimed, would also bolster national
defense, given the continuing disputes with the British over the southwestern border. The region's temperate climate made it ideal for settlement, according to Yang, and the area could accommodate up to 6,000
families. With settlement and the opening of schools, the government
could easily unify the language and promote nationalism.[99] Yang's optimistic assessment was almost certainly an exaggeration. Nevertheless,
Yang's proposal astutely appealed to government interest in developing
the frontiers. In 1938, the Finance Ministry received proposals from
tribal leaders to develop irrigation, mining, and agriculture in several
minority counties along the southern borders of Yunnan. The land was
not particularly fertile, these tribal leaders offered, which was why they
needed science to develop the region.[100]

––––––––

In 1938, the prominent Malaysian Chinese Liang Yugao (Leong Yew Koh)
submitted an eighty-one-page report on the development of border areas
in Yunnan and recommendations on border policies.[101] Liang Yugao was
born in Malaya in 1888 and belonged to an extensive network of overseas Chinese who moved between southern China and Southeast Asia.
He attended University of London and studied economics, sociology,
and political science. He returned to serve in the Republic of China in
1932 in various government positions, including as an advisor to the Executive Yuan (the executive branch of the government of the Republic

of China), before going back to Southeast Asia to lead the anti-Japanese movement, later becoming a founder of the Malayan Chinese Association in 1949. In short, Liang's life demonstrates how individuals and networks transcended the borders of nations and empires. The report he submitted in 1938 promoted railroad, agriculture, and mining in the southwestern borderlands. To fund these projects, Liang suggested raising 10 million yuan from overseas Chinese. The southern border with the British-controlled Burma had long been in contention. The remoteness and geography of the region made it difficult to administer, and the scattered indigenous populations showed little loyalty to either side. At a time of war, Liang argued, it was in the shared interest of both sides, the British and the Chinese, to finally come to an agreement on the border.

Liang emphasized the importance of opening an agricultural experimental station, with particular emphasis on research into cotton, tea, and tropical plants, including such economically valuable crops as rubber and coffee. In addition, he advocated the development of the mining industry. He suggested starting with mines already opened by indigenous peoples. It would be more economical, he recommended, to start with traditional methods for mining gold and silver, only turning to new mechanized technologies after viable veins had been located. Liang's status as a respected member of overseas Chinese groups ensured that his report was taken seriously by the Nationalist government. On August 12, 1938, at 9 a.m., representatives from various ministries and members of the committee on overseas Chinese met at the Interior Ministry's offices in Chongqing to discuss Liang's proposal. The group placed the Yunnan situation as of the highest importance to national security, even as the Nationalist's deteriorating military situation forestalled any immediate action to carry out Liang's plans.

The 1938 meeting in Chongqing and the 1942 meeting in Berlin discussed at the beginning of this chapter reveal the convergence of interests between scientists, social scientists, and technocrats in these governments on the two sides of the war. In both instances, the global circulation of ideas on economic development, science, and national defense came together in detailed settlement and development plans for the frontiers. Through the networks of science and the social sciences geo-modernity took root in both Germany and China. On opposite ends of the world, in Berlin and in the wartime ministries in Chongqing, officials met to discuss the reclamation and settlement of the borderlands, coopting the language of science and social science for the political project of reconstituting empire in the age of the nation-state. At a moment when the Germans were facing deteriorating conditions on the Eastern Front and the Chinese were barely clinging to survival against superior Japanese forces, both regimes nevertheless pushed forward with ambitious plans to settle the borderlands. That these plans rarely went beyond the paper stage spoke to the harsh realities of war rather than a lack of effort. For geographers and agronomists like Walter Christaller and Tang Qiyu, however, that distinction made all the difference for their postwar lives.

SEVEN

Cold War New Empires

The nation shattered, mountains and river remain
Grass grows high between cities.
国破山河在, 城春草木深.

Du Fu (712–770)

Ministers come and ministers go, even dictators die, but mountain ranges stand unperturbed.

Nicholas Spykman[1]

In the eighth century, a vast rebellion rocked the Tang dynasty and threatened to bring down the great empire. As cities lay in ruins, the poet Du Fu, now widely viewed as one of China's greatest poets, wrote of a desolate spring scene as he waited for word of loved ones. Reading the poem at age twenty, I thought it offered a glimmer of hope. The country may be broken, but the landscapes remain intact. Only years later did it occur to me to read the line as an expression of despair at the ephemerality of human existence. Wars begin and end, cities disappear into the weeds. The mountains and rivers remain, but not the humans who live so perilously in the landscape. The poet died in the year 770 AD, an itinerant in an empire wracked by unrest. Nicholas Spykman offered a similar observation in his 1942 book, at a moment when America was about to enter its golden age. He did not live to see it. He died from cancer a year later in 1943 at age forty-nine.

The insight that geography outlasts the lives of individuals and the

rise and fall of empires has crossed centuries and cultures. In the twentieth century, modern states turned to science as one of the preferred
means to project power and control territories and peoples, a project that
intensified after the end of World War II. Some of the geographers and
agronomists mentioned in previous chapters will come up again in this
chapter as the theorists for building a new world order after the devastation of a second global war within the span of three decades. In many
cases, however, they outlasted their usefulness and met tragic ends, dis-
carded by the very states they helped to establish. In the last chapter, I
traced the intersection of German and Chinese inner colonization plans
during the war. In this chapter, I turn to the divergent paths the United
States and China took towards empire building during the Cold War
period. While the two countries diverged on political ideology and what
constituted territorial sovereignty, they agreed on the primacy of science
in achieving their respective goals in their metaphorical and physical
frontiers.

The Most Powerful Geographer in the World

The cover of *Time* magazine from March 23, 1936, featured Isaiah
Bowman, then at the height of his renown and the president of Johns
Hopkins University. At the peak of his career, Bowman was known as
Roosevelt's geographer and one of the most powerful academics in the
US, with influence that crossed over from academia to the federal government. During World War II, from 1942 to 1945, Bowman served as
the chairman of the Territorial Committee of the State Department and
as special advisor to the Secretary of State. He was an official represen-
tative at the Dumbarton Oaks Conference in the summer of 1944. He
chaired the group of experts that advised the United States delegation
at the San Francisco conference where negotiations for the framing and
adoption of the Charter of the United Nations were completed. If the
"American Century," the term coined by *Time* publisher Henry Luce,
was set in motion by the global reordering of the world war, then Isaiah
Bowman was its consigliere. Although today Isaiah Bowman is no longer
a household name, he left a major legacy in how the United States engaged with the world in the second half of the twentieth century.

By the end of World War II, Bowman had redoubled his efforts to
center American foreign policy on a scientific basis. To the National

Academy of Sciences, Bowman presented his vision of science as an integral part of international affairs.[2] In more select circles, he pushed for the importance of geography for American military aims.[3] At the same time, Bowman consistently viewed internationalization as both inevitable and necessary for American policy. In a public address entitled, "Is an International Society Possible?" at the Princeton Bicentennial Celebration on October 14, 1946, Bowman optimistically offered that "in the field of politics, planetary thinking has permanently displaced parochial thinking for us and for our government and a world view becomes imperative in a time when all wars seem to promise world wars."[4] In this respect, Bowman's political agenda coincided with that of the major American philanthropic foundations, which had funded the organizations Bowman led over the course of his career.

In addition to a long list of domestic correspondents, Bowman also maintained strong connections internationally. Bowman's list of international correspondents included Hu Huanyong, then the director of the Research Institute of Geography at National Central University, which had relocated with the wartime government to Chongqing[5] and geographer Chang Chiyun (Zhang Zhiyun).[6] Bowman corresponded with German geographer Carl Troll throughout the 1930s and again after the war.[7] Another particularly important correspondent was philosopher Carsun Chang (Zhang Junmai), who originally arrived in the US as the Chinese delegate to the World Security Conference in San Francisco. The Chinese Ministry of Education tasked Carsun Chang to survey scientific development in the US. Chang sought out Bowman both because of his prominence as a geographer as well as his leadership of Johns Hopkins University and the federal Office of Scientific Research and Development during the war. In replying to Chang, Bowman suggested that China should focus its scientific development on those disciplines with practical applications for the country's current situation. He wrote, "I would think it very important that China should concentrate in the first instance on civil engineering, chemical and sanitary engineering. . . . chemical engineering should be directed, it seems to me, toward practical needs of Chinese agriculture and the development of mineral deposits in collaboration with first-class geologists."[8] A few years later, the Soviet Academy of Sciences made similar suggestions to a visiting delegation of Chinese scientists. The new communist regime in China revamped its scientific agenda to conform to these goals.

Secretary of State Cordell Hull shared Bowman's interest in deploying science to solve real-world problems. Both men viewed science as the necessary foundation of American power and influence. In a May 15, 1939, letter to Bowman, Hull wrote, "As science and its products contribute to the creation of new situations and new problems, science and its products must be called upon to contribute to the meeting of those situations and problems."[9] Hull remained keenly aware of the limits of science, as well as its destructive potentials. By the end of the war, however, men like Bowman and Hull would view the state sponsorship of scientific development as imperative. Influenced by Bowman, in July of 1945, Vannevar Bush (1890–1974), the director of the US Office of Scientific Research and Development, submitted a report to the president, "Science, the Endless Frontier," that set the course for postwar American science policy.[10] Bush was an engineer and later administrator at Massachusetts Institute of Technology (MIT).[11] Written during Bush's brief foray into government service, "Science, the Endless Frontier" argued for science as the cornerstone of American power, both domestically and overseas. Science and technology would serve as the underpinning of American power in the postwar world.

During the war, geographers' work both in the United States and around the world intersected with government interest in managing natural resources. Chinese geographers threw themselves into dangerous fieldwork in support of the wartime government and its search for resources. Japanese geographers provided the maps for the empire's continental expansion. In the United States, Edward Ackerman, a geographer at the University of Chicago, was placed in charge of instruction in geography for the Army Specialized Training Program by the General Headquarters of the Supreme Commander for the Allied Powers.[12] The American Geographical Society mass produced maps of Europe and Asia for the home front public to follow as American troops made their way to far-off battlefronts, as it had during World War I.[13]

Under Bowman's influence, American views of geography and territorial possession began to change. In his various academic positions during the interwar years, Bowman had developed a de-territorialized concept of empire based on the control of and access to natural resources and infrastructure rather than military occupation. These ideas, which first appeared in Bowman's 1921 work *The New World,* now began to influence American foreign policy. At the May 1940 meeting of the Pan American

Union in Washington, DC, President Roosevelt had emphasized the so-called Good Neighbor Policy, which emphasized cooperation and trade rather than military force in American relations with Latin America. American leaders had used the language of noninterference before, but they had consistently reneged on their promises of peaceful collaboration. This time, the Good Neighbor Policy was bolstered by the export of American expertise through governmental agencies and philanthropic organizations such as the Rockefeller and Carnegie Foundations. The Department of Interior became a key vehicle of enacting this policy of emphasizing mutually beneficial development, joining in the war effort to locate strategic minerals and aid in the development of resources in Latin American countries.

Interior experts, including geologists and engineers, fanned out across Central and South America, from Haiti and Costa Rica to Bolivia and Brazil, and compiled detailed reports on local conditions. These agents worked for the Department of the Interior but also reported on the costs and conditions of development to mining industries back home. In its official publications, the State Department argued that "technical cooperation is the direct opposite of imperialism. Its aim is the development of intellectual and physical self-reliance, and the conditions of basic economic strength which enable underdeveloped countries to resist foreign dominance or to cast off oppressive economic ties"[14] The idealistic language of development belied the program's origins during the war as part of the American government's efforts to secure strategic minerals for the war effort in Latin America.

The global search for mineral resources fundamentally altered American foreign policy calculations and represented a new de-territorialized concept of empire. Instead of sending troops to the Philippines, as the United States had done during the burst of imperial acquisition at the end of the nineteenth century and where they were bogged down in fighting insurgents on unfamiliar terrain, American federal agencies deployed experts, at taxpayer expense, to assist foreign governments in their search for the resources to develop their economies. The Americans could plausibly argue that the arrangement was beneficial for all parties and promoted development and the spread of democratization. These government-sponsored programs complemented the efforts of private American philanthropies like the Carnegie, Ford, and Rockefeller Foundations. Both the US State Department and private foundations subscribed to the view that fostering a global elite in science and technology would pave the way to democratization of countries around the world.

The vision that Bowman had of a new world order led by the United States came to fruition in the postwar period. The United States did not need to establish colonies because the expansion of corporate interests, subsidized by the American taxpayers, would do the job of empire instead by controlling vital resources overseas. Global power changed shape after World War II, from the global territorial empire modeled by the British—the sun did set after all in the age of decolonization—to one defined in economic terms. American *Lebensraum* would ultimately take shape as a form of economic imperialism, updating the Monroe Doctrine for the twentieth century by decoupling territory and physical boundaries from economic forms of domination and influence.[15] In this effort, as during the war, agency experts worked closely with American industry and private interests, providing critical intelligence and reports, all at the American taxpayers' expense.

In the end, Bowman's influence over US territoriality outlasted his influence as a disciplinary leader to geography. In 1948 Harvard University suddenly eliminated its geography department. In justifying the decision, Harvard president James Conant issued a statement that pointed to the lack of clarity on the field's disciplinary boundaries and the assessment that "geography is not a university subject."[16] At the time of the decision, Bowman was on the Board of Overseers at Harvard University and on friendly terms with Conant, yet he remained curiously quiet about the momentous decision by the university. Before Bowman could do anything more to salvage the discipline that he had advocated for his entire life, he died of a heart attack in January 1950, just over a year after his retirement from Johns Hopkins. These two events signaled the death knell of geography as an academic discipline in the United States at elite ivy league universities. Today, geography remains a thriving discipline in Europe, Asia, and in public universities in the US, but its purview has considerably shrunken.

China's Changing Territorialities

In 1943, the US Department of State sponsored six Chinese academics for a yearlong exchange in the United States as part of its program aimed at establishing and deepening cultural relations with wartime allies.

Among those brought to the US was Zhang Qiyun, the geographer from Zhejiang University. The other five academics, including famed sociologist Fei Xiaotong, had previously studied in the US; only Zhang had never been abroad. He received his spot through the recommendation of the Harvard-trained meteorologist Zhu Kezhen, at the time the president of Zhejiang University. After graduating from college, Zhang had joined Shanghai Commercial Press in the 1920s. In the four years he worked at the press, Zhang oversaw the writing of Chinese and world geography textbooks for high schools. During this time, he became close friends with Zhu, at whose recommendation he became a lecturer in geography at Central University in 1927. Zhang published prolifically during these decades. His works included a 1930 collaboration with Zhu Kezhen on a Ministry of Education–sanctioned geography textbook for high schools.[17]

Soon after Zhang joined the Nationalist Party in the early 1930s, he became a member of the National Defense Planning Commission. During this period, Zhang came to the personal attention of Chiang Kai-shek. Both men had come from the same hometown in Zhejiang; Chiang, like many educated Chinese at the time, treasured his atlas of China and viewed geography as an essential field of knowledge and key to the construction of Chinese nationalism.

In 1944, with a letter of introduction from the US Department of State, Zhang contacted Isaiah Bowman. After the two geographers exchanged letters, Zhang eventually went to Baltimore to meet Bowman. Zhang requested a preface from the senior scholar for his upcoming English-language book, targeted at Western readers, to be called *China in the New World: A Study in Political Geography.* At the time of Zhang's request, Bowman himself was reevaluating the ramifications of his earlier works, particularly in light of their apparent influence on the German Geopolitik school. Bowman had vigorously defended his own scholarship and attempted to demarcate his approach, which he considered "political geography," from geopolitics, in an essay in the *Geographical Review.*[18] In his correspondence with Zhang, Bowman commented on uncomfortable similarities between Zhang's views on China's future relationship with Southeast Asia and German geopolitical aims. In one letter, he wrote, "This is the line of argument that Germany has taken with reference to her people in the US and in South America. She took it during World War I, and still more aggressively in World War II." Bowman continued, "It seems to me that you have tried to do two things. First, to write an objective account of Chinese political geography; and second, plead China's cause before the world in terms of a future political program. However important political aspirations may be, they are aspirations and not science."[19] And so in the private letter with a Chinese scholar, Bowman finally broached the essential issue of the future direction of geography. He nevertheless agreed to write the preface and contacted the publisher Harcourt, Brace, and Company to gauge their interest in Zhang's book.[20] The planned English-language version with Bowman's preface never appeared, but the work was subsequently published in China.

Bowman's letter to Zhang revealed the profound contradictions of his version of American *Lebensraum*. Bowman had taken his time addressing the huge refugee issues created by World War II. Millions died because careful American studies of the refugee situation delayed opening the country to immigration for those fleeing the war. Bowman had argued that successful settlement required huge financial investments and continuing state support. The conclusion wasn't necessarily wrong—it takes a great deal of state support to successfully settle difficult terrains in wartime conditions, something the Soviet, German, Japanese, and Chinese governments could all confirm. But the inaction was also callous and cynical and underlined the racist underpinning of frontier studies. Only when commenting on someone else's work, in a field far removed from his own specialization, did he recognize the porous line between politics, state agenda, and geography and how difficult it was to separate a country's scientific agenda and nationalist goals.

Zhang's work was by no means exceptional among Chinese geographers. Bowman and Roosevelt both misread China's geopolitical ambitions. Roosevelt needed Chinese forces to keep millions of Japanese troops locked in conflict while the Americans built up their capacity to conduct the Pacific War. To that end, Roosevelt diverged from Churchill's open and racist contempt for the Chinese and advocated for their inclusion among the Great Powers. Even in the years before the US officially entered the war, Roosevelt had opened the spigot of American aid through the Lend-Lease program. Chiang realized the leverage his position afforded but also faced other more pressing domestic concerns, including the rival Communist camp in the Northwest. If at points the American strategic aim overlapped with the Chinese—in particular, the importance of holding onto the Northwest frontier—it is because on the Chinese side, such views had steadily reached crescendo from the 1920s

in ways that had nothing to do with American strategic aims. Throughout the Republican period, Chinese geographers uniformly included
disputed territories, including Mongolia, Xinjiang, and Tibet, in their
monographs and textbooks on Chinese geography. Years of resentment
against imperialist encroachment had steadily refashioned a twentieth-
century imperial ideology. And if the Chinese borrowed the language of
science and geography, they nevertheless also refashioned it according
to their own historical imagination.

After his return to China in 1945, Zhang Qiyun went back to work at
Zhejiang University as the dean of the College of Liberal Arts and concurrently the head of the Department of History and Geography. In the
twilight of the GMD regime in 1948, Zhang was ousted by leftist student
protesters.[21] As Communist forces closed in, Zhang's long-time mentor
and friend Zhu Kezhen decided to stay on the mainland, becoming the
vice president of the Chinese Academy of Sciences. Zhang, on the other
hand, decided to leave with the regime to Taiwan, where he served as
Minister of Education in the 1950s. The presence of Zhang and others
like him in the GMD government in Taiwan explains the considerable
overlap in territorial views on both sides of the straits and across the
1949 changing of regimes.

This territoriality could be seen in the writings of GMD official Zhu
Jiahua, a geologist by training who entered politics in the 1930s. During
the war, Zhu encouraged and supported research on frontier regions and
attempted to build a party structure in the Northwest, including in Xinjiang. Zhu had also been a key advocate for the Northwest Expedition,
a large-scale scientific expedition sponsored by the wartime government.[22] The political strategic thinking behind this plan was to counter
the growing popularity and spread of the Communist Party from its
base in Yan'an. In the 1940s, the Community Party had used the war's
reprieve to begin to implement land reform and political organization in
the arid and poverty-stricken northwestern area around their main base.
Having previously been driven to the Northwest by exigency, and to near
annihilation by Chiang Kai-shek's last "Bandit Suppression Campaign,"
the growing influence of the Communist base now ironically appeared
to reinforce the writings of geopolitical writers, including the British geographer and geopolitician James Fairgrieve, that future military threats
to the Chinese heartland would come from Central Asia and the vast flat
stretches of land to the west. In exile in Taiwan, Zhu Jiahua, like Zhang

Qiyun, continued to believe in maintaining the territorial expanse of the Chinese Empire. For the remainder of his life in Taiwan, Chiang Kai-shek persisted on including Mongolia and other borderland territories on his imagined map of China. Chiang would dismiss the independence movements in both Mongolia and Xinjiang as the result of foreign interference and the disastrous breaking of ranks in what should have been a unified anti-Communist front.

From Oracle Bones to Geopolitics

By the late 1930s, as the Japanese invasion continued and the situation in China began to look increasingly precarious, it was clear to Isaiah Bowman and other members of the Council on Foreign Relations that the war would once again remake the global map. At a confidential meeting of the council in April 1940, the council heard from Owen Lattimore, an Inner Asia specialist Bowman had personally hired at Johns Hopkins. Shortly thereafter, the Roosevelt administration would send Lattimore to China as a personal liaison with Chiang Kai-shek. In his remarks to the council, Lattimore pointed out that the Western powers had caused the Manchukuo debacle:

> Japan had destroyed the previous judicial principle of sovereignty in the Far East by setting up Manchukuo. But that principle itself had been imposed on the Far East by the West . . . The Japanese had insisted that Manchukuo was an independent state whether or not it wanted to be independent. In Outer Mongolia the Soviets supported an independent state without recognizing it as separate from China. This principle of regionalism might be played in many ways, the Japanese, Russian, Chinese, and American ways.[23]

Lattimore recognized that the events playing out in Asia were but one facet of the global tensions created by the rise of the nation-state. Empire never disappeared, but rather continued to cast its shadow on conflicts over sovereignty and borderlands. Although the Americans continued to sit on the fence regarding the escalating conflicts around the world until the last possible moment, it was clear that the war would alter the status quo ideas on sovereignty and state power.

Owen Lattimore was born on July 29, 1900, in Washington, DC, to parents who were at the time both high school teachers. In 1901, his father, David Lattimore, was appointed to teach French and English at Nanyang University in Shanghai. Lattimore's aunt (his father's older sister) had already lived in China for many years as a Presbyterian missionary. A peripatetic childhood saw him move to North China, when his father was appointed to the Zhili Higher Provincial Normal School, then a brief stint at boarding schools in Switzerland and in England. Upon his return to China after World War I, he worked at the British trading firm of Arnold and Company in Tianjin. As the firm's expert on business in the interior regions, Lattimore handled the export of such products as wool, straw, and peanuts. While Lattimore loved the travel involved in this line of work, his heart was never in commerce. Lattimore resigned from Arnold and Company in 1926 to travel in the interior and subsequently to pursue academic interests back in the United States.

When Lattimore returned to the US in 1928, it was his first visit since having left as an infant in 1901. After taking some classes at Harvard, in 1930, Lattimore returned to China with a fellowship from the Harvard-Yenching Institute, followed the next year by a Guggenheim Fellowship. In Beijing he began to intensively study the Mongolian language and traveled extensively around Inner Mongolia. During these travels, he witnessed firsthand efforts to reclaim the frontier territories by military officers under Zhang Xueliang's control and the eviction of Mongolian tribes from the borderlands in the name of civilization and progress. In 1938, while serving as editor of *Pacific Affairs*, a journal funded by the Rockefeller Foundation, Lattimore came into the orbit of Isaiah Bowman and was appointed director of the Walter Hines Page School of International Relations at Johns Hopkins.

Despite having never attended college, Lattimore possessed a unique set of skills. He spoke Chinese and various dialects of Mongolian fluently and was seen as the foremost authority in the Anglo-American world on Mongolia and the Northeast Chinese borderlands. He was gifted in the art of small talk and had an uncanny ability to pick up information from strangers on his travels. He was not closely associated with any faction or political party in China. In the spring of 1941, Lauchlin Currie, economic advisor to President Roosevelt, interviewed Lattimore and recommended his appointment as an American liaison to the faltering Nationalist leader Chiang Kai-shek. Currie found Lattimore's views "New Dealish" and thought he would exert a positive influence on Chiang Kai-shek, who at the time was rapidly becoming the United States' most important ally in Asia. The recommendation was approved by President Roosevelt and forwarded to Chongqing. In a letter from June 11, 1941, Finance Minister T. V. Soong issued a formal invitation to Lattimore to serve as Chiang's personal political advisor. Lattimore left for China by the first clipper in July 1941.

Lattimore had met Chiang Kai-shek during his previous stints living in China. A compact man with a stiff military bearing, Chiang had not been the obvious choice to succeed Sun Yat-sen upon his death in 1925 from cancer in Beijing. The handsome and urbane Wang Jingwei had more charisma and revolutionary credentials. But Chiang, who had attended a military academy in Japan and taught at the Whampao Military Academy in Guangzhou, had the loyalty of his men and the harder-to-discern quality of political shrewdness, along with the ability to take sudden and decisive action.[24] In a politically fractured country, Chiang's ability to balance his political enemies against each other made him the crucial factor in the Nationalist Party's (GMD) ascendance to power. In 1928, the GMD reestablished a national capital in Nanjing, which had last served as the capital in the Ming dynasty. Events outside of his control soon embroiled Chiang and all of China in a war for survival.

Upon his arrival in Chongqing in 1941, Lattimore settled into a close and cordial relationship with the Chinese leader. Their rapport was a marked contrast to Chiang's famously contentious relationship with the US military commander Joseph Stilwell later in the war.[25] Over the next several months, Chiang and Lattimore held a series of discussions on China's wartime situation and postwar plans. In one such conversation on July 31, 1941, Chiang questioned Lattimore closely on the issue of Xinjiang, Manchuria, and Mongolia. By that point, China had already been engaged in a war of resistance for four years. China remained isolated in its efforts despite expressions of sympathy from the Americans and the Soviet Union. Chiang and his American-educated wife, Song Meiling, both urged Lattimore to directly warn Roosevelt of an imminent Japanese campaign and turn to Southeast Asia, which he did. With that expectation, almost no one in either the US or China thought Japan would instead preemptively strike the US Navy on its base in Hawaii.

In October 1941, Lattimore traveled to Kunming and Dali in Yunnan. During the trip, Lattimore took careful note of the technical staff he encountered and put his skills in small talk to great use, eliciting from the people he met their transnational educational backgrounds and their careful attention to developing the country's wartime industrial potential from the borderlands. Among those he met was Wang Shou-Ching, the general manager of the National Resources Commission Machine Works in Kunming. Wang, then thirty-eight years old, had studied physics at Ts-inghua University in Beijing, which had strong connections to American missionaries from its founding. He continued his studies at Cornell, Harvard, and Columbia University, where he ultimately obtained his PhD in physics. Wang then received a Carnegie Fellowship in physics, the only foreign national to win the fellowship that year, which he spent at the University of Wisconsin. Wang returned to China to teach physics at Peking University. By the time that Lattimore met him, Wang had become a technical expert in mechanical engineering, having spent parts of 1933, 1934, and 1936 in Germany and Czechoslovakia. As late as 1936, Wang was in Germany as a technical expert attached to a Chinese military purchasing commission. The Machine Works he now ran in Kunming employed 2,000 workers, including 30 mostly university-educated technical staff, half of whom had studied outside of China. Wang informed Lattimore that, compared to the US, German technology was organized more compactly and better suited for use in China. Instead of the mass production standard in the US, the Germans specialized in semi-mass production.

Lattimore also talked to Tseng Yang-fu, who invented a modified diesel engine that burned tung oil, and K. Y. Two, the manager of the Hihlungpa hydroelectric plant, who had studied in the US. Two had worked in Manchuria for six years and firmly believed that China could solve its energy problem by building small hydroelectric units across the country. Lattimore additionally met the industrialist and banker Miao Yun-t'ai in Kunming. Miao had gone to the US on a scholarship to the University of Illinois before transferring to Minnesota for a degree in mining engineering. He returned to China around 1919. In the years since, he had become the successful owner of a tin mine and had opened a refinery in Yunnan to cut out Hong Kong middlemen. Although he was also the leading banker in Yunnan, Miao was a firm believer in state intervention in production and supported both rural and industrial cooperatives. After his return to Chongqing in November 1942, Lattimore met with geologist and wartime GMD official Weng Wenhao, who had just returned from a month in Dihua in Xinjiang. Weng updated Lattimore on the situation with the Xingjiang warlord Sheng Shicai.

Upon his return to Chongqing, in December, Lattimore had a breakfast meeting with Chiang Kai-shek. Lattimore predicted that the war and the logic of new technologies would create the right conditions for the Nationalist government to institute policies that had been identified with the left, including farming collectives. Despite his staunchly anti-Communist views, in private conversation with Lattimore, Chiang expressed approval of Stalin's domestic policies. Asked to present his ideas, Lattimore brought up the importance of the frontier territories and the need to incorporate these areas firmly in the Chinese national political structure. Lattimore suggested providing progressive education for minorities in their own languages. Lattimore viewed Soviet policy on minority nationalities as one of its outstanding successes. In response, Chiang praised Soviet policy but insisted that the borderlands were integral parts of China.[26] In Lattimore, Chiang had found not only a direct channel to Roosevelt but also an astute observer with whom to discuss the larger geopolitical situation in Asia.

The successful completion of the China assignment made Lattimore the go-to expert for the State Department. In 1944, Lattimore was named a member of a special delegation headed by Vice President Henry Wallace. They would travel to Russia, Mongolia, and China with the goal of enhancing friendly relations with a wartime ally. The group primarily focused on agriculture and accordingly scheduled stops to inspect agricultural experiment stations, collective farms, and research institutions. They made relatively few visits to military installations. On their return, members of the mission favorably described the scientific work being done in Soviet agriculture. The collective farms they toured applied technology "in no way inferior to the methods employed by the Federal and State Departments of Agriculture in the United States." The report was complimentary on the Soviet treatment of minorities, including the Buryats, Uzbeks, Khazaks, and Yukuts, explaining that "the Russians have gone to great pains to enlist the wholehearted support of the minorities in the Soviet program," while also promoting the language and culture of the minorities.[27] The only negative comment in the report noted the "primitive" condition of the toilets in some collectives. A decade later, in the context of the climate of US anti-communism, this positive assessment of the collective farms landed the mission and its members in political hot water.

Among the places the delegation visited was the Red Dawn Cooperatives, located about ten miles northwest of Irkutsk. One hundred forty-two families (572 individuals) lived on the cooperatives, where they cultivated 2,000 hectares of land to produce mostly grains (approximately 40 percent wheat, 50 percent rye, and 10 percent oats). In return for use of the land, the collective agreed to sell 60 percent of its total production to the government at about a quarter of the market price. In addition to the farmlands, the collective also cared for 3,338 cattle and 112 horses and leased nine tractors and three combines from the state. It maintained a school with 300 pupils, a fire station, and a church building, which, because it was impossible to locate a clergyman, was used as a grain store house. With most of the men away at war, 70 percent of the fieldwork was done by women. The Americans noted that another collective, the Telman Collective, used a type of silo which was first developed by the Wisconsin Experimental Station. Other experimental stations visited by the delegation conducted research on crops, vegetables, and fruits that could withstand the extreme temperatures common in the region. In Tashkent, the Commissar of Agriculture Kasyan Rakhymov stated that 1.5 million hectares of land were under cultivation, with 500,000 added since 1939. The Agro-Technical Experiment station studied ways to improve the cotton crop, while also experimenting with increasing the yield of onions, melons, tomatoes, and cucumbers.

What Wallace, Lattimore, and other members of the mission failed to realize was the extent to which the Soviets had prepared to welcome them by carefully staging Potemkin villages for their inspection.[28] The experimental stations and model farms they visited, what Wallace referred to as "a combination of TVA [Tennessee Valley Authority] and Hudson's Bay Company," were a carefully constructed façade. Just short walks away from these sites, laborers in the vast gulag system toiled behind barbed wire fences. At Magadan, a new mining center in the Kolyma Valley that the Wallace mission visited, thousands of prisoners extracted precious metals from ores mined nearby. In one such prison camp, the great plant hunter and geneticist Nicolai Vavilov had died in 1943, most likely from malnutrition. Over decades of global travel, Vavilov had collected a vast seedbank of plant varieties from sixty-four countries around the world. After he was arrested in 1940 and imprisoned, fellow scientists kept guard over the seeds he had so painstakingly gath-

ered and stored in Leningrad (now St. Petersburg). During the 872-day
Siege of Leningrad during World War II, they starved rather than touch
any of the tons of food they protected with their lives.[29]

Wallace publicized the mission's findings in a book, *Soviet Asia Mission,* which presented Soviet accomplishments in a positive light. Lattimore sold his own travel account to the *National Geographic.* Within a
decade, Wallace and Lattimore's glowing reports, along with their unfortunate comparisons of gulags to the Tennessee Valley Authority, fueled
suspicions of Lattimore's communist sympathies. Unbeknownst to Lattimore, by decade's end the FBI had already opened a file on him as a
suspected communist and briefly kept him under surveillance.[30] Within
a decade, his every word became grist for a trial in the US Senate led
by Senator Joseph McCarthy, who accused Lattimore of being the top
Soviet spy in the US. Although the congressional committee eventually
cleared Lattimore of the charges, his career was derailed by the hearings.
In 1953, Bowman's successor as president of Johns Hopkins University,
Detlev Bronk, announced the closing of the Walter Hines Page School,
and along with it, the elimination of Lattimore's position as its director to
appease the university's trustees, who had pushed him to fire Lattimore
outright. Although Hopkins never fired Lattimore, for the next decade, he
languished as a lecturer as his career in the US effectively came to an end.

While Lattimore went about his wartime missions, a Chinese historian had reached very similar conclusions about how China's geography
influenced its past and future. In 1948, the historian and oracle bone
expert Ding Shan (1902–1952) published a slim volume titled *Geography
and the Rise and Fall of Chinese Civilization* (*Dili yu zhonghua minzu zhi
shengshuai* 地理與中華民族之盛衰). In the work, Ding argued that geography is the key to history and civilization, a conclusion that the historian
Gu Jiegang (1893–1980) reinforced in the preface he penned to the work.
Gu Jiegang had written extensively on historical geography beginning
in the 1920s and in 1938 had coauthored a work of historical geography
entitled *A History of Change in China's Frontier Regions.*[31] The historical
geographer Tan Qixiang and Gu Jiegang, like their Western intellectual
counterparts, used history to legitimize conquest and incorporate imperial territories into the national body.[32]

In contrast to Lattimore, whose career peaked in the 1940s with his
State Department assignments, in the previous decades Ding's career
progressed largely outside of the limelight. Ding was born in 1901 in

rural Anhui province to a poor family. In 1924, he entered Peking University's graduate program in national studies *guoxue* 國學. In the following decades, he taught at Xiamen University, Zhongshan University, and Shandong University. He also worked as a research associate at the Institute of Philology at Academia Sinica from 1929 to 1932. His diary entries in the years from 1936 to 1951 record a broad range of readings in Western philosophy, anthropology, and sociology, including works by Ernst Grosse, Gustave Le Bon, and Edward Westermarck, as well as the classics of Chinese historical geography and history. Other than writing a series of lectures on ancient Chinese geography in 1936, however, he did not appear particularly invested in the field of geography.[33]

In a retrospective of Ding's life written in the 1980s, safely after the end of the Maoist era, and when scholars might once again study oracle bones and the archaeology of ancient civilizations, the author claimed that, before his death in Qingdao in 1952, Ding devoted himself to the study of Marxist-Leninist thought. This is certainly possible, given Ding's wide-ranging reading habits, but if so, there's no record of this intellectual turn late in his life. While geographers in Chongqing devoted themselves to fieldwork, trekking up mountains and to the dangerous upper reaches of rivers, Ding read histories. While members of the Warring State Clique published bombastic articles comparing the contemporary geopolitical conflict to the Warring States period, Ding worked on a manuscript on the ancient Shang civilization.

Even as his readings carried him to the remote past, time was not on Ding's side. Ding had tuberculosis in his youth. The hardships of the war years further exacerbated these health issues; his health rapidly deteriorated in the years before his death in Qingdao. As his health declined, his diary entries grew sparser and shorter. They recorded visits to the bank and to doctors, the changing weather, and often, his daily readings. From 1946 to the publication of *Geography* in 1948, Ding returned time and again to reading the Yuan dynasty classic *Wenxian Tongkao* 文獻通考 and the foundational text of Chinese historiography, the *Shi Ji* 史記. These entries provide little evidence that Ding had returned to his previous interest in historical geography. Yet, on the eve of the Communist victory, Ding Shan pulled together the various geographical threads of the previous decades, whether originating from left- or right-leaning intellectual circles, and synthesized them in a book that connected history, geography, and geopolitics.

Unlike many other works of geography published during the Republican period, Ding's *Geography* did not include a single map. Nor did he try to draw analogies between events in ancient China and the present. Instead, he drew out the geographical understanding that had always been present in Chinese histories but had largely been overshadowed in the twentieth century by the flood of New Geography and the visual impact of maps in these works. Ding argued that geography is the key to history and civilization. The connections he made between geography, history, and civilizational claims date to the late Qing period. By the time Ding Shan penned his book, geopolitical ideas had circulated widely in China for over four decades. Similarly, social Darwinian ideas of states engaged in wars for survival had been in circulation for more than half a century. Ding Shan brought all these ideas, scattered across various journals, newspaper articles, textbooks, and histories, into one book.

First, Ding pointed out that geographical differences led to cultural divisions. Starting with the First Emperor's unification of China, Ding argued, Chinese rulers overcame these geographical barriers by forced cultural homogenization. For Ding, the pinnacle of the Han dynasty's achievements came with the emperor Han Wudi's sponsorship of Zhang Qian's westward expeditions and wars of conquest in western regions. These military campaigns, however, exposed the Han nationality's (*minzu*) reliance on the power of horses, leading to Ding's second major point: the importance of horses in warfare and in the rise and demise of the early dynasties.

Next, Ding turned to north-south differences in Chinese geography, which he viewed as a long-term contributor to an unfortunate north-south tension in Chinese history.[34] Ding pointed to the successive southern remnants of northern empires.[35] Moving rapidly through dynasties, Ding saw the Qing's capable management of the border regions and Tibet as its greatest accomplishment.[36] For Ding Shan, the Qing's demise could be traced to its loss of control of productive power. The Industrial Revolution unleashed for the West a burst of dynamic impetus which brought down the Qing, much as the powerful horse-riding, nomadic peoples of the northwestern regions ran roughshod over the sedentary agricultural peoples of the Chinese cultural heartlands in the Han and Tang dynasties.

Ding posited that crises throughout Chinese history had been created by external forces. Before the Opium War, he argued, these external pressures frequently originated from the deserts of the Northwest; after the Opium War, they arrived over the seas.[37] Ding cited the 1915 work *Geography and World Power*, written by James Fairgrieve, one of Halford Mackinder's students, which had been translated into Chinese in 1937.[38] The very brevity and vagueness of Fairgrieve's discussion of China allowed his Chinese readers room for interpretation. In the short section on China, Fairgrieves made a standard geo-determinist argument, highlighting the importance of the railroad as an essential infrastructure connecting North China to Central Asia.[39] Ding slightly altered Fairgrieves's assessment by equating the Japanese invasion from the Northeast with historical invasions of the Chinese heartland from the Northwest. Time and again over the course of Chinese history, Ding argued, these border regions posed a strategic threat to Chinese civilization, one that if left unchecked spelled its doom. Written after the Japanese surrender, Ding already saw beyond the current war to the potential source of future conflict.

Like Owen Lattimore, Ding Shan recognized the importance of the frontier to the development of Chinese history. Both also recognized the impact of industrialization in unleashing new forces on the age-old dynamics of the frontier; of the sedentary, agriculturally based society in the core of Chinese civilization; of the mixed culture of the borderlands; and of the nomadic, horse-centered cultures beyond the pale. In his 1935 book on the Inner Asian frontiers, Owen Lattimore had put forward his "reservoir" theory of Manchuria. The territories on the other side of the Great Wall, Lattimore asserted, served as a reservoir for the successive waves of foreign invaders who eventually conquered China. Ding displayed the same concern over borderlands as a potential vulnerable opening for foreign invasion.

When the Nationalists lost the civil war and retreated to Taiwan in 1949, it would be the Communist regime that continued to carry out the territorial agenda foretold by Ding, Lattimore, and other geographers.[40] Ding, in particular, emphasized the role of technology in changing China's geopolitical calculus. Like Lattimore, he recognized that new developments in science and technology, initially the railroad and steamships, then later airplanes, shifted the balance of power between land and sea. Lattimore, too, recognized the significance of this shift for China, which "like India, Indonesia, Pakistan, Argentina, and Brazil—has been added to the countries which, combining large area, large population, and great diversified natural resources for internal industrial development, can no longer be dominated by across-the-ocean projection of either naval or naval-and-land power."[41] All of these developments enhanced the importance of the western frontiers for China.[42] A new age dawned, one that hearkened back to the ancient overland routes connecting Europe and Asia—but now the routes would be connected by air and rail. Air power, in other words, required that states adjust the balance of naval and land power. Long before the latest American incursions in Iraq and Afghanistan, Lattimore looked to the limited success of Japan's bombing efforts against Chongqing and Shanghai to argue that air power alone could not secure territories.

In *Geography*, Ding adapted these ideas on historical progress and technology by placing the discussion in the context of the longue durée of Chinese history from the Qin dynasty to the present. He reinterpreted this history with technology as the decisive factor in the fight over control of the Chinese borderlands. Like Kjellén at the turn of the century, Ding concisely and expertly brought together the larger intellectual currents of his time. Lattimore and Ding never met in person. Their ideas, however, converged and pointed to the geopolitical future of China.

The Mountains Remain

Anti-Communism campaigns in the United States and anti-imperialism campaigns in the Soviet Union and China formed a strange symmetry. While the territorial vision that saw the bifurcation of the world into capitalist and socialist blocs endured during these years, the people who crafted the vision, particularly geographers and other social scientists, fared less well. The mountains and rivers remained constant; people went into exile, were hounded, persecuted, imprisoned, and driven to suicide.

From 1949, the Communist Party's consolidation of power in China established stability for Chinese scientists and social scientists to once again conduct research in the frontier regions. Chinese geographical research in the 1950s continued efforts started during the war years under the Nationalists. Scientific organizations had rushed to aid the war effort to burnish their reputations by contributing to the patriotic defense of the nation. The Chinese Geographical Association was formed in the crucible of the war, in Beibei, a small village outside the wartime capital of Chongqing, where the rest of Academia Sinica relocated. One of the leading geographers in the country, Huang Guozhang 黃國璋 (1896–1966), contributed the preface to the inaugural issue of the *Journal of Geography* (*Dili* 地理), the association's primary publication. Like many of his fellow scientists, Huang had received his training overseas. A Hunan native, Huang had received his graduate degree in geography from the University of Chicago and returned to China in 1928 to take up a teaching post in Nanjing. Like many other leading intellectuals, Huang retreated with the GMD army into the interior after the Japanese invasion.[43]

Huang's preface introducing the new journal begins by acknowledging the ancient roots of geography in both the West and in China, although in his view, Chinese geography stagnated and failed to go through the revolutionary changes the field had undergone in the West in the nineteenth century. As a result, in his view, Chinese geography had only begun to catch up when Chinese students began studying abroad in large numbers. Universities in China had only begun to establish geography departments in the 1920s. According to Huang, "Modern geography seeks to establish the principles of the relationship between mankind and the earth. Geography is not only a theoretical science, but also a discipline that seeks to address practical ways of improving people's lives. It is particularly important to the education of citizens of the nation."[44] For Huang, geography could serve as a compass both for China's diplomatic efforts and its domestic policy. All organisms compete to survive and must adapt to their environment, according to Huang, but mankind goes a step further, having the ability not only to adapt to the environment, but also to exploit its value.[45] Huang explained that the *Journal of Geography* would contribute to Chinese survival by broadcasting geographers' efforts to a broader reading public, targeting in particular university students, middle school geography teachers, and all those with an interest in geographical research.[46]

Within three months of the Geographical Association's founding, the geographers formed two fieldwork groups. The first group spent nine months in the field working on the upper reaches of the Jialing River. A second group spent nine months in the field researching the valley region between the Da Ba mountains in northeastern Sichuan and Hubei. In 1941, the various groups in Academia Sinica organized six research teams. The largest of these was the Northwest research team. The Ministry of Forestry formed a research group for the Qinghai/Gansu region.

In 1946, then-president of the Chinese Geographical Association (Zhong-guo dili xuehui 中國地理學會) Li Chengsan 李承三 wrote a report on the current state of geography and the prospects for the field after almost a decade of war.[47] Li ended his report on an optimistic note, remarking that geography in China was still in its infancy. Many people, he wrote, still do not see geography as a science. As a result, the geographers would need to redouble their efforts to prove their worth as scientists.

The Chinese geographers cast their lot with the state. In the years to come they would pay dearly for this decision. Under the severe constraints of wartime conditions, the society continued its research program, carrying out surveys and participating in the long-term planning on the development of the Northwest. But despite the patriotic fervor with which Chinese geographers threw themselves into their research and their eagerness to contribute to the war effort, ominous signs had already appeared by war's end that the state viewed geography as essential but geographers as expendable. The geographers' staff morale plummeted when Academia Sinica moved back to Nanjing but left the geographers behind in Sichuan with no sense of when they might rejoin the larger organization. Their building in Beibei was sold, with the staff unceremoniously evicted and moved to a separate building several kilometers away.

For scientists and social scientists, it at first appeared that the end of the civil war and Communist victory would finally allow them the political stability to pursue their research and fieldwork. Many felt great optimism that they would contribute to the building of the nation in a new era of peace. In the initial phases of conquest, the Communist regime appeared much more open to the efforts of scholars to promote better relations between Han Chinese and minority groups on the frontiers. Under the People's Republic, Academia Sinica was renamed the Chinese Academy of Sciences and top Chinese scientists, like geologist Weng Wenhao and meteorologist Zhu Kezhen, were invited to return to the mainland, whatever their previous political affiliations. During the Japanese invasion, Weng had served as director of the Industrial and Mining Adjustment Administration for the GMD and oversaw the evacuation and relocation of Chinese industries.[48] Weng was the highest-level GMD official to repatriate. His return to the mainland marked a major coup for the new regime.

The considerable personnel overlap into the late 1950s underscores similarities between the wartime research agendas of scientific institutions under the GMD and that of the newly established academies in the People's Republic of China (PRC) in the 1950s. The last years of the civil war had proved exceptionally damaging to the scientific infrastructure in China and further decimated the scientific community's confidence in the GMD state. The fact that Weng Wenhao and Zhu Kezhen were both recruited to high positions with the newly reorganized Chinese Academy of Sciences must have been encouraging to the geography community. Yet almost immediately, starting in the early 1950s, ideological debates broke out to cleanse geography of its wartime connections to the suspect branches of geopolitics and environmental determinism. One could trace the transformation of the geographical community in the pages of the journal *Geographical Knowledge* (*Dili Zhishi* 地理知識).

The inaugural issue in 1950, published when the China Geographical Society had only recently moved back to Nanjing from Chongqing, set forth the new ideological foundations for the field in Communist China. Geography, the introduction intoned, must serve the masses. In the old China, geographical research was controlled by the ruling classes to serve their feudal objectives. The people's revolution, however, had now washed away old China and liberated geography.[49] Within months, Chinese Academy of Sciences vice president Zhu Kezhen delivered a harsh rebuke of the discipline. Zhu informed the geographers that the creation of an institute of geography at the Academy had been delayed because of the weak scientific nature of geography.

By 1951, the journal increasingly featured translations of Russian geographers rather than original research produced by Chinese geographers. Criticism of the field mounted from the top. In December 1951, the journal's operations were moved to the capital in Beijing. In that issue, the journal conducted a scathing set of self-criticisms, pointing out three fundamental errors in the discipline: (1) a vague political stance, (2) taking on a bourgeois perspective, and (3) working against the scientific truth.[50] Three months later, the journal published Zhu Kezhen's keynote address at the Chinese Geographical Association's first national congress. In the address, Zhu pointed to the checkered history of the field, with multiple associations formed between 1909 and 1940, including the founding of a China Geographical Research Institute in Chongqing. Zhu himself had actively participated in some of these endeavors, but under intense political pressure, Zhu now identified geography as a politically problematic discipline. As had Harvard president James Conant in his decision to shut down Harvard's geography department, Zhu cited geography's lack of a scientific foundation.

For the rest of the 1950s, each issue of *Geographical Knowledge* featured a photospread of different regions of the country, showcasing the conquest of nature accomplished by the masses, from terracing in Gansu, to great hydroelectric projects around the country, to the accomplishments of the first Five Year Plan. In 1952, Tian Meng translated a volume edited by the Soviet Academy of Science entitled *Geography in the Service of American Imperialism.* The work roundly excoriated geopolitics as a tool of American chauvinism, a cause of the recent worldwide conflicts, and an intellectual cover for economic exploitation.[51] The suspect nature of geography was made clear by a series of essays on the various shortcomings of geography as practiced in Western Europe and the US.

Over the next decade, the Chinese Academy of Sciences and the Chinese Geographical Society published a series of critiques against imperialist components within geography. A 1955 translated volume of essays by Soviet scientists specifically identified three aspects of bourgeois geography: geopolitics, Malthusian population discourse, and environmental determinism.[52] By the 1960s, the acceptable parameters of geography in China had narrowed to the study of soil composition and other practically oriented fields of physical geography (*ziran dili* 自然地理) and cartography. The determined practical focus of research at the Chinese Academy of Sciences (CAS) continued the prewar trend of emphasizing geology, surveying work, and research on natural resources. In 1956, the CAS formed an Interdisciplinary Committee for Exploration to create the institutional structure for scientists across various disciplines to collaborate on fieldwork and research devoted to exploiting natural resources. Along similar lines as the Chinese Communist Party's economic planning process, the CAS interdisciplinary committee established five-year plans and divided their research program into macro regions. The research agenda largely continued the wartime focus on border regions in the Northeast, the Northwest, and the Southwest.[53] Their work focused on the development of practical science on the frontiers, including surveys for developing the coal and oil industries and other natural resources essential to the national economy. The PRC's first major oil strike, on September 26, 1959, in the Songliao Basin in the Northeast, resulted from one of these surveys and resulted in the development of a national oil industry at Daqing.[54]

The establishment of a scientific infrastructure in frontier territories laid the groundwork for economic development in these regions. The CAS maintained a Xinjiang research team between 1956 and 1960; a Qinghai / Gansu research team in 1958–1960; and an Inner Mongolia / Ningxia research team in 1961–1966. The CAS's twelve-year, long-term plan furthermore called for the establishment of fourteen regional research institutes in the provincial capitals of Urumqi in Xinjiang and Hohhot in Inner Mongolia. These institutes of geographical, geological, soil science, animal, and plant sciences, along with institutes covering economic and historical research, formally launched between 1962 and 1965 with anywhere from twenty-two to sixty researchers at each location.[55] In 1957, CAS president Guo Moruo led a delegation of 120 CAS academicians to Moscow to consult Soviet experts on their long-term research plans. The Soviets' sixteen-member panel of experts criticized the CAS long-term plan as not setting sufficiently clear goals, but otherwise supported the Chinese research agenda. As a result, CAS redoubled its efforts in places like Xinjiang, with practically oriented research that would bear fruit for the development of agriculture, mining, and industry.[56]

After 1949, the agronomist Tang Qiyu continued to advocate for the inner colonization of the Chinese frontier. Unlike many geographers who promoted similar ideas about reinforcing the frontiers through Han settlement, and despite having served in various positions in the GMD wartime government, including as the deputy director of the Department of Reclamation in the Ministry of Agriculture and Forestry, Tang managed the Republican-PRC transition with minimal political exposure. He returned to Shanghai, where he was in the Agricultural Department's cadre school when a stroke forced him to retire. The health crisis turned out to be a blessing in disguise. Tang availed himself of the various resources in the Shanghai library to work on a massive agricultural history book and only stopped writing with the outbreak of the Cultural Revolution.[57] He passed away in 1978 in Shanghai after suffering another stroke. His son published his magnum opus on the longue durée history of Chinese agriculture posthumously in 1986.

Tang's ideas about inner colonization, which centered on settling excess Han Chinese population in the Northwest, had also been popular amongst geographers. The new regime's objections to this approach were already apparent in a grade-school textbook of geography written within the first months of Beijing's fall to Communist forces in 1949.[58] The textbook introduced the Marxist historical narrative of China's liberation from feudal oppression: "In the past the Han people represented the landlords. The capitalist political operatives promoted the 'Greater Han Ethnic Principle,' and oppressed the Mongolians, the Hui, the Tibetans, the Miao, the Yao and other minorities. Henceforth under the leadership of the Communist Party and the people, all ethnic minorities within the country could enjoy true freedom and equality."[59] The rousing rhetoric on equality, however, fell short of advocating for self-determination. The textbook taught, "We should follow the principle of ethnic equality, and offer them [the minorities] forceful help in the political, economic, and cultural arenas, bringing about a true unity of the ethnicities."[60] When push came to shove, it seems, the Chinese Communist Party was not quite willing to grant the ethnic minorities in the borderlands the full right of self-determination. Cloaked in Marxist rhetoric was the same program as the civilizing mission of the interwar years.

At least for Tang Qiyu, the disciplinary demarcations between the geographical and agronomical basis for inner colonialization turned out to be crucial. As an agronomist, Tang continued working well into the 1950s. His health, rather than past service in the GMD regime, led to his retirement. Geographers, on the other hand, quickly became embroiled in political attacks. Huang Guozhang, one of the founders of the wartime Institute of Geography, committed suicide with his wife in 1966. Noted human geographers Hu Huanyong and Li Xudan were labeled counterrevolutionaries in the 1950s and spent years in jail before being rehabilitated in the 1980s. Political scientist Lin Tongji, who received his PhD from UC Berkeley, was labeled a rightist in 1958. More "fortunate" members of that cohort of social scientists, including the geographer Sha Xuejun and Zhang Yintang, lived out the rest of their lives in exile in Taiwan and the United States respectively. The litany of tragic fates is at once a somber reminder of individual powerlessness against the relentless political upheavals in twentieth-century China and an intimation of a much larger epistemological shift at work since the nineteenth century, shaped by evolving ideas about the state, empire, and science.

Land of No Regrets

During the Ming dynasty, the state allowed soldiers to bring their families with them to garrison the southern frontiers. Despite these measures, the military had trouble keeping the soldier settlers in the mountainous region. The Qing state, on the other hand, forbade women from migrating to the borderlands. The gendered social hierarchy of the dynasty elevated the ideal of cloistered women.[61] As a result, Chinese migration, both internally to the borderlands and overseas in the Chinese diaspora, was highly gender imbalanced, with sojourning men and women who remained at home in the villages.[62] Twentieth-century population displacements challenged some of these patterns. The chaos of wartime drove men and women alike off their land. The new Communist regime would further challenge the gendered pattern of migration. The settlement of Xinjiang in the 1950s, which took place under the auspices of the People's Liberation Army, illustrates some of these fundamental breaks from earlier migration. While efforts at land reclamation (*kaiken* or *tunken*) followed imperial precedents, the PRC policy on women proved to be the most significant break from earlier practices.

After the end of World War II in 1945, the military situation for the GMD steadily eroded in the civil war with Communist forces. In 1946, the Nationalist (GMD) commander Tao Zhiyue (1892–1988) was appointed by Chiang Kai-shek to stabilize the situation in Xinjiang. Tao had attended military academy in Wuchang (present day Wuhan) and joined the revolutionary group *Tongmenghui* (Revolutionary Alliance) when unrest broke out in the city in 1911, which subsequently brought about the downfall of the Qing dynasty. In 1916, he graduated from the famed Baoding Military Academy. In September 1949, the Red Army general Wang Zhen (1908–1993) led the first People's Liberation Army (PLA) units into Xinjiang. Recognizing the inevitable, Tao severed relations with the Nationalist government. For his betrayal, Tao was rewarded by Mao and allowed to retain command of his reorganized troops. Approximately 89,000 PLA troops advanced on Xinjiang, combined with 71,000 Nationalist soldiers already stationed on the frontiers, plus some additional local ethnic troops, to make up a total force of 170,000 soldiers.[63] The newly established People's Republic of China immediately sought to turn the troops to productive labor along the frontiers. A mere two months after the founding of the People's Republic and

Mao's iconic moment atop Tiananmen Square on October 1, 1949, Mao issued a proclamation on troop participation in labor and production. The first order of business was land reclamation in the borderlands. The Reclaim Wastelands and Plant Crops campaign (*kaihuang zhongdi* 開荒種地) launched with the target of bringing 600,000 *mu* of wasteland under cultivation for 1950. The PLA exceeded this target and reclaimed over 960,000 *mu* in 1950.

As with wartime reclamation projects under the previous regime, the statistics of progress hid ugly conditions on the ground. The presence of nearly 200,000 soldiers in Xinjiang created an enormous gender disparity. Among the troops, men outnumbered women 160:1; among those older than thirty and unmarried, the ratio was 300:1. Efforts to recruit a youth corps to Xinjiang from May to October in 1949 netted over 10,000 recruits but, of these recruits, only 1,127, or roughly 11 percent, were women.[64] Unlike some Nationalist commanders during the war, who condoned and even encouraged relations with local women, Wang Zhen was adamant that ethnic Han troops not be allowed to marry non-Han women. Wang believed that such relations could potentially inflame tensions with indigenous populations. Such a skewed gender ratio was obviously untenable for long-term occupation, however, and Wang Zhen personally requested permission from Marshall Peng Dehuai to recruit women settlers to Xinjiang.

From the beginning, a cloak of secrecy surrounded the attempts to recruit women to the frontiers. The first efforts in Shaanxi and Gansu advertised openings for party cadre training. Without explicitly mentioning the army, the advertising succinctly advertised three months of training in Lanzhou in Gansu province. After a mere month of "training," at 3 a.m. on the morning of October 6, 1949, 1,500 recruits, including 150 fourteen- and fifteen-year-old girls, set off for Xinjiang. From Turfan they had to walk the last 1,800 kilometers to Kashi. As they passed through the Tianshan region, some number of recruits, including a few women, remained at each stop. Similar recruiting trips continued for several years, but they did little to correct the gender imbalance. Such was the scramble for marriageable women that, in a 1950 speech, the Second Army political cadre Wang Enmao issued a priority list for how the men would select wives. Comrades over the age of thirty should get the first picks, followed by the twenty-eight- or twenty-nine-year-olds, and then those older than twenty-five. When relatives and family were allowed to join the troops, they nevertheless amounted to only an additional 3,148 members of the Han Chinese population.

Both Wang Zhen and Tao Zhiyue hailed from Hunan. When it became clear that they needed to step up recruiting efforts to address the gender imbalance, they turned to their home province. Starting in January 1951, the *New Hunan News* (*Xin Hunan Bao*) published advertising every few days encouraging settlement in Xinjiang. In 1951, 3,000 women recruited from Hunan arrived in Xinjiang in thirteen groups.[65] In 1952, Wang Zhen also attempted to recruit from Shandong. Over the next few years, around 9,000 women from Shandong were recruited for Xinjiang. Thanks to these campaigns, the bulk of the female recruits in the 1950s came from Hunan and Shandong.

To attract potential settlers, recruiters downplayed the hardships involved and oversold the actual conditions of various "industries" in Xinjiang. Women were told that marriage was an essential duty of the revolution. The severe gender imbalance, however, created conditions ripe for abuse. Many recruits were ambushed with surprise weddings to strangers upon their arrival. Instead of the jobs in factories that some recruiters promised, the women, some underage, discovered the lack of even basic amenities, housing that consisted of holes dug into the ground, and little or no health services for those with mental or physical problems. On August 3, 1953, the situation was severe enough for the military district to issue a special report on emergency measures to address women's mental issues.

According to the report, women were to be educated about the national marital law, which mandated the legal age for marriage and allowed for divorce to be initiated by both parties. The legislation was considered the signal victory for Chinese feminists in the twentieth century in their fight for gender equality. On the ground, however, the new marital law encountered frequent opposition in rural areas, where men viewed it as undue state intervention with their women. In response to the mental health crisis, the report suggested sending those patients with conditions that could not be treated locally to Urumqi. Giving a hint of the extent of the problem, the report explicitly stated that restraining patients by tying them to bedframes is the wrong method of treatment.[66] The army also raised the age requirement for female recruits to at least twenty years old. Nevertheless, women who entered Xinjiang from the interior generally married by age sixteen or seventeen, significantly younger than the age mandated by the national marriage law. Rumors quickly spread among recruits about conditions in Xinjiang. To prevent escapes, including women's attempts to jump from trains, the train cars holding recruits were padlocked. Still, some women attempted to run. According to the official count, nearly forty women from Shandong died on the journey to Xinjiang between 1950 and 1954. [67]

Starting in the 1990s, members of this group of settlers began to publish oral interviews and celebratory volumes commemorating their settler experiences. A collection of oral interviews of women who moved to Xinjiang from Hunan is deeply revealing. In the published accounts, the women explain they were inspired to migrate to Xinjiang in the spirit of Nanniwan (the Communist *tunken* base in Yan'an.)[68] In account after account, women end the narrative of their life experiences with the expression, *wu yuan wuhui* 无怨无悔 (to have neither complaint nor regret), even when the actual content of these accounts appears to belie the notion of having neither complaint nor regret. One woman vividly recalled her shock upon discovering that her wedding to a stranger was arranged to occur immediately upon her arrival at her assigned work unit.[69] Other accounts referenced the pitiable lives of women for whom multiple arranged marriages failed.

The gender policies adopted by the new regime would continue to reverberate in the twenty-first century. By the 1980s, later arrivals in Xinjiang from cities like Shanghai longed to return home. Some did so, even without employment prospects, benefits, or legal status. They carried on long legal fights with the government for the right to return to what they viewed as their real homes.[70] The decision by top military and Communist party officials to discourage intermarriage meant that the waves of Han settlers who moved into Xinjiang since 1949 have never been integrated into local society and social networks. This blinkered and racialized view of frontier/borderland settlements was not unique to China. A geopolitical view of the world, determined by a select group of men, reduced people and individual motivations to moves on a chessboard and exacted a steep price for building geo-modernity on the frontiers.

———

The chapter opened with the unlikely intersection of Tang dynasty poet Du Fu and the twentieth-century American political scientist Nicholas Spykman; the story continued with the careers and lives of Isaiah

Bowman, Zhang Qiyun, Owen Lattimore, Ding Shan, Tang Qiyu, and the thousands of men and women who were recruited to settle the borderlands in Xinjiang beginning in the 1950s. These lives cut across the rise and fall of empires, the peak era of American postwar global hegemony, and China's Cold War–era military reclamation campaigns in the northwestern borderlands. In the clash of empires, individual lives fell to the wayside, buffeted by forces beyond their control.

In chapter 6, wartime German and Chinese reclamation plans converged through the invisible networks of social scientists and the theories that underpinned their planning for frontier development. In this chapter, two different opposing countries in the Cold War, the US and China, again shared surprising points of intersection in their pursuit of nontraditional empires. The mountains and rivers remain, but in the crisscrossing paths of these individual lives and the overlap of ideas we see not only how such global networks transcended the constraints of time and space but also the human cost of geo-modernity, paid for in lives lived far from home.

Epilogue

> It has been basic United States policy that Government should foster the opening of new frontiers. It opened the seas to clipper ships and furnished land for pioneers. Although these frontiers have more or less disappeared, the frontier of science remains. It is in keeping with the American tradition—one which has made the United States great—that new frontiers shall be made accessible for development by all American citizens.
>
> *Vannevar Bush, "Science, the Endless Frontier," 1945*

About an hour's drive north from Knoxville, Tennessee, on I-75, the entrance to the Cumberland Gap National Historical Park takes you straight to a vantage point where one could look out to the juncture of three states: Kentucky, Tennessee, and Virginia. Looking out upon these rolling green hills, as far as the eye can see, one might imagine the same vista greeting the first Anglo settlers. Early Anglo settlers pushed southwest across the Appalachians mountains through the Cumberland Gap. The reddish clay-like soil of these parts is not agriculturally productive, and so the settlers headed steadily south and westward to more fertile grounds. By the time I visited in 2012, that pioneering past was a distant memory. By the end of the nineteenth century, this push across the Appalachian Mountains was already a remote history. The West was won and the Cherokee peoples evicted from their homelands in these verdant mountains to the arid and flat stretches of Oklahoma. The key question of the age was no longer the opening of new lands but the more efficient development of existing agricultural lands.

A short distance away, hidden in a valley in the foothills of the Smoky Mountains is the Oak Ridge National Laboratories, where the Manhattan Project had achieved a crucial phase to its successful development of the first nuclear bomb. Anglo settlers had pushed Indian tribes from this land. In the 1940s, the American military removed the farming families in the valley and within months built a secret laboratory that drew more power than the island of Manhattan. In the early morning hours of November 4, 1943, the graphite reactor reached criticality. With criticality, the scientists knew that the bomb was within reach and a new atomic frontier of science opened.

In 2022, it's not nuclear science but the next supercomputer, one step closer to quantum computing, named Frontier, that has come to define the next phase of American scientific development. As the world's most powerful computer and the United States' first exascale computer, the Department of Energy touted Frontier as the crucial accelerant to American innovation in science and technology and US leadership in high-performance computing and artificial intelligence. When it reaches full capacity, Frontier will operate at five times the speed of the current fastest supercomputers in the world at an astonishing quintillion calculations per second. Several centuries have passed between one kind of frontier symbolized by the Cumberland Gap to the metaphorical frontiers at Oak Ridge, but both represent the centrality of the frontier to American identity and policy. The frontier closed but never ended.

In his account of the Cold War, Odd Arne Westad has argued that "science and education were at the heart of the project to build modern states in the Third World."[1] These methods did not originate with the Cold War but were crafted and refined in the age of empires. From the US side, these developmental ideas, some of which were pioneered by nongovernmental organizations like the Rockefeller Foundation as discussed in chapter 5, shaped the countryside of Afghanistan and India, Africa and South America, and formed the foundational conceptions behind US foreign policy in the twentieth century.[2] In many of these places both formal and informal US aid and investments were targeted at limiting the influence of Soviet intervention. Nor were these methods limited to the Cold War superpowers—I have tried to show that China and its reconceptualization of empire should be considered part of the global history of how science and frontiers transformed the modern world.

In the twentieth and twenty-first centuries, empire took on new forms: from transnational American corporations, the European Union, to the Belt and Road Initiative in China since 2013.[3] In recent years China has launched multiple efforts to expand its territorial claims from the South China Sea to the Himalayan highlands on the contested border with India. Rather than wait for international bodies like the UN to hand down decisions on its claims, China has simply built airstrips and entire villages on artificial islands. Commentators have viewed these land grabs as part of China's increasingly aggressive foreign policy in the wake of its rise as a global power.[4] A longer perspective reveals the historical context for these Chinese claims and how they emerged from a period of global flux as imperial concerns dueled with rising nationalism and the rethinking of territoriality and the purview of state power.

The kind of claims that China has made in recent years date to the late nineteenth and early twentieth centuries. The loss of Qing claims to Japan in Korea, Taiwan, and the Ryukyus, and other territories to Western powers including France, Britain, and Russia, was widely portrayed as a series of national humiliations.[5] Even as imperial language was jettisoned in favor of nationalistic claims, many Chinese intellectuals, including the foremost geographers and scientists of the period, sought to retain the imperial territories. In these efforts, the setting up of "reclamation" zones in the borderlands was viewed as an essential part of national defense. Although many of the intellectuals involved described these efforts as either rooted in antiquity or entirely modern and based on science, land reclamation projects in the twentieth century in many respects carried on late Qing efforts to reinforce its borderland territories. These projects survived the collapse of the last imperial dynasty and crossed the partisan divides of twentieth-century political regimes.

This work has shown the ways that geography and related fields of agricultural science contributed to a global geo-modernity. A new territoriality emerged, based on a fixation with frontiers but also reliant on the deployment of science to exploit natural resources and enact development schemes in contested territories. The countries discussed in this book, including the United States, Germany, China, and Japan, all participated in new forms of imperialism that depart from traditional empires and a strictly spatial concept of territory. From the nineteenth century Germany pioneered New Imperialism as empire ruled by technical and scientific expertise. Japan followed the German example as it extended its territories to the Asian mainland. In Manchuria Japanese imperialism reached its apotheosis—empire in the guise of a nation-state formed out of the principles of self-determination.[6] World War II brought about the dramatic downfalls of both the German Third Reich and the Japanese Empire. Rumors of the death throes of empire as a state-form, however, may have been exaggerated. In the postwar period, both the United States and China embarked on the reconstitution of empire by different means. In the former, corporate and nongovernment organizations took the lead in building a transnational technocratic elite; in the latter, Marxist ideology provided an ideological cover for the retention of empire by other names.

As we settle into the twenty-first century, it is worth noting that of all the countries that attempted to resurrect the empire as a state form in the preceding century, only China has retained its imperial expanse and is looking to actively expand. Yet, China, too, has had to contend with a deteriorating security situation in Xinjiang, a restive population in Tibet, and active pushback from neighboring states. In response to growing unrest in Xinjiang, the central government brought to bear the full force of new technologies of surveillance along with the old techniques of incarceration and reeducation. The draconian quarantine measures in the Chinese response to the Covid-19 outbreak draws from the same arsenal of intrusive surveillance measures. The governance methods developed in the experimental stations of the borderlands did not remain in the peripheries but made their way to become central tenets of Chinese Communist Party policy and enforced upon the population at large.

The tragic ends of many of the figures discussed in this book illustrate how the turn to mass politics in the twentieth century transformed the nature of political power. Securing the frontiers provided powerful fodder for political leaders who wished to appeal to popular sentiment and nationalism. People like Geopolitik advocate Karl Haushofer and Chinese geographer Huang Guozhang promoted what they believed to be an important science. From the nineteenth century the professionalization of geography was a global phenomenon, taking place in parallel with growing nationalism and an international legal system which privileged clearly defined borders and sovereignty. To reinforce their borders and extend control of frontier territories, states around the world deployed geographers to conduct surveys and investigate ethnographic conditions on the ground. At the same time, the development of geopolitics as its own field of study emphasized ascertaining the strategic location of resources and the potential for economic and agricultural development of borderlands. Agricultural experimental stations, promoted as the scientific study of agriculture, took on the added benefit of doubling up as a means of securing the frontiers.

As the frontiers turned into experimental zones, the men and women who settled there became the involuntary test subjects of the experiment. During World War II, on the Eastern Front in Europe the social scientists who planned for the remaking of the countryside viewed their work with blinders to the atrocities enacted to make possible the settlement of the newly acquired territories. The ethnic Germans brought in to populate these lands, however, had to face the wrath of local residents and the advancing Soviet army at the end of the war.[7] In the Japanese Empire, defeat and the end of the war left Japanese residents in its colonial outposts to fend for themselves. In Manchuria, some fleeing Japanese residents abandoned their children with local Chinese farmers. In Taiwan, Okinawans, many of whom spent most of their lives abroad, suddenly had to find any means possible to repatriate.[8] In China, both the Nationalist regime during the war years and the subsequent Communist regime viewed Han Chinese settlers on the frontiers as essential to national security, leaving unsaid that they provided the human buffers for potential invasions. Women were viewed as essential for the success of frontier policies in their role as wives and mothers and as stabilizing forces in frontier communities. The women themselves, however, played little role in the crafting of frontier policy and were systematically excluded from academic disciplines like agronomy and geography.

In these borderland experimental zones, geographers and agronomists saw the pyrrhic fruition of their vision. The ideas they promoted were incorporated into political campaigns and frontier policies. As individuals, however, these scientists and social scientists were deemed dispensable. Far from the mastermind of Nazi domination, Haushofer was powerless to prevent his son Albrecht's execution in the waning days of the war. Chinese geographers during the war saw their inclusion in Academia Sinica as the recognition of the field as a science for which they had long lobbied. That very inclusion, which continued after 1949, when Academia Sinica was renamed the Chinese Academy of Sciences, exposed leading geographers to political attacks in the 1950s and 1960s. The Cultural Revolution shut down the academy and led to the persecution of many scientists. Among scientists, geographers were especially politically exposed.

The tragic personal lives of those involved contrast with the continuing importance of empire as we settle into the twenty-first century. When the Chinese government launched its Open Up the West plan in 1999 and more recently with the Belt and Road Initiative, it took up a rallying cry that had first sounded during the Republican period, when social scientists first linked *kaifa*, *kaiken*, and *kaifang* (development, reclamation, and opening) as three interconnected strategies to reinforce national defense and conquer nature in inhospitable borderlands and to extract natural resources in the name of the nation. Successive movements in the twentieth century to develop and open the frontiers have resulted in a transformation of the environment in the borderlands.

In Europe, by the end of the twentieth century the European Union appeared to be the fulfillment of a century-long dream to form a continental economic bloc. The EU would provide the benefits of empire, allowing for seamless, borderless trade and the associated clout and increased leverage of a large territorial expanse, without the political baggage. The economic turmoil that caused the 2008 Great Recession, followed by the Covid-19 pandemic in 2020, gave lie to that ideal. Particularly after 2008, resentment built up against Germany, the EU's largest economy, and its fiscal conservatism. Budget cuts proved devastating for Greece and Italy, the weaker members of the union, which had to impose extreme austerity in the wake of the financial crisis. The 2020 pandemic brought back border controls and travel restrictions and further exposed the limits of the EU's structure and limits of its power. Finally, the Russian invasion of Ukraine in 2022 and Putin's effort to restore Soviet imperial territories brought war back to the heart of Europe. The global search for the next frontier will continue to define the twenty-first century.

NOTES

Preface

1. Justin Jacobs, *The Compensations of Plunder: How China Lost Its Treasures* (Chicago: University of Chicago Press, 2020).

2. Sigrid Schmalzer, *The People's Peking Man: Popular Science and Human Identity in Twentieth-Century China* (Chicago: University of Chicago Press, 2008); James Leibold, *Reconfiguring Chinese Nationalism: How the Qing Frontier and Its Indigenes Became Chinese* (New York: Palgrave Macmillan, 2007).

Introduction

1. Shellen Wu, *Empires of Coal: Fueling China's Entry into the Modern World Order, 1860–1920* (Stanford, CA: Stanford University Press, 2015); Shellen Wu, "The Search for Coal in the Age of Empires: Ferdinand von Richthofen's Odyssey in China, 1860–1920," *American Historical Review* 119, no. 2 (April 2014): 339–62.

2. For a broader discussion on translation, see Lydia Liu, *Translingual Practices: Literature, National Culture, and Translated Modernity–China, 1900–1937* (Stanford, CA: Stanford University Press, 1995).

3. Benjamin Hopkins termed this "frontier governmentality" in the peripheries of the British Empire. Benjamin D. Hopkins, *Ruling the Savage Periphery: Frontier Governance and the Making of the Modern State* (Cambridge, MA: Harvard University Press, 2020), 6.

4. John Mack Faragher, "Introduction," *Rereading Frederick Jackson Turner: The Significance of the Frontier in American History and Other Essays,* ed. John Mack Faragher (New York: Henry Holt, 1994), 2; Patricia Nelson Limerick, "Tur-

nerians All: The Dream of a Helpful History in an Intelligible World," *American Historical Review* 100, no. 3 (1995), 697–716; also Patricia Limerick, *The Legacy of Conquest: The Unbroken Past of the American West* (New York: Norton, 1987); Ned Blackhawk, *Violence over the Land: Indians and Empires in the Early American West* (Cambridge, MA: Harvard University Press, 2008); Pekka Hämäläinen, *The Comanche Empire* (New Haven, CT: Yale University Press, 2009); Elliot West, *The Last Indian War: The Nez Perce Story* (New York: Oxford University Press, 2011); Elliot West, *The Contested Plains: Indians, Goldseekers, and the Rush to Colorado* (Lawrence: University Press of Kansas, 1998); Pekka Hämäläinen and Samuel Truett, "On Borderlands," *Journal of American History* 98, no. 2 (Sept. 2011), 338–61.

5. Scott Montgomery, *Science in Translation: Movements of Knowledge through Cultures and Time* (Chicago and London: University of Chicago Press, 2000); Federico Masini, *The Formation of Modern Chinese Lexicon and Its Evolution toward a National Language: The Period from 1840 to 1898* (Berkeley: University of California Press, 1993); Michael Lackner, Iwo Amelung, and Joachim Kurtz, eds., *New Terms for New Ideas: Western Knowledge and Lexical Change in Late Imperial China* (Leiden: Brill, 2001).

6. Kumao Takaoka, *Die inner Kolonisation Japans* (Leipzig: Verlag von Duncker & Humblot, 1904). For discussion of the political alignments in German colonial circles, see Dörte Lerp, "Farmers to the Frontier: Settler Colonialism in the Eastern Prussian Provinces and German Southwest Africa," *Journal of Imperial and Commonwealth History* 41, no. 4 (2013): 567–83; Dörte Lerp, *Imperiale Grenzräume: Bevölkerungspolitiken in Duetsch-Südwestafrika und den östlichen Provinzen Preußens 1884–1914* (Frankfurt a. M: Campus Verlag, 2016).

7. For a discussion on Nitobe and his colonial views, see Alexis Dudden, *Japan's Colonization of Korea: Discourse and Power* (Honolulu: University of Hawai'i Press, 2005), 133–38; Kären Wigen, *A Malleable Map: Geographies of Restoration in Central Japan, 1600–1912* (Berkeley: University of California Press, 2010), 171; David Howell, *Geographies of Identity in Nineteenth-Century Japan* (Berkeley: University of California Press, 2005), 131.

8. It's not a coincidence that Nibote received his PhD in Germany. Robert Eskildsen, "Of Civilization and Savages: The Mimetic Imperialism of Japan's 1874 Expedition to Taiwan," *American Historical Review* 107, no. 2 (April 2002), 388–418.

9. *Deutsches Wörterbuch von Jacob und Wilhelm Grimm*, 16 Bde. In Teilbänden (Leipzig: 1854–1961). Online version: http://woerterbuchnetz.de/DWB/?sigle=DWB&mode=Vernetzung&lemid=GV03121#XGV03121.

10. Alexander Etkind, *Internal Colonization: Russia's Imperial Experience* (Cambridge: Polity Press, 2011), 21; Mark Bassin, "Turner, Solov'ev, and the 'Frontier Hypothesis': The Nationalist Signification of Open Spaces," *Journal of Modern History* 65, no. 3 (September 1993), 473–511.

11. The August 1912 document, *Mongol Treatment Provisions,* issued by President Yuan Shikai, specifically enjoined the Central Government from using terms like "dependent" (*lifan*) or "colonial" (*zhimin*) to refer to Mongolia. Justin

Tighe, *Constructing Suiyuan: The Politics of Northwestern Territory and Development in Early Twentieth-Century China* (Leiden: Brill, 2005), 193.

12. Qing documents referred to *tuntian* for military agricultural colonies on the frontiers, for example, in the Northeast. James Rearon-Anderson, *Reluctant Pioneers: China's Expansion Northward, 1644–1937* (Stanford, CA: Stanford University Press, 2005), 78–79; James Millward, *Beyond the Pass: Economy, Ethnicity, and Empire in Qing Central China, 1759–1864* (Stanford, CA: Stanford University Press, 1998), 40–41; Peter Perdue, *China Marches West: Qing Conquest of Central Eurasia* (Cambridge, MA: Belknap Press, 2005), 345; Yuxin Peng, *Qingdai tudi kaiken shi* (Beijing: Nongye chuban she, 1990).

13. Siberia in the Russian imagination similarly underwent significant change in the nineteenth century as a result of translations from the American literature on frontiers. See Mark Bassin, "Inventing Siberia: Visions of the Russian East in the Early Nineteenth Century," *American Historical Review* 96, no. 3 (June 1991): 763–94.

14. Bendict Anderson, *Imagined Communities: Reflections on the Origin and Spread of Nationalism* (London and New York: Verso, 1991), 19; Tessa Morris-Suzuki, "The Frontiers of Japanese Identity," in *Asian Forms of the Nation*, ed. Stein Tonnesson and Hans Antlöv (Richmond, Surrey: Curzon, 1996).

15. Stefan Tanaka, *History without Chronology* (Lever Press, 2019), 1.

16. Richard H. Grove, *Green Imperialism: Colonial Expansion, Tropical Island Edens, and the Origins of Environmentalism, 1600–1860* (Cambridge: Cambridge University Press, 1995); Alfred Rieber, *The Struggle for the Eurasian Borderlands: From the Rise of Early Modern Empires to the End of the First World War* (Cambridge: Cambridge University Press, 2014); John F. Richards, *The Unending Frontier: An Environmental History of the Early Modern World* (Berkeley: University of California Press, 2003); John C. Weaver, *The Great Land Rush and the Making of the Modern World, 1650–1900* (Montréal: McGill-Queen's University Press, 2003); Howard R. Lamar and Leonard M. Thompson, eds., *The Frontier in History: North America and Southern Africa Compared* (New Haven, CT: Yale University Press, 1981).

17. Marc Bloch, "A Contribution towards a Comparative History of European Societies," in *Land and Law in Medieval Europe: Selected Papers,* trans. J. E. Anderson (London: Routledge, 1967).

18. For an overview of this relatively new field of global history, see Sebastian Conrad, *What Is Global History?* (Princeton, NJ: Princeton University Press, 2016); Dominic Sachsenmaier, *Global Perspectives on Global History: Theories and Approaches in a Connected World* (Cambridge: Cambridge University Press, 2011).

19. Martin W. Lewis and Kären Wigen, *The Myth of Continents: A Critique of Metageography* (Berkeley: University of California Press, 1997).

20. Christopher L. Hill, *National History and the World of Nations: Capital, State, and the Rhetoric of History in Japan, France, and the United States* (Durham, NC: Duke University Press, 2008).

21. For an overview history of empires, see Jane Burbank and Frederick Cooper, *Empires in World History: Power and the Politics of Difference* (Princeton, NJ: Princeton University Press, 2011).

22. Ibid., 11.

23. Thomas Mullaney, *Coming to Terms with the Nation: Ethnic Classification in Modern China* (Berkeley: University of California Press, 2011).

24. For a good overview of the invention of an American national history, see Ian Tyrrell, "Making Nations / Making States: American Historians in the Context of Empire," *Journal of American History* 86, no. 3 (December 1999), 1015–44; on the periodic use and disuse of *empire* in American historical discourse, see Paul A. Kramer, "Power and Connection: Imperial Histories of the United States in the World," *American Historical Review* 116, no. 5 (2011): 1348–91.

25. Yoshihisa Tak Matsusaka, *The Making of Japanese Manchuria, 1904–1932* (Cambridge, MA: Harvard University Asia Center, 2001); Louise Young, *Total Empire: Manchuria and the Culture of the Wartime Imperialism* (Berkeley: University of California Press, 1998); Peter Duus, Ramon H. Myers, and Mark R. Peattie, eds., *The Japanese Informal Empire in China, 1895–1937* (Princeton, NJ: Princeton University Press, 1989); Mariko Asano Tamanoi, "Knowledge, Power, and Racial Classifications: The 'Japanese' in 'Manchuria,'" *Journal of Asian Studies* 59, no. 2 (May 2000), 248–76; Jun Unchida, *Brokers of Empire: Japanese Settler Colonialism in Korea, 1876–1945* (Cambridge, MA: Harvard University Asia Center, 2011).

26. David Blackbourn, *The Conquest of Nature: Water, Landscape and the Making of Modern Germany* (London: Jonathan Cape, 2006), 282–84; Shelley Baranowski, *Nazi Empire: German Colonialism and Imperialism from Bismarck to Hitler* (Cambridge: Cambridge University Press, 2011), 270; Vejas Liulevicious, *The German Myth of the East: 1800 to the Present* (Oxford: Oxford University Press, 2009), 114–23.

27. John Fitzgerald, *Awakening China: Politics, Culture, and Class in the Nationalist Revolution* (Stanford, CA: Stanford University Press, 1996), 128.

28. Evelyn Rawski first coined the term *New Qing History* in a 1996 presidential address to the Association of Asian Studies. Evelyn Rawski, "Re-envisioning the Qing: The Significance of the Qing Period in Chinese History," *Journal of Asian Studies* 55, no. 4 (1996): 829–50; Laura Hostetler's work, for example, juxtaposed Qing gazetteers and Miao albums with European engravings of the New World. See Laura Hostetler, "Qing Connections to the Early Modern World: Ethnography and Cartography in Eighteenth-Century China," *Modern Asian Studies* 32, no. 3 (2000): 623–62; Laura Hostetler, *Qing Colonial Enterprise: Ethnography and Cartography in Early Modern China* (Chicago: University of Chicago Press, 2001); Pamela Crossley, *A Translucent Mirror: History and Identity in Qing Imperial Ideology* (Berkeley: University of California Press, 1999.); Mark Elliot, *The Manchu Way: The Eight Banners and Ethnic Identity in Late Imperial China* (Stanford, CA: Stanford University Press, 2001). William Rowe's recent book provides a fine synthesis of the latest scholarship on Qing history in *China's Last Empire:*

The Great Qing (Cambridge, MA: Belknap Press of Harvard University Press, 2009). Emma Teng, *Taiwan's Imagined Geography: Chinese Colonial Travel Writing and Pictures, 1683–1895* (Cambridge, MA: Harvard East Asian Monographs, 2004); John Shepherd, *Statecraft and Political Economy on the Taiwan Frontier 1600–1800* (Stanford, CA: Stanford University Press, 1993); Millward, *Beyond the Pass*; James Millward, "'Coming onto the Map': Western Regions' Geography and Cartographic Nomenclature in the Making of Chinese Empire in Xinjiang," *Late Imperial China* 20, no. 2 (December 1999), 61–98; Mark Elliot, "The Limits of Tartary: Manchuria in Imperial and National Geographies," *Journal of Asian Studies* 59, no. 3 (August 2000), 603–46.

29. Perdue, *China Marches West*; James A. Millward, *New Qing Imperial History : The Making of Inner Asian Empire at Qing Chengde* (London: Routledge, 2004).

30. Prasenjit Duara, *Culture, Power, and the State: Rural North China, 1900–1942* (Stanford, CA: Stanford University Press, 1988), 3–4.

31. Philip Kuhn, "The Development of Local Government," in *Cambridge History of China, Vol. 13: Republican China 1912–1949*, Part 2, ed. John King Fairbank and Albert Feuerwerker (New York: Cambridge University Press, 1978).

32. Megan Black, *The Global Interior: Mineral Frontiers and American Power* (Cambridge, MA: Harvard University Press, 2018).

33. Rainer Eisfeld, "Mitteleuropa in Historical and Contemporary Perspective," *German Politics and Society*, no. 28 (1993): 39–52, http://www.jstor.org/stable/23735073.

34. Michael Burleigh, *Germany Turns Eastwards: A Study of Ostforschung in the Third Reich* (Cambridge: Cambridge University Press, 1988.)

35. Historians have examined the complex interactions between imperialism and nationalism in Manchuria. See Prasenjit Duara, *Sovereignty and Authenticity: Manchukuo and the East Asian Modern* (Lanham, MD: Rowman & Littlefield, 2003.)

36. Grove, *Green Imperialism*.

37. Ibid., 309.

38. Richards, *The Unending Frontier,* 4.

39. Weaver, *The Great Land Rush*, 347.

40. Charles Maier, "Consigning the Twentieth Century to History: Alternative Narratives for the Modern Era," *American Historical Review* 51, no. 1 (2000): 807–30, 825; for a broader discussion of modern territorial ideas, see Charles Maier, *Once within Borders: Territories of Power, Wealth, and Belonging since 1500* (Cambridge, MA: Belknap Press of Harvard University Press, 2016); Emily S. Rosenberg, *A World Connecting, 1870–1945* (Cambridge, MA: Belknap Press of Harvard University Press, 2012).

41. Lee Alan Dugatkin, *Mr. Jefferson and the Giant Moose: Natural History in Early America* (Chicago: University of Chicago Press, 2009).

42. Benjamin Elman, *On Their Own Terms: Science in China, 1550–1900* (Cambridge, MA: Harvard University Press, 2005), 90.

43. William Cronon, *Nature's Metropolis: Chicago and the Great West*, 1st ed. (New York: W. W. Norton, 1991); G. William Skinner, "Marketing and Social Structure in Rural China, Part I," *Journal of Asian Studies* 24, no. 1 (1964): 3–43; "Marketing and Social Structure in Rural China Part II," *Journal of Asian Studies* 24, no. 2 (1965): 195–228; "Marketing and Social Structure in Rural China, Part III," *Journal of Asian Studies* 24, no. 3 (1965): 363–99.

44. Walter Christaller, *Die zentralen Orte in Süddeutschland: eine ökonomisch-geographische Untersuchung über die Gesetz mässigkeit der Verbreitung und Entwicklung der Siedlungen mit städtischen Funktionen* (Jena: Gustav Fischer, 1933).

45. Lijing Jiang, "Retouching the Past with Living Things," *Historical Studies in the Natural Sciences* 46, no. 2 (2016): 154–206.

46. Zuoyue Wang, "Science and the State in Modern China," *Isis* 98, no. 3 (2007): 558–70, https://doi.org/10.1086/521158; Fa-ti Fan, "Redrawing the Map: Science in Twentieth-Century China," *Isis* 98, no. 3 (2007), 524–38.

47. The key points of this research are explained for general readers in Albert-Laszlo Barabasi, *Linked: How Everything Is Connected to Everything Else and What It Means for Business, Science, and Everyday Life* (New York: Basic Books, 2004). Network scientists and sociologists before them have posited that network nodes are not randomly distributed but that new nodes prefer to link to more connected nodes, a concept called *preferential attachment*. Albert-Laszlo Barabasi, *Network Science* (Cambridge: Cambridge University Press, 2016), chapter 5.

48. Anna Lowenhaupt Tsing, *The Mushroom at the End of the World: On the Possibility of Life in Capitalist Ruins* (Princeton, NJ: Princeton University Press, 2015); Merlin Sheldrake, *Entangled Life* (New York: Random House, 2020).

Chapter 1

1. Frederick Jackson Turner, "The Significance of History," *Rereading Frederick Jackson Turner: The Significance of the Frontier in American History and Other Essays,* ed. John Mack Faragher (New York: Henry Holt, 1994), 22.

2. Friedrich Engels and Florence Kelley, *The Condition of the Working-Class in England in 1844*, trans. Florence Kelley (London: S. Sonnenschein & Co., 1892).

3. Friedrich Engels and Karl Marx, *The Communist Manifesto* (Minneapolis, MN: Lerner Publishing Group, 2018).

4. Jonathan Spence, *God's Chinese Son: The Taiping Heavenly Kingdom of Hong Xiuquan* (New York: W. W. Norton & Company, 1996); Stephen Platt, *Autumn in the Heavenly Kingdom: China, the West, and the Epic Story of the Taiping Civil War* (New York: Knopf, 2012).

5. Pamela Crossley, *A Translucent Mirror: History and Identity in Qing Imperial Ideology* (Berkeley: University of California Press, 1999); William Rowe, *China's Last Empire: The Great Qing* (Cambridge, MA: Belknap Press of Harvard University Press, 2009).

6. Karl Marx, "Revolution in China and in Europe," June 14, 1853, in *Marx on*

China, 1853–1860: Articles from the New York Daily Tribune (London: Lawrence & Wishart, 1951).

7. Richard von Glahn, "The Changing Significance of Latin American Silver in the Chinese Economy, 16th–19th Centuries," *Revista de Historia Económica— Journal of Iberian and Latin American Economic History* (2019): 1–32.

8. Already in the late nineteenth century European historians realized the importance of this transition from wood to coal and argued that the exhaustion of wood through deforestation was *the* major incentive for industrialization. See Werner Sombart, *Der Moderne Kapitalismus*, vol. 2 (Munich, 1902), 1138. Mentioned in Wolfgang Schivelbusch, *The Railway Journey: The Industrialization of Time and Space in the Nineteenth Century* (Berkeley: University of California Press, 1986), 1–3; In *The Protestant Ethic and the Spirit of Capitalism*, Weber saw fossil fuels as the foundation of the modern economic order, discussed in Marshall Berman, *All That Is Solid Melts into Air: The Experience of Modernity* (New York: Viking Penguin, 1982; repr., 1988), 27; William Frederick Cottrell, *Energy and Society: The Relation between Energy, Social Change, and Economic Development* (New York: McGraw-Hill, 1955); E. A. Wrigley, *Continuity, Chance and Change: The Character of the Industrial Revolution in England* (Cambridge: Cambridge University Press, 1988); Rolf Peter Sieferle, *The Subterranean Forest: Energy Systems and the Industrial Revolution* (Cambridge: White Horse Press, 1982; repr., 2001).

9. Mark Elvin, "The High-Level Equilibrium Trap: The Causes of the Decline of Invention in the Traditional Chinese Textile Industries," in *Economic Organization in Chinese Society*, ed. W. E. Willmott (Stanford, CA: Stanford University Press, 1972).

10. Jason Moore, *Capitalism in the Web of Life* (New York: Verso, 2015).

11. Robert Marks, *China: Its Environment and History* (Lanham, MD: Rowan & Littlefield, 2011), 221.

12. William T. Rowe, *Saving the World: Chen Hongmou and Elite Consciousness in Eighteenth-Century China* (Stanford, CA: Stanford University Press, 2001).

13. Limin Bai, "*Gewu Zhizhi* and Curriculum Building," in *Re-Envisioning Chinese Education*, ed. Guoping Zhao and Zongyi Deng (London: Routledge, 2015), 55–73.

14. Mark Elvin, *The Retreat of the Elephants: An Environmental History of China* (New Haven, CT: Yale University Press, 2004), 466.

15. Gregory Cushman, *Guano and the Opening of the Pacific World: A Global Ecological History* (Cambridge: Cambridge University Press, 2013); Brett Clark and John Bellamy Foster, "Ecological Imperialism and the Global Metabolic Rift: Unequal Exchange and the Guano/Nitrates Trade," *International Journal of Comparative Sociology* 50, no. 3–4 (2009): 311–34.

16. Carl Trocki, "Drugs, Taxes, and Chinese Capitalism in Southeast Asia," in *Opium Regimes: China, Britain, and Japan, 1839–1952*, ed. Timothy Brook and Bob Tadashi Wakabayashi (Berkeley: University of California Press, 2000), 79–104.

17. Peter Lavelle, *The Profits of Nature: Colonial Development and the Quest for Resources in Nineteenth-Century China* (New York: Columbia University Press, 2020), 17–38.

18. Francesca Bray, *Science and Civilisation in China: Volume 6, Biology and Biological Technology, Part II, Agriculture* (Cambridge: Cambridge University Press, 1984), 56.

19. Benjamin Elman, *On Their Own Terms: Science in China, 1550–1900* (Cambridge, MA: Harvard University Press, 2005), 90.

20. Lavelle, *The Profits of Nature*, 63–64.

21. Peter Guardino, *The Dead March: A History of the Mexican-American War* (Cambridge, MA: Harvard University Press, 2017).

22. Horace Capron, "Memoirs of Horace Capron" in two volumes (unpublished, in the USDA library and copied by permission from original in the possession of his grandson, Horace M. Capron, 1423 Maple Avenue, Evanston, Illinois,) 92–93.

23. Ibid., 93.

24. Richard White, *Railroaded: The Transcontinentals and the Making of Modern America* (New York: W. W. Norton, 2011).

25. Merritt Starr, "General Horace Capron, 1804–1885," *Journal of the Illinois State Historical Society* (1908–1984) 18, no. 2 (July 1925), 259–349.

26. Capron, "Memoirs of Horace Capron," 67.

27. Horace Capron, in *The Plough, The Loom and the Anvil* (later renamed *American Agriculturist*), vol. 1 (1848–1849), J. S. Skinner & Sons, Philadelphia, 501.

28. Capron, "Memoirs of Horace Capron," 66.

29. Andrea Wulf, *The Founding Gardeners: The Revolutionary Generation, Nature, and the Shaping of the American Nation* (New York: Knopf, 2011).

30. USDA, "About the US Department of Agriculture," https://www.usda.gov/our-agency/about-usda (accessed October 15, 2020).

31. Robert A. Gross, *The Transcendentalists and Their World*, 1st ed. (New York: Farrar, Straus and Giroux, 2021), 165.

32. Capron, "Memoirs of Horace Capron," 75a and 75b.

33. Ibid., 81.

34. Ibid., 117.

35. Ned Blackhawk, *Violence over the Land: Indians and Empires in the Early American West* (Cambridge, MA: Harvard University Press, 2006).

36. Elliot West, *The Last Indian War: The Nez Perce Story* (Oxford: Oxford University Press, 2009).

37. Capron, "Memoirs of Horace Capron," 276.

38. Donald Roden, "In Search of the Real Horace Capron: An Historiographical Perspective on Japanese-American Relations," *Pacific Historical Review* 55, no. 4 (November 1986): 549–75, quoted on p. 553.

39. William S. Clark Papers, Series 2: Correspondence Box 4, Folder 2, letter dated March 7, 1851.

40. Margaret Rossiter, *The Emergence of Agricultural Science: Justus Liebig and the Americans, 1840–1880* (New Haven, CT: Yale University Press, 1975).

41. Raphael Pumpelly, *My Reminiscences* (New York: H. Holt and Company, 1918), 119.

42. Cora Lee Nollendorfs, "Alexander von Humboldt Centennial Celebrations in the United States: Controversies Concerning His Work," *Monatshefte* 80, no. 1 (Spring 1988): 59–66.

43. Elliot West, *The Contested Plains: Indians, Goldseekers, and the Rush to Colorado* (Lawrence: University Press of Kansas, 1998).

44. William S. Clark Papers, Series 2: Correspondence Box 4, Folder 2, letter dated March 7, 1851 from Hannover.

45. Denise Phillips, "Experimentation in the Agricultural Enlightenment: Place, Profit and Norms of Knowledge-Making in Eighteenth-Century Germany," *Notes and Records* 72, no. 2 (2018), 159–72.

46. Richard Hartshorne, "The Nature of Geography: A Critical Survey of Current Thought in the Light of the Past," *Annals of the Association of American Geographers* 29, no. 3 (1939): 173–412.

47. For a general overview of the Scientific Revolution, see Steven Shapin, *The Scientific Revolution* (Chicago: University of Chicago Press, 1996).

48. Michele Myatt Quinn and Robert B. Fairbanks, *Science as Service: Establishing and Reformulating American Land-Grant Universities, 1865–1930* (Tuscaloosa: University of Alabama Press, 2015).

49. William S. Clark Papers, Series 2: Correspondence Box 4, Folder 2, letter dated May 2, 1852 from Berlin.

50. Daniela Bleichmar, *Visible Empire: Botanical Expeditions and Visual Culture in the Hispanic Enlightenment* (Chicago and London: University of Chicago Press, 2012).

51. Courtney Fullilove, *The Profit of the Earth: The Global Seeds of American Agriculture* (Chicago: University of Chicago Press, 2017), 28.

52. Fullilove, *The Profit of the Earth*, 31–37.

53. Peter Shulman, *Coal and Empire* (Baltimore: Johns Hopkins University Press, 2015), 80.

54. Christopher Jones, "A Landscape of Energy Abundance: Anthracite Coal Canals and the Roots of American Energy Dependence, 1820–1860," *Environmental History* 15, no. 3 (July 2010): 449–84; Christopher Jones, *Routes of Power: Energy and Modern America* (Cambridge, MA: Harvard University Press, 2014).

55. Theodore Huters, *Bringing the World Home: Appropriating the West in Late Qing and Early Republican China* (Honolulu: University of Hawai'i Press, 2005); Meng Yue, *Shanghai and the Edges of Empires* (Minneapolis: University of Minnesota Press, 2006).

56. Bayard Taylor, *A Visit to India, China, and Japan in the Year 1853* (New York: G. P. Putnam & Co., 1855), 312–13.

57. Taylor, *A Visit*, 354.

58. *The Narrative of the Expedition of an American Squadron to the China*

Seas and Japan, Performed in the Years 1852, 1853, and 1854, under the command of Commodore M. C. Perry, United States Navy, compiled from the original notes and journals of Commodore Perry and his Officers (New York: D. Appleton and Company, 1856), 175.

59. *The Narrative of the Expedition,* 196.

60. Mark Ravina, *To Stand with the Nations of the World: Japan's Meiji Restoration in World History* (New York: Oxford University Press, 2017), 91–92.

61. Ravina, *To Stand with the Nations of the World*, 29.

62. Alexis Dudden, *Japan's Colonization of Korea: Discourse and Power* (Honolulu: University of Hawai'i Press, 2005).

63. Hiroko Matsuda, *Liminality of the Japanese Empire: Border Crossings from Okinawa to Colonial Taiwan* (Honolulu: University of Hawai'i Press, 2019), 8.

64. For some of those ties in the last millennium, see Ronald Findlay and Kevin O'Rourke, *Power and Plenty: Trade, War, and the World Economy in the Second Millennium* (Princeton, NJ: Princeton University Press, 2007).

Chapter 2

1. Horace Capron and His Foreign Assistants, *Reports and Official Letters to the Kaitakushi* (Tokei: Published by the Kaitakushi, 1875), 11.

2. Maki Fukuoka, *The Premise of Fidelity: Science, Visuality, and Representing the Real in Nineteenth-Century Japan* (Stanford, CA: Stanford University Press, 2012); Federico Marcon, *The Knowledge of Nature and the Nature of Knowledge in Early Modern Japan* (Chicago: University of Chicago Press, 2015).

3. Douglas Howland, *Borders of Chinese Civilization: Geography and History at Empire's End* (Durham, NC: Duke University Press, 1996).

4. Brett Walker, *The Conquest of Ainu Lands: Ecology and Culture in Japanese Expansion 1590–1800* (Berkeley: University of California Press, 2001), 74–75.

5. Walker, *The Conquest of Ainu Lands,* 227.

6. Robert Eskildsen, "Of Civilization and Savages: The Mimetic Imperialism of Japan's 1874 Expedition to Taiwan," *American Historical Review* 107, no. 2 (April 2002), 388–418.

7. Jeffery Jenkens, Lee Alton, and Kara Gorski, "Who Should Govern Congress? The Salary Grab of 1873 and the Coalition of Reform," Institute for Policy Research, Northwestern University, Working Paper Series, https://www.ipr.northwestern.edu/documents/working-papers/2005/IPR-WP-05-07.pdf (accessed on March 23, 2021).

8. Bogdan Mieczkowski and Seiko Mieczkowski, "Horace Capron and the Development of Hokkaido: A Reappraisal," *Journal of the Illinois State Historical Society (1908–1984)* 67, no. 5 (November 1974): 488.

9. Gordon H. Chang and Shelley Fisher Fishkin, eds., *The Chinese and the Iron Road: Building the Transcontinental Railroad* (Stanford, CA: Stanford University Press, 2019).

10. Capron, *Reports and Official Letters to the Kaitakushi.*

11. Raphael Pumpelly, *Travels and Adventures of Raphael Pumpelly, Mining Engineer, Geologist, Archaeologist and Explorer* (New York: Henry Holt and Company, 1920), 210–16.

12. Takehiko Hashimoto, "Introducing a French Technological System: The Origins and Early History of the Yokosuka Dockyard," *East Asian Science, Technology and Medicine* 16 (1999): 53–72.

13. Capron, *Reports and Official Letters to the Kaitakushi*, 40.

14. Mieczkowski and Mieczkowski, "Horace Capron and the Development of Hokkaido," 493.

15. Ian Tyrell, *True Gardens of the Gods: Californian-Australian Environmental Reforms, 1860–1930* (Berkeley: University of California Press, 1999).

16. Eiichiro Azuma, *In Search of Our Frontier: Japanese America and Settler Colonialism in the Construction of Japan's Borderless Empire* (Berkeley: University of California Press, 2019), 176.

17. William S. Clark Papers, Series 5: Box 19, Folder 1, letter from Clark to Kuroda dated September 8, 1871.

18. He then requested leave from the trustees at the Massachusetts Agricultural College. William S. Clark Papers, Series 2: Box 4, Folder 13, letter from Clark to trustees, dated January 12, 1876.

19. William S. Clark Papers, Series 2: Correspondence Box 4, Folder 14, letter from Clark to Sister Belle written from Sapporo, Hokkaido, dated August 5, 1876.

20. Eikoh Shimao, "Darwinism in Japan, 1877–1927," *Annals of Science* 38, no. 1: 93–102.

21. Scott Montgomery, *Science in Translation: Movements of Knowledge through Cultures and Time* (Chicago and London: University of Chicago Press, 2000), 217.

22. J. R. Bartholomew, *The Formation of Science in Japan* (New Haven, CT: Yale University Press, 1993), 71.

23. Daniel T. Rodgers, *Atlantic Crossings: Social Politics in a Progressive Age* (Cambridge, MA: Belknap Press of Harvard University Press, 1998).

24. Max Sering, *Die landwirtschaftliche Konkurrenz Nordamerikas in Gegenwart und Zukunft* (Leipzig: Verlag von Dunder & Humblot, 1887).

25. Max Sering, *Die innere Kolonisation im östlichen Deutschland* (Leipzig: Verlag von Dunder & Humblot, 1898).

26. Robert Nelson, "From Manitoba to the Memel: Max Sering, Inner Colonization and the German East," *Social History* 35, no. 4 (2010): 439–57.

27. Scott Eddie, "The Prussian Settlement Commission and Its Activities in the Land Market, 1886–1918," in *Germans, Poland, and Colonial Expansion to the East, 1850 Through the Present,* ed. Robert Nelson (Palgrave Macmillan, 2009), 39–63.

28. Geheimes Staatsarchiv Preußischer Kulturbesitz, Ha. I. 212, 801.

29. Gerd Fesser, *Der Traum vom Platz an der Sonne, Deutsche "Weltpolitik" 1897–1914* (Bremen: Donat, 1996), 25.

30. Mechthild Leutner and Klaus Mühlhahn, *Musterkolonie Kiautschou: die Expansion des Deutschen Reiches in China: deutsch-chinesische Beziehungen 1897 bis 1914: eine Quellensammlung* (Berlin: Akademie Verlag, 1997).

31. Sean McMeekin, *The Berlin-Baghdad Express: The Ottoman Empire and Germany's Bid for World Power* (Cambridge, MA: Harvard University Press, 2010).

32. Erik Grimmer-Solem, *Learning Empire: Globalization and the German Quest for World Status, 1875–1919* (Cambridge: Cambridge University Press, 2019), 346–47.

33. Bernd Martin, "Sichtweisen der Kolonialgeschichte von Kiautschou," in *Mit Kreuz und deutscher Flagge: 100 Jahre Evangelium im Süden Tanzanias; zum Wirken der Berliner Mission in Ostafrika; Beiträge der historischen Konsultation am 31. Mai und 1. Juni 1991 in Berlin* (Münster: Lit, 1993), 35; see also the annual reports published by the Navy, *Denkschrift betreffend die Entwickelung des Kaiutschou-Gebiet* (Berlin: Dietrich Reimer).

34. William C. Summers, *The Great Manchurian Plague of 1910–1911: The Geopolitics of an Epidemic Disease* (New Haven, CT: Yale University Press, 2012).

35. Kate Brown, *A Biography of No Place: From Ethnic Borderland to Soviet Heartland* (Cambridge, MA: Harvard University Press, 2004); and Kate Brown, "Gridded Lives: Why Kazakhstan and Montana Are Nearly the Same Place," *American Historical Review* 106, no. 1 (February 2001): 17–48.

36. Robert Paxton, *The Anatomy of Fascism* (New York: Knopf, 2004).

37. Christopher L. Hill, *National History and the World of Nations: Capital, State, and the Rhetoric of History in Japan, France, and the United States* (Durham, NC: Duke University Press, 2008); the German historicist school played a key role in promoting German nationalism. Frederick C. Beiser, *The German Historicist Tradition* (Oxford: Oxford University Press, 2011); the Chinese reformer Liang Qichao sought to reform the study of history. Qichao Liang, "Xin Shixue," *Yinbing shi wen ji* (Collected essays from the Ice-Water Studio), Vol. 9, *Yinbing shi heji* (Complete works from the Ice-Water Studio), Book 1, Zhonghua shuju, 1989.

38. Oleg Benesch, *Inventing the Way of the Samurai: Nationalism, Internationalism, and Bushido in Modern Japan* (Oxford: Oxford University Press, 2014).

39. Japanese reformers promoted the study of geography as a key subject for building a new nation and what separated them from the backward countries in Asia. Stefan Tanaka, *Japan's Orient: Rendering Pasts into History* (Berkeley: University of California Press, 1993), 63.

40. Sidney Xu Lu, *The Making of Japanese Settler Colonialism: Malthusianism and Trans-Pacific Migration, 1868–1961* (Cambridge: Cambridge University Press, 2019), 40.

41. Lu, *The Making of Japanese Settler Colonialism,* 160.

42. Ibid., 12.

43. This was, of course, one of James Scott's key arguments about modernizing states. See James C. Scott, *Seeing Like a State: How Certain Schemes to Im-*

prove the Human Condition Have Failed (New Haven, CT: Yale University Press, 1998).

44. Sidney Xu Lu, "A Great Convergence: The American Frontier and the Origins of Japanese Migration to Brazil," *Journal of Global History* 17, no. 1 (2022): 109–27.

45. Azuma, *In Search of Our Frontier,* 14.

46. Ibid., 159–61.

47. Lu, *The Making of Japanese Settler Colonialism,* 216–18.

48. Yoshihisa Tak Matsusaka, *The Making of Japanese Manchuria, 1904–1932* (Cambridge, MA: Harvard University Asia Center, 2001); Louise Young, *Total Empire: Manchuria and the Culture of the Wartime Imperialism* (Berkeley: University of California Press, 1998); Peter Duus, Ramon H. Myers, and Mark R. Peattie, eds., *The Japanese Informal Empire in China, 1895–1937* (Princeton, NJ: Princeton University Press, 1989); Mariko Asano Tamanoi, "Knowledge, Power, and Racial Classifications: The 'Japanese' in 'Manchuria,'" *Journal of Asian Studies* 59, no. 2 (May 2000), 248–76; Jun Unchida, *Brokers of Empire: Japanese Settler Colonialism in Korea, 1876–1945* (Cambridge, MA: Harvard University Asia Center, 2011).

49. Kumao Takaoka, *Die innere Kolonisation Japans* (Staats- und socialwissenschaftliche forschungen, 23. bd., 3. Hft. Leipzig: Duncker & Humblot, 1904.)

50. Stephen Vlastos, "Agrarianism without Tradition," in *Mirror of Modernity: Invented Traditions of Modern Japan,* ed. Stephen Vlastos (Berkeley: University of California Press, 1998), 79–94.

51. Miriam Kingsberg Kadia, *Into the Field: Human Scientists of Transwar Japan* (Stanford, CA: Stanford University Press, 2019), 144.

52. Laura Hostetler, *Qing Colonial Enterprise: Ethnography and Cartography in Early Modern China* (Chicago: University of Chicago Press, 2001); Laura Hostetler, "Qing Connections to the Early Modern World: Ethnography and Cartography in Eighteenth Century China," *Modern Asian Studies* 32, no. 3 (2000), 623–62.

53. Federico Masini, *The Formation of Modern Chinese Lexicon and Its Evolution toward a National Language: The Period from 1840 to 1898* (Project on Linguistic Analysis, University of California, 1993), 197.

54. Nianshen Song, *Making Borders in Modern East Asia: The Tumen River Demarcation, 1881–1919* (Cambridge University Press, 2018), 151.

55. Peter Lavelle, "Agricultural Improvement at China's First Agricultural Experiment Stations," in *New Perspectives on the History of Life Sciences and Agriculture,* ed. Denise Phillips and Sharon Kingsland (Dordrecht: Springer, 2015), 327.

56. Peter Lavelle, "Tools for Overcoming Crisis: Agriculture, Scarcity, and Ideas of Rural Mechanization in Late Qing China," *Agricultural History* 94, no. 3 (Summer 2020): 386–412.

57. Thanks to Ruth Mostern for pointing out gazetteers' role in bringing localities into the orbit of the imperial state in her presentation "Landscapes in

Motion: Modeling Spatial Dynamics in Chinese and Global Digital History," University of Tennessee, Knoxville, March 7, 2022.

58. Pierre-Etienne Will, "Chinese Local Gazetteers: An Historical and Practical Introduction," *Notes de Recherche Centre Chine,* No. 3 (Paris: Centre de recherches et de documentation sur la Chine contemporaine [EHESS], 1992).

59. *(Minguo) Dali Xian zhi gao* (民國)大理縣志稿, ed. Zhou Zonglin 周宗麟 and Zhang Peijue 張培爵 (1917).

60. Academica Historica, waijiao bu, zhongying dianmian jiewu 外交部: 中英滇緬界務, 410.2/0012: 1931 and 1936.

61. C. Pat Giersch, *Corporate Conquests: Business, the State, and the Origins of Ethnic Inequality in Southwest China* (Stanford, CA: Stanford University Press, 2020).

62. *Nong xue bao* (Shanghai: Nong xue bao guan, 1897).

63. *Linggui xian (Guangxi) zhi* 臨桂縣(廣西)志, eds. Wu Zheng'ao 吳征鼇 and Huang Mi 黃泌 (1905), 14.644.

64. Yi Wang, "Irrigation, Commercialization, and Social Change in Nineteenth-Century Inner Mongolia," *International Review of Social History* 59, no. 2 (2014): 215–46; Liping Wang, "From Masterly Brokers to Compliant Protégées: The Frontier Governance System and the Rise of Ethnic Confrontation in China—Inner Mongolia, 1900–1930," *American Journal of Sociology* 120, no. 6 (May 2015): 1641–89.

65. Kingsberg Kadia, *Into the Field*, 48–49.

66. Jonathan Schlesinger, *A World Trimmed with Fur: Wild Things, Pristine Places, and the Natural Fringes of Qing Rule* (Stanford, CA: Stanford: Stanford University Press, 2017); David Anthony Bello, *Across Forest, Steppe and Mountain: Environment, Identity and Empire in Qing China's Borderlands* (New York: Cambridge University Press, 2016).

67. Yingcong Dai, *The Sichuan Frontier and Tibet: Imperial Strategy in the Early Qing* (Seattle: University of Washington Press, 2009).

68. Matthew W. Mosca, *From Frontier Policy to Foreign Policy: The Question of India and the Transformation of Geopolitics in Qing China* (Stanford, CA: Stanford University Press, 2013).

69. Xiuyu Wang, *China's Last Imperial Frontier: Late Qing Expansion in Sichuan's Tibetan Borderlands* (Lanham, MD: Lexington Books, 2013), 102.

70. Xu, Guoqi, *China and the Great War: China's Pursuit of a New National Identity and Internationalization* (Cambridge: Cambridge University Press, 2005).

71. Robert Nelson, "Inner Colonization," in *Germans, Poland, and Colonial Expansion to the East: 1850 to the Present*, ed. Robert Nelson (New York: Palgrave Macmillan, 2009), 70.

72. Deborah Fitzgerald, *Every Farm a Factory: The Industrial Ideal in American Agriculture* (New Haven, CT: Yale University Press, 2003).

73. For a discussion on the changing concept of "wasteland" in early modern

Europe, see Vittoria Di Palma, *Wasteland: A History* (New Haven, CT: Yale University Press, 2014).

74. Azuma, *In Search of Our Frontier,* 10 (citing Ann Laura Stoler).

Chapter 3

1. Isaiah Bowman, "The Pioneer Fringe," *Foreign Affairs* 6, no. 1 (October 1927): 51.

2. Martin Lowsky, *Karl May* (Stuttgart: Metzler, 1987); Karl May, *Winnetou,* trans. David Koblick (Pullman: Washington State University Press, 1999), vii–xii.

3. Kristin Kopp, "Reinventing Poland as German Colonial Territory in the Nineteenth Century: Gustav Freytag's *Soll und Haben* as Colonial Novel," in *Germans, Poland, and Colonial Expansion to the East: 1850 to the Present*, ed. Robert Nelson, 11–38 (New York: Palgrave Macmillan, 2009).

4. David Wrobel, *Global West, American Frontier: Travel, Empire, and Exceptionalism from Manifest Destiny to the Great Depression* (Albuquerque: University of New Mexico Press, 2013), 43.

5. Wang Tao, Shangfan Chen, Shuhe Zhong, Gui Li, Shuchang Li, and Jianyin Xu, *Man You Sui Lu* (Changsha Shi: Yuelu shu she, 1985).

6. Xu Jianyin, *Ou you za lu* (Changsha: Hunan ren min chu ban she: Hunan Sheng xin hua shu dian fa xing, 1980).

7.. Geheimes Staatsarchiv Preußischer Kulturbesitz. I. Ha. Rep. 76, Sekt 1. Tit. XII Nr. 3 Bd. 3. Letter dated October 31, 1923.

8. Friedrich Ratzel and Stewart A. Stehlin, *Sketches of Urban and Cultural Life in North America* (New Brunswick, NJ: Rutgers University Press, 1988).

9. Friedrich Ratzel, *Politische Geographie* (München und Leipzig: R. Oldenbourg, 1897).

10. Friedrich Ratzel, *Der Lebensraum: eine biogeographische Studie* (Germany: H. Laupp, 1901); quote from David Thomas Murphy, *The Heroic Earth: Geopolitical Thought in Weimar Germany, 1918–1933* (Kent, Ohio, and London: Kent State University Press, 1997), 10.

11. Friedrich Ratzel, *Sketches of Urban and Cultural Life in North America*, 4.

12. William Cronon, *Nature's Metropolis: Chicago and the Great West* (New York: W. W. Norton, 1991).

13. On Barak, *Powering Empire: How Coal Made the Middle East and Sparked Global Carbonization* (Berkeley: University of California Press, 2020), 15.

14. David Wrobel, *The End of American Exceptionalism: Frontier Anxiety from the Old West to the New Deal* (Lawrence: University Press of Kansas, 1993), 38.

15. Ibid., 43.

16. Friedrich Ratzel, *Sketches of Urban and Cultural Life in North America,* 153.

17. Ibid., 161.

18. Andrew Zimmerman, *Anthropology and Antihumanism in Imperial Germany* (Chicago: University of Chicago Press, 2001), 204.

19. Friedrich Ratzel, *The History of Mankind,* Vol. 1, trans. from second German edition by A. J. Butler (London: Macmillan and Co. 1896), 68.

20. For a discussion on the various ways that energy made its way to popular discussions, see Anson Rabinbach, *The Human Motor: Energy, Fatigue, and the Origins of Modernity* (New York: Basic Books, 1990).

21. Susan Schulten, *The Geographical Imagination in America, 1880–1950* (Chicago: University of Chicago Press, 2001), 70.

22. Ellsworth Huntington Papers, Yale University Library, Group 1, Series IV, Box 21 Documents and Papers, Trips: Africa–China Folders 203–17.

23. Halford Mackinder papers, Oxford University, 1899 diaries. Entry date June 8, 1899.

24. Susan Schulten, *Mapping the Nation: History and Cartography in Nineteenth-Century America* (Chicago: University of Chicago Press, 2012), 162.

25. His correspondence has been digitized and made available online by the Johns Hopkins University Library Special Collections, https://jscholarship .library.jhu.edu/handle/1774.2/41445 (accessed November 15, 2021).

26. Ellsworth Huntington Papers, Yale University, Group 1, Series 1, Box 4. Letter to father from Vienna, 28th of April, 1903.

27. Ellen Semple Papers, University of Kentucky Special Collections, Box 10.

28. Albert-Laszlo Barabasi, *Network Science,* http://networksciencebook.com /chapter/5#growth (accessed August 29, 2022).

29. Innes M. Keighren, *Bringing Geography to Book: Ellen Semple and the Reception of Geographical Knowledge* (London: I. B. Tauris, 2010), 94.

30. Ellen Churchill Semple, *Influences of Geographic Environment on the Basis of Ratzel's System of Anthro-Geography* (New York: Henry Holt and Company, 1911), 139.

31. William Rowe, "Owen Lattimore, Asia, and Comparative History," *Journal of Asian Studies* 66, no. 3 (August 2007), 759–86.

32. Geoffrey J. Martin, *Ellsworth Huntington: His Life and Thought* (Hamden, CT: Archon Books, 1973), 177.

33. Samuel Huntington, *The Clash of Civilizations and the Remaking of World Order* (New York: Simon & Schuster, 1996), 13.

34. This interest in "civilization" was not exclusive to the West, as shown by Tessa Morris-Suzuki, "The Invention and Reinvention of 'Japanese Culture,'" *Journal of Asian Studies* 54, no. 3 (August 1995), 759–80.

35. The trend started with Thomas Parke Hughes, *Networks of Power: Electrification in Western Society, 1880–1930* (Baltimore: Johns Hopkins University Press, 1983) and more recently developed in works such as Barak, *Powering Empire* and Judd Kinzley, *Natural Resources and the New Frontier: Constructing Modern China's Borderlands* (Chicago: University of Chicago Press, 2018).

36. Leo K. Shin, *The Making of the Chinese State: Ethnicity and Expansion on the Ming Borderlands* (New York: Cambridge University Press, 2006), 8.

37. Joseph Needham, *Science and Civilisation in China. Vol.3. Mathematics*

and the Sciences of the Heavens and the Earth (Cambridge: Cambridge University Press, 1959), 495–680.

38. Shin, *The Making of the Chinese State.*

39. Timothy Brook, *Mr. Selden's Map of China* (London: Bloomsbury, 2013).

40. Willard J. Peterson, "The Life of Ku Yen-wu (1613–1682)," *Harvard Journal of Asiatic Studies* 29 (1969), 201–47.

41. Laura Hostetler, *Qing Colonial Enterprise: Ethnography and Cartography in Early Modern China* (Chicago: University of Chicago Press, 2001); Laura Hostetler, "Qing Connections to the Early Modern World: Ethnography and Cartography in Eighteenth Century China," *Modern Asian Studies* 32, no. 3 (2000): 623–62.

42. Mario Cams, *Companions in Geography : East-West Collaboration in the Mapping of Qing China (c. 1685–1735)* (Leiden; Boston: Brill, 2017), http://dx.doi.org/10.1163/9789004345362.

43. Jiajing Zhang, "The Art of Compromise: New Maps in Local Gazetteers in the Late Qing," *ISIS,* December 2022, Focus section; a different interpretation of the combined uses of traditional and imported cartographic technologies is presented in Iwo Amelung, " New Maps for the Modernizing State: Western Cartographic Knowledge and Its Application in 19th and 20th Century China," in *Graphics and Text in the Production of Technical Knowledge in China* (Leiden: Brill, 2007), 79, 685–726, https://doi.org/10.1163/ej.9789004160637.i-772.108.

44. Nianshen Song, *Making Borders in Modern East Asia: The Tumen River Demarcation, 1881–1919* (Cambridge: Cambridge University Press, 2018).

45. Yao Minghui and Yunlong Shen, *Menggu zhi: [3 juan]* (1875–1908).

46. Song, *Making Borders,* 36.

47. Arthur W. Hummel ed., *Eminent Chinese of the Ch'ing Period,* Vol. 2 (Washington, DC: United States Government Printing Office, 1943–44), 850–52.

48. Matthew Mosca, *From Frontier Policy to Foreign Policy: The Question of India and the Transformation of Geopolitics in Qing China* (Stanford, CA: Stanford University Press, 2013), 273–74.

49. James Bartholomew, *The Formation of Science in Japan: Building a Research Tradition* (New Haven, CT: Yale University Press, 1989).

50. Stefan Tanaka, *Japan's Orient: Rendering Pasts into History* (Berkeley: University of California Press, 1993).

51. Douglas Howland, *Translating the West: Language and Political Reason in Nineteenth-Century Japan* (Honolulu: University of Hawai'i Press, 2002), 33.

52. *Hubei xue bao* 4, no. 1 (1903): 28.

53. Ibid.

54. Ibid., 35.

55. Tu Ji, *Zhongguo dili xue jiaoke shu* (*Geographical Study of the Chinese Empire*) (Shanghai: Commercial Press, 1906).

56. Rune Svarverud, *International Law as World Order in Late Imperial China: Translation, Reception and Discourse, 1847–1911* (Leiden: Brill, 2007).

57. Alexis Dudden, *Japan's Colonization of Korea: Discourse and Power* (Honolulu: University of Hawai'i Press, 2005).

58. Tanaka, *Japan's Orient*, 63.

59. Yukichi Fukuzawa, *An Outline of a Theory of Civilization*, trans. David Dilworth and G. Cameron Hurst III (New York: Columbia University Press, 2009).

60. Kären Wigen, *A Malleable Map: Geographies of Restoration in Central Japan, 1600–1912* (Berkeley: University of California Press, 2010), 171; David Howell, *Geographies of Identity in Nineteenth-Century Japan* (Berkeley: University of California Press, 2005), 131.

61. Liang Qichao, "Zhongguoshi xulun," in *Yinbingshi wenji dianxiao*, ed. Wu Song et al. (Kunming: Yunnan Jiaoyu chuban she, 2001), 3:1620.

62. Ibid., 3:1802.

63. Rebecca Karl, *Staging the World: Chinese Nationalism at the Turn of the Twentieth Century* (Durham, NC: Duke University Press, 2002), 152.

64. As Peter Zarrow has argued, "Social Darwinism had become critical to Liang's thinking, and by the early 1900s he was taking the 'nation-state' as the unit of the struggle for survival. The nation-state for Liang did not mean a state composed exclusively or even predominantly of a single ethnic nation, but a state whose national identity was defined in patriotic and civic terms. . . . Liang reconceptualized the empire not as a nation-state but as a citizen-state." In *After Empire: The Conceptual Transformation of the Chinese State, 1885–1924* (Stanford, CA: Stanford University Press, 2012), 76.

65. China's New Citizens (pen name), "Dili yu wenmin zhi guanxi," *Xinmin Congbao*, no. 1 (1902).

66. Guan Yun, "Zhongguo yu wan yi wenti lun," *Xin min congbao*, 1903 (4).

67. Karl, *Staging the World*, 69.

68. Mats Norvenius, "Images of an Empire: Chinese Geography Textbooks of the Early 20th Century" (PhD dissertation, Stockholm University, 2012); Christopher Reed, *Gutenberg in Shanghai: Chinese Print Capitalism, 1876–1937* (Vancouver: University of British Columbia Press, 2004); Sabine Dabringhaus, *Territorialer Nationalismus in China: Historisch-geographisches Denken 1900–1949* (Köln: Böhlau Verlag, 2006).

69. Robert Culp, *Articulating Citizenship: Civic Education and Student Politics in Southeastern China, 1912–1940* (Cambridge, MA: Harvard University Press, 2007), 74; see also Peter Zarrow, "The Importance of Space," in *Educating China: Knowledge, Society, and Textbooks in a Modernizing World, 1902–1937*, chapter 7 (Cambridge: Cambridge University Press, 2015.) For definition of *geobody*, see Thongchai Winichakul, *Siam Mapped: A History of the Geo-body of a Nation* (Honolulu: University of Hawai'i Press, 1994); William A. Callahan, "The Cartography of National Humiliation and the Emergence of China's Geobody," *Public Culture* 21, no. 1 (2009), 141–73; Bill Hayton, "The Modern Origins of China's South China Sea Claims: Maps, Misunderstandings, and the Maritime Geobody," *Modern China* 45, no. 2 (2019): 127–70.

70. Another example of this image in Peter Zarrow, *Educating China: Knowl-*

edge, Society, and Textbooks in a Modernizing World, 1902–1937 (Cambridge: Cambridge University Press, 2015), 233.

71. *Zhongguo dili san zi jing* (Beijing: Renmin jiaoyu chuban she, 1963).

72. John Mack Faragher, "Introduction," in *Rereading Frederick Jackson Turner: The Significance of the Frontier in American History and Other Essays*, ed. John Mack Faragher (New York: Henry Holt, 1994), 2.

73. Schulten, *Mapping the Nation*, 185.

74. Ibid., 70.

75. Patricia Nelson Limerick, "Turnerians All: The Dream of a Helpful History in an Intelligible World," *American Historical Review* 100, no. 3 (June 1995), 697–716; also Patricia Limerick, *The Legacy of Conquest: The Unbroken Past of the American West* (New York: Norton, 1987). Ned Blackhawk, *Violence over the Land: Indians and Empires in the Early American West* (Cambridge, MA: Harvard University Press, 2008); Pekka Hämäläinen, *The Comanche Empire* (New Haven, CT: Yale University Press, 2009); Elliot West, *The Last Indian War: The Nez Perce Story* (New York: Oxford University Press, 2011); Elliot West, *The Contested Plains: Indians, Goldseekers, and the Rush to Colorado* (Lawrence: University Press of Kansas, 1998); Pekka Hämäläinen and Samuel Truett, "On Borderlands," *Journal of American History* 98, no. 2 (September 2011), 338–61.

76. Schulten, *The Geographical Imagination in America*, 39.

77. Ibid., 66.

78. James Belich, *Replenishing the Earth: The Settler Revolution and the Rise of the Angloworld* (New York: Oxford University Press, 2009).

79. Jeremy Adelman, *Frontier Development: Land, Labour, and Capital on the Wheatlands of Argentina and Canada, 1890–1914* (New York: Oxford University Press, 1994).

80. Alexander Etkind, *Internal Colonization: Russia's Imperial Experience* (Cambridge: Polity Press, 2011), 62.

81. Robert Nelson, "The Archive for Inner Colonization, The German East, and World War I," in *Germans, Poland, and Colonial Expansion to the East: 1850 to the Present*, ed. Robert Nelson (New York: Palgrave Macmillan, 2009), 66.

82. Andrew Offenburg, *Frontiers in the Gilded Age: Adventure, Capitalism, and Dispossession from Southern Africa to the US-Mexican Borderlands, 1880–1917* (New Haven, CT: Yale University Press, 2019), 43–44.

83. https://www.ndl.go.jp/exposition/e/s1/naikoku1.html (accessed November 15, 2021).

84. Eiichiro Azuma, *In Search of Our Frontier: Japanese America and Settler Colonialism in the Construction of Japan's Borderless Empire* (Berkeley: University of California Press, 2019), 88.

85. John C. Weaver, *The Great Landrush and the Making of the Modern World, 1650–1900* (Montréal: McGill-Queen's University Press, 2003), 18.

86. Lauren Benton, *A Search for Sovereignty: Law and Geography In European Empires, 1400–1900* (Cambridge: Cambridge University Press, 2010).

87. Weaver, *The Great Landrush*, 347.

88. *Zwanzig jahre deutscher kulturarbeit. Tätigkeit und aufgaben neupreussischer kolonisation in Westpreussen und Posen 1886–1906* (Berlin: W. Moeser, 1907); David Blackbourn, *The Conquest of Nature: Water, Landscape and the Making of Modern Germany* (London: Random House, 2006), 281–82; Prasenjit Duara, *Sovereignty and Authenticity: Manchukuo and the East Asian Modern* (Lanham, MD: Rowman & Littlefield, 2003); Prasenjit Duara, "The Discourse of Civilization and Pan-Asianism," *Journal of World History* 12, no. 1 (Spring 2001), 99–130. Hokkaido became a powerful early model for Japanese colonization efforts. See Sidney Xu Lu, "Colonizing Hokkaido and the Origin of Japanese Trans-Pacific Expansion, 1869–1894," *Japanese Studies* 36, no. 2 (2016): 251–74; Wigen, *A Malleable Map*, 171; Howell, *Geographies of Identity in Nineteenth-Century Japan*, 131; Anastasia A. Fedotova and Marina V. Loskutova, "Forests, Climate, and the Rise of Scientific Forestry in Russia: From Local Knowledge and Natural History to Modern Experiments (1840s–early 1890s), in *New Perspectives on the History of Life Sciences and Agriculture*, ed. Denise Phillips and Sharon Kingsland, 113–38 (Dordrecht: Springer, 2015); Marina V. Loskutova and Anastasia A. Fedotova, "The Rise of Applied Entomology in the Russian Empire: Governmental, Public, and Academic Responses to Insect Pest Outbreaks from 1840 to 1894," in *New Perspectives on the History of Life Sciences and Agriculture*, ed. Denise Phillips and Sharon Kingsland, 139–62 (Dordrecht: Springer, 2015).

89. Erik Grimmer-Solem, *Learning Empire: Globalization and the German Quest for World Status, 1875–1919* (Cambridge: Cambridge University Press, 2019), 399.

Chapter 4

1. Liang Qichao, *Ouyou xinying lu* (Hong Kong: San da chu ban she, 1963), 22–23.

2. Erik Grimmer-Solem, *Learning Empire: Globalization and the German Quest for World Status, 1875–1919* (Cambridge: Cambridge University Press, 2019), 229; Sven Beckert, "American Danger: United States Empire, Eurafrica, and the Territorialization of Industrial Capitalism, 1870–1950," *American Historical Review* 122, no. 4 (2017), 1137–70.

3. Gregory James Kasza, *The Conscription Society: Administered Mass Organizations* (New Haven, CT: Yale University Press, 1995).

4. Erez Manela, *The Wilsonian Moment: Self-Determination and the International Origins of Anti-colonial Nationalism* (New York: Oxford University Press, 2007).

5. Klaus Mühlhahn, *Herrschaft und Widerstand in der "Musterkolonie" Kiautschou: Interaktionen zwischen China und Deutschland 1897–1914* (München: Oldenbourg, 2000); Edwin Hoyt, *The Fall of Tsingtao* (London: Arthur Barker Limited, 1975), 135–38.

6. Vera Schwarcz, *The Chinese Enlightenment: Intellectuals and the Legacy of the May Fourth Movement of 1919* (Berkeley: University of California Press, 1986).

7. Shigenobu Okuma, "Illusions of the White Race" (1921), http://afe.easia
.columbia.edu/ps/japan/illusions.pdf (accessed on November 1, 2021).

8. Susan Pedersen, *The Guardians: The League of Nations and the Crisis of Empire* (New York: Oxford University Press, 2015).

9. Courtney Fullilove, *The Profit of the Earth: The Global Seeds of American Agriculture* (Chicago: University of Chicago Press, 2017), 110–14.

10. David Moon, *The American Steppes: The Unexpected Russian Roots of Great Plains Agriculture, 1870s–1930s* (Cambridge and New York: Cambridge University Press, 2020), 129.

11. IB, Box 1.1.

12. Neil Smith, *American Empire: Roosevelt's Geographer and the Prelude to Globalization* (Berkeley: University of California Press, 2003), 122.

13. Innes Keighren, *Bringing Geography to Book: Ellen Semple and the Reception of Geographical Knowledge* (London: I. B. Tauris, 2010), 139.

14. Neil Smith, "Bowman's New World and the Council on Foreign Relations," *Geographical Review* 76, no. 4 (1986): 438–60.

15. Isaiah Bowman, *The New World: Problems in Political Geography* (World Book Company, 1921), 16.

16. Ibid., 191.

17. Ibid., 219.

18. Quinn Slobodian, *The Globalists: The End of Empire and the Birth of Neoliberalism* (Cambridge, MA: Harvard University Press, 2018), 8.

19. Ibid., 150.

20. Bowman, *The New World*, 354.

21. Isaiah Bowman, "The Pioneer Fringe," *Foreign Affairs* 6, no. 1 (October 1927): 49–66.

22. Ibid., 51.

23. Smith, *American Empire*, 319.

24. He defended his position in Isaiah Bowman, "Geography vs. Geopolitics," *Geographical Review* 32, no. 4 (1942), 646–58.

25. Quoted in Gerry Kearns, *Geopolitics and Empire: The Legacy of Halford Mackinder* (Oxford: Oxford University Press, 2009), 21.

26. IB, Box 6.1. Address to the Council on Foreign Relations.

27. IB, Box 4.4. Letter from O. E. Baker, February 25, 1930.

28. IB, Box 6.1. Letter dated March 23, 1939.

29. Jean Gottman, "The Background of Geopolitics," *Military Affairs* 6 (1942): 205.

30. Karl Haushofer Papers, N 1122, Bd. 155 2.

31. Christian W. Spang, *Karl Haushofer Und Japan: Die Rezeption Seiner Geopolitischen Theorien In Der Deutschen Und Japanischen Politik* (München: Iudicium, 2013).

32. Karl Hausofer Papers, N 1122, Bd. 66.

33. Including Karl Haushofer, *Geopolitik des Pazifischen Ozeans* (Berlin,

1927). Karl Haushofer, *Japans Werdegang als Weltmacht und Empire* (Berlin, Leipzig, 1933).

34. *Zeitschrift für Geopolitik* (Germany: Kurt Vowinckel) 2 (1925), 400.

35. Karl Haushofer Papers, N 1122, Bd. 110.

36. IB, Series 1, Personal Box 1.3, Folder 2.

37. IB, Box 3.1.

38. Benjamin Schwartz, *In Search of Wealth and Power* (Cambridge, MA: Harvard University Press, 1964); David Wright, "Yan Fu and the Tasks of the Translator," in *New Terms for New Ideas: Western Knowledge and Lexical Change in Late Imperial China*, ed. Iwo Amelung Michael Lackner and Joachim Kurtz (Leiden: Brill, 2001), 240–44; Sean Hsiang-lin Lei, "The Dawn of Science as Cultural Authority in China: *Tianyanlun* (*On Heavenly Evolution*) in the Post-1895 Debate over the Engagement with Western Civilization," *East Asian Science, Technology and Society: An International Journal* 16, no. 3 (2022), 408–32, DOI: 10.1080/18752160.2022.2095102.

39. Rebecca E. Karl, *Staging the World: Chinese Nationalism at the Turn of the Twentieth Century* (Durham, NC: Duke University Press, 2002).

40. Liu Hongdiao, *Zhengzhi Dili* 政治地理 (Hunan: Fazhen biji she, 1905.9.29), preface.

41. Ibid., 2.

42. Ibid., 181.

43. The relationship between nature and the spread of capitalism has been explored by geographers, including David Harvey, *Justice, Nature, and the Geography of Difference* (Malden, MA: Blackwell, 1996); Neil Smith, *Uneven Development: Nature, Capital, and the Production of Space*, 3rd ed. (Athens: University of Georgia Press, 2008); Bruce Braun, "Producing Vertical Territory: Geology and Governmentality in Late Victorian Canada," *Ecumene* 7, no. 1 (2000): 7–46; Jason W. Moore, *Capitalism in the Web of Life* (New York: Verso, 2015).

44. Boris Torgasheff, *The Mineral Industry of the Far East* (Shanghai: Chali Company, 1930), 1–3.

45. Ibid., 56–57.

46. Hu Rongquan 胡榮銓, *Zhongguo Meikuang* 中國煤礦 (Shanghai: Shangwu yinshu guan, 1935).

47. Ellen Semple and Chen Jianmin, trans., *Dili huanjing zhi yinxiang* (Shanghai: Shangwu chu ban she, 1937).

48. From Halford Mackinder, "The Scope and Methods of Geography," *Proceedings of the Royal Geographical Society* 9 (1887), 141–60; Halford Mackinder, "The Geographical Pivot of History," *Geographical Journal* 21 (1904), 421–37; and finally, what might be the culmination of his ideas in Halford Mackinder, *Democratic Ideals and Reality* (New York: H. Holt and Company, 1942). Alfred Thayer Mahan, *The Influence of Sea Power upon History: 1660–1783* (New York: Hill and Wang, 1957).

49. James Fairgrieve, *Geography and World Power* (London: University of London Press, 1924), 232.

50. SHAC, 393-359.

51. The war created severe shortages of raw materials for industries, in addition to millions of refugees who were displaced from their homes. See Micah Muscolino, "Refugees, Land Reclamation, and Militarized Landscapes in Wartime China: Huanglongshan, Shaanxi, 1937–45," *Journal of Asian Studies* 69, no. 2 (May 2010): 453–78.

52. Hu Huanyong, *Guofang Dili* (Guomin zhengfu jushi weiyuan hui zhengzhibu bianyin, August 21, 1938), 2.

53. Ibid., section 5.

54. Grace Yen Shen, *Unearthing the Nation: Modern Geology and Nationalism in Republican China* (Chicago: University of Chicago Press, 2014), 155.

55. IMH, Zhu Jiahua papers, 301-01-15-018; 301-01-15-019.

56. Jiang Pei, *Zhanguo cepai: Sichao yanjiu* (Tianjin: Tianjin People's Publishing House, 2001), 11–12.

57. In addition to Jiang's monograph on the Warring States Clique, discussion of members of the group also appears in Edmund Fung, *The Intellectual Foundations of Chinese Modernity: Cultural and Political Thought in the Republican Era* (Cambridge: Cambridge University Press, 2010), 120–26; Ye Juan, *Ling yizhong xixue: Zhongguo xiandai liuderen jiqi dui deguo wenhua de jieshou* (Beijing: Beijing University Press, 2005), chap. 4.

58. Lin Tongji, "The Replay of the Warring States Era," *Warring States Policies*, no. 1 (1940): 7.

59. Hong Siqi, "The War in Norway: Topography and Military Strategy," *Warring States Policies,* no. 3, 23–26; Hong Siqi, "Geography and National Strategy," *Warring States Policies,* no. 4, 12–14; Hong Siqi, "If Hitler Were to Win," *Warring States Polices*, no. 5, 1–7.

60. Kearns, *Geopolitics and Empire,* 20.

61. Jiang, *Zhanguo cepai*, 13.

62. Sha Xuejun, *Guofang dili xinlun* (Chongqing: Shangwu yinshu guan, 1943), 11.

63. Ibid., 9.

64. Karl Haushofer, *Guofang dili xue*, trans. Zhou Guangda (Chongqing: Shangwu Yinshu guan, 1945).

65. *Zhongjian,* 3, no. 11 (August 1947).

66. *Junshi Zazhi*, no. 201 (1948): 97.

67. He Yongji, "Cong tianxia zhi diyuan guo," *Guancha* 2, no. 19 (1947): 12–14.

68. Eric Fischer Carl Troll, "Geographic Science in Germany during the Period 1933–1945: A Critique and Justification," *Annals of the Association of American Geographers* 39 (1949): 103.

Chapter 5

1. Isaiah Bowman, *The Pioneer Fringe* (American Geographical Society Special Publication No. 13, 1931), preface, v.

2. David Blackbourn, *The Conquest of Nature: Water, Landscape and the*

Making of Modern Germany. London: Jonathan Cape, 2006), 282–84; Shelley Baranowski, *Nazi Empire: German Colonialism and Imperialism from Bismarck to Hitler* (Cambridge: Cambridge University Press, 2011), 270; Vejas Liulevicious, *The German Myth of the East: 1800 to the Present* (Oxford: Oxford University Press, 2009), 114–23.

3. Kiran Klaus Patel, *The New Deal: A Global History* (Princeton, NJ: Princeton University Press, 2016).

4. Ann Laura Stoler, "Tense and Tender Ties: The Politics of Comparison in North American History and (Post) Colonial Studies," *Journal of American History* 88, no. 3 (December 2001), 829–65.

5. Quinn Slobodian, *Globalists: The End of Empire and the Birth of Neoliberalism* (Cambridge, MA: Harvard University Press, 2018), 68.

6. RF Archives, No. 26, Series 1, Box 27: International Education Board.

7. Inderjeet Parmar, *Foundations of the American Century: The Ford, Carnegie, and Rockefeller Foundations in the Rise of American Power* (New York: Columbia University Press, 2012), 68.

8. Mary Augusta Brazelton, "Western Medical Education on Trial: The Endurance of Peking Union Medical College, 1949–1985," *Twentieth-Century China* 40, no. 2 (2015): 126–45.

9. Gabriela Soto Laveaga, "Beyond Borlaug's Shadow: Octavio Paz, Indian Farmers, and the Challenge of Narrating the Green Revolution," *Agricultural History* 95, no. 4 (2021): 576–608; Prakash Kumar, "'Modernization' and Agrarian Development in India, 1912–52," *Journal of Asian Studies* 79, no. 3 (2020): 633–58.

10. Harry Houser Lover and John Henry Reisner, *The Cornell-Nanking Story: The First International Technical Cooperation Program in Agriculture by Cornell University* (Ithaca, NY: The Internet-First University Press, 2012).

11. Xu Yinglian, Li Jingxi, and Duan Jili, eds., *Quanguo xiangcun jianshe yundong gaikuang* (Zouping: Shandong xiangcun jianshe yanjiu yuan chu ban gushou, 1935).

12. Charles W. Hayford, *To the People: James Yen and Village China* (New York: Columbia University Press, 1990).

13. RF Archives, RG 1 Projects, Series 601, Box 12, Folder 125. Letter dated December 16, 1932, from Selskar Gunn to Warren Weaver from Shanghai.

14. Laurence Schneider, *Biology and Revolution in Twentieth-Century China* (Lanham, MD: Rowman & Littlefield, 2003), 72.

15. RF Archives, RG 1 Projects, Series 601, Box 9, Folder 67.

16. RF Archives, RG 1 Projects, Series 601, Box 10, Folder 98.

17. Ibid., Folders 99–100.

18. Hayford, *To the People,* 19–21.

19. Ibid., 154.

20. Both Yen and Liang were leading proselytizers of progressive rural modernization, a vision backed by a number of American philanthropists with Christian leanings, including Henry Ford and John D. Rockefeller. See Kate

Merkel-Hess, *The Rural Modern: Reconstructing the Self and State in Republican China* (Chicago: University of Chicago Press, 2016), 50.

21. RF Archives, RG 1 Projects, Series 601, Box 9, Folder 69.

22. Ibid., Folder 70.

23. RF Archives, RG 1 Projects, Box 8, Folder 78.

24. Ibid., Folder 80.

25. "Marshall Balfour, Population Expert," Obituary, *New York Times*, March 23, 1976, 30.

26. RF Archives, RG 1 Projects, Box 9, Folder 73. Letter from Balfour to Yen dated July 17, 1940.

27. Ibid., Letter dated September 9, 1940, from Gunn to Balfour.

28. RF Archives, RG 1 Projects, Series 601, Box 13, Folder 133. Balfour to Interdivisional China Committee, dated April 3, 1944.

29. RF Archives, RG 1 Projects, Series 601, Box 9, Folder 75.

30. RF Archives, RG 1 Projects, Series 601, Box 11.

31. Micah S. Muscolino, *The Ecology of War in China: Henan Province, the Yellow River, and Beyond, 1938–1950* (New York: Cambridge University Press, 2015), 31.

32. Randall Stross, *The Stubborn Earth: American Agriculturalists on Chinese Soil, 1898–1937* (Berkeley: University of California Press, 1986, 199.

33. Tore Olsson, *Agrarian Crossings: Reformers and the Remaking of the US and Mexican Countryside* (Princeton, NJ: Princeton University Press, 2017).

34. Jonathan Harwood, "Whatever Happened to the Mexican Green Revolution?" *Agroecology and Sustainable Food Systems* 44, no. 9 (2020): 1243–52, DOI: 10.1080/21683565.2020.1752350.

35. Stross, *The Stubborn Earth,* 213.

36. RF Archives, RG 1 Projects, Box 8, Folder 82.

37. Hayford, *To the People,* 220.

38. James Lin, "Sowing Seeds and Knowledge: Agricultural Development in the US, Taiwan, and the World, 1949–1975," *East Asian Science, Technology and Society* (EASTS) 9 (June 2015): 127–49.

39. Quoted in Parmar, *Foundations of the American Century*, 12.

40. Sigrid Schmalzer, *Red Revolution, Green Revolution: Scientific Farming in Socialist China* (Chicago: University of Chicago Press, 2016).

41. Hao Hu, Funing Zhong, and Calum G. Turvey, eds., *Chinese Agriculture in the 1930s: Investigations into John Lossing Buck's Rediscovered "Land Utilization in China" Microdata* (London: Palgrave Macmillan, 2019).

42. John Lossing Buck, *Land Utilization in China, a Study of 16,786 Farms in 168 Localities, and 38,256 Farm Families in Twenty-Two Provinces in China, 1929–1933* (Shanghai, China: The Commercial Press, Ltd., 1937).

43. Zuoyue Wang, "Saving China through Science: The Science Society of China, Scientific Nationalism, and Civil Society in Republican China." *Osiris* 17 (2002): 291–322.

44. Yi Wang, "Irrigation, Commercialization, and Social Change in

Nineteenth-Century Inner Mongolia," *International Review of Social History* 59, no. 2 (2014), 215–46; Ding Changqing, "The Development of Capitalism in Modern Chinese Agriculture," in *The Chinese Economy in the Early Twentieth Century*, ed. Tim Wright (New York: St. Martin's Press, 1992), 134–51.

45. Xiuyu Wang, *China's Last Imperial Frontier: Late Qing Expansion in Sichuan's Tibetan Borderlands* (Lanham, MD: Lexington Books, 2013), 211–12.

46. Ding Changqing, "The Development of Capitalism in Modern Chinese Agriculture," 134–51.

47. Peter Lavelle, *Profits of Nature: Colonial Development and the Quest for Resources in Nineteenth-Century China* (New York: Columbia University Press, 2020), 102.

48. SHAC, 23-1251.

49. Ibid., 59.

50. Zou Zuohua, *Tunken qianshuo* (Xing An Tunken gongshu, 1928).

51. James Reardon-Anderson, *Reluctant Pioneers: China's Expansion Northward, 1644–1937* (Stanford, CA: Stanford University Press, 2005); Thomas Gottschang and Diana Lary, *Swallows and Settlers: The Great Migration from North China to Manchuria* (Ann Arbor: Center for Chinese Studies, University of Michigan, 2000).

52. Gottschang and Lary, *Swallows and Settlers*, 2.

53. Yoshihisa Tak Matsusaka, *The Making of Japanese Manchuria, 1904–1932.* (Cambridge, MA: Harvard University Asia Center, 2001), 4–5.

54. Louise Young, *Japan's Total Empire: Manchuria and the Culture of Wartime Imperialism* (Berkeley: University of California Press, 1998).

55. The Japanese opened an agricultural experimental station in the borderlands between China and Korea as early as 1907. Nianshen Song, *Making Borders in Modern East Asia: The Tumen River Demarcation, 1881–1919* (Cambridge: Cambridge University Press, 2018), 149–51.

56. *Xing An Tunken Bureau Report* (XTB), Year 1, 82 (National Library of China).

57. Ibid, 4.

58. Ibid., 5.

59. Ibid., 28.

60. Ibid., 52.

61. Ibid., 156–65.

62. Ibid., 273.

63. Daqing Yang, *Technology of Empire: Telecommunications and Japanese Expansion in Asia, 1883–1945* (Cambridge, MA: Harvard University Asia Center, 2010).

64. Owen Lattimore, *The Diluv Khutagt: Memoirs and Autobiography of a Mongol Buddhist Reincarnation in Religion and Revolution* (Wiesbaden: Harrassowitz, 1982), 2. Quoted in James Cotton, *Asian Frontier Nationalism: Owen Lattimore and the American Policy Debate* (Atlantic Highlands, NJ: Humanities Press International, 1989), 10.

65. XTB, 256.

66. Reardon-Anderson, *Reluctant Pioneer,* 148.

67. Yutaka Kurimoto, *Kōan tonkonku jijō* (Dairen: Minami Manshū Tetsudō Kabushiki Kaisha, 1929).

68. Yi Wang, "Irrigation, Commercialization, and Social Change in Nineteenth-Century Inner Mongolia," 215–46; Liping Wang, "From Masterly Brokers to Compliant Protégées: The Frontier Governance System and the Rise of Ethnic Confrontation in China–Inner Mongolia, 1900–1930," *American Journal of Sociology* 120, no. 6 (May 2015): 1641–89.

69. Justin Tighe, *Constructing Suiyuan: The Politics of Northwestern Territory and Development in Early Twentieth-Century China* (Leiden: Brill, 2005), 100–102, 122–24.

70. *Xibei Wenti,* No. 1 (April 1929).

71. Ibid., 11. Yajun Mo has argued that the founding Chinese tourism industry also reaffirmed the territorial expanse of the country. See Yajun Mo, *Touring China: A History of Travel Culture, 1912–1949* (Ithaca, NY: Cornell University Press, 2021).

72. Robert Nelson, "The *Archive for Inner Colonization*: The German East, and World War I," in *Germans, Poland, and Colonial Expansion to the East: 1850 to the Present*, ed. Robert Nelson (New York: Palgrave Macmillan, 2009), 74.

73. IMH, 03-32-204-03-037, Beiyang zhengfu waijiaobu.

74. Guo Weiping, "kaifa xibei tan," in *Kaifa Xibei zhi xian jue wenti,* no. 3–4 (1932) Xibei xue hui zonghui, 9.

75. Suiyuan tong zhi guan, *Suiyuan tong zhi gao, 100 juan* (Huhehaote Shi: Nei Menggu ren min chu ban she, 2007).

76. Donald Gillin, *Warlord: Yen Hsi-shan in Shansi Province, 1911–1949* (Princeton, NJ: Princeton University Press, 1967), 75.

77. Ibid., 93.

78. Party Committee on the History of Datong Coalmines, "1918–1936 niande datong meikuang," *Lishi Jiaoyu* (*History Teaching*), no. 2 (1962), 26–35.

79. Both the Qing and the subsequent Republican government attempted to develop the Suiyuan region agriculturally, yet in the 1930s, it was still widely known as an impoverished backwater. Tighe, *Constructing Suiyuan,* 100–102, 122–24.

80. Yan was not the only one attuned to the popular calls for rural revival. See Merkel-Hess, *The Rural Modern*; Margherita Zanasi, "Western Utopias, Missionary Economics, and the Chinese Village," *Journal of World History* 24, no. 2 (June 2013), 359–87.

81. Gillin, *Warlord,* 128.

82. Kiran Klaus Patel, *The New Deal: A Global History* (Princeton, NJ: Princeton University Press, 2016), 214.

83. Suiyuan Tunken Bureau (SYTB), Year One Report (Y1), 234.

84. SYTB, Y1, 257.

85. SYTB, Y1, 266–67.

86. SYTB, Y1, 251.

87. SYTB, Y1, 269.

88. SYTB, Y1, 275.

89. SYTB, Y1, 283.

90. Suiyuan Tunken Bureau (SYTB), Year Two Report (Y2), 213.

91. SYTB, Y2, 316–17.

92. SYTB, Y2, 387.

93. SYTB, Y2, 390–91.

94. Suiyuan Tunken Bureau (SYTB), Year Three Report (Y3), 7.

95. SYTB, Y3, 122.

96. SYTB, Y3, 152.

97. Suiyuan Tunken Bureau (SYTB), Year Four Report (Y4), 51.

98. SYTB, Y4, 253.

99. SYTB, Y4, 323–25

100. *Xin Nongcun,* 6.15, 1933 (1). Taiyuan, Shanxi. National Library of China, Beijing collection.

101. Gillin, *Warlord,* 215.

Chapter 6

1. Paul Rohrbach, *Um des Teufels Handschrift: Zwei Menschenalter erlebter Weltgeschichte* (Hamburg: Hans Dulk, 1953), 488.

2. Jeffrey Herf, *Reactionary Modernism: Technology, Culture, and Politics in Weimar and the Third Reich* (Cambridge: Cambridge University Press, 1984).

3. *Zwanzig jahre deutscher kulturarbeit. Tätigkeit und aufgaben neupreussischer kolonisation in Westpreussen und Posen 1886–1906* (Berlin: W. Moeser, 1907).

4. Robert Nelson, "The *Archive for Inner Colonization,* the German East, and World War I," in *Germans, Poland, and Colonial Expansion to the East: 1850 to the Present,* ed. Robert Nelson (New York: Palgrave Macmillan, 2009), 66–93, 84.

5. Susan Pedersen, *The Guardians: The League of Nations and the Crisis of Empire* (New York: Oxford University Press, 2015), 284.

6. Carl Schmitt and G. L. Ulmen, *The Nomos of the Earth in the International Law of the Jus Publicum Europaeum* (New York: Telos Press, 2003); Stephen Legg, *Spatiality, Sovereignty and Carl Schmitt: Geographies of the Nomos* (Abingdon, Oxon: Routledge, 2011).

7. Pedersen, *The Guardians,* 340.

8. Max Sering Papers, N 1210/3.

9. Pedersen, *The Guardians,* 333.

10. Sven Beckert, "American Danger: United States Empire, Eurafrica, and the Territorialization of Industrial Capitalism, 1870–1950," *American Historical Review* 122, no. 4 (October 2017): 1137–70.

11. Pedersen, *The Guardians,* 344–46.

12. German Federal Archives (BA), Berlin-Lichterfelde, R 6/104.

13. Ibid., R 6/102.

14. Ibid., R 6/109.

15. Ibid., R 6/431.

16. Ibid., R 6/19.

17. Michael Burleigh, *Germany Turns Eastwards: A Study of Ostforschung in the Third Reich* (Cambridge: Cambridge University Press, 1988).

18. Shelley Baranowski, *Nazi Empire: German Colonialism and Imperialism from Bismarck to Hitler* (Cambridge: Cambridge University Press, 2011), 339.

19. Sebastian Conrad, *German Colonialism: A Short History* (Cambridge: Cambridge University Press, 2012), 125.

20. Jonathan Harwood, *Styles of Scientific Thought: The German Genetics Community 1900–1933* (Chicago: University of Chicago Press, 1993), 222–23.

21. Walter Christaller and Carlisle Whiteford Baskin, *Central Places in Southern Germany* (Englewood Cliffs, NJ: Prentice-Hall, 1966).

22. M. Rössler, "Applied Geography and Area Research in Nazi Society: Central Place Theory and Planning, 1933 to 1945." *Environment and Planning D: Society and Space* 7, no. 4 (December 1989): 419–31.

23. *Trials of War Criminals before the Nuremberg Military Tribunals under Control Council Law No. 10, October 1946–April 1949*, Vol. 5, 156–57.

24. G. William Skinner, "Marketing and Social Structure in Rural China, Part I," *Journal of Asian Studies* 24, no. 1 (1964): 3–43; "Marketing and Social Structure in Rural China Part II," *Journal of Asian Studies* 24, no. 2 (1965): 195–228; "Marketing and Social Structure in Rural China, Part III," *Journal of Asian Studies* 24, no. 3 (1965): 363–99.

25. G. William Skinner, "Presidential Address: The Structure of Chinese History," *Journal of Asian Studies* 44, no. 2 (1985): 271–92.

26. Karl Haushofer Papers, N 1122, Bd. 110.

27. Carl Troll, "Geographic Science in Germany during the Period 1933–1945: A Critique and Justification," *Annals of the Association of American Geographers* 39 (1949): 133.

28. Ibid., 103.

29. Walter Mogk, *Paul Rohrbach und das „Größere Deutschland" Ethischer Imperialismus im Wilhelminischen Zeitalter* (München: Wilhelm Goldmann Verlag, 1972), 15.

30. Rohrbach, *Um des Teufels Handschrift*, 13.

31. Shellen Wu, "The Search for Coal in the Age of Empires: Ferdinand von Richthofen's Odyssey in China, 1860–1920," *American Historical Review* 119, no. 2 (April 2014): 339–62.

32. Rohrbach, *Um des Teufels Handschrift*, 16.

33. Mogk, *Paul Rohrbach*, 61.

34. Rohrbach, *Um des Teufels Handschrift*, 7.

35. Fritz Fischer, *Germany's Aims in the First World War* (New York: Norton & Norton, 1967), 275.

36. Rohrbach, *Um des Teufels Handschrift*, 199.

37. Ibid., 19.

38. Paul Rohrbach, *Deutschland unter den Weltvőlkern, Materialien zur aus-wärtigen Politik* (Germany: J. Engelhorns, 1921), 107.

39. In 2021, the German government finally formally acknowledged the colonial-era genocide during its occupation of Namibia and offered financial compensation, https://www.bbc.com/news/world-europe-57279008 (accessed September 14, 2022).

40. Tilman Dedering, "The German-Herero War of 1904: Revisionism of Genocide or Imaginary Historiography?" *Journal of Southern African Studies* 19, no. 1 (March 1993): 87.

41. Paul A. Cohen, *History in Three Keys: The Boxers as Event, Experience, and Myth* (New York: Columbia University Press, 1997).

42. Rohrbach, *Um des Teufels Handschrift,* 64.

43. Ibid., letter from 1905, 69.

44. Paul Rohrbach, *Deutschlands koloniale Forderung* (Hamburg: Han-seatische Verlagsanstalt, 1935),110–13.

45. Isabel V. Hull, *Absolute Destruction: Military Culture and the Practices of War in Imperial Germany* (Ithaca, NY: Cornell University Press, 2005), 328.

46. Mogk, *Paul Rohrbach,* 111–13.

47. Ibid., 64–65.

48. Rohrbach, *Deutschland unter den Weltvőlkern,* 20–21.

49. Rohrbach, *Deutsche Gedanke in der Welt* (Germany: K. R. Langewiesche, 1912), 52.

50. Ibid., 66.

51. Paul Rohrbach, „Russland und wir" in *Das Grőssere Deutschland,* no. 39, Dezember 24, 1914.

52. Friedrich Röder, Deutsch-Ukrainische herder-Gesellschaft, *Dem Anden-ken Paul Rohrbachs: ein Beitrag zur osteuropäischen Problematik* (München: Verlag Ukraine, 1949), 49.

53. Ibid., 66.

54. Horst Bieber, *Paul Rohrbach—Ein konservativer Publizist und Kritiker der Weimarer Republik* (Berlin and Műnchen: Verlag Dokumentation, 1972), 67.

55. Rohrbach, *Um des Teufels Handschrift,* 308.

56. Paul Rohrbach, *Deutschtum in Not! die Schicksale der Deutschen in Europa ausserhalb des Reiches* (Berlin-Schmargendorf: W. Andermann, 1926).

57. For an extended discussion of Himmler's pet project, "Heim ins Reich" program see Götz Aly and Susanne Heim, *Architects of Annihilation: Aus-chwitz and the Logic of Destruction.* (Princeton, NJ: Princeton University Press, 1991); and Götz Aly, *'Endlősung': Vőlkerverschiebung und der Mord an den eu-ropaischen Juden.* (Frankfurt am Main: Fischer Verlag, 1995).

58. Rohrbach, *Deutschland! Tod oder Leben?* (München: F. Bruckmann, 1930), 165.

59. Henry Cord Meyer Papers, Box 1.

60. Nevertheless, the evocative title of his memoir has captured the attention of German historians, see George Steinmetz, *The Devil's Handwriting: Precolo-*

niality and the German Colonial State in Qingdao, Samoa, and Southwest Africa (Chicago: University of Chicago Press, 2007).

61. Rohrbach, *Um des Teufels Handschrift,* 54.

62. IMH and the GMD Party Archives both contain materials related to these *tunken* plans. IMH (20-11-14-11; 20-11-83-2; 20-00-61-6-3; 20-16-45-14; 20-26-8-22); GMD (5.2/20/1/2; 3.1/20/23/2).

63. SHAC, 23-23, *nonglin bu kuaiji chu.*

64. In addition to internal Party documents, writers also published propaganda books promoting *tunken.* Huang Fensheng, *Bianjiang tunken renyuan shouce* (Nanjing: Zhongyang qingnian yinshua suo, 1946).

65. SHAC, 23-3104.

66. The tunken zones were also viewed as a solution to the refugee problem. See Micah Muscolino, "Refugees, Land Reclamation, and Militarized Landscapes in Wartime China: Huanglongshan, Shaanxi, 1937–45," *Journal of Asian Studies* 69, no. 2 (May 2010): 453–78.

67. IMH 20-87-141-03.

68. IMH 20-87-143-04.

69. IMH 20-87-149-05.

70. IMH 20-87-157-09.

71. Zuoyue Wang, "Saving China through Science: The Science Society of China, Scientific Nationalism and Civil Society in Republican China," *Osiris* 17 (2002): 291–322.

72. Chi Yu Tang (Tang Qiyu), "An Economic Study of Chinese Agriculture" (PhD dissertation, Cornell University, 1924).

73. Ibid., 272.

74. Ibid., 274.

75. Justin Tighe, *Constructing Suiyuan: The Politics of Northwestern Territory and Development in Early Twentieth-Century China* (Leiden: Brill, 2005), 122–23.

76. SHAC, 23-3150.

77. SHAC, 23-3092.

78. Tang Qiyu, *Lidai tunken yanjiu* (Shanghai: Zhongzheng shuju, 1945).

79. He Weizhong, *Nanniwan tunken ji* (Tianjin: Tianjin Renmin Chubanshe, 1959).

80. James Leibold, *Reconfiguring Chinese Nationalism: How the Qing Frontier and Its Indigenes Became Chinese* (New York: Palgrave Macmillan, 2007), 107.

81. SHAC, 23-1977.

82. SHAC, 12-14178.

83. SHAC, 5.147.

84. SHAC, 23-2937.

85. SHAC, 4.30269.

86. SHAC, 12.6.14178.

87. SHAC, 4.9183.

88. SHAC, 23-1253.

89. IMH 20-87-206-06

90. IMH 20-87-219-04.

91. IMH 20-87-219-06.

92. IMH 20-87-219-12, 20-87-219-07.

93. IMH 20-87-219-13.

94. SHAC, 23-2140.

95. Joseph Lawson, *A Frontier Made Lawless: Violence in Upland Southwest China, 1800–1956* (Vancouver: University of British Columbia Press, 2017), 166.

96. Ibid., 163.

97. SHAC, 12.6.10562.

98. SHAC, 5.128.

99. SHAC, 12.6.14370.

100. SHAC, 4.30062.

101. SHAC, 12-2045.

Chapter 7

1. Nicholas J. Spykman, *America's Strategy in World Politics: The United States and the Balance of Power* (New York: Harcourt, Brace, and Co., 1942), 41.

2. IB, Box 3.5. Public address delivered on April 22, 1946, National Academy of Sciences, Washington, DC.

3. IB, Box 3.5. Address on September 30, 1946, to US State Department, "Impact of Geography on National Power" (marked "Secret").

4. IB, Box 3.5. Public address at Princeton University, October 14, 1946.

5. IB, Box 2.22.

6. IB, Box 2.10.

7. IB, Box 2.43.

8. IB, Box 2.10. Letter dated October 16, 1945, from Bowman to Chang in response to inquiry about American institutions of science.

9. IB, Box 2.22, Correspondences. Letter dated May 15, 1939, from Hull to Bowman.

10. Vannevar Bush, *Science: The Endless Frontier* (Washington: US Government Printing Office, 1945).

11. Johnny Miri, "The Fall of Vannevar Bush: The Forgotten War for Control of Science Policy in Postwar America," *Historical Studies in the Natural Sciences* 51, no. 4 (2021): 507–41.

12. IB, Box 2.9.

13. William Rankin, *After the Map: Cartography, Navigation, and the Transformation of Territory in the Twentieth Century* (Chicago: University of Chicago Press, 2016), 85.

14. IB, Box 6.4. "World Economic Progress through Cooperative Technical Assistance: The Point 4 Program," The Department of State Publication 3454, released April 1949.

15. Megan Black, *The Global Interior: Mineral Frontiers and American Power* (Cambridge, MA: Harvard University Press, 2018), 118.

16. Neil Smith, "'Academic War over the Field of Geography': The Elimina-

tion of Geography at Harvard, 1947–1951," *Annals of the Association of American Geographers* 77, no. 2 (June 1987), 155–72.

17. Zhang Qiyun and Zhu Kezhen, *Benguo Dili* (xin zhongxue zhijiao gaokeji shu, Shangwu yinshuguan, 1930).

18. He defended his position in Isaiah Bowman, "Geography vs. Geopolitics," *Geographical Review* 32, no. 4 (October, 1942): 646–58.

19. IB, Box 2.10. Letter dated November 13, 1944, from Bowman to Zhang.

20. IB, Box 2.10. Letter dated December 26, 1944, from Harcourt, Brace, and Co. editor Lambert Davis to Bowman explaining that they have to turn down Zhang's manuscript because they are already publishing David Nelson Rowe's *China among the Powers.*

21. Fangyu He, "From Scholar to Bureaucrat: The Political Choice of the Historical Geographer Zhang Qiyun," *Journal of Modern Chinese History* 10, no. 1 (2016): 35–51.

22. IMH, Zhu Jiahua papers, 301-01-15-018; 301-01-15-019.

23. IB, Boxes 6.3 and 6.3a. April 1940 meeting records.

24. Rana Mitter, *Forgotten Ally: China's World War II, 1937–1945* (Boston: Houghton Mifflin Harcourt, 2013), 38.

25. Barbara Tuchman, *Stilwell and the American Experience in China, 1911–45* (New York: Macmillan, 1970).

26. Owen Lattimore Papers, Box 27, Folder 1.

27. Owen Lattimore Papers, Box 26, Folder 15.

28. Robert P. Newman, *Owen Lattimore and the "Loss" of China* (Berkeley: University of California Press, 1992), 109.

29. E. A. Aronova (Elena Aleksandrovna), *Scientific History: Experiments in History and Politics from the Bolshevik Revolution to the End of the Cold War* (Chicago: University of Chicago Press, 2021), 60–86.

30. Reports from the 1940s–1950s espionage investigation of Owen Lattimore conducted as a result of allegations linking him to Soviet espionage, http://foia .fbi.gov/foiaindex/owenlatt.htm (last accessed September 16, 2022 from the Princeton University Library catalog.)

31. Gu Jiegang and Shi Nianhai, *Zhongguo Jiangyu Yangeshi* (Shangwu Chubanshe, March 1938).

32. Peter Perdue, *China Marches West: The Qing Conquest of Central Eurasia* (Cambridge, MA: Harvard University Press, 2005), 336, 384.

33. Ding Shan, *Ding Shan Ri Ji* (Beijing Shi: Guo jia tu shu guan chu ban she, 2018), 32.

34. Ding Shan, *Dili yu zhonghua minzu zhi shengshuai* (Shanghai: Da Zhongguo tushu ju, 1948), 30.

35. Ibid., 40.

36. Ibid., 64.

37. Ibid., 72.

38. James Fairgrieve and Zhang Fukang, trans., *Dili yu shijie ba quan* (Shanghai: Shangwu yinshu guan, 1937).

39. James Fairgrieve, *Geography and World Power*, 2nd ed. (New York: E. P. Dutton & Co., 1917), 225–46.

40. Sun Honglie et al., ed., *Zhongguo ziran ziyuan zonghe kexue kaocha yu yanjiu* (Beijing: Shangwu yinshu guan, 2007); Zhang Jiuchen, *Ziran ziyuan zonghe kaocha weiyuan hui yanjiu* (Beijing: Kexue chubanshe, 2013).

41. Owen Lattimore, *The Inner Asian Frontiers* (New York: Oxford University Press, 1940), xxi.

42. Lattimore, *The Inner Asian Frontiers,* xxiii.

43. Huang Guozhang, *Dili* 1, no. 1 (1941): 3.

44. Ibid., 1.

45. Ibid., 2.

46. Ibid., 3.

47. SHAC, 393-2102.

48. Grace Yen Shen, *Unearthing the Nation: Modern Geology and Nationalism in Republican China* (Chicago: University of Chicago Press, 2014), 140.

49. *Dili Zhishi*, no. 1 (1950): 1.

50. *Dili Zhishi,* December 1951, 275–76.

51. Soviet Academy of Sciences Geographical Research Institute, ed., Tian Meng, trans., *Wei mei di fuwu de zichan jieji dilixue* (*Bourgeois Geography in the Service of American Imperialism*) (Beijing, 1952).

52. Zhongguo dili xuehui zhishi bianji weiyuanhui (Chinese Geographical Society Geographical Knowledge Editorial Committee), *Guanyu zichan jieji dili sixiang de pipan* (*Critique of Bourgeois Geographical Thinking*) (Shanghai, 1955).

53. Sun Honglie, *Zhongguo ziran*; Zhang Jiuchen, *Ziran ziyuan zonghe kaocha weiyuan hui yanjiu* (Beijing: Kexue chubanshe, 2013).

54. Li Hou, *Building for Oil: Daqing and the Formation of the Chinese Socialist State* (Cambridge, MA: Harvard University Asia Center, 2018), 33.

55. Zhang Jiuchen, *Ziran ziyuan,* 88.

56. Ibid., 89–91.

57. Tang Qiyu, *Zhongguo nongshi gao* (Beijing: nongye chubanshe, 1985); Tang Qiyu, *Zhongguo zuowu caipei shigao* (Beijing: nongye chubanshe, 1986).

58. Xiang Ruoyu, ed., *Xinbian gaoji xiaoxue dili keben*, 4 vols. (Beiping: Haubei lianhe chubanshe, 1949).

59. Ibid., 1:2.

60. Ibid., 3:21.

61. Susan L. Mann, *Gender and Sexuality in Modern Chinese History* (New York: Cambridge University Press, 2011).

62. Shelly Chan, *Diaspora's Homeland: Modern China in the Age of Global Migration* (Durham, NC: Duke University Press, 2018).

63. Li Fusheng and Fang Yingkai, *Xinjiang bingtuan tunken shubian shi,* 2 vols. (Urumqi: Xinjiang ke ji wei sheng chu ban she 1997).

64. Yong Yao, *Xiang lu nu bing zai Xinjiang* (Beijing: Guang ming ribao chuban she, 2012), 22.

65. Ibid., 33.

66. Ibid., 75.

67. *Xinjiang shengchan jianshe bintuan shiliao xuanji*, vol. 13 (Urumqi: Xinjian renmin chuban she, 2003), 361.

68. Ou Changfu and Dai Qingyuan, *Ba qian Xiang nü jin Jiang hui yi lu* (Changsha Shi: Hunan ren min chu ban she, 2010).

69. Ibid., 391.

70. Bin Xu, "Historically Remaining Issues: The Shanghai-Xinjiang Zhiqing Migration Program and the Tangled Legacies of the Mao Era in China, 1980–2017," *Modern China* 48, no. 4 (2021): 1–33.

Epilogue

1. Odd Arne Westad, *The Global Cold War: Third World Interventions and the Making of Our Times* (Cambridge, MA: Harvard University Press, 2005), 93.

2. Nick Cullather, *The Hungry World: America's Cold War Battle against Poverty in Asia* (Cambridge, MA: Harvard University Press, 2010); David Ekbladh, *The Great American Mission: Modernization and the Construction of an American World Order* (Princeton, NJ: Princeton University Press, 2011).

3. Min Ye, *The Belt Road and Beyond: State-Mobilized Globalization in China: 1998–2018* (Cambridge: Cambridge University Press, 2020).

4. Jennifer M. Rudolph and Michael Szonyi, eds., *The China Questions: Critical Insights into a Rising Power* (Cambridge, MA: Harvard University Press, 2018).

5. Peter Gue Zarrow, *After Empire: The Conceptual Transformation of the Chinese State, 1885–1924* (Stanford, CA: Stanford University Press, 2012).

6. See Prasenjit Duara, *Sovereignty and Authenticity: Manchukuo and the East Asian Modern* (Lanham, MD: Rowman & Littlefield Publishers, 2003).

7. Timothy Snyder, *Bloodlands: Europe between Hitler and Stalin* (New York: Basic Books, 2010).

8. Barak Kushner and Sherzod Muminov, *Overcoming Empire in Post-Imperial East Asia: Repatriation, Redress and Rebuilding* (London; New York: Bloomsbury Academic, 2020).

ARCHIVES AND LIBRARIES CONSULTED

Isaiah Bowman (IB) Papers, Special Collections, Johns Hopkins University
Box 1.1; Box 1.3: Personal; Box 2.9: Correspondences; Box 2.10:
Correspondences; Box 2.21: Correspondences; Box 2.22: Correspondences; Box
2.23; Box 2.25: Correspondence; Box 2.33; Box 2.34; Box 2.43: Correspondences;
Box 3.1: Series 3: Speeches; Box 3.2: Speeches; Box 3.5: Speeches; Box 3.6:
Speeches; Box 3.7: Speeches; Box 4.4: Writings; Box 4.19: Writings; Box 5.6:
Research Notes; Box 5.10: Research Notes; Box 6.1: Organizations; Box. 6.3;
Box 6.3a; Box 6.4: Organizations / Commissions (Marshall Plan, Overseas
Territories); Box. 6.5; Box 9.2: Project M; Box 9.7; Box 9.8; Box 9.10; Box 9.18:
Project M; Box 9.19: Project M; Box 9.20: Project M; Box 9.21: Project M; Box
9.22: Project M; Box 13.1: Paris Peace Conference; Box 13.3; Box 13.4; Box
14.3: State Department Advisory Committee; Boxes 14.10 and 14.11: State
Department Advisory Committee

Ellsworth Huntington Papers, Special Collections, Yale University
Group 1, Series 1, Box 4; Group 1, Series 1, Box 5; Group 1, Series IV, Box 4;
Group 1, Series IV, Box 21; Group 1, Series X, Box 2; Group 1, Series XI, Box 2;
Group 1, Series XII, Box 1

Ellen Semple Papers, Special Collections,
University of Kentucky, Lexington

Halford Mackinder Papers, Special Collections, Oxford University

William Smith Clark Papers (RG 3/1–1867). Special Collections and University Archives, W.E.B. Du Bois Library, University of Massachusetts Amherst
Series 2: Correspondence Box 4, Folders 1–17; Series 5: Hokkaido University / UMass relations

Foreign Ministry Archives, Academia Historica, Taipei, Taiwan
410.2/0012

Institute of Modern History Archives, Academia Sinica, Taipei, Taiwan (IMH)
301-01-07-027: Zhu Jiahua Papers. Call numbers indicate various ministries, including Ministries of Forestry and Defense: 03-32-204-03-037; 28-03-02-001-06; 01-24-005-03-012; 02-16-008-04-005; 301-01-05-006; 301-01-06-022; 301-01-06-288; 301-01-06-289; 301-01-06-473; 301-01-06-474; 301-01-09-076; 301-01-15-018; 301-01-15-019; 301-01-15-020; 301-01-15-021; 301-01-15-024; 301-01-15-025; 301-01-15-026; 301-01-23-764; 301-01-23-783; 20-00-48-1; 20-00-61-6-1; 20-00-61-6-3; 20-11-14-11; 20–11-83–2; 20-16-45-14; 20-26-6-27; 20-26-8-22; 20-26-8-28; 20-26-9-7; 20-26-21-4; 20-26-21-5; 20-26-21-6 ; 20-26-21-7; 20-26-21-9; 20-26-21-11; 20-26-21-12; 20-26-101-3; 20-26-101-8; 20-87-090-08; 20-87-133-04; 20-87-133-05; 20-87-141-03; 20-87-143-04; 20-87-146-06; 20-87-146-07; 20-87-149-05; 20-87-157-09; 20-87-158-01; 20-87-158-02; 20-87-158-03; 20-87-158-10; 20-87-159-09; 20-87-160-05; 20-87-165-05; 20-87-204-06; 20-87-206-06; 20-87-206-07; 20-87-219-04; 20-87-219-06; 20-87-219-07; 20-87-219-12; 20-87-219-13; 20-87-220-01; 20-87-220-02; 20-87-220-03; 20-87-220-06; 20-88-010-01; 27-07-5-12; 20-26-74-21

GMD Party Archives, Taipei, Taiwan
5.2/20/1/2; 3.1/20/23/2

Shanghai Library, Republican Collections, Shanghai, China

Second Historical Archives of China, Nanjing (SHAC)
12.1.612; 23.2937; 23.2722; 23.2723; 393.2090; 23.150; 4.30269; 12.6.14178; 12.6.10197; 12.6.16848; 12.6.12659; 12.1.367; 783.308; 783.152; 4.9196; 12.6.8391; 4.9183; 12.6.8387; 4.10261;12.6.12662; 4.30263; 12.6.14370; 12.6.16849; 12.6.10562; 4.30062; 12.1.213; 12.6.19223; 12.6.10535; 12.6.9677; 783.310; 783–152; 783.309; 783.311; 783.313; 12.6.10196; 783.307; 783.312; 5.6793; 12.6.3492; 12.6.2093; 4.3956; 4.9282; 5.10839; 783.484; 12.6.12579;12.6.19841. 11.1934; 4.15453; 12.6.9547; 12.4.661; 5.6794; 12.6.8383;12.6.9895; 12.6.12649; 393-57; 393-56; 23-2843; 393-82; 23-2242; 393-2119; 393-50; 393-107; 393-131; 787.2088; 393-48; 393-71; 393-49; 393-54; 393-119; 393-442; 393-466; 393-420; 5.128; 12-2045; 393-55; 23-3150; 23-3108; 12-14277; 12-14363; 23-3094; 393-359; 5.1741; 23-2140; 12-14178; 393-2611; 23-3; 23-1977; 393-2612; 23-1253; 5.147; 12-10197; 23-

3104; 23-132; 23-1251; 393-2613; 393-2148; 393-2614; 393-2643; 23-2893;12-12575; 23-2842; 393-2102; 5.6795; 393-1476; 23-2710; 23-2689; 23-304; 23-2687; 23-123; 393-2616; 12-10629; 23-2180; 23-20; 12-10631; 783-152; 23-467; 23-464; 23-2824; 23-136; 3093, 23-3093; 393-2729; 23-2673; 23-3092; 23-23

Max Sering Papers, German Federal Archives, Koblenz, Germany
N 1210/1, 1935–1938, Schriftwechsel: Internationale Agrarkonferenz; N 1210/3, 1931–1934, Internationale Agrarkonferenz; N 1210/24; N 1210/119: Correspondence; N 1210/132 (2); N 1210/17: 1914–1918, Siedlungsland im Baltikum; N 1210/18 from 1896, Innere Kolonisation; N 1210/19: 1909–1912, Gesellschaft zur Förderung der inneren Kolonisation; N 1210 / 23; N 1210/26, 1936; N 1210/27, 1920s; N 1210/28, Gesellschaft zur Förderung der Inneren Kolonisation; N 1210/48, 1920s; N 1210/164

Karl Haushofer Papers, German Federal Archives, Koblenz, Germany
N 1122/1, Bd. 155 Folder. Japan Schriftwechsel und andere Briefe aus dem fernen Osten; N 1122/2, Bd. 155 Folder. Militär Berichte aus Japan 1909–1910; N 1122/6, 1926–1944. Korrespondenz; Deutsche Akademie 1926–1944; Deutsche akademische Auslandstelle München e.V. 1934–1939; Deutscher akademischer Austauschdienst Berlin 1937–1939; Deutsches Auslandsinstitut Stuttgart, 1927–1944; N1122 /23; 1924–1944. Korrespondenz: Nakmura A. 1927; Korrespondenz der NSDAP 1935–1944; Dr. Oskar Ritter von Niedermeyer 1924–1944; Ulrich Noack 1938–1943; N 1122/25, Bd. 1918–1943. In Dr. Rudolf Pechel 1926–1933; Wilhelm Frhr. von Pechmann 1918–1943; Justus Perthes 1933–1942; N 1122/35, Bd. 1921–1944. Weltpolitische Montsberichte, Dr. Max Wiedemann; N 1122/40, Bd. 1923–1944. *Zeitschrift für Geopolitik*; N 1122/58, Bd. 1938–1944. Korrespondenz Albrecht Haushofer; N 1122/61, Bd. 1903–1944. Wissenschaftliche Korrespondenz; N 1122/66, Bd. 1930–1939. Beziehungen zu Japan; N 1122/67, Bd. 1934–1939. Schreiben von Ministern und hohen Militärs; N 1122/103, Bd. 1930–1944; 1909. Dt. Akademie; Karl Haushofer u. Wissenschaft; Japan; N 1122/110, 1923–1928. Geopolitk: Autoren, Korrespondenten; N1122/110, Bd. Aufsätze, etc.; N 1122/123, Besprechungen und Briefe über Japan Buch "Dai Nihon"; N 1122/123, 1919–1929. Martha an Karl; N 1122/129; N 1122/142; N 1122/152, 1.12.09–31.3.10 Zeitübersicht der 1. Ausbildungsperiode des 22. FAR Eindrücke während der ersten Rekrutenzeit. Military reports in Japan–persönliche Eindrücke; N 1122/154, Bd. Japanreise/ Militärberichte

Geheimes Staatsarchiv Preußischer Kulturbesitz, Berlin, Germany
I. Ha. Rep. 194, 140; I. Ha. Rep. 89, 15650 and 1913–1914. "Ostasiatischer Verein Deutsch-Chinesischer Verband"; Ha. I Rep. 212, 6094; Ha. I Rep. 212, 6098. Reichsarchiv Posen Ansiedlungskommission Generalia; Ha. I Rep. 212, 801; Ha. I Rep. 212, 6097; Ha. I Rep. 212, 863; Ha. I Rep. 212, 864. 1913–1915. Teilungspläne; I. Ha. Rep. 76, Sekt 1. Tit. XI Nr. 9 Bd. 1. 1873. die deutsche

Gesellschaft für Natur und Völkerkunde Ostasiens; I. Ha. Rep. 76 Sekt. 1 Tit. XI Nr. 10 Bd. 2; Ha. I Rep. 212, 5222. 1886–1906. Zwanzig Jahre deutscher Kulturarbeit. 1886–1906; Ha. I Rep. 212, 799; Ha. I Rep. 212, 800. 1887/88–1888/89. Ansiedlungs Kommission: die Ausiedelungspläne für die in den Provinzen Westpreußen und Posen belegenen Güter; Ha. I Rep. 212, 802; Ha. I Rep. 212, 525; Ha. I Rep. 212, 6115; Ha. I Rep. 212, 5220; Ha. I Rep. 212, 865. 1916. Teilungspläne; Ha. I Rep. 212, 5221; Ha. I Rep. 212, 4767. 1919–1924. Besiedlungswesen allgemeines; I. Ha. Rep. 76, Sekt. 1 Tit. XI, Nr. 10 Bd. 1 and Bd. 3; I. Ha. Rep. 76, Sekt 1. Tit. XII Nr. 3 Bd. 1 and 2 and 3. 1874–1904; 1905; 1910–. Technische Hochschule; I. Ha. Rep. 76 Va, Sekt 1. Tit. X Nr. 6. 1908–1922. Das Studium junger Chinesen auf preußischen Hochschulen

German Federal Archives, Berlin, Lichterfelde (BA)
R 6/9; R 6/19; R 6/23; R 6/102; R 6/104; R 6/109; R 6/206; R 6/426; R 6/431; R 6/511; R 6/512; R 6/516; R 6/517; R 6/567; R 6/576; R 6/604; R 6/605; R 6/634; R 6/626

Rockefeller Foundation (RF) Archives, China
Rural Reconstruction Initiative
RG 1 Projects, Series 601, Box 8; RG 1 Projects, Series 601, Box 9; RG 1 Projects, Series 601, Box 10; RG 1 Projects, Series 601, Box 11; RG 1 Projects, Series 601, Box 12; RG 1 Projects, Series 601, Box 13; RG 1 Projects, Series 601, Box 14; RG 1 Projects, Series 601, Box 15; No. 26, Series 1, Box 27: International Education Board

Owen Lattimore Papers, Library of Congress, Washington, DC
Box 26, Folder 15, 1944. "Special Mission #42."
Box 27, Folder 1, October 1941–November 1942. "War Time Activities Biographical Assessments and Summaries of Conversations."

Henry Cord Meyer Papers, Hoover Institution
Library and Archives, Stanford University

INDEX

India: border with China, 242; Rockefeller Foundation programs, 149
Indians: removal, 5, 39, 40, 45, 164,
241; romanticized, 88; White settlers and, 5; Wild West Show, 111
Indigenous peoples: Ainu, 39–40, 55,
106, 114; atrocities committed by
imperial powers, 189, 276n39, g;
Herero Rebellion, 180, 187, 188,
189; in Japanese Empire, 114, 164;
land taken from, 17, 58, 63, 189,
219; stereotypes, 40; in Taiwan,
106, 114; treatment of, 5, 17, 106,
164. *See also* Indians
Indigenous peoples, in Chinese borderlands: effects of Han settlement,
162, 164, 167, 219; ethnic categories, 102; ethnological accounts,
101–2; historical relationships with
central power, 101, 102, 107–8;
Liang Qichao on, 107–8; Nationalist policies toward, 139, 163; PRC
minorities policy, 12, 14, 234; traditional lifestyles, 163; in Xinjiang,
x–xii, 236, 238; in Yunnan, 206
Industrialization: agricultural, 37,
113, 129–30; in Britain, 28; in
1850s, 51; energy sources, 3, 28, 35,
136, 253n8; exhibitions at World's
Fairs, 114; fuel needs, 136; impact,
91, 226, 227; in Manchuria, 162;
transportation improvements, 91–
92; in United States, 38, 45, 85, 91.
See also Technology
Inner colonization: abandoned
settlers, 244; Chinese terms, 6–7,
197; experiments, 84; interest in,
68, 167; in Japanese Empire, 71–
73, 162, 164, 167, 244; promoted
by Tang Qiyu, 197–99, 233–34;
terminology, 6. *See also* Chinese
borderlands, Han settlement; East
Prussia; Hokkaido; *Tunken*
Inner Mongolia, 163, 197, 219, 233

Institute of Geography, 140, 234
International Geographical Union,
130–31
International law, 50–51, 85, 106, 243
International nationalism, 84

Jäckh, Ernst, 190, 191
Japan: agriculture, 58, 74; education,
62, 83, 106–7, 161, 168–69; emigration to Americas, 72, 73, 114;
expansion, 75; foreign experts, 57,
59–62, 70; geography in, 12, 104–5,
106–7, 110, 258n39; geopolitics in,
135, 142; industrial exhibitions,
114; Meiji government, 55–62,
104–5, 106–7; Meiji Restoration,
50, 54, 55, 57; military, 57, 182;
modernization, 54, 57, 61; modern
science introduced, 6, 54, 61, 62,
104–5; natural resources, 57; overpopulation, 74; Rohrbach's visit,
191–92; Ryukyu Domain, 50–51;
social sciences, 69–70, 72, 73, 100–
101; Tokugawa shogunate, 53–55,
57, 72, 74; treaty with Perry, 50, 61
Japanese Empire: agricultural experimental stations, 74–75, 272n55;
defeat in World War II, 5, 243, 244;
expansion, 4, 5, 12, 73, 85, 87, 242–
43; expansion in China, 7, 12, 13,
73; First Sino-Japanese War, 107,
134, 140–41; frontier discourse,
72–73, 87; indigenous peoples, 114,
164; inner colonization programs,
71–73, 162, 164, 167, 244; international law used by, 106; knowledge
networks, 62; as knowledge transfer hub, 62; labor migration, 51, 72,
74; Manchukuo, 59, 146, 166, 218,
243; map, xviii; military government, 146; mimetic imperialism,
55; natural resources access, 129;
Okinawa's place in, 51; power, 134;
relations with Western powers,

Technology (*cont.*)
  reclamation and rural development projects, 129–30, 163–64, 170–74; Nazi interest in, 177; settlement and, 2–3, 17; supercomputers, 241; surveillance, xi, 243; transportation, 33, 116; at World's Fairs, 113–14. *See also* Agronomy; Industrialization
Tennessee Valley Authority (TVA), 147, 223, 224
Territoriality, Chinese: claims in South China Sea, 110, 138–39, 242; historical basis, 161, 177; nationalism and, 22, 83–84, 138–39; Nationalist claims, 7, 13, 109, 216–18; in twentieth century, 11, 13, 20, 21–22, 147, 199, 242; in twenty-first century, 110–11, 242. *See also* Chinese borderlands
Territory, *see* Borderlands; Borders; Geography
Thünen, Heinrich von, 91
Tian Meng, 232
Tibet: as autonomous zone, 12; Han settlement efforts, 160; independence supporters, 122; in Qing period, 82–83, 103; rural development efforts, 160; unrest, 243. *See also* Chinese borderlands
Time, history and, 8–9
Ting Hsien, *see* Ding County Experimental Zone
Tokugawa shogunate: "Dutch learning" (*Rangaku*), 54, 72, 74; Ezo colonization, 54–55, 57; foreign experts, 57; foreign trade, 53–54
Torgasheff, Boris, 136–37
Trade: agricultural, 44, 91, 126; with China, 28, 49, 51, 53–54, 102; in Chinese borderlands, 82; global routes, 28, 44, 51
Transportation: air, 228; fuel needs, 47, 50, 57, 92; hubs, 116; industrial-

ization and, 91–92; maritime, 47, 50, 57, 92, 116; railroads, 56, 65, 91–92, 116, 162, 169, 227; technological advances, 33, 35, 116
Travel: accounts, 89–90, 91, 95, 102; to Chinese borderlands, xi–xii; by educated elites, 89–90, 95, 96–97, 98–99, 102
Troll, Carl, 143, 185, 211
Trotha, Lothar von, 187–88
Tseng Yang-fu, 221
Tu Ji, 105–6
Tunken (military colonies): advocates, 199; challenges for settlers, 199–201, 204; Guizhou Six Dragons, 201, 202 (fig.), 203 (fig.); historical background, 70–71, 161, 172, 198–99; as inner colonization, 197–98; Nanniwan, 199, 238; in PRC, 235–36; regulations, 201; schools, 204; in Suiyuan, 166, 169–72, 171 (fig.), 173 (fig.), 175; use of term, 6–7, 71, 163; for veterans, 194–96, 205; in wartime, 199–201, 204–5, 277n66; Xing An, 161, 162–66, 165 (fig.). *See also* Land reclamation projects
Tuntian, 6–7, 161, 199, 249n12. *See also Tunken*
Turner, Frederick Jackson, 4, 25, 93, 95, 111–12, 114, 115, 129
TVA, *see* Tennessee Valley Authority
Two, K. Y., 221

Udagawa Yōan, 74
Ukraine, 123, 180–82, 190, 245
United Nations, 210
United States: African Americans, 39, 47, 93, 128; agriculture and agronomy, 36–38, 45, 93, 113; anti-Communist campaigns, 224, 228; censuses, 111–12, 114, 115; China Hands, 159; Chinese laborers, 29, 56; Chinese students, 150, 151, 152, 157, 158, 196–97, 221, 229;

CPSIA information can be obtained
at www.ICGtesting.com
Printed in the USA
JSHW080215100723
44367JS00002B/2